Exploring Multilingual Hawai'i

Exploring Multilingual Hawai'i

Language Use and Language Ideologies in a Diverse Society

Scott Saft

LEXINGTON BOOKS
Lanham • Boulder • New York • London

Published by Lexington Books
An imprint of The Rowman & Littlefield Publishing Group, Inc.
4501 Forbes Boulevard, Suite 200, Lanham, Maryland 20706
www.rowman.com

6 Tinworth Street, London SE11 5AL, United Kingdom

Copyright © 2019 by The Rowman & Littlefield Publishing Group, Inc.

All rights reserved. No part of this book may be reproduced in any form or by any electronic or mechanical means, including information storage and retrieval systems, without written permission from the publisher, except by a reviewer who may quote passages in a review.

British Library Cataloguing in Publication Information Available

Library of Congress Cataloging-in-Publication Data

Names: Saft, Scott, author.
Title: Exploring multilingual Hawai'i : language use and language ideologies in a diverse society / Scott Saft.
Description: Lanham : Lexington Books, [2019] | Includes bibliographical references and index.
Identifiers: LCCN 2018060484 (print) | LCCN 2019004101 (ebook)
Subjects: LCSH: Multilingualism—Hawaii. | Languages in contact—Hawaii. | Language and culture—Hawaii.
Classification: LCC P35.5.U6 (ebook) | LCC P35.5.U6 S24 2019 (print) | DDC 306.44/609969—dc23
LC record available at https://lccn.loc.gov/2018060484

ISBN: 9781498561181 (cloth)
ISBN: 9781498561204 (pbk.)
ISBN: 9781498561198 (electronic)

Contents

Acknowledgments		vii
Introduction		1
1	The Development of Hawai'i as a Multilingual Society	21
2	Hawaiian: Lost (Almost) and Found	55
3	Pidgin: The Local(s) Voice	93
4	Heteroglossic Language Practice in Hawaiian Society	125
5	The Many Japanese Voices in Hawai'i	155
6	Ideology and the Latest Arrivals: The Construction of "Filipino" and "Micronesian" in Newspaper Discourse	191
Conclusion		221
Bibliography		233
Index		257
About the Author		263

Acknowledgments

Providing appropriate acknowledgments to all of the people who helped with this project is a nearly impossible task. Nonetheless, I will attempt to do so here by first thanking my students at the University of Hawai'i at Hilo (UHH) for pushing me to see aspects of the linguistic landscape in Hawai'i that I would have otherwise missed. In particular, I owe much gratitude and at least a few "pepsis" to Hannah Lockwood, Dylon Koehn, Gabriel Tebow, Ronald Santos, Dylan Sugimoto, Alexander Kaetsu, Sierra Boulos, Ami Lu, Vivianne Yamanishi, and Lehua Akano. Through their work as research assistants and/or informants, they have been invaluable to the completion of the book.

I will also be forever grateful to the editorial team at Lexington Books for their patience and gentle guidance in helping me navigate the publication process. Without the assistance and constant encouragement from Jana Hodges-Kluck and Trevor Crowell, publication would never have become a reality.

Much appreciation also goes to those who graciously allowed me to employ their databases for my analyses. This includes the overseers of the Clinton Kanahele Collection at Brigham Young University-Hawai'i, those in charge of the video clips at 'Ōiwi TV, and those involved with ulukau.org. Access to these data sources was absolutely crucial in terms of allowing a focus on the situated usage of language.

In addition, I am indebted to my colleagues at UHH for their tremendous insights into language and culture in Hawai'i. Especially, I am grateful to my friends and co-workers at the Ka Haka 'Ula o Ke'elikōlani College of Hawaiian Language for continuously testing the limits of my understanding of languages such as Hawaiian, Pidgin, and Japanese. While their "tests" have enhanced my ability to produce the analyses within this book, I emphasize that I alone am responsible for any errors and inaccuracies that remain.

I also have benefitted greatly from a diverse group of people in the community of Hilo who provide daily "lessons" in the complex and varied usages of language on the Big Island of Hawai'i, usually free of charge. Since arriving in Hilo in 2004 for the first time, I have been extremely fortunate to experience their tremendous warmth and humor, frequently while sharing some 'ono grindz and cold beer. In particular, I am thankful for the Hilo basketball connection, including Da Next Level, the YSY crew at Waiākea Uka, da Thursday night gang at Andrews Gym, and the annual Vulcans Camp gatherings. Without this "comraderie," it is doubtful I would have had the fortitude to engage in and complete this project.

Much of the content of this book has been influenced by those in Hawai'i who stand resolute in using the languages specific to this beautiful 'āina. Friends and colleagues such as Larry Kimura, Pila Wilson, Kauanoe Kamanā, Iota Cabral, Hiapo Perreira, Kekoa Harman, Kaliko Trapp, Aolani Ka'ilihou, Kamalani Johnson, and Keiki Kawai'ae'a have shown me day in and day out the absolute necessity of revitalizing indigenous languages such as Hawaiian. I likewise have been greatly influenced by advocates of the local language known as Pidgin. While I do not know people such as Billy Kenoi, Andy Bumatai, and Lee Tonouchi on a personal level, my students and I have drawn much inspiration from their commitment to the usage of Pidgin across various social situations. Such activism on behalf of Hawaiian and Pidgin helps ensure the place of these languages in modern Hawaiian society.

I also express my utmost appreciation to the members of the Fujino family for opening their doors to me. My interactions with Eiko-san, Gordon, Gayle, Garret, Annie, Tony, Taylor, Lauren, and Asia have been some of my most delightful experiences on the Big Island. With their skillful mixture of English and Pidgin, as well as smatterings of Hawaiian, Japanese, Mandarin, Cantonese, Tagalog, and Ilocano, they provide the type of linguistic education that cannot be found in books. Of all the family members, though, I am most grateful to Glynis, my partner in crime, whose love and support has guided me throughout this project.

Finally, I recognize the contributions of my son Sebi, who was born and raised (mostly) in Hawai'i, first on O'ahu and later on the Big Island. Observing his development on a daily basis into a well-adjusted young adult with profiencies in multiple languages and an identity that crosses ethnic boundaries has served as a constant reminder of the beauty, complexity, and utter uniqueness of multilingual Hawai'i.

Introduction

A typical day in the town of Hilo on the Island of Hawaiʻi, where I live and work, may go as follows:

1) In the morning, upon arriving at my office in the College of Hawaiian Language at the University of Hawaiʻi, I receive the following greeting in Hawaiian from a colleague:
 Aloha mai kāua. Pehea ʻoe i kēia kakahiaka? ("Greetings. How are you this morning?")
2) Next, as I walk across campus later in the morning, I see a group of Marshallese students relaxing between classes and overhear the following:
 Mottan jete class rainin? ("How many more classes do you have today?")
3) At lunchtime, I join some of my colleagues at a local restaurant run by speakers of Mandarin who say to each other:
 Cài hái méi zhōu hǎo ("The food is not done cooking yet.")
4) If by chance it is Wednesday, one of the days of the Farmer's Market in the downtown area (the other day is Saturday), we might stop by on our lunch hour to pick up some cheap produce and hear some of the Filipino vendors talking among each other in Ilocano:
 Dagijay nateng ko ket nalaka ("My vegetables are very cheap.")
5) After leaving work in the afternoon, I go for a workout at the gym in the downtown area where I hear two men speaking in the local vernacular known as Pidgin:
 Da battery wen make en so da machine stay all hamajang now. ("The battery died and so the machine does not work now.")
6) I then see someone who thanks me in a mix of languages that includes English, Hawaiian, and Pidgin for helping him register for a university course:
 Mahalo nui for your kōkua. I never knew how fo register fo wan course before. ("Thank you for your help. I never knew how to register for a course before.")

1

7) After the gym, I stop at the local supermarket where I see tourists from Japan marveling at the amount of Japanese foodstuffs displayed:
   Koko de mochi mo utte iru n da ne ("they sell mochi here too")
8) Finally, I might settle at my house and watch the local Hawaiian news being broadcast in English.
   Tonight we bring you your local news . . .

The everyday experiences of people in Hawai'i undoubtedly differ, with language usage itself varying from community to community and even from island to island. Still, on most islands and in most communities, there are many people living and visiting who, like me, run across a variety of languages on a daily basis. Many will also regularly experience the mixing of languages shown in number 6. This book endeavors to describe Hawai'i as a multilingual society, concentrating on how it developed as such, the functions and usage of language in society, including the mixing of languages, and attitudes and beliefs toward various languages and speakers of those languages that at times place them in hierarchical relationships of power and prestige.

Multilingualism has been defined in a way that applies to both individuals and also societies:

> Multilingualism conveys the ability of societies, institutions, groups, and individuals to have regular use of more than one language in their everyday lives over space and time. (Franceschini 2011, 346)

Both societal and individual multilingualism is a common part of the world in which we live; it is estimated that at least half of the world's population is proficient in at least two languages (Bhatia and Ritchie 2013; Braunmuller and Gabriel 2012; Fishman 1980; Grosjean 2010; Romaine 2013; Li Wei 2008). In addition to my own experiences, there is significant evidence of multilingualism in Hawai'i.

1. The data report of 2011 notes that 24.8 of households in Hawai'i speak a language other than English at home (data report 2011). Tagalog, Japanese, Ilocano, and Chinese are listed as the four most common household languages other English, with Spanish, Hawaiian, and Korean not far behind.
2. In 2014 the availability of the driver's license exam was expanded to 13 languages, Chinese, Japanese, Korean, Vietnamese, Tongan, Samoan, Tagalog, Ilocano, Hawaiian, Spanish, Chuukese, Marshallese, and English (State of Hawai'i: Department of Transportation).
3. Although the Hawaiian language was banned as a medium of education in 1896 as part of the colonization process (Wilson and Kamanā 2001),

changes in the legislature as well as the development of a strong revitalization movement have resulted in the opening of schools where the primary language of instruction is Hawaiian. In fact, in what is being referred to as a P-20 intiative (Wilson and Kamanā 2014), programs have been put in place so that individuals can be educated in Hawaiian from pre-school to the doctoral level (Kawaiʻaeʻa and Wilson 2007). Where Hawaiian was once thought to be on the verge of extinction in the 1960s and 1970s with less than 50 children speakers of the language (Kimura, Kamanā, and Wilson 2003), it is now noted that as many 15,000 people use or understand Hawaiian (McCarty 2008 based on personal communication with William Wilson), with some of them referred to as "new native speakers" who have begun acquiring Hawaiian as a first language (Brenzinger and Heinrich 2013, 9).
4. The increase in Hawaiian speakers grew partly out of the decision in 1978 at the Hawaiʻi Constitutional Convention to name Hawaiian as one of the two official languages (together with English) of the state. Until Alaska put 20 indigenous languages on a par with English as official state languages in 2014, Hawaiʻi was the only the state to have a language other than English recognized at the state level.
5. Despite being criticized regularly as a mere substandard form of English (Hargrove and Sakoda 1999; Tamura 1996), Pidgin is gaining appreciation as a language unto itself. While it has not been given official status at the state level, it has been recognized by the U.S. Census Bureau as a language of Hawaiʻi. This fits the observations of language specialists who have noted that nearly half of the population, approximately 600,000 people, are speakers of Pidgin (Sakoda and Siegel 2003).
6. Due to an 1986 agreement (the Compact of Free Association) between the United States and over 1,000 small islands in the Western Pacific known by the term "Micronesia," about 30 percent of the Micronesians have left their homelands to travel to the United States and U.S. territories, with the majority landing in Hawaiʻi and Guam. A report in 2008 from the University of Hawaiʻi System states that "Micronesians are among the fastest growing migrant groups in the state of Hawaiʻi." This influx of people has made languages such as Yapese, Kosraen, Chuukese, Marshallese, and Pohnpeian fairly recent additions to an already multilingual society.
7. In addition to housing a large number of residents who speak various languages, Hawaiʻi is also well known for a tourism industry that brings in people from different countries on a daily basis. According to statistics released by the Hawaiʻi Tourism Authority in 2015, of the 8,282,680 people who visited in 2014, 3,306,254 came from places outside of the United States, with 1,510,938 from Japan alone. A vibrant tourism industry not

only increases the diversity of languages that enter Hawaiian society, but also intensifies the need of a workforce of multilingual people who can provide services to those visitors.

This list mentions numerous languages and many contexts of language usage, including the home, social services such as driving exams, education, business, and also politics. This study will unfortunately not be able to discuss all the languages found in Hawai'i, nor will it be able to cover all sectors of society affected by these languages, but it will provide understanding of the general importance of multiple languages in Hawaiian society as well as some points of intersection of those languages.

Prior research on language in Hawai'i has decribed the historical developments that brought various languages to the islands (Reinecke 1969). There are also detailed accounts of the emergence and evolution of specific languages in Hawai'i, sometimes together with general developments concerning specific ethnic groups. This includes work focusing on Hawaiian (Elbert and Pukui 1979; Huebner 1984; Schütz 1994), Pidgin (Sakoda and Siegel 2003; Vellupillai 2003), Japanese (Asato 2006; Odo 2008; Okamura 2014; Yoshida 2007); Chinese (Young 1972), Filipino (Labrador 2015; Poblete 2014), and also English (Tamura 1993a, 1993b, 1996). There is also significant research considering the history and organization of different aspects of Hawaiian society, such as politics (Mykkanen 2003; Silva 2004; Tsujimura 2016), education (Bayer 2009; Benham and Heck 1998), sports (Bowman et al. 2005; Walker 2011), gender (Chun 2006; 'Iwalani et al. 2007), protest (Mast and Mast 1996; Reinecke 1996), and business/tourism (Desmond 1999; Diamond 2008; Jung 2006). Furthermore, there is a detailed edited volume which reflects on the multicultural nature of Hawai'i through a "stewpot" model (McDermott and Andrade 2011). In doing so, it offers a psychocultural profile of a large majority of the ethnic groups in Hawai'i, providing information about the social structure(s), gender and generational relations, occupational and educational patterns, political strategies, and central values of each group (McDermott and Andrade 2011). Information gained through this volume and the other available studies will serve as valuable resources in this study as it examines language usage in Hawaiian society from the perspective of multilingualism.

By focusing on Hawai'i as a multilingual society, this work is meant to be situated within the growing interest in linguistics and related fields on multilingualism and linguistic diversity. The term superdiversity has been recently invoked to describe and discuss the tendencies of people and languages to move across cultural and geographical boundaries (Arnaut et al. 2016; Blommaert 2015; Blommaert and Rampton 2011; Duarte and Gogolin

2013; Meissner and Vertovec 2015). Although the world has always been a diverse place, the ease with which people can now travel and communicate has created a "diversity within diversity" (Blommaert 2012, 8), and it has also created a need to understand what this diversity means for the present and future of languages and for human beings in general.

One interesting and seemingly ironic effect of this heightened ability to transcend boundaries is an increase in concern for the extinction and endangerment of languages. As contact among humans become simpler to accomplish, more people are abandoning their ancestral tongues in favor of so-called world languages such as English that are perceived to hold more potential for success in a globalized world. Michael Krauss, for example, once famously predicted that half of its 7,000 or so languages will no longer be spoken by the end of the twenty-first century (Krauss 1992; see also Walsh 2005 for discussion). This fear of losing languages has given rise to movements among linguists and language activists to document and teach endangered languages, actions which are deemed crucial to protecting and sustaining the world's linguistic and cultural diversity (Grenoble and Whaley 2006; Harrison 2007, 2010; Hinton 2013). As Harrison (2007) has maintained, each language contains within it a vast amount of knowledge about not just cultural practices and the naming of objects, land, and people but also different ways of interacting with the world. The loss of languages thus means the loss of important epistemological perspectives about human engagement with other people as well as with natural resources. In this sense, then, an increase in global diversity has led to even more anxiety about the future of linguistic diversity and also, to some, the prospects for the human race. With one language, Hawaiian, that is considered endangered but currently benefitting from a strong revitalization movement, another language, Pidgin, that was created locally but has been much maligned, and at least one language, English, whose dominance has greatly impacted island life, Hawai'i should be a prime location for enhancing our understanding of the complexities, problems, and possibilities associated with the diversity of a multilingual society.

THE HAWAIIAN CONTEXT

In order to move a step closer to beginning an analysis of the nexus of languages in Hawai'i, it will be helpful to make note of some features of the Hawaiian context that are relevant to its multilingualism. First, Hawai'i covers a relatively small geographical area with eight primary islands that are isolated in the Pacific Ocean approximately 4,000 kilometers (2,500 miles) from the nearest mass of land (the coast of California). While residents frequently construct smaller communities based on shared languages and backgrounds—there are, for example, communities known to be primarily Japanese and Filipino, these communities are located in close proximity to one another, making it very difficult to avoid contact with others. The only way to get significant distance between communities is to leave the state (or at least the island).

Second, prior to being "discovered" by Europeans in the late 1700s, the people in Hawai'i had existed in an essentially monolingual and monocultural society since arriving by canoe from other Polynesian islands approximately 1,000 years ago. As Wilson (1998a, 126) notes, "Hawai'i is the most isolated aboriginally inhabited island chain in the world, and Hawaiian developed with little outside influence for countless generations." Hawaiian continued to be the language of all politics, business, religion, and the like, that occurred prior to the late 1700s and early 1800s. While Hawaiian monolingualism continued for nearly 1,000 years, it only took a relatively short amount of time, approximately 100 years, to transform into a multilingual society.

Third, the diversity of languages in Hawai'i cuts across a wide range of linguistic families. Of the languages referred to in the personal experiences listed at the outset of this chapter, only English falls into the language group of Indo-European, considered the language family with the most speakers in the world. Mandarin is the only representative of the second largest language family, Sino-Tibetan, which includes Cantonese and the other varieties of Chinese. Hawaiian, Marshallese, and Ilocano all fall under the same language family of Austronesian, but they are typically placed in different subgroupings within that family. Hawaiian is Polynesian, Marshallese is a Micronesian language, and Ilocano is either grouped together with Indonesian languages or placed in its own separate subgrouping. The classification of Japanese into a language family has been controversial, but it would not fall into any of the categories mentioned here. Then there is Pidgin, another distinct language variety which stands by itself as a creole language that was created uniquely in Hawai'i, albeit with influences from several existing languages that include Hawaiian, English, Chinese, and Portuguese (Sakoda and Siegel 2003). It is quite remarkable to think that such a diverse set of language families have all come together on this small chain of islands.

Moreover, the previous list of languages does not even begin to do justice to the number of tongues that have played a role in the historical development as well as the evolving present situation of Hawai'i. Speakers of European languages such as Spanish, Portuguese, Russian, German, and Swedish have made their way to Hawai'i to live and work. The same is true for speakers of Asian languages such as Cambodian, Thai, and Vietnamese; Polynesian languages that include Sāmoan, Tahitian, and Tongan; and as already noted, Micronesian languages such as Chuukese, Pohnpeian, and Yapese.

Finally, it is worth noting that multilingualism is pervasive in Hawai'i despite the implementation of an American educational system that gives precedence to English. To be sure, Hawai'i in this sense is no different from the rest of the United States, where educational prerogatives focusing on English stand in strong contrast to not just the multilingual history of the United States but also a population that is growing in diversity. This book does not focus on education per se, but a strongly American educational system surely impacts the attitudes toward languages as well as decisions about which language(s) to use. As will be noted in some of the chapters of this study, attitudes that are encouraged through education can be advantageous for speakers of certain languages while disadvantaging speakers of others.

While some of the features just described are not necessarily special to Hawai'i, they undoubtedly all contribute to making Hawai'i a unique yet potentially important context for studying multilingualism. They also lead to several questions: How did a group of small islands once occupied by monolingual speakers of Hawaiian become a breeding ground for such a diverse group of languages? How are the prevalent languages in society currently used in daily life? Relatedly, what types of innovative usages arise from this intersection of languages, particularly when languages are mixed? What is the connection of these languages to the construction of identity and a sense of cultural belonging, especially in a place where the number of people of mixed ethnicity is high? What are the atttidues toward these languages and how do these attitudes figure in positioning the population vis-a-vis one another and in maintaining social relations? Finally, how might the Hawaiian linguistic situation inform our understanding concerning multilingualism and diversity, especially in a world that features a "diversity within diversity" (Blommaert 2012, 8). These are some of the primary questions that have led to the writing of this book, and, while I am not confident that all of them will be satisfactorily answered here, the pursuit of answers will hopefully move us closer to understanding Hawai'i as a multilingual society. The next section describes the research framework to be followed throughout.

MULTILINGUALISM: FINDING A RESEARCH FRAMEWORK

Previous research on multilingualism has been interdisciplinary in nature and has cut across disciplines such as linguistics, anthropology, sociology, psychology, and education. While the wide breadth of prior research has contributed greatly to our understanding of multilingualism, it nonetheless makes it difficult to find a specific research perspective that can account for the complexities of particular societies that are dynamic and fluid in nature. As Baker and Prys Jones (1998, 99, also quoted in Romaine 2013, 447) note in reference to the study of bilingual communities, "there is no preferred term that is capable of summing up all the complexity, dynamism and color of bilinguals existing in groups." The same is certainly true for a context such as Hawai'i with its multiple languages and unique contextual features.

Research concentrating specifically on multilingualism at the societal level has often attempted to depict the relationship of languages to the larger entities to which they belong, such as nations, states, and also communities (Romaine 2013). As Romaine notes, this vantage point has often led to reliance "on census data and various typologies to determine the linguistic composition of these units" (Romaine 2013, 449). It also resulted in the usage of terms such as territorial bilingualism that attempt to pinpoint the location of language borders that might exist within one nation, in order to understand where the reach of one language ceases and another starts (Hamers and Blanc 2000). Belgium and Switzerland have been offered as examples of parts of the world with territorial bilingualism, and Canada has also been discussed as another place where this concept applies (Pons-Ridler and Ridler 1989). Diglossia is another term that has been employed to capture territorial language usage, except in this case the languages overlap in the same territory. However, they still remain separate from one another in the sense that they perform different, even complementary roles within a community, with one typically having high prestige and thus used in formal, public situations and the other low prestige and employed in casual, private contexts (Ferguson 1959; Fishman 1967; Romaine 2013). Paraguay is frequently given as an example of diglossia with Spanish serving as the high prestige language and Guarani the low one (Fishman 1967).

These ideas of borders, territories, and diglossia apply, at least in part, to the situation in Hawai'i. The fact that Hawai'i consists of islands makes it, theoretically anyway, easy to pinpoint the greater borders of language use. For instance, prior to western contact it was thought that each island had its own variety, or dialect, of Hawaiian. The islands themselves, in other words, served as the borders. Additionally, statistical data works in terms of gaining an understanding of not only the dominance of English in Hawai'i but also some of the other languages that are spoken and the frequency with which they are used. Territorial bilingualism exists to a certain degree with the different local communities that are dominated by a specific language. Moreover, there is one privately owned island, Ni'ihau, which has been basically closed to the public so that Hawaiian can remain the primary language.

When Hawaiian was thought to be near extinction, Ni'ihau represented "the" Hawaiian language territory, although that is certainly changing in current society as advocates work to reclaim a place for Hawaiian in everyday society. Finally, diglossia is seemingly applicable at times, particularly to the role of Pidgin in society. With Pidgin known mostly as a language for private conversations among friends and family and also for joking around, there is social expectation that Pidgin speakers will employ English in their formal, public interactions. Additionally, it may not be a stretch to use diglossia to describe certain expectations within the evolving Hawaiian language revitalization movement as Hawaiian speakers fall into a routine whereby they use Hawaiian with other speakers and English with non-speakers. In that sense, Hawaiian has developed a form of prestige, at least in certain sectors of society, that makes it visible which members of society have the capacity to speak the language regarded as indigenous to the islands.

However, despite the statistical and descriptive value of delineating borders and employing terms such as territorial bilingualism and diglossia, these perspectives ultimately fall short of appreciating the dynamism that constitutes modern Hawaiian society. Terms such as diglossia and territorial bilingualism depict fairly fixed relationships between and among languages, and they do not really account for the sometimes rapid changes from language to language as well as the innovative and even hybrid forms of speech that can be heard and seen frequently around town as people mix their languages. One example that will be discussed in more detail later in the book is the case of Billy Kenoi, the mayor of Hilo from 2008 to 2016, who is known for using Pidgin in his formal, public speeches. He was referred to as "the Shakespeare of Pidgin" and in fact had a penchant for mixing English, Pidgin, and Hawaiian when speaking in public. Such usages can only be adequately explored through an analysis of situated language usage that also understands the greater social meanings that those languages have to the people living and working in that community.

Without claiming to have discovered "the" way to understand multilingualism and especially multilingual Hawai'i, I adopt in this book an approach that places an emphasis, as much as possible, on situated language usage and that is flexible and broad enough to allow for consideration of the attitudes about languages that influence their employment within society. My approach draws inspiration largely from two schools of thought, language ecology and linguistic ethnography. The perspective of language ecology is attributed to the Norwegian-American linguist, Einar Haugen (i.e., Haugen 1972), and defined "as the study of interactions between any given language and its environment" (Haugen 1972, 325). As Ansaldo (2015) notes, the emergence of Haugen's ideas in the late 1960s and early 1970s can be viewed in light of the tremendous influence at the time within linguistics of Chomsky and his colleagues, who were promoting a uniquely cognitive view of language. While Haugen did profess to having an interest in the cognitive side of language, it was clear that language ecology was not going to treat "the speech community of a language as nothing more than a bit of incidental background" (Garner 2005, 92). As Haugen wrote (1972, 375), "another part of its ecology is sociological: its interaction within the society in which it functions as a medium of communication. The ecology of a language is determined primarily by the people who learn it, use it, and transmit it to others." This last sentence is telling because it seemingly encourages researchers to concentrate on the actual usage of language in episodes of interaction as it is transmitted from person to person.

Language ecology was exceptional at that time not only because it brought language out of the minds of individuals but also because it offered an early challenge to a linguistics that was, to quote Fransceschini (2011, 352), "born out of the spirit of monolingualism." Language ecology looked to examine the intersection of languages in a society; as Garner (2005, 91) explains, it was "primarily concerned with the ways in which different languages, in their spoken and written forms, co-exist and interact in a multilingual community." In its focus on multiple languages, language ecology was praised for opening up an "infinite world of possibilities" (Barron, Bruce, and Nunan 2002, 10) that related to aspects of language such as human interaction, language policy and planning, and classroom language teaching, to name just a few (Creese, Martin, and Hornberger 2008). Creese, Martin, and Hornberger (2008, i) take this even a step further in pointing out possible critical applications: "the study of language ecology is the study of diversity within specific socio-political settings where the processes of language use create, reflect and challenge particular hierarchies and hegemonies, however transient they may be." Such a statement is a reminder that an approach focusing on the usage of multiple languages in society must also consider the socio-political relationships among the languages as well.

Language ecology has been criticized for providing little in terms of direction for actual research. Garner (2005, 98) captures part of this critique by writing that "language ecology has not lived up to the promise of the original proposal by Haugen. It has remained a marginal and ill-defined approach, mainly in the study of multilingual societies." Muhlhausler (1996) notes a series of 10 questions that Haugen asks in his 1972 work that could serve as a research guide, but he also laments that except for a few studies such as Mackey (1980) and Enninger and Haynes (1984), language ecology has been of "quite marginal importance to the concerns of linguistic theoreticians" and has generally "failed" to make a "greater impact" (Muhlhausler 1995, 4).

Indeed, in attempting to research and write about multilingualism in Hawai'i, language ecology has not provided much practical guidance in terms of research design and methodology. Nonetheless, Haugen's ideas have served as an inspiration to pursue a study such as this that focuses on the usage of multiple languages in a single society with consideration of the attitudes toward and the social histories of those languages. In this sense, I agree with Garner when he writes, "I found the general perspective on the dynamic, interactive nature of language and community very valuable in integrating a range of social, cultural, and historical characteristics of the communities under study and relating them to a range of observed linguistic features." Following language ecology, this book devotes one chapter, chapter 2, to detailing the historical developments that had the greatest effect on making multilingual Hawai'i, with descriptions of language practices in other chapters remaining aware of the ways in which language use is constitutive of the social, cultural, and political features of the communities in Hawai'i.

In seeking a concrete method to research and present findings concerning the relationships among languages in Hawai'i, I found myself engaging more and more with an emerging area referred to as Linguistic Ethnography (Copland and Creese 2015; Rampton et al. 2004; Rampton, Maybin, and Roberts 2014). Borne out of the collaboration of researchers in the UK in the British Association of Applied Linguistics (BAAL), Linguistic Ethnography holds "that to a considerable degree, language and the social world are mutually shaping, and that close analysis of situated language use can provide both fundamental and distinctive insights into the mechanisms and dynamics of social and cultural production in everyday activity" (Rampton et al. 2004, 2). Drawing greatly on Hymes's ethnography of communication (Rampton 2007) and also the insights of researchers of the nexus of language, culture, interaction and identity such as Duranti (2003), Hanks (1996), and the Goodwins (Goodwin 2000; Goodwin and Goodwin 2004) as well as those associated with the work of Gumperz (1982, 1986) and interactional sociolinguistics, linguistic ethnography maintains that the linguistics and the ethnography are not supposed to be separate-but-connected realms of inquiry. In other words, ethnographic techniques are not meant merely to fill in background pieces of information about language usage. Instead, linguistic practices and sociocultural features are in a mutually constitutive, dialectic relationship that is constantly in flux (Blommaert 2012). Such a view sees situated language practices as actions that help construct the social and cultural worlds of the participants, not as actions that are the result of already in-place features of society and culture. Researching this dialectic relationship requires simultaneous understanding of the linguistic features as well as the ethnographic details in which they are embedded.

One important aspect of linguistic ethnography is the incorporation of the beliefs of post-structuralism. Embracing the ideas of critics such as Anderson (1983), Bakhtin (1981), Voloshinov (1973), and Foucalt (1972), linguistic ethnography problematizes concepts such as language, culture, and identity rather than assume them as stable objects of analysis. The acceptance prior to the analysis that participants are speaking a specific language while inhabiting a particular culture and possessing a certain identity is seen as a form of essentialism that prevents researchers from understanding the processes of "how humans come to inhabit these social categories" (Rampton, Maybin, and Roberts 2014, 5). As Rampton, Maybin, and Roberts (2014, 5) explain in describing the evolution of modern linguistics from its structuralist beginnings:

> The critique associated with post-structuralism has of course entailed much more than just dislodging linguistics from its former pre-eminence. Received notions like "society," "nation," "community," "gender" and "ethnicity" have also been the subject of extensive reassessment, so that now, rather than being seen as natural and unchangeable entities or identities, the default position in a great deal of social science is that these are social constructions, produced in discourse and ideology. (see e.g., Anderson 1981; Foucalt 1972)

One example of this "extensive reassessment" is a rethinking of the status of languages as autonomous systems represented by labels such as "English," "Japanese," or "Spanish" (Makoni and Pennycook 2005, 2006; Rampton 2015; Toolan 2003). To some critics, these labels are human inventions—as Makoni and Pennycook (2006, 18) note in making reference to Muhlhauser (2000), "the notion of a 'language' is a recent culture-specific notion associated with the rise of European nation States and the Enlightenment." Language categories are thus created by people via language by assigning labels to an assemblage of features assumed to constitute a system, which thus makes analyses of the social construction of these language categories an interesting topic in and of itself.

In linguistic ethnography, one outcome of this suspicion about language labels is an interest in hybrid forms of language in which participants mix languages to produce innovations not only in their usage of language but also in their construction of identities (Perez-Milans 2016; Rampton 2015). Terms such as heteroglossia, crossing, stylizing, and translanguaging have all been employed in order to examine and understand some of the dynamic and even ambiguous language practices actually being used by participants in society.

This book is not necessarily going to challenge language labels such as "Hawaiian," "Pidgin," "Japanese," "Portuguese," that have long been used in daily social life in Hawai'i. Yet, this post-structuralist critique of such language labels will prove relevant in at least two ways. First, one chapter of the book, chapter 5, is devoted to heteroglossic uses of language in public sectors of Hawai'i, including an analysis of public speeches made by Billy Kenoi, the local politician mentioned earlier. The analysis will show how the politician moves in and out of three supposedly stable languages, English, Pidgin, and Hawaiian, employing the non-referential, socially derived meanings of each one to create an innovative style of speaking. Second, in relation especially to language activism in Hawai'i to revitalize Hawaiian and to appreciate the locally constructed Pidgin, the analysis will include a focus on how discourse in and about these languages has constructed them as important aspects of Hawaiian society. In particular, part of the analysis in chapter 5 will show how public discourse in Hawai'i constructs language categories as relevant by treating them as accepted and typical aspects of society.

The previous quotation from Rampton, Maybin, and Roberts (2014, 5) asserts that notions such as language, culture, and identity are "produced in discourse and ideology." In fact, these two concepts, discourse and ideology, are key to the presentation of findings throughout this book. Chapters 3–7 utilize examples of actual discourse to describe the relationship among languages and also the relationships of those languages to the identities of their speakers; and likewise, the chapters also probe the ideologies that may be expressed explicitly or underlie the discourse.

To say, however, that this study will contain analyses of discourse does not necessarily paint a clear picture of the research methodology as there are several approaches to discourse analysis, including but not limited to "critical discourse analysis," "conversation analysis," "media discourse," "membership category analysis," and "narrative analysis." Some of these focus specifically on spoken discourse, some on written, and others include both spoken and written, and they all tend to diverge slightly from one another in terms of goals and focus. These differences, though, are not a significant obstacle in linguistic ethnography because of a mindset that remains open to the incorporation of different approaches to discourse as part of an "interdisciplinary relevance" (Rampton, Maybin, and Roberts 2014, 13). Rampton (2007, 585) makes this apparent when he states, "linguistic ethnography is in itself neither a paradigm, a cohesive 'school' nor some kind of definitive synthesis. Instead it is more accurately described as a site of encounter where a number of established lines of research interact, pushed together by circumstance, open to the recognition of new affinities, and sufficiently familiar with one another to treat differences with equanimity." For instance, even though perspectives such as critical discourse analysis and conversation analysis have been at epistemological odds concerning the inclusion of ethnographic information into analyses (see the discussion/debate between Schegloff 1999a and Billig

1999; also Koole 2007 and Wetherell 1998), linguistic ethnographers have suggested that such methodological paradigms "can be mixed as long as one is careful and willing to separate findings and methods from the explanations and interpretations with which they are conventionally packaged" (Rampton, Maybin, and Roberts 2014, 15).

Toward the goal of understanding the intersection of languages in Hawai'i, this book will make use of different approaches to situated language usage. In order to understand how categories of language and identity are constructed and negotiated in society, parts of the study will employ membership category analysis (i.e., Sacks 1992; Sacks and Schegloff 1979; Schegloff 2007). Membership category analysis will be employed, for example, to demonstrate in chapter 5 how people orient to the relevancy of language categories such as "Hawaiian," "Pidgin," and "Japanese," and it will be used again in chapter 6 to describe how interviewees negotiate Japanese identities. In other parts of this study, especially chapter 3, analysis of spoken discourse data will follow a turn-by-turn analysis that is associated with conversation analysis (i.e., Sacks, Schegloff, and Jefferson 1974). Such an analysis will be applied to conversations among elder speakers of Hawaiian and combined with insights from ethnopoetics (Auden 2009; Blommaert 2006; Hymes 2003) in order to reveal the different epistemological approach to speaking held by traditional speakers of Hawaiian. Additionally, elements of critical discourse analysis (Fairclough 1989, 1995) will be employed to show the role of newspaper discourse in reinforcing the social stigma attached to newer arrivals to Hawai'i from Micronesia (Huot et al. 2016; Tekin 2010). Finally, this study will also invoke ideas from the theory of metaphor that originated from the work of George Lakoff. Metaphor theory will not necessarily be applied to actual discourse but it will be employed in chapter 2 in discussing how English speakers in Hawai'i made use of metaphors to construct ideological beliefs that placed immigrant workers at a disadvantage. The combination of these methods, which both examine and analyze the usage of language in Hawai'i and also consider the positions of different ethnic groups in society, will work together to fulfill the larger goal of this study, namely understanding Hawai'i as a multilingual society.

The notion of ideology also occupies an important place in this study in terms of understanding the development and changes in the language ecologies in Hawai'i. Ideology, like discourse analysis, has been approached in various ways (Verschueren 2012). This study is especially interested in ideologies about languages and people and how they affect language usage and ultimately factor into situating languages and people in hierarchical relationships within society. For the purposes of this book, I rely on the definition of language ideology given by Jourdan and Angeli (2014), who draw greatly from Makihara (2004) and Kroskrity (2000) when they write:

> Language ideologies can be defined as cultural conceptions of languages (Makihara 2004). They are culturally shaped attitudes about the nature of language, the way it should be USED (i.e. when, where, and by whom), the VALUE of particular languages and linguistic varieties, their ORIGINS, and their FUTURE. (emphasis in the original)

As attitudes about language, language ideologies can greatly influence individual decisions about which language to use in particular situations, and they also serve as the basis of our evaluations of the people we come across on a daily basis. They play a role in education as parents sometimes decide which school to send their children based on language ideologies. This is especially true in Hawai'i, which now offers increasing opportunities to educate youth through Hawaiian. Language ideologies also reach into business and politics as people themselves constantly make decisions about how to speak while also judging how others speak.

Researchers have emphasized that multiple language ideologies can exist simultaneously within a single community, with some of them being in a contrastive relationship (Field and Kroskrity 2009; Kroskrity 2000, 2009). This is important point in Hawai'i, where beliefs differ concerning the various languages. Language ideologies may even diverge in a community concerning individual languages. For example, while advocates of Pidgin are growing in number, negative attitudes are still prevalent and play a strong role in keeping Pidgin out of certain sectors of society such as education.

Likewise, prior studies have made it clear that language ideologies may change over time. For example, Jourdan and Angel (2014) describe how the independence of the Solomon Islands in 1978 resulted in "new language ideologies" that began to realign the hierarchy that had traditionally given more prestige to English than to the locally created creole language known as Pijin. Similarly, Makihara (2004, 2007) found in Rapa Nui the breakdown of an ideology of "colonial diglossia" in which Spanish, the language of the people from Chile who annexed Rapa Nui, was seen as dominant over the Rapa Nui language. The political successes of a local indigenous movement helped shift the language ideology and allowed for the rise of Rapa Nui syncretic languages practices. This notion of shifting language ideologies will be important in understanding both the rise of the Hawaiian language revitalization movement, the ambivalent attitudes and future prospects for Pidgin, and also the prospects for "newer" languages to Hawai'i such as the Filipino and Micronesian languages.

In some cases, the language ideologies in Hawai'i will be readily apparent in overt expressions in discourse (i.e., "I think Pidgin should not be spoken in schools."). In other cases, they will not be as obvious, only being visible in the common sense inferences made by people in their daily interactions. This point about "uncovering" ideology is made by Verschueren (2012, 7) when he notes, "ideology is associated with underlying patterns of meaning, framing of interpretation, world views, or forms of everyday thinking and explanation. Thus the way in which beliefs, ideas, or opinions are discursively used, i.e., their forms of expression as well as the rhetorical purposes they serve, are just as important for ideology as the contents of thinking for which these three terms serve as labels." Language ideologies, then, as underlying patterns of meaning, can play an important role in encouraging audiences of readers and/or listerns to arrive at certain conclusions based on features of language present in discourse. An example would be when the discourse encourages an audience to view certain languages and the people who speak them as "outsiders" or "others" (Huot et al. 2016; Tekin 2010). The analysis of situated language in discourse in this study will thus become important to uncovering and discussing ideologies in Hawai'i toward language and their effects on the development of a multilingual society.

Lastly about ideologies, it should be noted that while this book is largely interested in ideologies about language, understanding multilingual Hawai'i necessitates consideration of beliefs about the speakers of languages as well. A significant portion of chapter 2, for example, will explicate the ideologies disseminated by English speakers about immigrants who arrived to work on the plantations and who brought with them various languages. Likewise, I will endeavor in chapter 7 to pinpoint the ideological beliefs expressed in public discourse concerning some of the people who arrived more recently in Hawai'i.

ORGANIZATION OF THIS BOOK

This book consists of a total of eight chapters, including this introduction. Chapter 1 adopts a historical approach as it describes the development of multilingual Hawai'i, beginning with the arrival of the first westerners in 1778. It details some of the major events that led not only to the introduction of a diverse range of languages into society, but also to the emergence of Pidgin, the rise to power of English, and the demise of Hawaiian. This chapter is not based on the analysis of discourse, but it does attempt to describe the origins of some of the beliefs toward certain languages as well as toward the speakers of those languages. It relies on the writings of those who have produced detailed research on the history of languages in Hawai'i, such as Reinecke (1969) and Schütz (1994), and also others who have discussed the history and situations of specific immigrant groups. By using this prior research to examine the origins of Hawai'i's diversity, this chapter will further set the stage for examination in subsequent chapters of some of the situated usages of the various languages as well as the ideological beliefs that underlie current Hawaiian society.

Chapter 2 centers on the Hawaiian language, starting from the period in the early 1970s that has generally been referred to as the Hawaiian Renaissance. This chapter places an emphasis on the development of a strong revitalization movement in the last 40 years, describing how Hawaiian has reemerged as a visible language in society. Two analyses of discourse are presented, the first of which focuses on repetition in Hawaiian conversational discourse of elder speakers in order to demonstrate how the Hawaiian language brings with it a different epistemological approach to human interaction. This analysis emphasizes the contribution of Hawaiian to the diversity of knowledge in multilingual Hawai'i. The second analysis speaks to concerns about the authenticity of the reemerging Hawaiian language as it focuses on the expression of agency in the speech of younger Hawaiian speakers who are products of the revitalization movement.

Chapter 3 is devoted specifically to Pidgin and endeavors to understand and explain the complex place of Pidgin in Hawai'i. This chapter draws largely from a growing literature focused on attitudes toward Pidgin in Hawai'i, some of which is showing that beliefs about Pidgin, which have traditionally been negative, may becoming more positive. This chapter includes an analysis, first of all, of the speech of Billy Kenoi during his time as mayor to underscore the degree to which Pidgin may be used as an effective resource in the public sphere. Additionally, a second analysis is offered, this time of Pidgin in radio advertisements, in order to gain further insight into the usage of Pidgin in the public sphere. The analysis makes use of the idea of indexicality (Ochs 1992, 2012; Silverstein 2003) to indicate the connection between Pidgin and the notion of "local" and to show how the use of Pidgin, a language mostly thought to be a language restricted to informal, private situations, contributes to the creation of a local style that appeals to an audience that is local or at least familiar with Pidgin.

Chapter 4 focuses on the phenomenon of heteroglossia (Bakhtin 1981) and particularly examines discourse in which Hawaiian, Pidgin, and English are used together. This chapter presents three analyses, with the first focusing on university commencement speeches made by Billy Kenoi. This analysis describes how he is able, through the usage of resources from three languages, to invoke different ideological beliefs, specifically, the prestige associated with Hawaiian, the formality of English, and the casual, private, and even joking side of Pidgin, to create innovative speech full of humor that also fulfills the serious functions of political and public discourse. The second analysis looks at written discourse on the website of Kamehameha Schools, the largest private school system in Hawai'i, and describes how creative mixtures of English and Hawaiian allow the school system to cater to people of a Hawaiian ethnic background who are interested in formal education in Hawai'i. The third analysis focuses on the significance of these innovate language mixings for language usage in Hawai'i, and employs some insights from membership category analysis to compare and contrast these emerging hybrid forms to traditional language categories such as "Hawaiian" and "Japanese." Discussion of the analyses in this chapter centers on the idea that investigation of heteroglossic language practices in Hawai'i holds greats promise in terms of understanding the complexities of language usage in a multilingual place such as Hawai'i.

Chapter 5 investigates the Japanese language as an example of an immigrant language, that is, a language that is not necessarily indigenous to Hawai'i but nevertheless has played an important role in history and the development of modern society. Employing an analysis of four sets of interviews with people of different backgrounds with the Japanese language, this chapter highlights the problematic nature of the label of "Japanese" in reference to both a language and an identity in current Hawaiian society. More specifically, the analysis shows that the category "Japanese" is invoked to refer to a diverse range of language varieties and identities. Discussion of the analysis draws connections to the concept of heteroglossia presented in chapter 4, which enables understanding of how a category such as Japanese has become constituted by a mixture of languages and identities since the first arrival of immigrants from Japan in the 1800s.

Chapter 6 focuses on two fairly diverse groups of languages and their speakers, represented by the categories "Filipino" and "Micronesian." These are considered together in the same chapter because they are, relatively speaking, two of the newer sets of groups to Hawai'i, even though the people and languages of Micronesian are considerably more recent. This chapter consists of one analysis, a critical discourse analysis of newspaper articles, that intends to bring to light to the ideological beliefs about the categories "Filipino" and "Micronesian" that exist in current society. The analysis compares the newspaper discourse to the relatively short histories of both groups in Hawai'i, histories which indicate that, as later arrivals, both were subjected to othering from those already integrated into the society. By examining the way discourse is structured about these languages and their speakers, the analysis uncovers the ideological beliefs that may serve as obstacles to more complete participation in a multilingual society.

The conclusion works to tie the analyses together toward an overall assessment of the Hawaiian context and of the idea of a "multilingual Hawai'i." It furthermore endeavors to connect the issues raised in each chapter to the concept of multilingualism and express the greater contributions of the methodology and the results to our understanding of the significance of diversity in Hawai'i.

FINAL COMMENTS

Before moving to the chapters of analysis, I should let readers know that a significant portion of the data and the observations in this book come from my place of residence and employment, the town of Hilo on the Big Island of Hawai'i. While the findings are meant to serve, as much as possible, as generalizations about the Hawaiian context, questions may of course be raised in terms of the degree to which the observations apply to the different communities on all islands. Some familiar with the situations in other parts of state might argue that certain uses of language are not reflective of their communities. Such a potential criticism, however, actually speaks to one of the main points of the book, namely, that Hawai'i, despite its remote location and relatively small population, is indeed a diverse place saturated with various languages and different beliefs. While it is impossible to capture all aspects of its diversity in one book, it is hoped that this work will push us forward toward understanding what this diversity means for Hawai'i as a multilingual society.

Chapter One

The Development of Hawai'i as a Multilingual Society

The language situation in Hawaii is unique. The population is made up of many races, speaking distinctly different languages. Sometimes more than one foreign tongue is spoken within a single home. The situation is further complicated by the fact that "pidgin" is the language of the street, and is almost universally spoken and understood by the whole population. Probably nowhere else in the world, certainly in no other area under the American flag, is there a language situation paralleling that in Hawaii. Education officials are alive to the seriousness of the problems involved and are experimenting with methods designed to further their solution. (Cook 1938, ix)

Americans know that their impressionable children, literally surrounded throughout the school- day and at playtime by these swarms of Orientals, will unconsciously pick up and adopt Oriental manners and mannerisms. . . . The American child will be held back to the pace of the Oriental, who is studious indeed but toiling under a terrific weight of lack of English words and word-images to respond to the efforts of the teacher. Anonymous school authority of Hawai'i, 1921 (quoted in Allen 1921 and also Young 2002)

INTRODUCTION: MULTILINGUALISM AS A SOCIAL PROBLEM

In their introduction to the book "The Multilingual Challenge," Jessner and Kramsch (2015, 2–5) note that multilingualism may be viewed as "an opportunity," "an advantage," and also "as a sign of vitality." However, as suggested by these two quotations, multilingualism in Hawai'i has traditionally been viewed as a problem.[1] While the quotations refer specifically to an educational context, the plurality of languages in Hawai'i has caused problems throughout other public sectors of society as well, even in modern Hawai'i. Although the previous chapter mentioned the availability of the driver's test in multiple language, this was only made possible following a lawsuit in 2013 on behalf of speakers of other languages, which forced governmental leaders to recognize Hawai'i's multilingualism and allow tests in multiple languages (Kelleher 2014a). As reported in the newspapers, the state began offering the exam in several languages in 2001, but when the English version of the test was updated shortly thereafter, the state stopped offering the translated exams (Kelleher 2014b). Multilingualism has also raised challenges in the court system, where it has been difficult to meet the increased demand for interpreters for a diverse number of languages with a limited supply of qualified workers (Viotti 2003). Additionally, even though Hawaiian was named an official language of the state in 1978, requests by Hawaiian-English bilinguals to employ Hawaiian in court have not been met with approval (Hofschneider 2018; Wong and Perry 2017). These are language issues caused by multilingualism that reverberate throughout political, economical, as well as educational sectors of Hawaiian society.

This purpose of this chapter to provide a historical introduction to multilingualism in Hawai'i by adopting a critical perspective that explains the "multilingualism as problem" viewpoint that developed throughout history and still exists today. In order to do so, the chapter is divided into two basic sections, one that provides a description in chronological order of the major events that moved Hawai'i from a monolingual society to one marked by multiple languages, and another that focuses on the ideological beliefs that became attached to the languages and their speakers. It will be shown that these ideologies contribute to the process of "othering" used by the western colonizers in Hawai'i to construct non-English speakers as "different." Othering is related to Said's work on Orientalism as well as critical research on colonialism and is described as a process that results in "moral and political judgments of superiority and inferiority between in-groups and outgroups ('us' and 'them'), and within groups" (Dervin 2015). Othering constructs groups and the individuals placed in those groups not only as "different" but also as "exotic" and even "deficient," and thus allows those initiating the "othering" to claim their own superiority. The process of othering, which the European "discoverers" started applying first to the native Hawaiians and later to the various groups of immigrants, will be important to understanding how even in a modern world where many linguists and other activists fight to preserve the world's languages, multilingualism can still be viewed as a problem.

One of the reasons for emphasizing a critical approach in the early stages of this book is to separate this work from the tendency to portray Hawai'i as a paragon of racial harmony. This view has been referred to as "the Hawai'i multicultural model" and it supposedly distinguishes Hawai'i from other parts of the world based on its "tolerance, equality, and harmony" (Okamura 2008, 7). Such a model was promoted by academics in the early 1900s, with the scholar Romanzo Adams credited as the first—but not the last—to refer to Hawai'i as a "racial melting pot" (Adams 1926; Okamura 2008, 8). Such an image of Hawai'i has been reinforced by some influential historical figures. Martin Luther King Jr., in a visit to the islands soon after Hawai'i was officially declared a state of the United States in 1959, made the following remarks:

> As I think of the struggle that we are engaged in in the South land, we look to you for inspiration and as a noble example, where you have already accomplished in the area of racial harmony and racial justice, what we are struggling to accomplish in other sections of the country, and you can never know what it means to those of us caught for the moment in the tragic and often dark midnight of man's inhumanity to man, to come to a place where we see the glowing daybreak of freedom and dignity and racial justice. (Dekneef 2016)

More recently, former president Barack Obama, considered an authority on Hawai'i because he was born and partly raised on the island of O'ahu, supported this depiction when he stated that Hawai'i "comes about as close as you'll come to a true melting pot of cultures, where people live and work together in mutual trust and mutual respect" (reported by Epstein 2011). This image of harmony reaches back to the World War II period, when, despite the fact that the authorities placed some people of Japanese descent in internment camps in Hawai'i, *Life* magazine in 1945 labeled Hawai'i as "the world's most successful experiment in mixed breeding, a sociologist's dream of interracial cultures" (reported by Berman 2015).

To be clear, the purpose here is not to paint a picture of Hawai'i as a place of social unrest. My own personal experience has made it evident that the diverse combination of people, many of whom are themselves of mixed ethnicity, often interact smoothly and harmoniously in both private and public sectors of society. As Haas (1998, 51) comments, "somehow the competitive coexistence of Hawai's ethnic groups seems to work without embittered rancor despite occasional flare-ups." Nonetheless, any discussion of multilingualism in Hawai'i that does not consider the underlying beliefs that have left English as the dominant language of the islands and placed other languages and their speakers at a disadvantage and sometimes even in peril would be far from complete. I begin the following description with the event considered responsible for introducing Hawai'i to the Western world, namely, the landing of the British Captain James Cook on the shores of Hawai'i in 1778.

A BASIC TIMELINE: THE BIRTH AND DEVELOPMENT OF MULTILINGUALISM

First Arrivals: The Introduction of Writing and English

When Cook arrived at the island of Kaua'i in 1778, he found a population of Hawaiian speakers. At that time, Hawaiian flourished as a dynamic language used for all communication with dialectical variations across the islands (Wilson 1998a). The Hawaiian language provided a foundation for a system of communal land usage, a complex system of law, and all the different aspects of communication, including chanting and the hula, which allowed the people to pass along oral histories without the need of a formal written language (Holmes, Leong, and Yoo 2012).

While Cook's arrival is regarded as the beginning of Western influence in Hawai'i, scholars note that the appearance of Cook and his men did not usher in immediate changes to the linguistic situation (Reinecke 1969; Schütz 1994). Reinecke (1969, 25) writes that "before approximately 1810 linguistic communication between foreign seamen and native Hawaiians was intermittent and comparatively restricted," and Schütz (1994) likewise notes that there were no subsequent recorded visits from the outside for nearly 10 years. Interaction with the outside world did increase beginning in 1810, as whaling and the sandalwood trade brought numerous sailors to the islands (Kuykendall 1965; Reinecke 1969), but the year 1820, when American missionaries started coming to Hawai'i in order to "save" the natives from their religious beliefs and so-called heathen ways, serves as a much more important date in terms of language and linguistic change in the islands. Interestingly, their arrival came one year after the death of King Kamehamehama I, the man who united the islands and started the Hawaiian Kingdom, and one year after King Kamehamehama II lifted the religous kapu that had made it illegal for women and men to eat together. It has been suggested that the timing made many Hawaiians, including some in the royal family, open to new ideas (see Kamele'ehiwa 1992 for a detailed, critical discussion of the events surrounding the removal of the kapu).

The missionaries brought the English language with them, but as Bickerton (1998) notes, their initial purpose was not to force the natives to abandon Hawaiian for English. In fact, the missionaries originally looked at the Hawaiian language as a resource that could help them spread their religious views. In order to do so, they endeavored to develop a standardized way of writing Hawaiian, which is thought to have previously been solely an oral language.[2] The missionaries demonstrated quick success as they introduced the idea of printing as well as printing presses. In the words of Reinecke (1969, 27–28):

Only twenty months after entering the islands, the missionaries had partially fixed the Hawaiian orthography and were able to print a spelling book in the vernacular. One month after the printing press began to function, the chief Kuakini was able to write a letter in his own language. He was followed by thousands . . . Hawaiian had become overnight a written language.

Credit is typically given to the missionaries for introducing writing to the Hawaiians, but the adoption of writing is largely owed to the willingness and ability of the Hawaiians to learn how to both read and write their own language as it was written in the Western orthography. King Kauikeaouli, otherwise known as King Kamehameha III, reportedly declared in 1824 "*He aupuni palapala koʻu*" 'Mine shall be a kingdom of literacy' (Kamakau 2001). Within a relatively short period of time, the Hawaiian population developed a high rate of literacy (Huebner 1984; Kloss 1977).

With the help of the missionaries, the first Hawaiian language newspaper was established in 1834 at the Lahainaluna School on Maui. Through 1948, there were over one hundred newspapers in Hawaiian, which made it possible not only for Hawaiian speakers to voice their opinions about their changing society but also to document information about the history and customs of their land, information that had previously passed down orally (Geracimos-Chapin 1998). As Charlot (1998, 55) writes, "Hawaiian-language newspapers provide thousands of pages of information on all aspects of Hawaiian culture."

Even with the presence and rising status of the English speaking missionaries, Hawaiian still remained the dominant language of society in the early and middle 1800s (Bickerton 1998; Buck 1993; Roberts 1995). However, English did start to make its mark on the linguistic landscape in Hawaiʻi. The first English language newspaper appeared in 1836, two years after the first Hawaiian language publication. In addition, English was being learned by the Hawaiian elite, including the royals, the chiefs, and the children of both groups. Moreover, as early as the 1840s, laws and other governmental documents were being drafted first in English and then in Hawaiian (Buck 1993).

And more than just increased visibility in certain aspects of society, English, according to Reinecke (1969), began exerting an influence on the Hawaiian language. Reinecke (1969) offers the example of English-speaking translators of the Bible and religious materials, who allowed English idioms to creep into their work and who created expressions from a Western perspective that may not have been previously employed in Hawaiian. Reinecke also lamented that contact with English was resulting in the loss of traditional ways of speaking (Reinecke 1969, 29):

The attention of the nation to the *palapala* and to the foreign culture which accompanied it could not but have a destructive influence upon the preservation of, and further composition in, the elevated, extraordinarily allusive, and obscure poetic and religious special language. . . . The cultural changes also destroyed such secret dialects as the *kake* (described as, in at least one form, "a jargon used by criminals").

The missionaries may not have intended to put the Hawaiian language in peril, but these seemingly minor linguistic changes foretold major linguistic and social changes on the horizon.

THE PLANTATION ERA AND THE ARRIVAL OF FOREIGN LABORERS

Both whaling and the sandalwood trade brought numerous sailors to the islands, particularly between the years of 1810–1860, but the business that is most responsible for the rise of multilingualism in Hawai'i is sugar cane, beginning with the first plantation in 1835 on Koloa, Kaua'i, under the supervision of William Hooper from Boston (Takaki 1983). The plantation was made possible by a lease obtained by Ladd & Company, an American firm that had set up shop in Honolulu. At the time of this first plantation, it was not possible for foreigners to own land outrightly in Hawai'i. This, however, changed soon thereafter in 1848 through an event known as the Great Mahele, which permanently altered the traditional practices for dividing land in Hawai'i (see detailed discussion in Kame'eleihiwa 1992 for a Hawaiian perspective). It led to legislature in 1850 that made land available to both Hawaiian commoners and foreigners on a fee-simple basis. This new way of dividing land made it possible for caucasian businessmen not only to lease but also to own the lands and establish their own planter businesses. Employing the word "haole," which can be a derogatory reference to caucasians (Rohrer 2010), Okihiro (1991, 6–7) explains the effects of the Great Mahele by writing, "After the Great Mahele and the 1850 land act, foreigners eagerly bought and cheated their way into ownership of large estates; by 1886, two-thirds of government land and much of the land of chiefs and commoners had passed into *Haole* hands."

However, despite the potential for profit through these plantations, expansion within the United States, specifically the establishment of California as a state, made it difficult to export sugar without paying significant tariffs. Accordingly, sugar plantations struggled to find success in Hawai'i. Beechert (1985, 58) points out that "by 1856, there were only five plantations operating in all of Hawai'i," a situation which changed very little through 1874, when "in reality the Hawaiian economy was at a standstill" (Beechert 1985, 78). 1876, though, was a fortuitous year for the sugar planters, as a reciprocity treaty was signed with the United States that lifted tariffs on exporting sugar from Hawai'i to the United States. This treaty led to a boom in the sugar business and an increase in the number of plantations. According to Beechert (1985, 80), "while there had been a total of twenty plantations in 1875, there were sixty-three in 1880."

When the plantations began in 1835, the owners first looked to the native Hawaiian population for labor, typically giving them contracts of five years (with a change later to three years). With the relatively small number of plantations prior to 1876, it was possible to accomplish the work with a workforce comprised mostly of Hawaiians. Still, there were two essential problems. First, diseases introduced through contact with the Westerners had begun decimating the native population. According to estimations, the native population decreased from approximately 300,000 in 1778, when Cook landed, to about 71,000 in 1850 (Takaki 1983). Furthermore, by the end of the nineteenth century, statistics show that the native population decreased by 95 percent in the approximately 100 years since Cook's arrival (Osorio 2002; Rohrer 2010; Stannard 1989). Therefore, Hawaiian workers were growing increasingly scarce. Second, the Hawaiians discovered that the plantation work was hard labor with little compensation and thus began to avoid the plantations as much as possible. They opted to do other work that allowed more creativity and also higher pay (Beechart 1985).

Realizing that new sources of labor were necessary, the sugar planters turned to the Chinese, who were already familiar with Hawai'i through the sandalwood trade (Nordyke and Lee 1989). There was reportedly a small population of Chinese in Hawai'i, some of whom had already been involved in sugar planting and sugar milling (Char 1975). As Takaki (1983, 13) notes, Hooper had considered the Chinese to be a viable option on the plantation he supervised in Koloa in 1835, "in Hooper's view, the Chinese had more experience in milling and were more reliable factory operatives than the Hawaiians."

With an initially positive evaluation of Chinese workers, sugar planters recruited male workers from China, especially Kwangtung and Fukien in the southeastern part of mainland China, to come to Hawai'i to work on the plantations. In 1852, Captain John Cass delivered 195 workers to Hawai'i (Nordyke and Lee 1989), hence starting what would be a significantly large-scale immigration of Chinese to Hawai'i. According to Reinecke (1969), the census recorded 364 Chinese in Hawai'i in 1853, 700 in 1860, and 2,038 in 1872. Beechert further notes that these numbers increased quite drastically following the reciprocity treat of 1876, with 48,816 Chinese arriving in Hawai'i between 1879 and 1898.

These new arrivals brought language with them from their homelands, which given the language situation in China, made for an interesting dynamic in Hawai'i. The Chinese immigrants came from different parts of China and thus spoke dialects of Chinese, including Cantonese, Hakka, and later Mandarin, that were not necessarily mutually intelligible (Nordyke and Lee 1989; Char and Char 1975). This led to a situation in which Chinese immigrants sometimes found it easier to employ Hawaiian with each rather than their own dialects in order to make commuication easier. Nordyke and Lee (1989, 199) report the following observation made by Reverand William Speer in 1856, "One of the amusing sights I have seen on the islands has been Canton men and Amoy men resorting to the dialect of the Hawaiians as the only medium of ready communication with each other."

Some Chinese elected to return to China at the end of their contracts, but many also chose to stay in Hawai'i. Of those who remained, some moved away from the hard labor on the plantations and found other forms of work such as as farm hands, vegetable stands, and laundry helpers. Moreover, some even became involved in businesses such as merchantry, trade, carpentry, and shoemaking, that had previously been occupied by the caucasians, and they subsequently created an area in Honolulu for themselves that came to be known as Chinatown (Nordyke and Lee 1989). The Chinese were, in fact, the first immigrant group "to leave the plantations and to urbanize" (Nordyke and Lee 1989, 204). While many of the Chinese learned Hawaiian, this urbanization meant that a language other than English and Hawaiian was to be heard regularly outside of the plantations. It also was to set the stage for later immigrant groups in terms of seeking work outside of the plantations and inserting themselves into society.

Given the rapid increase in Chinese immigration in the late 1850s and 1860, reports stated that "by the middle of the eighteen sixties there were more Chinese men than white men at the islands" (Daws 1968, 181). With this large population branching out into some businesses that had been previously worked by caucasians, the Chinese, who had been initially viewed as good workers (Nordyke and Lee 1989), were now seen as a threat by the caucasian population, therefore prompting the sugar planters to step up their efforts to "recruit" sources of labor from other countries. In 1868, a single shipload of Japanese workers was sent over, but due to difficult living conditions and low pay, the workers, who had come from the urban area of Yokohama (Okamura 2014; Okihiro 1991), filed complaints with the Hawaiian Bureau of Immigration and returned to Japan. This led to a decision by the Japanese government not to send additional citizens to Hawai'i to work in the fields. At approximately the same time, people from islands in the Pacific were brought in to work as plantation laborers. According to Reinecke

(1969), 2,448 Pacific Islanders arrived between 1869 and 1885. All of them were from Micronesia with approximately 1,800 from the Gilbert Islands. Reinecke (1969, 66) also notes that most returned to their native islands as soon as they could, and he likewise suggests that those who stayed "were lost among the native Hawaiian population" and "learned to speak the Hawaiian language fluently." In other words, they had little effect on the linguistic situation of the islands.

With the Reciprocity Treaty in 1876 enabling sugar planters to expand their businesses, they began recruiting workers from two sets of islands off the coast of Portugal, the Madeira Islands and the Azores. The idea to do so came via a recommendation from Dr. William Hillebrand, a botanist and former physician to Hawai'i's royal families who had been appointed by King Kalākaua to serve as commissioner of immigration. The Madeira Islands and the Azores had a climate similar to Hawai'i and were also strongly agricultural, suggesting that workers from those places would be a good fit on the plantations. Between 1878 and 1913, approximately 25,000 Portuguese men, women, and children came as plantation contract laborers (Andrade and Nishimura 2011). Not all of them stayed in Hawai'i; some moved quickly on to California (Reinecke 1969), but those who stayed were reportedly quick to integrate themselves into local Hawaiian society. Unlike the Chinese and the one group of Japanese who came before them, many of them brought their families and then added to their families once moving to Hawai'i. As Sakoda and Siegel note, "in 1896, they made up over half of the locally born immigrant population" (Sakoda and Siegel 2003, 13).

In the meantime, Hawai'i continued to urge Japan to allow its citizens to come to Hawai'i to work in the fields. Following a visit to Japan from King Kalākaua in 1881 and a message from special envoy John Kapena that stated "Hawai'i holds out her loving hand and heart to Japan and desires that your people may come and cast in their lots with ours and repeople our island home" (Okihiro 1991, 24), Japan agreed and Japanese immigration began anew in 1885 with mostly male workers from rural areas. According to Okamura (2014), between 1885 and 1924, approximately 214,000 Japanese went to Hawai'i, including 159,000 men, nearly 50,000 women, and less than 5,000 children. Okamura (2014) further notes by the year 1900, the Japanese had become by far the largest group in the islands, constituting 39.7 percent of the population. By comparison, the native Hawaiians were listed at 24.4, the Chinese at 16.7, the Portuguese at 11.9, and the whites at 5.4.

The Chinese, Japanese, and Portuguese represent the largest immigrant groups prior to 1900, but they were by no means the only groups who were brought in around that time to work on the plantations. It is also reported, for example, that between 1882 and 1885, 1,052 Germans came to Hawai'i to work as laborers with the majority of them concentrated on a plantation in Lihue on the island of Maui (Reinecke 1969). Other Europeans include 615 Norwegians in 1881, 3,000 Russians from 1906 to 1912, Spanish speakers mostly from Malaga province between 1907 and 1913, Spanish-speaking workers from Puerto Rico in 1900 and 1901, and also laborers from Sweden, Denmark, and Poland who came in the late 1800s and early 1900s (Reinecke 1969). Reinecke (1969) emphasizes that the linguistic influence of the languages brought in by these workers was relatively minimal, but their arrival in Hawai'i does reflect the degree to which the Hawaiian cultural and linguistic landscape had changed in the one hundred some years since contact with Cook and his men.

In terms of Asia, there was significant immigration from Korea from 1904 through 1905. Chung-Do, Huh, and Kang (2011, 177) state that "by 1905, some 7,900 Korean immigrants were living and working in Hawai'i. About 90 percent of these immigrants were males, 6 percent children, and 4 percent women." In addition, there was also immigration on a large scale from Okinawa that began in 1900. It is estimated that "twenty-five thousand people emigrated from Okinawa to Hawai'i between 1900 and 1924" (Higashionna, Ikehara, and Matsukawa 2011, 131). Okinawan immigration is often subsumed under the label of "Japanese," but this is not entirely accurate given that Okinawa, prior to being taken over by Japan, was an independent kingdom, much like Hawai'i. Many ancestors of the immigrants identify as Okinawan and have created their own Okinawan associations and cultural centers and have begun to learn the indigenous languages of the Okinawan islands (Yuuji 2018).

Economic, Educational, and Linguistic Changes

At the same time that these workers were arriving from the outside, power was shifting within Hawaiian society, leading to some dramatic social changes. As the plantation owners gained profits by using cheap immigrant labor, an economic system came into place to serve the plantations that was dominated by mercantile houses known as the Big Five: Alexander & Baldwin, American Factors, C. Brewer and Company, Castle and Cooke, and Theo H. Davies & Company. The power and influence of the Big Five crossed over into the political arena and culminated in 1893 with the overthrow of the Hawaiian Kingdom by American businessmen with the support of American soldiers. Hawai'i was subsequently annexed by the United States in 1898 and officially became a territory in 1900.

The overthrow of the Hawaiian Kingdom coincided with major changes in the linguistic situation as well, especially in the languages used in education. When education was made compulsory in 1840, the majority of schooling was through Hawaiian, which helped the literacy rate reach an even higher level (Huebner 1984; Kloss 1977). While English language education had been available for the children of missionaries and for "elite" Hawaiians of a royal or chiefly background, English medium education became more readily accessible in 1853 when the legislature approved funds for the establishment of English medium schools for Hawaiians (Huebner 1984). As more Hawaiian students went to English schools, there was a steady decline in the number of students receiving education through the medium of Hawaiian. Huebner provides the following statistics (1984, 83):

> In 1854, there had been 412 common schools with a total population of 11,782 pupils, who received instruction in Hawaiian by Hawaiian teachers (Kuykendall 1968b, 109). By 1874, the number of common schools declined to 196, with only 5,522 students enrolled (71% of the student population). By 1878, 61% of the students were still enrolled in Hawaiian medium schools. By 1882, that figure dropped to 33% (Kloss 1977, 204). By 1888, less than 16% were found in such schools, with the number of common schools falling to sixty-three (Wist 1940, 72). Only seven years later, in the year of the overthrow of the Liliʻuokalani government by Americans in the community, the enrollment in Hawaiian medium schools had dropped to less than three percent of all students in public schools in Hawaiʻi.[3]

The decrease in influence of public schools in society was accompanied by the development of private schools, most of which consisted of education offered through the medium of English. The first private school, Punahou School, began in 1841 as a school primarily serving the children of the missionaries. In 1887 another school, Kamehameha School was founded from the will of Bernice Pauahi Pākī Bishop, great granddaughter of Kamehameha I, to further the education of the diminishing Hawaiian population. However, the Kamehameha School case is telling of the linguistic situation of that time in history because, despite being established specifically for Hawaiians, the school chose English from the outset as its medium of education (Eyre 2004). The decision on the part of Kamehahema Schools to focus on English education was followed nine years later by legislature in 1896 that required education to be carried out through English in all public and private schools. The law actually stated that schools had the option not to follow it, but in such cases, the schools would not be recognized by the new American-controlled government (Lucas 2000). As Lucas (2000) notes, by 1902 there were no longer any Hawaiian medium schools.

Pidgin and the Plight of Other Non-English Languages

English may have risen to the top of the hierarchy of languages in mainstream Hawaiian society, but it was clear at the same time that the diverse mixture of ethnic backgrounds was having an effect on the linguistic situation as pidgin languages developed. As Bickerton (1998) reminds us, the first pidgin that developed differed greatly from the Pidgin heard today because it was a pidgin Hawaiian. In Bickerton's (1998, 53) words, "the linguistic history of contact between Native Hawaiians and Caucasians, known locally as *haoles* . . . , was for almost a century primarily a story of *haole* accommodation to the Hawaiian language rather than Hawaiian accommodation to English." Bickerton (1998) includes the missionaries of 1820 as some of the speakers of this pidgin Hawaiian. Moreover, Bickerton and Wilson (1987) suggest that the Chinese as well as other immigrant groups who arrived later also employed pidgin Hawaiian.

In contrast to beliefs that the Pidgin of current Hawai'i society grew out of some form of broken English spoken by Hawaiians and then immigrant laborers as they tried to conform to the wishes of the haole elite (Carr 1972, Reinecke 1969), Bickerton (1998; also see Bickerton and Wilson 1987 and Roberts 1995) believes that a pidgin English emerged separately in society as pidgin Hawaiian remained relatively stable. One reason given for this is that despite a diminished Hawaiian population and growing American influence, the strength of the Hawaiian language endured even as the Hawaiian Kingdom was overturned in 1893 (Bickerton 1998; Bickerton and Wilson 1987). In fact, Bickerton (1998, 57) suggests that the precursor to Pidgin was not necessarily English per se but rather "a macaronic pidgin" that was "a structureless jumble of words drawn from several languages." This macaronic pidgin emerged by the mid-1880s as the Hawaiian language still predominated but "as more and more English-speaking supervisory staff entered the plantation system" (Bickerton 1998, 57). Eventually, then, it was not that pidgin English took over pidgin Hawaiian but rather a "gradual transition" occurred "between the pidgins" "including, probably, a period in which they were indistinguishable from one another" (Bickerton and Wilson 1987, 71). This pidgin then continued taking on lexical, phonological, and grammatical features that resembled English and became stabilized as the immigrants gave birth to children who grew up speaking this emerging pidgin, often together with the first languages of their parents. And once children started speaking it, Hawai'i had itself, in the words of Bickerton (1998, 53), "a novel creole language," in other words, what is known today as Pidgin. Reinecke (1969) gives a general time frame of 1905–1920 for the full stabilization of Pidgin as a creole. Although educators, politicians, and business leaders of the early 1900s had hoped that English would replace Hawaiian as the primary language of the islands, Pidgin became the language that many people preferred to use, particularly in more informal aspects of society. Chapter 3 of this book provides a more detailed description of the grammatical features of Pidgin as well as the social implications for the emergence of a language that was not welcomed by the newly formed American government.

In addition to Pidgin, further evidence of the effects of multilingualism on society is found in the concern that developed among many residents for heritage languages, including Hawaiian. Realizing that few children were learning Hawaiian, legislature was passed in 1919 amending the 1896 law to state that "the Hawaiian language shall be taught in addition to English in all normal and high schools of the territory" (Lucas 2000, 10). Despite the vague wording "the Hawaiian language shall be taught," this did not mean that Hawaiian was once again to become the medium of education. Instead, Hawaiian became a school subject to be taught mostly through English (Schütz 1994). Shortly thereafter, Hawaiian also became a subject at the University of Hawai'i (Schütz 1994). At roughly the same time, parents and other members in the Japanese, Chinese, and Korean communities established schools, the so-called language schools, where children could learn their heritage languages. These schools were typically taught through the heritage languages and were attended by students in addition to their regular English schools. Students usually went in the afternoons after their regular schools ended or on weekends. Statistics show that in 1922 there were 1,314 students in Chinese language schools, 21,448 in Japanese schools, and 126 in Korean schools (Asato 2006). These figures increased through 1934 to 2,714; 41,192; and 646, respectively (Asato 2006).

With the increase in these language schools and with the formation of Pidgin as a creole language, this period of Hawaiian history in the 1920 is a particularly dynamic one in terms of language. At the same time, this is a period in which the haole elite stepped up their efforts to problematize Hawai'i's multilingualism, especially at the educational level. At the center of these efforts was the desire to promote English, which led to the establishment of a series of schools known as as "English Standard Schools." These schools were established in 1924 as the number of people moving to Hawai'i from the mainland continued to increase. Unlike the wealthy landowners, these new haole arrivals did not have the means to send their children to the available private schools and so they "demanded education specifically for their children" (Higgins 2010, 33, paraphrasing Aspinwall 1960 and Benham and Heck 1998). The schools, thus, were created with two overlapping purposes in mind, enable haole children to attend schools that were free of Pidgin and prevent them from, in the words of a report published in 1948, "mingling with social inferiors" who attended the regular public schools (Hawaii's Standard Schools Report No. 3 1948).

In order to attend the English Standard Schools students were required to pass an oral examination, with children demonstrating features of Pidgin in their speech denied entry. Students unable to pass the test were then sent (back) to the regular public school system. The message transmitted by these schools was quite clear; Pidgin was, at least in the eyes of the newly arriving haoles, an unacceptable language. As Romaine (1999, 289) asserts, "by institutionalizing what was essentially racial discrimination along linguistic lines, the schools managed to keep creole speakers in their 'place.'"

The English Standard Schools were largely a reaction to the emergence of Pidgin, but they also accompanied a growing fear of other languages, particularly Japanese, which became construed as an enemy language as relations between the United States and Japan soured prior to World War II (Taylor 2011). The English Standard Schools helped insulate English speaking children from the influences of the Japanese and other languages and cultures. As Hughes (1993, 76) notes, "a second articulated goal of the English standard system was to assure that children of English-speaking parents learned Western, not Asian, values and behavior." The English Standard Schools were dismantled soon after the conclusion of World War II, but these schools represent the complex and conflicted attitudes toward multilingualism that emerged in the 1900s in Hawai'i. Heritage language schools were established to appreciate and promote multiple languages within an increasingly Americanized Hawai'i while the English Standard Schools were part of an Americanization movement that viewed multilingualism as a social dilemma.

Further Immigration

Although Hawai'i's multilingualism was already on display in the early 1900s, the linguistic landscape was to become even more saturated with languages. The Japanese, once thought to be model laborers who could replace the Chinese, grew increasingly discontent with conditions on the plantations and began to organize and engage in strikes. The sugar planters, who had grown even stronger with the creation of the Hawaiian Sugar Planters' Association (HSPA), began recruiting workers from other parts of the world. Like Hawai'i, Puerto Rico had recently been named a territory of the United States, and, due to severe weather and poor economic conditions, people in Puerto Rico were open to leaving their homes to work. The first Puerto Rican workers left for Hawai'i at the end of 1900 and, according to Camacho Souza (1984, 167; also see Poblete 2014), employment records showed that by June 30, 1901, "there were already 1,772 men and 623 women (a total of 2,395) working on 40 plantations on Oahu, Maui, Hawaii, Kauai." Additionally, as noted earlier, Korea and Okinawa were two places in Asia from which workers began arriving in the early 1900s.

The arrival of workers from Puerto Rico and Korea was considerably short-lived, but the HSPA soon focused on the Philippines, which was already a territory of the United States. The first Filipino workers arrived in 1906, and as Okamura (2016, 37) states, "Filipino labor recruitment was firmly established in 1909, hastened by a major strike organized by Japanese workers." Between 1909 and 1946, about 126,000 Filipinos immigrated to Hawai'i, most of them single, uneducated males from rural parts of the Philippines (Okamura 2016). By 1922, the Filipinos became the largest ethnic group in the plantation workforce at 41 percent, and in the 1930s that percentage reached about 70 percent (Lind 1980; Okamura 2016).

The timing of their arrival is important because it meant that the Filipino workers already had, in a sense, two strikes against them; they did not speak English, the language that might allow them to make vertical movement in society, nor did they speak Pidgin, which would have allowed them to assimilate more easily into the local community. In particular, the Chinese and Japanese, despite sharing the difficulties of plantation life, demonstrated little sympathy for the latest group of laborers. The Chinese and Japanese who already moved into aspects of business in Hawai'i were reluctant to work together with the latest immigrant group. Additionally, the effects of the Great Depression of the 1920s were also felt in Hawai'i, making it difficult for the Filipinos to find a way to start their own businesses, even if they wanted to do so.

Filipino immigration represents the last big group that came to work on the sugar plantations, but this does not mean that immigration to Hawai'i began to cease. The number of people from Sāmoa has increased significantly from 5,733 in 1970 to approximately 16,000 or even 28,000 if part-Sāmoans are included (Bond and Soli 2011). In addition, the 2000 U.S. census reports that there were 7,900 Vietnamese in Hawai'i as well as an additional 2,100 people who identified themselves as being part-Vietnamese. This makes them the largest Southeast Asian group in Hawai'i (Su and Tran 2011). In addition to Vietnam, immigration has occurred from other parts of Southeast Asia, most notably Thailand and Camobodia (Fukuda and Carriker 2011; Su 2011).

The other large group to arrive in Hawai'i are those grouped together under the category of "Micronesian." This is a category that will be considered in further depth in chapter 7, but for now it can be noted that since 1986, when the Compact of Free Association was approved, over 15,000 people have moved to Hawai'i from the Federated States of Micronesia, the Republic of the Marshall Islands and the Republic of Palau, the places that fall into this category of COFA nations (Blair 2015). These newer arrivals have increased the visibility of multilingualism as a problem in Hawai'i because the government has been forced to provide services such as driver's license examinations, English language education, and court interpreting in languages that include Marshallese, Yapese, Chuukese, Kosraen, and Pohnpeian.

From Sugar to Tourism

Agricultural employment went into sharp decline in the 1950s and sugar plantations began to close (Beechert 1985). There were several reasons for this, including a weakening of protections against tariffs and stronger unions that made it more difficult for the sugar planters to compete at an international level. Perhaps the biggest reason, though, was the rise of the tourism industry as many landowners and enterpreneurs found that they could make more money building hotels and condominiums. The tourism industry was bolstered by the introduction of commercial jet service in Hawai'i in 1959, which, not coincidentally, was also the year that Hawai'i was officially made a state of the United States (Latzko 2004). As Latzko (2004, 67) notes, "by reducing the money and time costs of travelling to Hawaii the jet plane touched off an era of rapid growth in tourism to Hawaii." The number of visitors increased from 171,367 in 1958 to 242,994 in 1959 and topped one million in 1967, two million in 1972, three million in 1976, and six million in 1988. More recent statistics show a record 8.3 million visitors in 2014 with those tourists spending 14.7 billion dollars in Hawai'i (Hawai'i Tourism Authority). The 2014 report from the Hawai'i Tourism industry indicates that speakers of various different languages contribute to this multibillion dollar industry. The Japanese language is the most common language outside of English, brought in by approximately 1.5 visitors from Japan, but speakers of Chinese, Korean, Spanish, French, Portuguese, and German also visited in significant number. These visitors contribute to a multilingual Hawaiian society by not only bringing their languages with them to the islands but also prompting local businesses to find workers who are capable of speaking these languages in order to attract profits from these visitors. This includes staff at hotels and restaurants but it also reaches out to other aspects of society such as radio and television broadcasting. An initiative sponsored by the University of Hawai'i Mānoa called the Hawai'i Language Roadmap Initiative reported in 2013 the existence of eight radio stations and four television stations with programming in a language other than English. These languages include Chinese, Japanese, Korean, Ilocanco, Filipino, Spanish, Tongan, Samoan, Vietnamese, Laotian, Okinawan, Marshallese, Pohnpeian, and Chuukese (Hawai'i Language Roadmap Initiative 2013).

The 1970s brought still another twist to multilingualism in Hawai'i through a renewed interest in the Hawaiian culture and language. Due to this interest, this period has been referred to as "The Hawaiian Renassaince" (Kanahele

1982, 1986), and featured an emphasis on music, hula, canoe-voyaging, lei-making, Hawaiian history, and numerous other aspects of the Hawaiian culture. It also sparked activism that helped lead to the declaration of the Hawaiian language in 1978 as one of the two official languages of the state (with English being the other). This set the stage for the Hawaiian language revitalization movement that increased the visibility of the Hawaiian language throughout society. This movement will be explained in further detail in chapter 2.

IDEOLOGIES ABOUT LANGUAGES AND THEIR SPEAKERS

The previous section provides an overview of the development of Hawai'i as a multilingual society. In doing so, it offers a sense of how English came to be the most commonly heard language in society, especially in public sectors such as politics, business, and education. This section intends to expand on this understanding by focusing on some of the ideas propagated by English speakers that led to the denigration of other languages and their speakers, thus enabling English to rise in power and prestige within society. Since the time of Captain Cook's first arrival in 1778, Westerners in Hawai'i were intrigued by the people and the language they encountered and had a propensity for writing down their beliefs and attitudes about their new surroundings. It is in their words and the writings of later visitors and residents that we can see the ideologies that would later serve to advantage English speakers and disadvantage the speakers of other languages. This section does not necessarily center specifically on language, but the working premise is that any committed attempt to comprehend multilingualism in Hawai'i must be grounded in an explication of the ideological beliefs that undergird the relationships among the speakers of the different languages found in the islands. This section begins with the beliefs expressed toward speakers of Hawaiian, and then continues with the four largest groups of immigrant plantation workers, namely the Chinese, Japanese, Portuguese, and Filipinos.

The "Childish" Hawaiians

The early Westerners who arrived found a Polynesian language very different from English and other European languages to which they were accustomed. The Hawaiian language consists of a comparatively small inventory of sounds, five vowels and eight consonants. In particular, the small number of consonants represents a point of departure from the languages they knew.

Moreover, one of the recognized consonants is actually a small pause in breath, referred to as a glottal stop (represented by the symbol ' and referred to in Hawaiian as '*okina*). It took the Western academic world a considerably long time to acknowledge that the 'okina should be included as a consonant of the Hawaiian language (Schütz 1994).

Unfamiliar with Hawaiian and other Polynesian languages, the European and American visitors alike, in their eagerness to document what they were hearing, employed terms such as "childlike," "primitive," "simple," and "underdeveloped" (Schütz 1994). For example, writing in 1837 but basing his impressions on visits to various islands in Polynesia in 1816–1817, Adelbert von Chamisso placed Polynesian languages into one singular category when expressing that "it is a pleasant childish babble that can hardly be called a language." He then specifically singled out Hawaiian, referring to Hawai'i by the name given to it by Cook in honor of the Earl of Sandwich, for its childlike character: "The language of the Sandwich Islands really did seem much more childish to us than the dialect of Tonga appears in its grammar" (Schütz 1994, 23).

These sentiments were also found in the writings of those who visited later in the 1800s: "Hawaiian sounds feeble, indistinct, and unsatisfying" (Donne 1866, 84–85, also Schütz 1994, 16). Manley Hopkins expanded on this idea of Hawaiian as unsatisfying:

> The language may . . . be considered as pleasing and agreeable to the ear after a time, though at first it sounds childish, indistinct and insipid. It lacks, of course, everything like force and expression . . . though it never offends the ear, always leaves us unsatisfied.

One last quotation comes from Otto Jespersen, one of the most famous and respected linguists of his time. As reported in Schütz (1994, 27), Jespersen made the following comments about Hawaiian in a book published in 1905 (Jespersen 1905):

> Can any one be in doubt that even if such a language sound pleasantly [sic] and be full of music and harmony the total impression is childlike and effeminate? You do not expect much vigour or energy in a people speaking such a language; it seems adapted only to inhabitants of sunny regions where the soil requires scarcely any labour on the part of man to yield him everything he wants, and where life therefore does not bear the stamp of a hard struggle against nature and against fellow creatures.

Jespersen's comments are striking because he relates his impressions of the language to the supposed character of its speakers, suggesting a lack of "vigour" and "energy."

There may be a temptation to dismiss these connections as mere reflections of an earlier time when it was not uncommon for academics to refer to people as "savages" and employ descriptors such as "uncivilized," "childlike," and "undeveloped." However, doing so would underestimate the power and durability of language and the ideological beliefs that underlie its usage. A term such as "childish" serves as a metaphor that, in comparing a group of people such as the Hawaiians to children, allows extensions to be made so that various characteristics of children can be applied to the target group. In the theory of metaphor developed by George Lakoff and his colleagues (Lakoff 1987; Lakoff and Johnson 1980; Santa Ana 2002), which details how human cognition can be affected by metaphorical language, the child is the "source domain" that is mapped onto the "target domain" of the Hawaiians. As more attributes are mapped and as the metaphor penetrates the consciousness of a society, people begin to view the target group in terms of the metaphor. For example, if an attribute of children is that they are not of a high enough maturity level to make responsible decisions and govern their own lives, then this may be applied to the target domain and persuade people that a certain group are not fit to fulfill leadership roles.

Indeed, this is what happened in Hawai'i as this description of the Hawaiians as "childish," which began in the late 1700s, was ultimately employed by the American colonizers to help rationalize their takeover of Hawai'i in 1893. Reverend Sereno E. Bishop, who was the son of Reverend Artemus Bishop and who was born and raised in Hawai'i as the son of a missionary, summed up the sentiment that was used to rationalize this move when he referred to the Hawaiians as "babes in character and intellect" and explained, "the common people were not intrusted with rule, because in their childishness and general incapacity, they were totally unfit for such rule" (quoted in Fuchs 1961, 34; Okihiro 1991, 12). This sentiment was echoed by Samuel Dole, the first territorial governor of Hawai'i, who referred to the Hawaiians as "irresponsible people" (Okihiro 1991,12). This metaphorical mapping through a descriptor such as "childish" served to rationalize the seizing of power by those who deemed themselves to be more fit to make decisions.

Moreover, not only did such a metaphor function as rationale for needing to govern "on behalf" of the Hawaiians, but it was also extended to the realm of religion as a reason for "saving" the Hawaiians. The logic here is that children who do not have proper guidance can lapse into deprivation and squalor, thus necessitating a parental figure to save them. Hiram Bingham, one of the first missionaries that arrived in 1820, embodied the attitude of a savior when he wrote the following in his memoirs:

> As we proceeded to shore, the multitudinous, shouting, and almost naked natives . . . exhibited the appalling darkness of the land which we had come to

enlighten. Here . . . appeared a just representation of a nation in a deep degradation, ignorance, pollution, and destitution as if the riches of salvation . . . had never been provided to enrich and enlighten their souls. (Bingham 1969, 86)

Bingham in fact emphasized just how much of a challenge and how much effort "saving" the native population would require:

> By what means shall the knowledge of the arts and sciences be acquired by a nation so stupid and ignorant, whose destination seemed almost to forbid their progress, while it imperatively required it, and whose spiritual wants, first to be met, demanded more attention than the missionaries could give. (Bingham 1969, 171)

Here the Hawaiians are not just depicted as uncivilized and savage-like but are explicitly called "stupid" and "ignorant," suggesting just how difficult a task it would be to save them.

Not surprisingly, the missionaries also rationalized their attempts to write the Hawaiian language in terms of a need to save the natives from their own "limited" language and linguistic practices. One of the chief translators of the Bible, Artemas Bishop explained in 1844 (quoted in Reinecke 1969, 29):

> We were able to form new words to an indefinite extent, in perfect accordance with the genius of the language, and intelligible to the native reader. The constant use of this power enabled us to meet and overcome nearly every difficulty arising from the paucity of Hawaiian words, besides enriching the language with hundreds of new terms, which are now in common use throughout the archipelago.

Bingham's voice is loud and clear in this area as well:

> In place of authentic history they had obscure oral traditions, national or party songs, rude narratives of successions of kings, wars, victories, exploits of gods, heroes, priests, sorcerers, the giants of iniquity and antiquity, embracing conjecture, romance, and the general absurdities of Polytheism. (Bingham 1969, 2)

In addition to "enriching" the Hawaiian's language, the missionaries gave them writing and thus saved them from "obscure oral traditions," "rude narratives," and "general absurdities." The missionaries thus credited themselves as saviors by disparaging the language and traditional linguistic practices. Of course, what they ignore in their self-congratulatory remarks is that for centuries the Hawaiians had passed down their histories skillfully and successfully through highly developed oratory practices (see Perreira 2013 for discussion). Moreover, most writers also fail to credit the Hawaiians for the swiftness with which they adopted writing into their culture and became fully literate, resulting in a rich tradition of writing that can be found in the old Hawaiian newspapers and also in selected books (see Brown 2016; Kamakau 1992; Malo 1987; Silva 2017). The missionaries may have introduced writing but there was nothing childish or lazy about the vigor and diligence with which the Hawaiians incorporated writing into their society.

One final extension of this metaphorical mapping of the qualities associated with "childish" onto the Hawaiians can be traced back to the employment of Hawaiians as a chief source of labor on the plantations. William Hooper reportedly stated after observing workers on his plantation: "A gang of Sandwich Island men are like a gang of School Boys. When their master is with them they mind their lessons, but when he is absent it is 'Hurra boys.' They display so little interest for their employment that it makes my heart ache" (reported in Takaki 1983, 11). The difficulty, then, of accomplishing the work of the plantations on the back of the Hawaiians was attributed to the childlike qualities of the Hawaiians, specifically their inability to do the work without supervision. Being childish, they necessitated a parental figure, namely a "master," in order to perform the required work. Such a depiction of the Hawaiians was certainly beneficial to the planters because it allowed them to further deprecate the Hawaiians and at the same time argue for the need to import workers from other countries who would be willing to do the work for less pay. Here, too, though, there is another side to this story as Hawaiian labor easily served as a scapegoat for the early problems the sugar planters had in initiating their businesses. As Beechart notes, "rather than analyze their failure in terms of the relevant commercial factors, many Europeans preferred to blame everything on the laziness, stupidity, and obstinancy of the islanders" (1985, 23).

There is evidence that this metaphor of the childish and lazy Hawaiian remained pervasive in the minds of people in Hawai'i. An anthropologist at the University of Hawai'i at Mānoa named Ernest Beaglehole reported in 1937 in research titled "Some Modern Hawaiians" (Beaglehole 1937) the self-assessments made by some members of the community with Hawaiian blood. He found that a woman with Hawaiian blood stated "seriously that all Hawaiians are lazy" which was blamed on "habits of indolence." Beaglehole also reported that many Hawaiians agreed that "in general, the Hawaiian lacks ambition" (reported in Kanahele 1986, 355). Later in the 1960s another professor at the University of Hawai'i, Joseph C. Finney, in putting together findings from his large-scale study of the attitudes of ethnic groups in Hawai'i toward one another, made the following generalizations based on what was said about the Hawaiians.

> As being dependent; as working no harder than they have to; as not being ambitious; as not being conscientious in carrying out responsibilities or fulfilling duties

and obligations;—and as being warm, friendly, fun loving and not serious. (Finney 1961–1962; also reported in Kanahele 1986, 315)

These assessments were published nearly 200 years after Cook's arrival and thus demonstrate the enduring quality of early comparisons of the Hawaiians to children. Despite centuries of successful self-government, people, including some Hawaiians themselves, became convinced of their childlike attributes, which in turned allowed the Westerners to rationalize the overthrow of the Hawaiian Kingdom and leave the Hawaiian language and the Hawaiians themselves at a disadvantage in their own indigenous land.

The Chinese: An Odd Commodity

There were early reports that praised the Chinese as good workers (Nordyke and Lee 1989), and there were also reports about how well some of the Chinese immigrants intergrated into the predominantly Hawaiian society due to their hard work and graciousness (Kai 1974). For example, Kai (1974) tells of a "Chinaman" named Aiko who found his way to Hawai'i prior to the start of immigration in 1852, made himself a business, got married, and was considered "a very kind-hearted man" (Kai 1974, 55). However, as the number of Chinese immigrants increased rapidly, it did not take long for the differences between the Chinese and the haole planters of the islands to lead to negative beliefs. These beliefs began with observations about the dress and appearance of the Chinese such as the following by a Yale professor named Francis Olmsted in 1841 on a whaling trip to Hawai'i:

> Among the foreigners resident in Honolulu, are several Chinese, the singularity of whose costume cannot fail of attracting one's attention. It consists of a large frock with ample sleeves, reaching down about midway between the waist and the knee. For the lower dress, they wear a pair of pantaloons made very full, and these together with peaked shoes having thick, wooden soles, complete their costumes. Their black hair is braid in a tail, a yard long, which usually hangs down the back and vibrates from side to side, like a pendulum, as they walk through the streets; a loss of these tails, which many of them coil up around their heads, would be regarded as a great disgrace. (Olmsted 1969, 212–213; reported in Char 1974, 5)

While the description is not necessarily meant to be negative, the inclusion of concrete details about Chinese fashion expresses a feeling of exoticness that marks the Chinese as different and strange. Even the usage of the term "costume" relays an attitude of oddness that "cannot fail of attracting one's attention."

More than just portrayed as being different, the Chinese were also vilified as one of the causes of social discord in Hawai'i. As the Chinese started moving from the plantations into towns, the *Pacific Commercial Advertiser* complained at the end of the 1850s that:

> nothing but "insecurity to life and property" resulted from the presence of the Chinese in town, "some of the vilest coolies that ever escaped hanging in their own countries. The thoughtless importation of coolies, a few years ago, because they were cheap labor, is now producing some lamentable fruit in the shape of burglary and murder." (Daws (1968, 180)

Glick (1938, 13) notes that "anti-Chinese feeling, like the stream of Chinese migration itself, developed slowly at first and rose to its greatest intensity during the late seventies and the eighties." Referring to the "Biennial Report of the President Board of Immigration" in 1890, Glick further relates how the Chinese, even 40 years after being brought over as workers, were considered different and thus viewed negatively:

> A Chinaman is unprogressive. He remains a Chinaman as long as he lives, and wherever he lives; he retains his Chinese dress; his habits; his method; his religion; his hopes, aspirations, and desires. . . . The Chinese are secretive, systematically shielding and assisting Chinese criminals. (1938, 19)

This growing anti-Chinese sentiment seemed to correspond with the increased population of Chinese on the islands and also with the increased movement of the Chinese into urban areas of society.

It is relevant to note here that research on Hawaiian society in the 1800s has made a distinction between the treatment of the Hawaiians and that of the immigrants from Asia, especially the Chinese as the first large Asian group. The Hawaiians were, in the words of Merry (2000, 127–131), "regarded as 'our' natives by the whites and treated childlike but benign, lazy, irresponsible with money, and friendly, although too sensuous," but the Chinese, as foreigners to the land, "were constructed as 'servile,' 'cheap labor' unfit for permanent settlement and citizenship, precisely for which they were desired and disdained" (also quoted Jung 2006, 70). Even the term often employed to refer to the Chinese, "coolies," which was used generally to refer to contract laborers from China and India, separated them from the Hawaiian workers and thus helped to distinguish the Chinese as the foreign "other." Despite earlier hopes that the Chinese could be integrated into society, the extent of the differences suggested that they were to be feared, not welcomed. The expanding haole society "objected that 'coolies' had a morally corrupting influence on their population, blaming the Chinese for bringing disease, opium, gambling, violence, and given the extreme gender imbalance, sexual depravity" (Jung 2006, 70).

Okamura (2014, 23) observes the tendency of the white planters to objectify the Chinese and other Asian immigrant workers in Hawai'i as commodities: "they did not consider nonwhite laborers as fully human beings like themselves; instead, they dehumanized them so they could rationalize their racist treatment, such as providing workers with low wages and substandard housing and sanitation facilities because nonwhites did not require a higher standard of living like haoles." As further evidence, Okamura points to a letter in 1930 in the newspaper the Honolulu Star-Bulletin from the president of the HSPA stating "from a strictly ethical standpoint, I can see little difference between the importation of foreign laborers and the importation of Jute bags from India" (Okamura 2014, 23). Likewise, a Theo Davies and Co. official is noted to have responded to an order for "bone meal, canvas, Japanese laborers, macaroni and a Chinaman" (Okamura 2014, 23). In short, the Asian worker as commodity is another metaphor that justified treatment of the immigrants as objects, such as jute bags, bone meal, canvas, and macaroni.

And working with this metaphor that Asian laborers were commodities imported from a foreign land, it was relatively easy for the haole planters, driven by a fear of the "exotic" and "different" Chinese, to decide to curtail immigration in much the same way a business owner would stop importing a commodity no longer wanted. Although the leaders in Hawai'i did not go as far as the United States, where a similar fear prompted the passing of a Chinese exclusion act in 1882, they took measures to gradually phase out immigration from China. As reported by Nordyke and Lee (1989, 204):

> In 1883, the Hawaiian Cabinet Council, concerned that the Chinese had secured too strong a representation in the labor market, passed a resolution to restrict Chinese immigration to 2,400 men a year and to require Chinese leaving the Islands to obtain a passport to prove previous residence if they expected to return. In 1885, harsher regulations limited passports to Chinese who had been in trade or who had conducted business for at least one year of residence, and no return passports were to be issued to departing laborers. Further government regulations introduced between 1886 to 1892 virtually ended Chinese contract labor immigration by restricting passports to business people who had resided in the Islands, to Chinese women and children, and to a few persons in China who were specifically invited by the minister of foreign affairs, such as clergy, teachers, and some businessmen. A limited number of Chinese laborers were permitted to enter Hawai'i under conditional work permits for agricultural purposes, provided that they left the Islands after five years.

Nordyke and Lee (1989) note that these procedures, while not eliminating immigration from China, were effective in preventing a further increase in the Chinese population in Hawai'i.

The Japanese: From Good Citizen to "Menace"

The handling of immigrant workers from Japan was similar in many ways to that of the Chinese. As another group of immigrant laborers from Asia, the Japanese were at first often grouped together with the Chinese not just as commodities but as general targets of racial discrimination. The HSPA put out a statement explaining why people from Asia were better suited to do hard labor. As quoted in Okamura (2014, 23), "whites were constitutionally and temperamentally unfitted for labor" in a tropical climate, while Asians and "brown" men were "peculiarly adapted to the extractions of tropical labor" (also cited in Takaki 1983, 66). Similarly, a report issued in 1906 on labor statistics concluded that, "the old customs and habit of regarding the Japanese and other Orientals as people of inferior civil status as compared with whites still prevail in Hawai'i and manifest themselves in a hundred unconscious acts of on the part of managers and overseers" (quoted in Okamura 2014, 23).

Unlike the Chinese, however, the Japanese became known for organizing strikes in order to push for better conditions and wages. The sugar planters responded by pitting the immigrant groups against each other. For example, when the Japanese organized a strike in 1909, the HSPA brought in Chinese, Hawaiians, Koreans, Portuguese, and Puerto Ricans to work as strikebreakers, offering them double the wages that were being received by the Japanese (Okamura 2014). Another tactic used by the planters in an attempt to prevent further strikes was to placate them through "paternalism." As Okamura (2014, 26) writes, "consistent with their racist attitudes toward their employees, the planters racialized them as somewhat like overgrown children whose every activity, including sleeping, was subject to constant monitoring and control." Murayama (1988, 96) writes based on firsthand experience, "everything was over-organized. There were sports to keep you busy and happy in your spare time. Even the churches seemed part of the scheme to keep you contented. Mr. Nelson (the plantation manager) knew each of us by first name, knew each family, and asked each time anxiously about the family. He acted like a father, and he looked after you and cared for you provided you didn't disobey." In addition, there were police on the camps whose job was to keep people considered as undesirable, for instance, pimps, gamblers, and labor organizers, away from the plantations (Okamura 2014). Like children, the Japanese would, if left without proper parental guidance, be unable to avoid trouble.

This treatment of the Japanese as children is thus not unlike the approach adopted toward other groups including the Hawaiians. Yet, one of the interesting sides to the development of Hawaiian society in the early 1900s is a growing belief in, and fear of, the mental fortitude of the Japanese. In 1926, Porteus and Babcock published a survey of the haole elite's beliefs of "six racial groups in Hawai'i." Surveying 25 haole judges, the Japanese scored very highly on a variety of traits; they scored first in "planning capacity," "resolution," "stability of interest," and "self control" and second in "prudence," self determination," and "dependability" (cited in Jung 2006, 82). Despite a lower score in the category of "tact," the Japanese earned the highest scored of 85.5 on a 100-point scale, except for the haole who presumably would score a perfect 100 percent (Jung 2006, 82). The Japanese were rated higher than the Portuguese despite the fact that the Portuguese typically held higher positions on the plantations than the Japanese (Jung 2006).

In fact, it was this high regard for the capabilities of the Japanese that eventually turned them from potential "good citizens" to political "menace." As Japan became a threat to the United States due to Japan's military aggression in Asia, politicians and military advisors in the United States became increasingly concerned with the large Japanese presence in Hawai'i. The paranoia of the Japanese that ensued was largely based on a concern of what the Japanese might be capable of. As Jung puts it (2006, 82), "anti-Japanese racism was not based on an assured belief that the Japanese were inferior but on a fear that they were not" (Jung 2006, 82). As the Japanese were taking part in an especially visible strike in 1920, there were heightened racial attacks in Hawai'i against the Japanese that linked the strikes to a desire on the part of Japanese to seize control of the entire sugar industry. Okamura (2014, 38) writes that, "the two main Honolulu newspapers demonized Japanese Americans as a political threat insofar as they were supposedly engaged not in a real strike but in a racial conflict to destabilize the sugar industry so that Japan could take over Hawai'i." The Honolulu Star-Bulletin asked at that time, "is control of the industrialism of Hawaii to remain in the hands of Anglo-Saxons or is it to pass into those of alien Japanese agitators?" (Okamura 2014, 38). It also continued to state, "what the alien Japanese priests, editors and educators are aiming at, in our opinion, is general recognition of their claim that they can absolutely control the 25,000 Japanese plantation laborers of this territory" (Okihiro 1991, 78). The other newspaper, the Honolulu Advertiser similarly expressed, "The Japanese Government is back of the strike; it is back of the organization of Japanese labor in the American Territory of Hawaii; it reaches out its arms and directs the energies and activities of its nationals here in these American islands" (also quoted in Takaki 1983, 172; Okamura 2014, 38).

Political leaders in Hawai'i could no longer afford to view the Japanese through the metaphor of "children" who could be controlled through paternalism. The Japanese were "alien" and "agitators," whose ultimate plan was not just to achieve control of business but instead to attain total domination in Hawai'i. The governor of Hawai'i at that time, Wallace Farrington, wrote in response to the strike of 1920 and also to militaristic movements of Japan within Asia:

> Seventy-five percent of the common labor of our agricultural industries is performed by a single alien element, and a very determined section of that alien element has shown a disposition to assume a position that threatens the American control of Hawaii's agricultural industries . . . the Japanese used every art they could command of threat, and appeal to racial and national solidarity, to establish, consolidate and perpetuate their control of industry, which would mean eventual economic and political control. (Okihiro 1991, 93)

Military reports likewise supported this paranoid view of the Japanese. Major Merrian of the U.S. military submitted a report in 1918 that outlined a series of ways that the Japanese in Hawai'i were promoting Japanese nationalism, including Japanese language schools and religion, specifically Buddhism. The report concluded that the presence of the Japanese in Hawai'i "was alien and antagonistic to the American way of life, posing a danger to national security" (Okihiro 1991, 105). A similar report from Captain Philip Spalding in 1919 stated that "this situation, if allowed to continue, will create a condition in the not so distant future where local politics will be controlled by Japanese-Americans who have been carefully schooled in ideas of patriotism to Japanese and not to the United States" (Okihiro 1991, 107). The Japanese problem, then, "had taken on epic proportions: a battle for the control of Hawaii" (Okihiro 1991, 108) and led to a paranoia that would extend from the Japanese immigrants to their *nisei* children, resulting in the internment of many *nisei* leaders as a result of World War II. In addition to internment, the Japanese language schools were shut down and Japanese Americans at that time were basically forced to abandon attempts to pass the Japanese language down to future generations in order to follow an Americanization movement and demonstrate their loyalty to the United States (Okihiro 1991).

THE PORTUGUESE: THE MEN IN THE MIDDLE

The Portuguese provide a contrast because unlike the Chinese, Japanese, and the Filipino immigrants, who struggled due to racial discrimination, the Portuguese, according to many reports, were able to make advances in society at a much swifter pace. As Geschwender, Carroll-Seguin, and Brill (1988, 518) state, "the best plantation jobs largely went to Haoles, but the Portuguese rapidly climbed from general labor to positions of luna (first-line supervisor) and craft worker." Andrade and Nishimura (2011, 84) confirm how this rapid rise also led to success beyond plantation life:

> The first-generation Portuguese, who stayed on the plantation after their contracts ended, had steadily risen up the ranks to be field supervisors, or luna. Many more saved significant portions of their earnings and left the plantations when their contracts ended to lease and purchase land in rural communities, establishing their own farms, ranches, and dairies; some became commercial fishermen; and others moved to the city and towns, becoming skilled laborers, or they opened bakeries and shops to apply their trades.

There has been a tendency to credit their success to the fact that they came from Europe and not Asia, and thus were much closer to the haole planters in terms of appearance and culture. While there is some truth to this, the situation was actually much more complex as the Portuguese were generally considered different from the haole and also from the other Asian immigrants. Fuchs (1961), for example, argues that Portuguese were indeed favored because they were from Europe but not because they were similar to haoles. In fact, categorization of the Portuguese in Hawai'i has not been consistent. Weinstein, Manicas, and Leon (1990, 305) note that "while Portuguese are not haoles, they are definitely Caucasian." Andrade and Nishimura seem to basically agree that they are "white but not haole" (Andrade and Nishimura 2011, 83), but Lasalle (2016) insists that they be referred to as "Caucasian but not white" (Lasalle 2016).

Although the purpose here is not to haggle over these categories, it is important to note that while the Portuguese were favored and were even encouraged to emulate the haole planters, they were in fact denied many haole privileges. Geschwender, Carroll-Seguin, and Brill (1988, 525) relates this to Wiley's (1967) "ethnic mobility trap":

> Apparent favoritism carried over to those Portuguese who left the plantations. Portuguese-Americans selected a strategy for advancement shaped by advantages believed to come from Haole favoritism. . . . Initially, it appeared to pay off in collective advancement, but its continued success depended on the continuation of a plantation society dominated by Haoles. . . . Still, Haoles remain disproportionately concentrated in the economic elite and Portuguese-Americans have experienced limited mobility. They are less well educated, have lower status occupations, and earn less than Haoles.

Daws (1968, 315) expresses this even more bluntly when he writes, "for a Portuguese, a job as a luna, but nothing more. The plantation manager and his immediate subordinates would always be white men, haoles, and in the islands the Portuguese, even though they were Europeans by name, were never counted as haoles."

The earlier long quotation from Geschwender, Carroll-Seguin, and Brill (1988) suggests that the Portuguese-Americans "selected" their own "strategy for advancement." However, rather than allowing the Portuguese to select strategies as they pleased, others have painted a picture in which "the haole elite manipulated Portuguese racialization to fit their various needs" (Rohrer 2010, 55; also see Lasalle 2016). Lasalle (2016) expresses a related idea but does so in a way that suggests that the Portuguese were rewarded for their willingness to obey the Haole planters: "with the patriarchal system in place in many plantations, the Portuguese were viewed somewhat like good, obedient children." This notion of childlike obedience is also apparent in the following report in 1902 from the Commisioner of Labor and Industry in Hawaii, which states, "These people are an exceedingly hopeful element of the population. They are both industrious and frugal, and their vices are not of a sort to injure their efficiency as workers. They make good citizens, and though those of the first generation are usually illiterate and averse to sending their children to the public schools, they rapidly become Americanized" (Lasalle 2016). There is thus here a common theme throughout the stories of the non-haole groups, including the Hawaiians. As long as they chose to act like obedient children and follow the voice of the haole, they would be fine.

The Portuguese, however, paid a price for their desire to be considered close to the haoles. As lunas on the plantations, they acted as middlemen between the haoles and other workers, and therefore were often resented because it was their job to maintain control over the workers. Within the oppressive context of the plantations, "the stifled rage of Asians against their haole bosses was displaced to their Portuguese man-in-the-middle supervisors. This harsh work environment spawned the stereotype of the sadistic, whip-wielding Portuguese luna, who in reality was an exaggeration and symbolic representation of the unfairness, racism, and brutal conditions of plantation life" (Andrade and Nishimura 2011, 89). From this hierarchical relationship, with the haole at the top, the Asian laborers at the bottom, and Portuguese in the middle, was born the notion of the "dumb Pawdagee" as scapegoat and also as the butt of ethnic humor (Andrade and Nishimura 2011; Geschwender, Carroll-Seguin, and Brill 1988; Mejer 1987). Indeed, so-called Portuguese jokes are still a point of controversy in society (Cataluna 2000a, 2000b; Labrador 2004).

THE FILIPINOS: INFERIOR FROM THE START

When the Filipinos arrived to work on the plantations in 1906, they already had a rather big strike against them, namely, they were coming from a land, the Philippines, that had been colonized by the United States. Hence, even prior to their arrival in Hawai'i, the people of the Philippines were objects of racialized discourse that portrayed them as unfit to govern for themselves. According to Hoganson (2000, 134–137), the discourse referenced gender and "presented the Filipinos as lacking the manly character seen as necessary for self-government."

Therefore, even though the Philippines consists of a diverse set of islands and even though Filipino immigrants were actually a heterogenous mix of Visayans, Ilocanos, and Tagalogs, they were lumped together in Hawai'i as one inferior racial group. As Jung (2006, 84) writes, "in contrast to the Japanese, Filipinos were believed by haole and nearly all non-Filipinos in prewar Hawai'i to be unequivocally inferior." Jung points to the same report from Porteus and Babcock in 1926 that had rated the Japanese so highly as evaluating the Filipinos as "extremely short sighted, suggestible, impulsive, irresolute, overemotional, unstable in their interests, and undendable (Jung 2006, 84; Porteus and Babcock 1926, 84). The Porteous and Babcock report arrived at the following conclusion: "summing up these characteristics we may say that the Filipinos represent a fine example of a race in an adolescent stage of development" that "are so like children" (quoted in Jung 2006, 84–85). At some point, thus, it seems that all of the non-haole groups in Hawai'i were constructed in some way as children, a metaphor that, with all of its possible extensions, allowed the haole elites to put themselves in the position of parents whose job was to lead the others.

Having arrived in Hawai'i after the Chinese, Japanese, and Portuguese, the Filipino workers suffered discrimination at the hands of not only the haole planters but also the other immigrant groups who had begun to establish roots in Hawai'i and who felt threatened by this new source of labor. Here, the Filipinos were resented by the other groups for their willingness to work for lower wages, thus creating a rift because it made it difficult for the other groups to negotiate for better working conditions. Reinecke (1996, 3) writes "between the Filipinos and other ethnic groups there was a wide social distance. . . . A great part of the population stereotyped them as hotheaded, knife-wielding, overdressed, sex-hungry young men. They were commonly subjected to slurs like 'poke poke' and 'poke knife' for their putative propensity to engage in violence, especially with knives, and feared as sexual predators." Labrador (2015, 63) notes that even currently the media and especially local comedians perpetuate "representations that have depicted Filipinos as a 'sex danger,' criminally inclined, and prone to violence, which have their origins in the plantation era." As Jung (2006) points out in a footnote (pp. 216), this connection between knives and Filipinos might have arisen due to the fact that it was primarily the Filipinos who were seen in the 1920s and

1930s out in the sugarcane fields working with knives. Nonetheless, this image of the Filipinos as hotheads and sexual predators fit the needs of the haole planters as well as other immigrants because it made it possible to keep these newer immigrants positioned as scapegoats underserving of advancement in society.

Despite hardships, the families of the early Filipino immigrants persevered and made Hawai'i their homes, but the situation is complicated by the fact that immigration from the Philippines has continued in current Hawaiian society. Since 1970, Filipinos have constituted the majority of the immigrants arriving annually to Hawai'i (Labrador 2015). Thus, while many residents of Filipino ancestry fall into the category of "local" and speak both Pidgin and English, those who arrived later are still viewed as "fresh off the boat" and subjected to othering for their cultural and linguistic differences (Labrador 2015). Labrador (2015) describes how jokes about eating dog and also "mock Filipino," which exaggerates certain pronunciations that cause speakers of Filipino languages to mispronounce words in English, construct the Filipinos as the foreign other. As Labrador (2015, 50) writes, "mock Filipino is a strategy often employed by Local comedians to differentiate the speakers of Philippine languages from speakers of Pidgin," and thus construct the Filipinos as something other than "local." Hence, despite a large representation in the islands, Filipinos may still be depicted as outsiders. A later chapter, chapter 6, explores in more depth the depiction of Filipino immigrants in society, together with another group of recent immigrants, namely, those from Micronesia, through an analysis of local newspapers.

CONCLUSIONS

This chapter began by describing the treatment of multilingualism in Hawai'i as a problem, and it concluded with a focus on how the presence of various immigrant groups, even though their arrivals were at the behest of the haole sugar planters, was likewise constructed to be problematic. Nonetheless, despite attempts to curtail the usage of some languages, what developed since 1778 is a society marked by the presence of speakers of multiple languages. Large-scale immigration brought in speakers of English, Chinese (both Mandarin and Cantonese), Portuguese, Japanese, Okinawan, Visayan, Tagalog, Ilocano, Korean, Samoan, Marshallese, and Chuukese, among others. Moreover, the addition of workers from different parts of the world gave birth to Pidgin, the creole language of Hawai'i, which itself has origins in at least two types of pidgin languages, a Hawaiian pidgin and a macaronic pidgin. In a very real sense, then, the ebbs and flows of history are responsible for turning

Hawai'i from a monolingual Hawaiian society into a remarkably multilingual one.

One theme of this chapter that mostly went unstated is the division of people, as well as languages, into groups such as "Hawaiian," "Chinese," "Filipino," and "Micronesian." Although contemporary approaches to identity assert the fluidity of identity construction and thus warn against the assumption of predetermined categories, much discussion of the development of modern Hawaiian society has focused on the contrast among groups referred to as "haole," "local," "Filipino," "Japanese," etc. As Jung (2006) notes (also see Okamura 1994), rather than grouping people from Asia together under one larger category of "Asian" and later "Asian American," people have been traditionally divided according to categories such as "Chinese," "Japanese," "Korean," and "Filipino." Likewise, even though immigrants from China came from different parts of China and even spoke different dialects, some of which were not mutually intelligible, they were most commonly grouped together as one group, "Chinese." The same is true for the "Japanese" and also the "Filipinos," who were actually an eclectic group of people speaking different languages. The rest of this book will mostly follow this practice of group reference, but it will also provide further discussion of these categories, especially in chapters 4, 5, and 6, in order to attempt a deeper understanding of the effects of multilingualism in contemporary Hawai'i.

A theme that was discussed more explicitly in this chapter is that the rise of multilingualism in Hawai'i occurred at the same time that English grew to be the language of power. The dominance of English led to the demise of the Hawaiian language and to attempts by the haole elite to discourage and, at times, even prevent residents from having access to other languages. Nonetheless, the fact that Hawai'i not only emerged as a multilingual society but also continues to seek ways (although sometimes begrudgingly) to deal with the needs of multilingual residents through interpreter and driver's license services speaks to the enduring quality of Hawai'i's multilingualism. As Bickerton (1998, 53–54) writes about attempts to suppress multilingualism: "efforts to impose monolingualism failed completely," and, as he continues, "regardless of what they were told, residents of Hawai'i, including many who paid lip service to the propoganda of their rulers, have continued in practice to do their own thing, or rather; things." The remaining chapters in this book continue to describe how speakers of some of the languages in Hawai'i have continued to do "their own things" despite the desire of officials in Hawai'i to promote English.

A final important theme of this chapter has been a focus on the ideologies about not just languages but also about the people who came to populate Hawai'i, including the indigenous Hawaiians. This story was told mostly through the eyes of the Western English speakers, as their dispersion of ideological beliefs corresponded with their growing power within Hawaiian society. There were differences in the beliefs that were applied to the different groups of people: the Hawaiians were immature, lazy, and undependable; the Chinese were odd in behavior and appearance and even prone to criminal behavior; the Japanese were insidious political menaces; the Portuguese were middlemen who cowtowed to the haoles; and the Filipinos were outrightly inferior. But there were also similarities, in particular, the frequent comparisons to children, a metaphor that enabled the haoles to situate themselves as rightful leaders of the land and to expect obedience from their childish subordinates. The haoles needed to appropriate the land and promote their language as a way of saving the others, who, by extension of the childish metaphor, were not of the maturity nor intelligence level necessary to govern on their own. Ideologies will continue to be a focus for the remaining chapters, particularly chapter 6, which attempts to understand the ideological beliefs expressed in newspapers toward the Filipinos and Micronesians and the effects of those beliefs not only on those groups but also on current Hawaiian society.

NOTES

1. Indeed, there have been other discussions of multilingualism as a general problem and also in specific parts of the world (Auer and Li Wei 2008; also see Blommaeert, Leppanen, and Spotti's [2012] discussion of a Finnish context).

2. The idea that there was no indigenous writing system in Hawai'i has been contested. See Reichl (2008, 2017) for discussion of the relationship of Hawaiian petroglyphs to writing.

3. There is no bibiliographic information included for Kuykendall 1968b in Huebner (1984). I believe this is the same book referred to in this work as Kuykendall 1965.

Chapter Two

Hawaiian

Lost (Almost) and Found

INTRODUCTION

The Hawaiian language is accepted as the indigenous language of the Hawaiian archipelago. Unfortunately, it is currently listed on the UNESCO Atlas of the World's Languages in Danger as a critically endangered language, a categorization that may lead to questions about its relevance within modern Hawaiian society. The author of a recent article in *The Honolulu Magazine*, for example, relates her mostly futile attempts to observe usage of Hawaiian in everyday social events (Hale 2013).

> I didn't hear more than *Hiki nō?* (Can do?) at the Acquarium's *Ke Kani o Ke Kai* concert. And I didn't hear a shred of *kūkākūkā* (conversation) at the Lili'uokalani Church lū'au in Hale'iwa. The only place I found an actual discussion in Hawaiian was in a room at UH Mānoa's Kuykendall Hall, where a Master's candidate in Hawaiian language was defending her thesis to a total of nine graduate students and professors.

Based on the outcome of her search, the author asks whether Hawaiian is "just Latin for Hawai'i—a language spoken only by priests and the faithful," and she also remarks that the language "may be cool, but it rarely helps you get a job, rent an apartment or fall in love" (Hale 2013, 55).

Although it may be true that Hawaiian is not "heard" as commonly as other languages in Hawai'i, especially English, it should be recognized, on the one hand, that the unequal distribution of languages is a regular feature of multilingual societies. In fact, terms such as "community language," "lesser-used language," and "minority language" are used to capture imbalances in relationships between and among languages in bilingual and multilingual parts of the world (Romaine 2013). Even the term "diglossia" implies an unequal partnership in which one language is considered more prestigious and more prevalent in certain sectors of society.

On the other hand, any discussion of the current place of Hawaiian in society must appreciate the fact that the language is in the midst of a revitalization movement that is producing a rather remarkable increase in the number of speakers as well as in the contexts in which Hawaiian is used. Around town in Hilo, for instance, I frequently hear Hawaiian spoken at local grocery stores by families and friends doing their shopping; many stores also have staff who speak Hawaiian. The same is true for many restaurants, as it is often possible to order and receive food and then pay the bill all through Hawaiian. In fact, there are even some places where Hawaiian has become the norm. The Hawaiian medium schools are one example, as is my place of employment, the Hawaiian Language College at the University of Hawai'i at Hilo, which conducts all of its affairs in Hawaiian, including formal and informal staff meetings, emails, and public lectures and other functions. Students, faculty, and staff speak with each other in Hawaiian in other parts of the university as well as outside in the community. Hence, it is not just that an occasional thesis defense occurs in Hawaiian in educational domains; Hawaiian has become the primary, accepted, and thus "normal" language in some educational institutions. In addition, though not numerous, there are local radio programs in Hawaiian, and Hawaiian can also be found on cable TV and in the social media. Moreover, the written language is seen on a regular basis throughout the islands on street signs and also in the names of various business establishments. It may not be on the same level as English in terms of being pervasive in the community, but Hawaiian definitely has a place in Hawai'i's current multilingual landscape, a point which Silva (2017, 2) has emphasized: "A child can conceivably now receive an education from an Hawaiian immersion preschool in Pūnana Leo to a PhD in programs conducted in Hawaiian or which are Hawaiian centered, and spend her time in voyaging, lo'i farming, hula, or other Hawaiian arts, and thus, while still surrounded by a hegemonic American culture, live a life that is substantially based in Hawaiian culture."

This chapter discusses the role of Hawaiian in society by first focusing on the language revitalization movement in more detail before offering two analyses intended to stress the importance of the Hawaiian language to society. The first analysis focuses on repetition in the discourse of elder speakers and suggests that Hawaiian speakers develop speaking skills that may be distinct from speakers of other languages, thus adding to the diversity of speaking repertoires available within society. The second analysis attempts to demonstrate that despite concerns about the authenticity of the re-emerging

Hawaiian language, younger members of society are speaking Hawaiian in a way that reflects "traditional" approaches to social interaction.

THE REVITALIZATION MOVEMENT

It should be stressed that the increase in the usage of Hawaiian is a relatively recent development. Although Hawaiian flourished as the language of the archipelago for several hundreds of years, the arrival of Captain Cook in 1778 and the subsequent influx of missionaries beginning in 1820 resulted in an extended period of colonization that has left Hawaiian on the verge of extinction for a large part of the twentieth century. As noted earlier, it was estimated that there were fewer than 50 child speakers of the language in the 1980s (Kimura, Kamanā, and Wilson 2003), and at least one linguist, Richard Benton in 1981, predicted that Hawaiian would become the first Polynesian language to be completely replaced by a European language (Benton 1981; also noted in Wilson and Kamanā 2001).

However, due to a strong revitalization program that has placed an emphasis on creating schools in which Hawaiian serves as the medium of education, the Hawaiian language has been growing in strength and number of speakers since the mid-1980s. Following a model of preschools in New Zealand for Māori, leaders of the Hawaiian movement created the nonprofit organization ʻAha Pūnana Leo in 1983 as a precursor to opening the first ʻAha Pūnana Leo preschool in 1984 in Kekaha Kauaʻi. This then led to the construction of several other preschools, and later, after working with legislators to eradicate the law of 1896 that banned the teaching of Hawaiian in schools, education through Hawaiian was extended to the elementary, junior high, and high school levels (Wilson and Kamanā 2001). Currently, in what has been called a P–20 system (Kamanā and Wilson 2014), Hawaiian language medium education is now available from the preschool level all the way through the undergraduate and graduate levels of university education. In fact, a doctoral program instituted in 2006 at the University of Hawaiʻi at Hilo has made it possible to earn a PhD through Hawaiian with a focus on indigenous language and culture revitalization. This educational system has sparked a major increase in speakers; Wilson in personal communication with McCarty (2008) suggests that there are approximately 15,000 people who use and understand Hawaiian, with some of them referred to as "new native speakers" who have begun acquiring Hawaiian as a first language (Brenzinger and Heinrich 2013, 9).

Although there have been various advocates and contributors from across the globe, the revitalization movement has essentially been a grassroots movement from a community of people mostly of Hawaiian ethnicity. The movement has required perseverance and strength of will in order to stand up to those in power who were often reluctant to acknowledge a place in society for Hawaiian as a spoken language. Likewise, it has necessitated an eloquence of tongue necessary to convince people of the importance of the Hawaiian language and culture. Finally, it has put on display the ingenuity to create educational systems and structures that provide contexts in which the language and culture can once again flourish. It goes without saying, then, that the intense efforts to organize the revitalization movement fly very much in the face of the stereotypes of Hawaiians as lazy and content that were discussed in the previous chapter. Due to the hard work of those dedicated to the language, revitalization efforts have attracted interest and praise from around the globe with Hawai'i now recognized as one of the most successful sites of language revitalization not only in the United States but also throughout the world (Cowell 2012; Grenoble and Whaley 2006; Lomawaina and McCarty 2006). Wilson and Kamanā (2001, 147) note that "Hawai'i has the most developed movement in indigenous language-medium education in the United States," and Lomawaina and McCarty remark that it "may be the most dramatic success story . . . to date" (Lomawaina and McCarty 2006, 138).

Educational programs have been at the forefront of Hawaiian revitalization, but credit also must be extended to those who worked on behalf of the language and culture during the period of time beginning in the 1960s and 1970s that has been labeled the Hawaiian Renaissance (Kanahele 1982, 1986). As noted previously, the Hawaiian Renaissance was marked by renewed interest in and dedication to aspects of the Hawaiian culture that include but are not limited to music, dance, food, canoe voyaging, and crafts. It was also a time of activism, as people of Hawaiian blood organized to contest some of the injustices bestowed upon them by the forces of colonialism. Activists fought against evictions of Hawaiian families for the purpose of building high-priced homes, they resisted the lack of access to water on Maui Island, and they also actively opposed the occupation and use as a bombing range by the American military of the island of Kaho'olawe, among other causes (see the articles in Goodyear-Ka'ōpua, Hussey, and Kahunawaika'ala 2014, also Goodyear-Ka'ōpua 2017). It was also during this time that a Hawaiian movement for independence and sovereignty gained strength (Trask 1999), a movement bolstered by writers of Hawaiian ethnicity who began countering Western academic perspectives by developing critical academic approaches that reexamined Hawaiian history, law, politics, culture, as well as colonialism from an indigenous Hawaiian viewpoint (Kame'eleihiwa 1992; Kanahele 1986; Osorio 2002; Silva 2004; Trask 1999).

This period of activism, in fact, helped create the political environment that led to the declaration in 1978 at the Hawai'i State Constitutional Convention of the Hawaiian language as an official language, together with English, of the state. It was the first time in the United States that an indigenous language was recognized as an official language, a status which made it easier for the language activists and educators in the 1980s to make a strong push for the establishment of Hawaiian language medium schools. If English, as an official state language, served as the medium of education for schools in Hawai'i, then it would follow that education through Hawaiian should also be allowed to match its "equal" status as an official language.

This activism should also be credited with changing attitudes about the Hawaiian language and culture, especially among those who identify as native Hawaiian. American colonization had left many people of Hawaiian ethnicity unproud of their Hawaiian heritage and believing that the language was useless, beliefs that had long been reinforced through education, including actual corporal punishment for speaking Hawaiian in school (Eyre 2004; Lipe 2016; Lucas 2000; Moon 2014; Wilson and Kamanā 2006). The Hawaiian Renassiance, however, led people to realize the importance of feeling proud to possess a Hawaiian identity and to practice the language. Quoting Ledward (2007), Snyder-Frey (2013, 234–235) notes that there was a "reawakening of Hawaiian dignity . . . as new perspectives surfaced about Hawaiian culture and history" and that "Hawaiian-ess had become an asset rather than a liability." Speaking specifically about language, Snyder-Frey (2013, 235) observes that "while it had previously been position as inferior to English, associated with rural, backward, lazy natives, it was now becoming a sign of cultural pride and knowledge, and probably indicated a certain level of education, as so many of the classes offered were at the university." Hawaiian thus went from a source of punishment to being considered, in the words of Kawai'ae'a, Housman, and Alencastre (2007, 186), "the jewel of our culture."

Hawaiian is therefore a good example of a language that has undergone a change in ideological beliefs in a relatively short period of time. This change in language ideologies has been essential for leaders of the Hawaiian language revitalization movement because it has brought to the movement an increasing number of younger people who are proud of their heritage and who possess a desire to perpetuate the language. Wilson and Kawai'ae'a (2007, 38) term this desire "crucial disposition" and credit it with prompting young people learning the language to become willing, first of all, to employ Hawaiian with their peers outside of school even under pressure to speak English. Second, this "crucial disposition" has also led younger Hawaiians to work in the Hawaiian medium schools and, perhaps even more crucially, to be willing to want to teach their own children Hawaiian, thus restarting the cycle of intergenerational transmission that had been disrupted. Kawai'ae'a, Housman, and Alencastre (2007) describe the efforts within their own families to transmit the language across three generations, starting with the parents who were founding members of the language revitalization movement to their children who attended some of the first Hawaiian medium schools and finally to their grandchildren who have been speaking Hawaiian since birth and who have been in the Hawaiian medium educational system since preschool.

THE HAWAIIAN LANGUAGE AND INDIGENOUS KNOWLEDGE

The revitalization of the language has helped to allow people of Hawaiian ancestry to reconnect with their cultural heritage and reinvigorate a Hawaiian identity. This alone is certainly more than enough of a reason to engage in and endure the struggles necessary to revitalize the language. Yet, to gain further understanding of the role of Hawaiian in a multilingual society, it is necessary to acknowledge that as much as the language revitalization movement is about reestablishing a spiritual reconnection, it is also about regaining access to the indigenous knowledge possessed by speakers of Hawaiian about not just language but also how to interact with the land and with the world in general. As Kanahele (2011, xiii–xiv) notes in discussing a certain *mele* (song), "the primary source for all Hawaiian knowledge is the *kūpuna*, the ancestors and the keepers of Native Hawaiian intellect from time immemorial" (also see Kikiloi 2010 for discussion of "ancestral memories"). Usage of the language in schools and in society is one way to attempt to reconnect with the knowledge held by the ancestors, knowledge that could not be passed down without the language. The re-introduction of this local, indigenous knowledge is one way that the revitalization of the Hawaiian language is contributing to a multilingual society, where a plurality of languages means more sources of knowledge.

In fact, scholars promoting language preservation such as Joshua Fishman (1991, 2001) and K. David Harrison (2007) have been steadfast in arguing for the need to fight on behalf of endangered languages due to the vast amount of knowledge contained within each language. They point out that each of the approximately 7,000 languages currently spoken throughout the world contain potentially different types of knowledge about our world, a diversity of knowledge that must be preserved. Harrison (2007, 15) writes that "much—if not most—of what humankind knows about the natural world lies outside of science textbooks, libraries, and databases, existing only in unwritten languages in people's memories," and he likewise points out that "it is only one generation from extinction and always in jeopardy of not being passed on. This immense knowledge base remains largely unexplored and uncatalogued" (2007, 15). This knowledge may be in the lexicon of a language, with words telling us how speakers of that language categorize their social world. It can be in the types of expressions, with idioms and proverbs letting us know what aspects of the world speakers find to be especially important, and it can also be in the syntax of the language, providing us insight into the way speakers organize their thoughts and process language. The content of the knowledge may be about our physical world concerning plants, trees, animals, traditional medicines, geographical space, and to like, that could potentially house answers to questions about environmental and even health issues. It may be related to knowledge about ways of engaging with the world and interacting with other humans (and possibly nonhumans) that may help humans promote peace and harmony throughout the world, and it may also be knowledge that heightens our understanding of the creative capabilities of the human brain.

An example from Hawaiian is the practice of naming places. As Elbert notes in the preface to the book on place names he co-authored with Mary Kawehi Pukui (Elbert, Pukui, and Moʻokini 1974, x), Hawaiians traditionally named places as well as "taro patches, rocks and trees that represented deities and ancestors, sites of houses and *heiau* (sites of worship), canoe landings, fishing stations in the sea, resting places in the forests, and the tiniest spots where miraculous or interesting events are believed to have taken place." Frequently included in the names are the history of the people and the place, including stories about the origin of the names. In the words of Kikiloi (2010, 75), "place names are important cultural signatures etched into the Hawaiian landscape and are embedded with traditional histories and stories that document how our ancestors felt about a particular area, its features, or phenomena." Moreover, they often told those stories through *kaona* ("hidden meanings") that are part of the rich tradition of storytelling in Hawaiian poetry, music, and oration (McDougall 2014, 2016; Silva 2017). Unfortunately, however, as the Hawaiian population diminished rapidly due to the colonization process and as the naming of places, buildings, and so on. was taken over by speakers of English, the number of people capable of understanding the histories of places and also the hidden meanings in place names has been greatly reduced (Wood 1999). Considering that, according to Elbert, Pukui, and Moʻokini (1974), the Hawaiians had named hundreds of thousands, even possibly millions of places, the inability to know, understand, interpret, and then relay the histories behind those places constitutes a serious loss of indigenous knowledge about how the Hawaiians interacted with their physical world. The potential loss of the language robs us of this chance to see and probe the indigenous perspectives toward living and interacting with the land, which was traditionally of the utmost importance to the Hawaiians.

Hawaiian naming practices have been discussed to a certain extent in other sources (Elbert, Pukui, and Moʻokini 1974; Kikiloi 2010; Oliveira 2014), and therefore I would like to pursue this point through an analysis of another linguistic phenomenon that provides a further example of how Hawaiian speakers interact with their social world. The analysis focuses on repetition as it was used in interviews with elder speakers of Hawaiian, people who are referred to as *kūpuna* and arguably are the last native speakers of the language (Kimura 2012). The analysis takes insights from two separate lines of inquiry, conversation analysis and ethnopoetics. Conversation analysis (CA) informs understanding of how interaction is organized into turns by self and other speakers (Sacks, Schegloff, and Jefferson 1974), and ethnopoetics is an area of linguistic anthropology that seeks to appreciate and understand stories and narratives as forms of verbal art (Blommaert 2006; Webster and Kroskrity 2013). The next section describes briefly how the integration of insights from the two will aid in understanding repetition in Hawaiian discourse.

CA, ETHNOPOETICS AND REPETITION IN HAWAIIAN

As developed by Harvey Sacks and his colleagues Emanuel Schegloff and Gail Jefferson, CA is known particularly for its focus on the minute details of social interaction, for example, how turns at talk are allocated as part of the sequential development of talk (Sacks, Schegloff, and Jefferson 1974). In fact, it has been noted that Sacks looked only minimally at the greater ethnographic context in order to discover "the organization of talk-in-interaction *in its own right*, as a 'machinery' independent of individual speakers" (Hutchby and Wooffitt 1998, 35, emphasis in the original). Yet, even though the place of contextual information in CA has been at times contested (Hopper 1990/1991; Mandelbaum 1990/1991; Nelson 1994), Moerman (1988) notes, in what he called a "culturally contexted conversation analysis," that "it is in interaction that people encounter, experience, and learn the principles, institutions, and ideals that characterized their society and culture" (1988, 2). The following analysis will go beyond what CA researchers are typically comfortable saying in terms of cultural knowledge, but it will begin by attempting to apply CA ideas to repetition in Hawaiian interaction, and it will likewise suggest that the use of repetition is a cultural skill learned by speakers of Hawaiian.

In fact, even though CA and ethnopoetics come from different intellectual origins, they are both similarly interested in the structure of language as it is actually used for communicative purposes. Ethnopoetics has links to Jakobsen's efforts to describe poetic language not only in poetry but also in other uses of language including spoken dialogue (Jakobsen 1960, 1966), and it also can be traced to Hymes's attempts to explain that the communicative competence exhibited by speakers extends beyond their ability to express just referential content (Blommaert 2006; Hymes 1964, 2003; Silverstein 2010). As Auden (2009, 1) notes in an introduction to the study of Navajo poetry, "if ethnopoetics has taught us anything, it is that while the 'what' of story (the content) is important, the 'how' of the story (the poetic structuring) is of equal importance." This focus on "the presentational form" of narratives makes it possible "to explicate their rhetorical power as verbal art" (Silverstein 2010, 933). Moreover, it is through the analysis of this verbal art that we attain a deeper understanding of culture and cultural practices. As Blommart (2006, 233) notes, "ethnopoetic analysis, we shall see, attempts to unearth culturally embedded ways of speaking." Observing that elder speakers of Hawaiian frequently engage in repetition in co-constructing stories about their life experiences, I follow this ethnopoetic perspective by attempting to understand repetition as a form of verbal art that both reveals the linguistic skills of the Hawaiian speakers and represents a culturally embedded way of approaching language and social interaction.

Although not necessarily aligned with the perspectives of CA and ethnopoetics, it is worth noting that there is a fairly extensive list of research on repetition that has focused primarily on the functions of repetition in discourse. These functions include agreement, repair, emphasis, coherence, confirmation, displays of participation and support, topic maintenance, ratifying listenership, humor, stalling, and also competition and asserting rights to information (see Johnstone 1994; Kim 2002; Norrick 1987; Stivers 2005; Tannen 1987, 1989). Furthermore, research shows that many of these functions apply not just to discourse in English but carry over to language usage in a variety of languages that include Chinese (Tsai 2001), Hindi (Abbi 1975), Italian (Duranti and Ochs 1979), Antiguan Creole (Shepherd 1985), New Guinea Pidgin (Grimes 1972), and Javanese (Becker 1984).

In fact, although studies of the Hawaiian language are still few in number, those that do exist suggest the importance of repetition in the Hawaiian language. Elbert and Mahoe (1970), for instance, point out that Hawaiian employs numerous full and partial reduplications in the construction of words and point out several in the translation of the song "Santa Claus Is Coming to Town." They note that "of the six content words in the first three lines of the third stanza, four of them are reduplications, so easy to learn and pleasantly repetitive: ʻoluʻolu ("kind"), ʻumiʻumi ("beard"), pūhuluhulu ("hairy"), ʻulaʻula ("red")" (Elbert and Mahoe 1970, 12). Elbert and Mahoe's usage in this description of terms such as "easy" and "pleasant" suggests a positive evaluation of repetition from a Hawaiian perspective.

Furthermore, as early as 1951, the linguist Samuel Elbert praised Hawaiian speakers for the frequent inclusion of repetition in Hawaiian tales expressed originally orally but also written down in Hawaiian newspapers between 1870 and 1890 (Elbert 1951). In his words, "repetition of key words in successive verses is much admired" and, given the length of some of the oral tales, serves as "proof that intellectual virtuosity was much esteemed in the culture" (Elbert 1951, 350). More recently, Hawaiian scholars such as Kimura (2002, 2012) and Perreira (2013) employ the Hawaiian term *pīnaʻi* ("repetition") and list repetition as one of the foundational features of a Hawaiian oratory that is manifested in chants, songs, poems, tales, and literature. These features, which are collectively referred to as *meiwi* from the two terms *mele* ("song") and *iwi* ("bones" or "core"), are what constitutes the cultural perspective of a Hawaiian oratory style (Kimura 2002; Perreira 2013). In particular, *pīnaʻi* ("repetition") can help give *mana* ("power") to the repeated parts of a story (Perreira 2013, 69). The analysis to follow will further show how speakers of Hawaiian added *mana* to their speech as a part of demonstrating their "intellectual virtuosity" and verbal artistry.

Analysis 1: Repetition in the Speech of Hawaiian Elders

The data for this analysis come from two sets of interviews of elder native speakers that were conducted in the early 1970s. One set of data was recorded by the Hawaiian educator Clinton Kanahele, who traveled to different parts of the islands to interview and document the speech of elder speakers of the language, and the other set is from interviews conducted by Larry Kimura, a Hawaiian language activist who has taught Hawaiian at both the University of Hawaiʻi at Mānoa and the University of Hawaiʻi at Hilo, as part of a radio show devoted to the Hawaiian language and broadcast through the Mānoa campus.[1]

I begin the analysis by noting that the distinction between speech made by the "self" and by "others" was important in early work in CA, particularly in research on repair (Schegloff, Jefferson, and Sacks 1977). Using this distinction, Schegloff, Jefferson, and Sacks, in fact showed that speakers prefer to engage in self-correction rather than wait for other speakers to correct them. Repair and correction are social actions related to repetition not only because repetition is often used to accomplish repair (Norrick 1987), but more specifically because both repair and repetition require two (or more) utterances in order to be accomplished as social actions. In other words, just as a repair requires a second utterance, either by self or other, to do the repair, so does a repetition necessitate a second utterance in order to constitute a repetition. Like repair, a repetition can be accomplished by a self or an other.

In her efforts to explicate the organization of repetition in interaction, Wong (2000) divides repetition into "first and second sayings." This division allows her to tie this organization of first and second sayings back to the notions of "self" and "other." Here is what she writes about repetition in interaction involving North American speakers of English:

> A repetition produced by another speaker achieves a different sort of action from one initiated by the same speaker, accomplishing tasks such as initiating repair (on a just prior trouble source utterance); registering receipt (of information, a story, an announcement, etc.); signaling rejection, correction, or disalignment (cf. Pomerantz, 1984); and "confirming allusions" (of a candidate understanding and its inexplicit mode of delivery; Schegloff, 1996a, 1997). Forms of same-speaker repetition perform different sorts of actions and are not restricted to the sort that I discuss here (cf. Schegloff, 1999, in press). Some same-speaker repetitions are in the nature of "suppressions" (Schegloff, in press), recycled turn beginnings (Schegloff, 1987), and so on. Different interactional tasks are brought to bear depending on who is responsible for the repeated element.[2]

I take the time to point out these distinctions between first and second sayings and also self and other because it is seemingly possible to see both in the interviews with elder Hawaiian speakers. Excerpt (1) from an interview of Solomon Kupihea (SK) by Clinton Kanahele (CK) offers an example that shows both types of repetition.[3]

Excerpt (1): Interview with Solomon Kupihea
1   CK: *kama'āina nō   'oe i   kēia 'āina. Lō'ihi nō   kēia noho ['ana*
         familiar   EP you O this land   long   EP this staying
         "You are familiar with this land. You have been staying here long"
2   SK: [*'ae lō'ihi*
                                                          yes long
3   *lō'ihi lō'ihi kēia- ko'u noho 'ana ma kēia 'āina*
         long   long   this   my staying on this land
         "Yes, long, long, my staying here on this land has been long"

The interviewer CK in line 1 puts forth two statements, first that "you" (*'oe* in Hawaiian) are familiar with this land and second that "this" (*kēia*) stay has been long (*lō'ihi*). As CK nears a point of possible completion in line 1, SK begins his response by uttering in overlap in line 2 the word 'ae ("yes"), an action which indicates an orientation to CK's utterance as deserving of a yes/no confirmation.[4] SK then continues in lines 2–3 by repeating the term *lō'ihi* that was uttered by CK and then stating it two more times before producing the term *kēia* that was also used by CK. He then cuts himself off after *kēia* and produces the first person possessive term *koʻu* ("my") as a part of stating that his staying there has been long. In doing so, all of the terms chosen by the elder SK, except for the possessive term *koʻu*, are repeats of words used by CK. It is, in other words, an example of other-repetition. In addition, SK, by uttering the word *lōʻihi* three times in succession has engaged in a self-repetition that is integrated into his other-repetition.

Yet, SK's action in line 3 is at least slightly difficult to categorize in terms of first and second sayings and also "self" and "other." His repetition of *lōʻihi* in line 2 is a second saying, but what about his third and fourth sayings in line 3. They are repetitions of the term *lōʻihi* that he himself just stated as a part of repeating part of CK's utterance. They are, in short, seemingly both self and other repetitions at the same time. Excerpt (2) provides a further example that speaks to the frequency of repetition in the data as well as the nuances involved in categorizing repetitions according to "self" and "other." The excerpt is also taken from the Kanahele collection as CK is interviewing another elder speaker, Gus Kaleohana (GK) about the place where the elder had been living.

Excerpt (2): Interview with Gus Kaleohana
1 CK: *ma laila   kanu ʻia   ke kalo*
         at there   plant PASS   the taro
         "the taro was planted there"
2 GK: *kanu ʻia   ke kalo*
         plant PASS the taro
         "The taro was planted"
((one comment about the river that provided water))
3 CK: *ma mua   kahe mau   kēlā kahawai*
         at before flow constantly   that river
         "before, the river flowed constantly"
4 GK: *wai   kahe mau,   kahe mau,   ʻaʻole loaʻa i ka ʻāina*
         water flow constantly   flow constantly not   reach to the land
5   *kanu   kalo i kai*
         plant taro at ocean
         "The water flowed constantly, flowed constantly, it did not reach the land where taro was planted by the ocean"

CK in line 1 makes a statement about the taro being planted there and GK confirms this information in line 2 by repeating verbatim the phrase *kanu ʻia ke kalo* ("it was planted"), omitting only the place *ma laila* ("there") that it was planted. This response in line 2 seems easily characterized as a second saying done by an other participant, in short, as an other-repetition. However, GK's next repetition is not so neatly categorized. In response to line 3, where CK makes a statement about the river flowing constantly, GK confirms in line

4 by repeating *wai* ("water"), which is one part of the word *kahawai* ("river") that was uttered by CK in line 3, and then by repeating twice the phrase *kahe mau* ("flowed constantly"). In terms of repetition, GK's usage of *wai* is quite ambiguous; it is a morpheme of *kahawai*, but it stands alone as a different word. Furthermore, GK's first uttering of *kahe mau* in line 4 may be a second saying by an other participant but his second repetition of *kahe mau* can be classified as both a self and an other-repetition.

This excerpt does show that the participants do more than repetition in their responses as GK continues in lines 4 and 5 to add more information related to the current topic of the planting of the taro and the water needed to assist in its development. He states *'a'ole loa'a i ka 'āina kanu kalo i kai* ("it did not reach the land where the taro was planted by the ocean"). Still, as excerpts (1) and (2) indicate, it was common for the elder interviewees to engage in repetition, even though their repetitive speech is sometimes difficult to divide into the categories of "self" and "other."

Based on the data thus far, it would be possible to suggest that repetition in Hawaiian serves some of the functions mentioned in earlier research on repetition in other languages. For instance, the other-repetition produced by SK and GK in excerpts (1) and (2) serves the purpose of confirming information and could also be taken as expressions of emphasis as well as demonstrations of participation and involvement. Yet, the same could be also be said for the self-repetitions, which arguably serve as signals of emphasis and also possibly as signs of involvement and support for a prior utterance. In other words, in contrast to Wong's (2000) observations about North American English data, it may not be viable to draw a similar distinction between "self" and "other" in repetitions in the Hawaiian interviews. To be sure, repetition may indeed be performing the functions noted in prior research, but instead of focusing on specific functions, I would like to pursue here the possibility that repetition in Hawaiian, whether self or other-produced, is a valued verbal skill that is part of the linguistic repertoire of Hawaiian speakers. Excerpt (3) begins to speak to this point. It is taken from the database created by Larry Kimura (LK) in his radio interviews with elder speakers.

Excerpt (3): Interview with Abigail Kāka'e Kaleiheana
1 LK: a   pehea kēia 'ōlelo no'eau, 'a'ohe u-
       and how this wise saying   no
       "and how about this wise saying, there is not"
2 AKK: 'a'ohe u'i   [(**)
       no   beauty
       "There is no beauty (**)"
3 LK: [(**) hele wale o Kohala
                          go   just   Kohala
       "in just going to Kohala"

4 AKK: 'ae (.) kēlā 'ōlelo   he 'ōlelo kēlā no ka po'e (.) a (.) kūpuna e a'o aku
       yes   that saying   saying that for the people   elders   teach
5   ai kāu mo'opuna.   Pehea lā kou u'i   a   hele nō me   ka lako,
       PS   grandchildren how   PS beauty and go   EP with the supplies
6   hele nō me ke ō,   Hele nō me ka 'a'ahu. Hele nō a   kahi e kipa
       go   EP with the food   go   EP with the clothes   go   EP and place to visit
7   ai, he 'ai nō   kāu, he i'a, 'a'ohe he hemahema ka hele 'ana, he kapa
               food EP PS   fish not have problems   the going   beddings
8   nō (*) 'o ia ka mea   i 'ōlelo 'ia ai, 'a'ohe u'i   hele wale o Kohala
       EP   that the thing PST say   Pass   no beauty go   just   Kohala
       "yes (.) that saying, it is a saying for the people, the elders to teach
       their grandchildren. How is your beauty, go with the proper supplies, go
       the food, go with clothes, go with a place to visit, you will have food, you
       will have fish, you will not have trouble in your going, you will have
       blankets (*) that is what this is saying, there is no beauty in just going
       without anything."
9 LK: 'ae
       yes
       "yes"
10 AKK: hele nō me ka 'ope'ope.
        Go   EP with the bundles
        "Go with bundles of stuff"
11 LK: 'ae, 'ae. A   'o ia ka ho'opuka 'ana.
        Yes yes and this the saying   NOM
        "Yes, yes, that is what they say"

As the interviewer LK is in the process of producing a question in line 1, the elder AKK anticipates that he is going to ask about the Hawaiian proverb *'a'ohe u'i ka hele wale o Kohala* ("there is no beauty in just going to Kohala"). The two of them then overlap in lines 2 and 3 as LK finishes the proverb in line 3. This prompts AKK to explain in the form of a narrative in lines 4–8 this proverb as something important the elders teach the grandchildren. In doing so, she employs the same form *hele nō*, which consists of the verb *hele* ("go") and the emphatic particle *nō* four times in lines 5 and 6 to explain that the proverb means that one should go with the proper supplies (*hele nō me ka lako*), go with food (*hele nō me ke ō*), go with clothing (*hele nō me ka 'a'ahu*), and go with a place in mind to visit (*hele nō a kahi e kipa ai*). This is, as she notes, in line 8 what this proverb means. And she even accentuates this with a further parallel structure in line 10, *Hele nō me ka 'ope'ope* ("go with bundles of stuff").

Note, though, that this type of structured repetition does not stop with the structure *hele nō* in line 6. AKK uses a different pattern in line 6 but continues this type of structural repetition. She utters *he 'ai nō kāu* ("you will have food") in line 7 and then continues with this possessive form with *he i'a* ("you will have fish"), and *he kapa nō* ("you will have blankets"). Even the utterance between *he i'a* and *he kapa nō*, *'a'ohe he hemahema ka hele 'ana* ("you will not have trouble in your travel") serves as a congruent structure since it is the negative form (with the he seen following the negative marker *'a'ohe*).

In terms of function, it may be possible to view these repetitions as a form of emphasis; AKK is in a sense emphasizing that these are the components that constitute the meaning of this particular proverb. Yet, what is striking here is the extent to which the elder speaker AKK employs distinctly parallel grammatical structures in constructing this short explanation. Grammatical parallelism has been a topic in the study of linguistics and has often been applied to the study of poetry and literature. However, Jakobsen (1960, 1966) challenged the notion that grammatical parallelism was only to be found in poetic language, leading him to posit a poetic function of language that extended beyond poetry and literature into everyday uses of language. Excerpt (4) from the same set of data compiled by Larry Kimura speaks to the frequency with which this grammatical parallelism was employed by the Hawaiian elders that contributed to his radio program.

Excerpt (4): Interview with Lilly Bilamour

1 LB: nā mea   a pau, 'ai maka, 'ōlelo *, ku'u makuakāne pēia
        Pl things all   eat raw   say   PS father   this
        "we ate everything raw, my father would say this"

2 LK: 'ai maka
        eat raw
        "eat raw?"

3 LB: mamake wau iā   'oukou e (.) a'o. A'o ana wau iā   'oukou.
        Want   I   O   you   to learn teach I   O   you
4   'ai 'oukou i   ka i'a maka. Nā mea a pau ua hā'awi iā   'oukou
        eat you   O   the fish raw Pl things all   Pst give   O   you
5   e 'ai 'a'ole wau kuke ana. 'A'ole wau pūlehu ana.
        To eat not I   cook   not I   broil
6   'a'ole wau palai ana. 'A'ole wau lāwalu ana.   Ho'oku'u ana
        not   I   fry   not   I   cook with tea leaves let go
7   wau iā   'oukou 'ai, 'ai maka. 'Ai maka mākou ka 'o'opu.
        I   O   you eat, eat raw eat raw we   the type of fish
        "I want you to learn. I am going to teach you. You will eat raw fish. Everything I give you to eat. I am not going to cook it. I am not going to broil it. I am not going to fry it. I am not going to cook it by wrapping it with tea leaves. I am just going to let you go and eat it raw. We ate those 'o'opu raw."

8 LK: i   ka 'o'opu?   Auē nō ho'i.
        O   the type of fish? Wow EP EP
        "the 'o'opu? Oh wow."

Beginning in line 3, LB embodies the voice of her father through the first person plural *wau* ("I") as she begins to explain what her father used to tell her and her siblings about eating food without cooking it. As a part of doing so, she employs the negative form *'a'ole* four consecutive times in line 5 to state *'a'ole wau kuke ana* ("I am not going to cook"), *'a'ole wau pūlehu ana* ("I am not going to broil"), *'a'ole wau palai ana* ("I am not going to fry"), and *'a'ole wau lāwalu ana* ("I am not going to cook with tea leaves"). These utterances cover only two lines, but there is an obvious parallelism created through the repetition of the same negative marker.

Moreover, we can see the construction of a slightly different type of parallelism by LB after she explains in lines 5–6 the different methods through which the food will not be cooked. As she finishes embodying the words of her father, she repeats the verb *'ai* ("eat") in lines 6–7 in stating "*Ho'oku'u ana wau iā 'oukou 'ai, 'ai maka. 'Ai maka mākou ka 'o'opu*" ("I am going to allow you to eat, to eat it raw, and we ate the 'opu'u raw"). In so stating, there is a kind of buildup where she ends her first utterance of *'ai* ("eat") with just *'ai*, then repeats the verb with the word *maka* ("raw") following it, and then she repeats both *'ai* and *maka* in creating the full sentence *'ai maka mākou ka 'o'opu* ("we eat the 'o'opu raw"). While this type of repetition is slightly different from the others noted in this excerpt and also in excerpt (4) because each subsequent repetition of *'ai* is followed by a gradual increase in the amount of words, it is just as noteworthy for the type of rhythm that it adds to the narrative, which is arguably just as poetic in nature and just effective in terms of expression as the parallelism of the other examples.

Excerpt (5) offers another example that consists of multiple grammatical parallisms from a different interview in Kimura's database.

Excerpt (5): Interview with John Keoni Kameaaloha Almeida
1 JKKA: *hau'oli nō ho'i ka pepeiao o ka po'e   ke   ho'olohe*
          happy EP EP the ears   of the people when listen
2   *mai.*
          DIR
          "it was pleasing to the ears of the people when they listen."
3 LK: *nāu nō i haku   ke ea   me ka [(*)*
          you EP pst composed the essence with the
          "You were the one who composed the essence with the (*)"
4 JKKA: *['ae. Na'u ka ea,*
                                                  yes I   the essence
5   *na'u ka leo, a, na'u ka wala'au 'ana.*
          I   the voice and I   the speaking

6 LK: 'ē.
          Yes
          "yes"
7 JKKA: i loko o kēlā, (1) mele Pua 'Ōhai (1.5) e (1) 'o nā pila e-
          within of that   song Pua 'Ōhai   Pl instruments
8   'ehā pila   a'u i   pā'ani ai, 'o ia ho'i, ma mua, ma mua o ke
          four instruments I pst play   that EM   before   before of the
9   kani, a   o ko'u hīmeni 'ana, kani ka mandolin, a, kani ke kīkā,
          sound and of PS singing   play the mandolin   play the guitar
10   kani ka 'ukulele, kani ka bass.
          Play the ukulele, play the bass
          "within that (1) song Pua 'Ōhai (1.5) e (1) the four instruments that I
          would play, they were, before, before the sound, my singing, I would play
          the mandolin, play the guitar, play the ukulele, and play the bass.
11 LK: a ho'ohui   'ia.
          And put together Pass
          "and they would be all put together"

The interviewer LK asks in line 3 whether the interviewee JKKA was the one who composed the essence of a certain song. In doing so, LK uses a grammatical pattern that, with the word *nāu* "you," both topicalizes and emphasizes JKKA as the subject of the action of composing (*haku*). In constructing his response that starts in line 4 and continues in line 5, JKKA employs the first person form *na'u* of the same grammatical structure to state that "I created the essence" (*na'u ka 'ea*), "I am responsible for the voice" (*na'u ka leo*), and "I am responsible for the talking" (*na'u ka wala'au*). This is yet a different grammatical pattern from the ones used by the elder speakers in excerpts (3) and (4), but the parallelism created through the repetition of a grammatical pattern is consistent in all three of these excerpts.

Furthermore, JKK's usage of parallelism in excerpt (5) does not end in lines 4–5 with the pattern beginning with *na'u*. Shortly thereafter, as he explains in lines 7–10 about a particular song called *Pua 'Ōhai*, he repeats the verb *kani* ("to sound or to play") as he notes that he plays four instruments, namely, the mandolin (*kani ka mandolin*), the guitar (*kani ke kīkā*), the ukulele (*kani ka 'ukulele*), and also the bass (*kani ka bass*). While this is a repetition of particular verb, it nonetheless creates a similar type of parallelism in his expression.

One last example that highlights the verbal artistry of the repetition employed by elder Hawaiian speakers comes from an interview by Kimura of Rachel Nahale'elua Mahuiki. In the three lines shown next, which contain part of Mahuiki's explanation of how to make poi bread, it does not take her long to construct a visible parallelism in her speech.

Excerpt (6): Interview with Rachel Nahale'elua Mahuiki
1 RNM: *aia nō a   mo'a   pono kāu wai, poe- paila 'oe i kēia wai*
         exist EP and prepare well your water   boil you O this water
2   *a   huli   a   huli   a   huli   a   mo'a pono, 'a'ole momona ka*
         and search and search and search and cook right not   sweet   the
3   *palaoa inā 'a'ole mo'a pono ka wai   wela, momona ana kāu palaoa*
         bread if   not   cook right the water not sweet   your bread
        "As soon as the water is prepared well, you boil this water
         and check and check and check and it is cooked right, then your bread
         will not be sweet, if your hot water is not prepared properly, your bread is
         going to be sweet"

At the beginning of line 1, RNM employs the phrase *mo'a pono kāu wai* ("prepare properly the water") to assert that the cooking of the poi bread depends on proper preparation of the water. She then employs her first repetition by repeating the term *huli* ("check") twice in line 2 to emphasize the need to check the water as it boils. Next, she repeats the term *mo'a pono* near the end of line 2 as a part of stating through line 3 that if (the water) is prepared properly, then the bread will not be sweet (*'a'ole momona ka palaoa*). Next in line 3, she repeats again *mo'a pono* but adds the negative *'a'ole* to note that if the water is not prepared to a proper heat, then the bread will be sweet, something that is not desired. In making this statement in line 3, she repeats the phrase *momona kāu palaoa* but without the negative.

There is thus a clever piece of symmetry in these three lines; RNM first remarks that if the water is *mo'a pono* ("boiled properly"), then *'a'ole momona ka palaoa* ("the bread will not be too sweet"), but she then shifts the position of the negative marker *'a'ole* to say that if (*inā*) *'a'ole mo'a pono* ("not boiled properly"), then *momona (ana) ka palaoa* ("the bread will be too sweet"). This is a bit of a subtle switch in position of the negative marker *'a'ole*, but it adds a kind of poetic and symmetrical quality to RNM's explanation.

These last four excerpts from Kimura's database exemplify first the frequency with which repetition was used by the elder speakers. If anything, these last four examples may be classified as self-repetitions since they basically show a single speaker repeater her/himself. However, at this stage of the analysis, I hesitate to assign any primacy to self-repetitions since the first two excerpts from Kanahele's database showed instances that could be fit into either the "self" or "other" together. Hence, rather than making a self-other distinction, I would like to emphasize the second point of the analysis, namely, that these instances of repetition exhibit interesting patterns of semantic and grammatical parallelism. Parallelism was realized by repeating of specific words and also grammatical structures, and it was also accomplished via a gradual increase of words following a particular grammatical pattern as in excerpt (4) and via a playful switching of the position of a negative marker as with 'a'ole in excerpt (6). This creative usage of repetition displays not only a lack of fear of being "repetitive" but also a quick and deft skill in arranging the repetition in such a symmetrical manner.

It should be noted that, even though at least one of the elder speakers in these excerpts, JKKA in excerpt (5) was a well-known Hawaiian musician and thus skilled at song composition, the interviewees were not necessarily selected because of their exceptional oratory skills. Instead, they were chosen because they were some of the few remaining native speakers of Hawaiian who were still living and available for interview. This then suggests that this skillful construction of parallelism through repetition is an ability that the Hawaiian elders acquired as a part of employing the language throughout their lifetime. The ability to employ repetition to construct this type of verbal expression is, in other words, part of the indigenous knowledge that goes together with their ability to speak the Hawaiian language, and it is, likewise, the type of verbal skill that would be lost should the language cease to be used in society.

This analysis therefore suggests that an important role of the Hawaiian language in multilingual Hawai'i is the diversity it brings in terms of interacting with the world. Just as an understanding of place names enhances our knowledge of the relationship between people and the land, so does an understanding of the skillfullness with which Hawaiian speakers employ repetition increase our knowledge of how people can organize and express their thoughts. In contrast to a sometimes negative image of repetition as indicating "sloppy" or "disfluent" speech from a Western perspective (see Tannen 1989 for discussion),[5] the Hawaiian perspective offers a view of repetition as a verbal art that can add to the parallelism and symmetry of speech.

THE HAWAIIAN LANGUAGE AND THE QUESTION OF AUTHENTICITY

While the previous analysis demonstrates a possible contribution of Hawaiian to the diversity of expression within society, the fact that the analysis just presented focuses on elder speakers in the 1970s raises questions about the current state of the language. The elder speakers in those two data sets are no longer with us and, with their passing, have given way to fluent speakers of Hawaiian who have been raised in a society dominated by English. How much, then, of the verbal artistry seen in the analysis is being transmitted to the younger speakers of Hawaiian who have primarily learned the language in schools and who are attempting to perpetuate the language and pass it on to subsequent generations?

This is a question related to the issue of authenticy, which has been a topic of discussion in Hawaiian language revitalization (Wong 1999a, 2006, 2011) and also in general research related to language endangerment and language revitalization (Dorian 1994; Henze and Davis 1999; Hinton and Ahlers 1999; Huffines 1989; Scully 2010). Authenticity becomes an issue with languages that have lost intergenerational transmission because in the process of revitalizing a language, it is often necessary to coin new words that can be employed in teaching a language to younger generations in a modern society. Concerns can arise as to whether the newly coined words appropriately reflect traditional cultural perspectives. In cases where there has been close contact with a dominant language, the fear is that the new coinages might represent the values of the dominant culture and not the indigenous one. Indeed, this possibility was raised by Reinecke (1969) (discussed in chapter 1), who noted Hawaiian expressions started to receive influence from English soon after the arrival of the missionaries and as the Bible was being translated into Hawaiian.

One of the solutions to this problem in the movement to revitalize the Hawaiian language was to create a "lexicon committee" that consists of elder native speakers as well as university-educated fluent speakers and that is tasked with creating words to be used in educational settings. Kimura and Councellor (2009) explain the close connection between the establishment of schools and word creation:

> New words needed to be coined for such concepts as a gathering circle to start and end the day (*lina poepoe*), a snack (*mea'ai māmā*) in the morning and afternoon, independent activities (*hana 'ae'oia*), to trace a figure (*ho'omahaka*), or "playing house" (*pā'ani 'anakē*). These words grew out of necessity and were immediately put to use with the start of the first Pūnana Leo School Hawaiian medium preschool in 1984.

As the Hawaiian medium school system expanded to reach higher levels of education, the need for word construction became even greater. The lexicon committee has published and updated a new words dictionary called *Māmaka Kaiao* in 1996, 1998, and 2003 with over 6,500 entries (Kimura and Councellor 2009).

Kimura and Councellor (2009) describes in detail the processes employed by the Hawaiian lexicon committee to coin new words, but questions about the authenticity of the Hawaiian language emerging in current society have tended to go beyond the word level, with the strongest criticism pointing to a distinction between a "traditional" Hawaiian and a "neo Hawaiian" that is now being spoken in current society (NeSmith 2005). Critics of the "new Hawaiian" recognize that language change over time is a natural phenomenon, but they nonetheless fear that placing the revitalization of the Hawaiian language in the hands of speakers who learned the language in schools is having adverse effects on not just the language but also culture and identity. In the words of NeSmith (2005, 3):

> Typically, NEO speakers acquire the language at schools that employ other NEO speakers, while TRAD speakers acquire Hawaiian as a first language spoken in the home. This has resulted, albeit inadvertently, in differences in Hawaiian cultural values, and ultimately, in different cultural identities, which have led to conflicts or misunderstandings between the two intersecting groups. In addition, I propose that NEO speakers are changing the way the Hawaiian language (and by extension, Hawaiian cultural values) is understood, expressed, and embodied. This change is transforming Hawaiian identity.

Thus, while there is a new generation of Hawaiian speakers that include "new native speakers" (Brenzinger and Heinrich 2013), the concern of critics is that new speakers are acquiring NEO Hawaiian because they are learning the language from speakers who learned it at school, and therefore are failing to acquire a traditional cultural identity. As Wong (2011, 153) notes, "language is commonly recognized as a marker of identity, but what is the point of putting in the effort to learn Hawaiian if it merely results in the ability to speak English in Hawaiian."

NeSmith (2005) lists a set of 17 linguistic characteristics, ranging from phonology to syntax, that supposedly set traditional Hawaiian apart from NEO Hawaiian and demonstrate how NEO speakers have changed the language. Included in this list is the tendency of NEO speakers to rely on only a limited set of grammatical structures (NeSmith 2005, 8–9); there is a "high value placed on a limited, prescriptive set of grammatical structures and rules, as learned in the classroom and/or from grammar texts." The concern here is that some of the important yet sometimes subtle connections between language and worldview may be missed by learners of language. As Wong aptly explains (2011, 152), "mastery of grammar and lexicon alone without the concomitant mastery of more subtle ways of speaking . . . signficantly limits the ability of the speaker to function appropriately in the target language and ultimately contributes to an overall shift in the defining linguistic and related social characteristic of the language." Wong (2011, 152–153) accentuates this point by stating "in this case, the shift moves away from Hawaiian and toward English and tests the link between language and identity."

These concerns about the authenticity of revitalized Hawaiian are, of course, understandable for an indigenous, endangered language such as

Hawaiian that has existed in a multilingual society for approximately 200 years, especially given the longstanding relationship with a language like English that has become dominant in society. Indeed, in my examination of repetitions, I did a quick search in some of the more commonly employed Hawaiian language textbooks and found very little, if any, information about the process of repeating from a Hawaiian perspective. To be sure, repetition may be considered a higher level oratory device that is beyond the coverage of most beginning level textbooks. Nonetheless, the fact that elder speakers employed repetition with such a regular frequency suggests a need to provide such information to learners attempting to revitalize Hawaiian speaking and cultural practices.

At the same time, however, inspection of more recent Hawaiian language data does reveal aspects of language usage that seem to preserve a Hawaiian way of interacting with the world. Here, I turn to the second analysis of this chapter, which focuses on the Hawaiian employed in a media initiative known as ʻŌiwi TV that appears on cable television in Hawaiʻi and also on the Internet. ʻŌiwi TV was begun by speakers of Hawaiian who largely learned the language in school and thus may be considered NEO Hawaiians speakers in NeSmith's definition. The data for the analysis are taken from video clips available on the Internet that feature interviews of Hawaiian speakers by reporters who also provide narration in Hawaiian about different topics. Both the reporters and the majority of the interviewees would fall into the NeSmith's (2005) category of NEO speaker.

Analysis 2: Expression of Agency in the Hawaiian Language on ʻŌiwi TV

According to its website, "ʻŌiwi TV produces top-quality documentaries, news and multimedia content from a uniquely Hawaiian perspective" that are "shaped by our aspiration to revitalize and affirm a positive native Hawaiian worldview." Accordingly, it will be interesting to see if the Hawaiian language employed also reflects a "uniquely Hawaiian perspective" and "native Hawaiian worldview."[6]

Not all of the videos feature speakers of the Hawaiian language, but the website states that, as of September 30, 2016, 1,250 videos have been produced, 925 of which are in the Hawaiian language. Some of the videos are of considerable length, approximately one hour, but the majority of the videos on the website are much shorter clips, in the range of three to seven minutes.

Of the Hawaiian videos, many consist of a mixture of English and Hawaiian, a result of the fact that many of the people interviewed in the videos are not fluent speakers of Hawaiian. Often, a video will begin with a narrator speaking Hawaiian as part of introducing the topic, then feature interviews with different people, some of whom might speak Hawaiian and some English, and then return to the narrator for further explanation in Hawaiian. Frequently, the videos also show English subtitles that make them understandable to non-Hawaiian speakers. Likewise, some of the English parts of a video provide subtitles in Hawaiian.

As videos that feature both visual images and spoken language, there are numerous resources employed toward the goal of promoting a Hawaiian worldview. The choice of topic, for instance, is one way a video can do this. Many of the videos focus on the relationship between people and the land and also between people and the ocean, which is suggestive of the emphasis placed in the Hawaiian worldview on protecting and making a living from nature. There is also a heavy concentration on language and also the arts, including music and dance.

Within the Hawaiian language as well, there are numerous resources for promoting a Hawaiian way of thinking, including vocabulary, proverbs, and grammatical patterns used to construct actions such as chants and songs that also appear in the videos. In this analysis, I am going to focus particularly on grammatical resources employed in Hawaiian for the expression of agency. More specifically, I am going to examine how speakers of Hawaiian formulate the occurrence of a particular action or result with an emphasis on the degree to which they explicitly state the agent, or doer, of the action. In doing so, the analysis draws on ideas from Duranti's (1994) investigation of Samoan political discourse which describes Samoan grammatical structures such as ergativity that figured prominently in the expression of agency. Duranti (1994, 125) defines an agent as a semantic role that is "the willful initiator of an event that is depicted as having consequences for either an object or animate patient," but I am going to follow Wong (2006, 2011) and loosen the definition here to include not just "willful initiators" but also "anyone or anything that does something (i.e., executes an action) or is in some way (other than overt action) responsible for the occurrence of a particular state of affairs" (Wong 2006, ix). Hence, even though "the boy" in the sentence "The boy saw the dog" would be considered an "experiencer" and not an "agent" in some taxonomies of semantic roles (see Duranti 1994), "the boy" is the doer of the action of "seeing" and thus will be considered as an agent for the purposes of this analysis.

Moreover, the analysis also adopts a functional perspective to linguistic structure associated with the work of Halliday (1985, 2003) and subsequent scholars (Billig 2008; Maynard 1999; Schroder 2002) in that it examines how specific grammatical features, especially passives, nominalization, and stative verbs, function within the media to express information in a way that is consistent with a Hawaiian approach to interaction. More specifically, the analysis will show a connection between these structures and the way that agency is articulated in the ʻŌiwi TV video clips.

The reason for choosing this topic as well as this general definition of agency is a sense that there is a preference in a Hawaiian perspective for expressing actions and or states of being without explicitly attributing those actions or states to particular actors. This idea is discussed in considerable detail by Laiana Wong in his dissertation (Wong 2006) and a subsequent publication (Wong 2011). Wong (2011, 153) writes, "it has been my contention (Wong 2006) that, in Hawaiian, indirection is the norm when it comes to pointing at grammatical agents, especially those that denote humans." Wong further explains that explicit pointing to an agent singles out that person from the rest of the group, an action that can do harm to the harmony of the group. In Wong's (2011, 159) words, "the overt indication of an individual, even for the purposes of praise, can often engender feelings of discomfort because it elevates that individual above his or her peers and, in doing so, isolates that individual from the rest of the group."

This way of expression, therefore, fits with the traditional Hawaiian notion of *hana pono* ("right behavior") (Pukui, Haertig, and Lee 1972). According to Pukui, Haertig, and Lee (1972), children in a Hawaiian worldview are taught to stay in the background and "observe, listen, and keep quiet." They are taught that to talk too much and to brag is to be *maha'oi* (lit. "thrust the temple forward") and not acceptable. Likewise, they are taught to be indirect in speech and use *kaona* ("hidden meanings"), particularly to veil speech that might be viewed as criticism (Pukui, Haertig, and Lee 1972, 225). Speaking in a Hawaiian perspective is more than just communicating a meaning; it is a powerful action in and of itself that can cause harm to those mentioned if words are not carefully chosen. A common Hawaiian *'ōlelo no'eau* ("wise saying") is *he mana ko ka 'ōlelo* ("there is power in language") (see Oliveira 2011), which means that one's words can directly cause states of affairs, such as sickness, disaster, and death, to occur.

Given this cultural perspective, it is not surprising that Wong (2006) found in his study that agents were expressed quite indirectly in some of the content published in Hawaiian language newspapers in the 1800s and early 1900s. One question that arises from such an observation is the degree to which such indirect patterns of expression have been passed on to subsequent generations of Hawaiian speakers. Excerpt (7) starts to answer such a question by demonstrating the methods chosen by Hawaiian speakers in the videos published by 'Ōiwi TV to express agents of actions. It is from a clip which reports that February was approved as Hawaiian language month.

Excerpt (7): http://oiwi.tv/politics/he-mahina-kuhelu-ko-ka-olelo-hawaii/
1   Reporter: *'akahi a 'āpono   'ia   ka pila SB409 e   ke kia'āina 'o Neil*
                 recently approve PASS   the bill   by the governor

2		*Abercrombie i mea*	*e*	*ho'ola'a*	*'ia*	*ai nō*	*ka mahina*
		in order to anoint			PASS	EMP	the month
3		*'o Pepeluali 'o ia ka mahina 'ōlelo*			*Hawai'i kūhelu ma*		
		February that the month language Hawai'i official in					
4		*Hawai'i nei*					
		Hawai'i DIR					

"Bill SB409 was just approved by Governor Neil Abercrombie so that the month of February may be annointed officially as the month of the Hawaiian language here in Hawai'i"

((a few seconds in which the speech of others is featured))

12	Reporter:	*i loko nō*	*o kēia paipai*	*'ana*	*ua*	*kāhiko 'ia*	*nō*	
		within EMP	of this encourage	NOM	PST	adorn PASS	EMP	
13		*kā*	*kākou 'ōlelo*	*Hawai'i me kekahi lei hou*			*aku o*	
		PS	we language	Hawai'i with a		lei more	DIR of	
14		*ka lanakila ma kēia piha makahiki he kanakolu o*					*ke aukahi*	
		the victory in this full year thirty					of the movement	
15		*ho'ōla*	*'ōlelo*	*Hawai'i ma lalo*		*ho'i o*	*ka*	
		Revitalize	language	Hawai'i in below		EMP of	the	
16		*'Aha Pūnana Leo.*						
		'Aha Pūnāna Leo						

"Within this encouragement, our Hawaiian language was adorned with another victory lei in this 30th year of the movement to revitalize the Hawaiian language under the guidance of the 'Aha Pūnana Leo"

In explaining lines 1–4 that the approval of legislative bill SB 409 means the annointment of February as "Hawaiian language month," the reporter explicitly states in lines 1–2 that the act of approval was done by the governor, Neil Abercrombie. This is accomplished via a passive construction that consists of the verb *'āpono* ("approve") followed by the passive marker *'ia* as a separate morpheme. It is important to note here that Hawaiian is considered a verb-initial language where the verb is typically followed by the subject. Accordingly in the passive construction in line 1, the passive form of the verb *'āpono 'ia* is followed by the subject *ka pila SB409* ("bill SB 409"). As a passive form, though, the subject is not the doer of the action; it is the actual object. In order for the agent of the action to be expressed as part of the passive construction, the marker *e* needs to be used, as in line 1 where it is stated *e ke kia'āina 'o Neil Abercrombie* ("by the governor Neil Abercrombie"). This utterance in line 1, then, is basically the passive construction in its prototypical format.

The reporter employs another passive form in line 2, *ho'ola'a 'ia* ("was anointed"), which states that the subject of this passive, *ka mahina 'o Pepeluali* ("the month of February") was anointed as the official month of the Hawaiian language. However, this time, there is no overt agent expressed through a noun phrase marked by *e*. There is, however, a phrase *i mea e* ("in order to") just prior to the verb and an also an anaphoric *ai* following the passive marker that makes it possible to discern agency of the verb anointing. More specifically, this phrase together with the anaphoric *ai* tells us that "the approving of the bill by the governor" is what anoints February as Hawaiian language month.

Although it possible to see agency in these two uses of the passive construction, there are two more instances in this excerpt in which it is difficult to find agents for action verbs. In line 12, the reporter follows the verb *paipai* ("encourage") with the marker *'ana*, which works to nominalize the verb to mean something like "within the encouraging" without mentioning explicitly who in fact was doing the encouraging. Finally, the reporter employs one more passive construction in the same line (line 12), *kāhiko 'ia* ("adorn"), to note through a metaphor of lei-giving that the Hawaiian language was given another lei of victory. It may be possible to infer that both of these verbs refer back to the approval of February as Hawaiian language month as the agents of this "encouraging" and "adorning," but there is no agent explicitly attributed to these two actions.

This first excerpt, thus, shows some of the complexities involved in expressing agency in Hawaiian. Although it is possible to make explicit reference to the doer of the action through the passive construction (and nominalization as well), such constructions also allow for agents to be left unstated, although they can often be inferred from the discourse. This is in fact appears to be a common way of expression in these Hawaiian clips. Excerpt (8) is from a video clip reporting on a dissertation defense by Kekuewa Kikiloi focusing on temples built in the Northwestern Hawaiian Islands. The reporter, it can be seen, employs several passive constructions through the marker *'ia*.

Excerpt (8): https://oiwi.tv/culture/kekuewa-kikilois-doctoral-defense/

1 Reporter: *i ka mahina nei, ua mālama 'ia kā Kekuewa Kikiloi*
in the month DIR PST hold PASS PS Kekuea Kikiloi
2 *kūpale pepa lae'ula ma kēia kumuhana hoihoi nō.*
Defense paper PhD on this topic interest EP
3 *ko'ako'a 'ia me nā koehana o kahiko, he ahuwale*
supply PASS with the artifacts of old obvious
4 *ua noho 'ia 'o Mokumanamana a me Nīhoa e nā kūpuna*
PST live PASS Mokumanamana and Nīhoa by the elders
5 *o ka wā kahiko, ua noho 'ia no kekahi wā lō'ihi i mea*
of the time old PST live PASS for some time long so that
6 *e kūkulu 'ia ai i ua mau moku lā. Eia na'e, 'o ka*

	build	PASS	O	that PL	islands	here though		the
7	*nīnau,*	*'o ia nō,*	*no ke aha i*		*kūkulu 'ia*		*ai 'o*	
	question that	EM	why		PST build	PASS		
8	*Mokumanamana lāua me Nīhoa, nā 'āina pāmalō loa o*
	Mokumanamana and	Nīhoa the land dry	most of
9	*Hawai'i pae 'āina?*
	Hawai'i archipelago

"Last month, Kekuewa Kikiloi's dissertation defense was held on this interesting topic. Well-supplied with the artifacts of old, it is obvious that Mokumanamana a Nīhoa were occupied by the elders of olden times, they were occupied for a long time so that the islands could be built. However, the question is indeed this, why were Mokumanamna and Nīhoa, the driest lands of the Hawaiian archipelago, built?"

The reporter begins in line 1 with the passive form *mālama 'ia* ("was held") to note that Kikiloi's dissertation defense was held last month. This passive construction tells us what was held, but the verb *mālama* does not have an explicitly stated agent that performed this action. The reporter next employs the passive marker *'ia* with the verb *ko'ako'a* ("supply") in line 3 and continues with the passive of *noho* ("live") in line 4 to state these two islands, Mokumanamana and Nīhoa, were well supplied with artifacts and inhabited by the Hawaiian people of olden times. In doing so, he makes his first and only reference to an actor by mentioning the Hawaiians of olden times through the phrase *e nā kūpuna o ka wā kahiko* ("the elders of olden times"). He then employs two more passives in lines 5 and 6, *noho 'ia* again and *kukulu 'ia* ("was built"), to report that the places were inhabited for a long time so that they could be built up with temples. Finally, he employs the passive *kūkulu 'ia* one more time in line 7 to ask why these places of land were chosen for the building of the temples. In total, then, the reporter has employed the passive marker *'ia* six times in this short passage while attributing agency only once to the ancient Hawaiians. While agency can be implied, mostly that it was the Hawaiians of old who did the actions of "living" and "building," usage of the passive form allows the reporter to leave this information unstated most of the time.

The argument to be constructed here is that the frequent usage of passive constructions fits a traditional Hawaiian perspective on speaking, but we may also want to consider the relationship between passive constructions and the language register of reporting news. More specifically, given the fact that Hawaiian, as an endangered language not spoken in many social domains for most of the 1900s, it is true that Hawaiian never really had a chance to develop a broadcasting/reporting register until recent news initiatives such as 'Ōiwi TV. Accordingly, perhaps the reporters' usage of passive constructions is a product of the Hawaiian speakers attempting to construct a newly emerging reporting register of the Hawaiian language. In such a case, we may ask whether the reporters' speech reflects traditional patterns of expression or whether it represents the reporters' attempts to constitute a formal reporting register, in which passive forms may be equated with formality.

While further research is necessary to understand how the originators of 'Ōiwi TV dealt with a lack of precedence of a broadcast register in Hawaiian, I would nonetheless like to suggest that this usage of passives to present information without explicitly attributing actorship is congruent with traditional patterns of expression, specifically, the usage of indirection to express agency. Evidence that this is the case comes from the fact that in the 'Ōiwi TV data it is not just the reporters who employ frequent resources such as passives but also other Hawaiian speakers appearing in the clips. Excerpts (9) and (10) show examples. Excerpt (9) is taken from a clip describing a program called 'Āina Ulu that is sponsored by the Kamehameha Schools. The excerpt occurs after the reporter introduced the program and as a participant in the program, Kihei, is describing the land that was set aside for the program. Excerpt (10) is from a clip reporting on a debate that was held at the University of Hawai'i at Hilo and it features first Hiapo, a participant in the debates, and then the voice of the reporter, who adds further explanation.

Excerpt (9): http://oiwi.tv/ks/huli-ka-lima-i-lalo/
1 Kihei: 'o ia paha   ke kumu o ka mālama 'ia   kēia mau 'āina
          this probably the reason of the preserve PASS this PL land
2   ma kēia 'ano 'a'ole ho'ohana 'ia   no ka development no
          in this way not   use   PASS for the   for
3   ka kū'ai aku, kūkulu hale, kūlana kauhale a   pēlā wale aku
          the selling   building houses towns   and the like
          "This is probably the reasons that these pieces of land have been preserved like this, not used for development, for selling, building houses, towns, and the like"

Excerpt (10): http://oiwi.tv/culture/paio-kalaimana'o-hawaiian-langauge-college-holds-a-second-teach-in/
1 Hiapo: 'o kēia ka lua   o ka 'aha   a'o kūloko e mālama 'ia   nei
           this the second of the event teach inside is holding PASS
2   'o ka mua ua   mālama 'ia   kēlā makahiki kula   aku nei
               the first PST hold   PASS that year   school DIR DIR
3   i ka wā nō   i hahana loa ai ke kūpale 'ana iā
           at the time EMP PST heat   very the defend NOM O

4		*Maunakea*
		Mauna Kea
		"This is the second of our teach-in meetings that is being held. The first was held last school year at the time when 'defend Mauna Kea' became a hot topic."
5	Reporter:	*me ke kākoʻo o ke kulanui o Hawaiʻi ma Hilo i mālama*
		With the support of the university of Hawaiʻi at Hilo PST hold
6		*ʻia ai he ʻaha hou me ke kumuhana ʻo ka paio*
		PASS a event again with the topic the contest
7		*kālaimanaʻo he mākau a haʻawina i ʻike ʻia mai loko*
		thought a skill and lesson PST see PASS from within
8		*mai o nā hanana e kū nei no ke kūkulu ʻohe nānā ʻana*
		from of the events standing for the build telescope NOM
9		*ma Maunakea.*
		on Mauna Kea
		"With the support of the University of Hawaiʻi at Hilo, another meeting was held with the focus on debate; it is a skill and a lesson observed from the events surrounding the building of a telescope on Mauna Kea."

In excerpt (9), the interviewee Kihei first employs the passive marker *ʻia* in line 1 with the form *mālama* ("preserve") to explain the land was preserved in such a way for a program such as "this" one. He then continues in lines 2 by employing *ʻia* again, this time with the verb *hoʻohana* ("use"), to note that it (the land) was not used for a list of activities that include developing, selling, and making houses and towns. In doing so, he has not explicity named the doers of the actions of preserving and using.

Excerpt (10) provides several further examples of passive constructions, with Hiapo employing two with the verb *mālama* ("hold"), one in line 1 and the other in line 2, to explain about the "holding" of the two teach-in events. Next, the reporter elaborates on Hiapo's explanation by employing the passive *mālama ʻia* in lines 5 and 6 and then the passive *ʻike ʻia* in line 7 to state that the most recent event was being held with the support of the university to develop the skills of debate observed in the events concerning the building of a telescope on the mountain of Mauna Kea. There are no explicit agents attributed to the verbs *mālama* ("hold") and *ʻike* ("see").

In addition, there is further support in these two excerpts for this idea that a Hawaiian preferred mode of expression is not to overtly state agents. In excerpt (9), Kihei does not use the nominalization marker *ʻana*, but he nonetheless nominalizes the verb "development" in line 2 as well as the verbs *kūʻai aku* ("sell") and *kūkulu* ("build") in lines 3 as part of saying that the land will not be used for the developing, selling, and constructing houses and towns.

Through this form of nominalization, Kihei mentions these actions but he does not specify who the actors are. Likewise, in excerpt (10), Hiapo uses the nominalizer *'ana* in line 3 with the verb *kūpale* ("defend") to discuss the defending of Mauna Kea but without saying who specifically was doing the defending. The reporter also employs nominalization in line 8 with the phrase *kūkulu 'ohe nānā 'ana* ("constructing telescope") to refer to the attempts to construct a telescope on Mauna Kea without stating the doer of the construction. In the case of these last two, one motive for not explicitly expressing the actors of the actions might lie in the controversy surrounding the building of a telescope on sacred land, but it nonetheless fits what seems to be a general pattern of not attributing agency.

Indeed, this usage of a combination of grammatical resources to obscure actorship is a common aspect of the language found on the 'Ōiwi TV videoclips. Excerpt (11) shows the usage of passives together with stative verbs which, according to Elbert and Pukui (1979), are the most common types of verbs in Hawaiian. Stative verbs allow speakers to refer to a state of affairs without expressing how those affairs came to be, in others words, without stating a "doer" or "actor" who put those affairs into place. This excerpt is also taken from the clip of the teach-in at the University of Hawai'i at Hilo and it focuses on the speech of Ka'ikena, who explains that he was asked to compose a song for the event.

Excerpt (11): http://oiwi.tv/culture/paio-kalaimana'o-hawaiian-langauge-college-holds-a-second-teach-in/

```
1 Ka'ikena: ua noi 'ia    au e haku   i kekahi leo   hou kekahi ea    hou
            PST ask PASS I  compose O  some  voice new some breath new
2           no kekahi po'aiapili hou no kēia mele (.) ua   pa'a ka 'ike
            for some  context    new for this song      PST solid the knowledge
3           kupuna ua   pa'a kekahi 'ike       Hawai'i i loko o kēia mele
            elders PST solid some   knowledge Hawai'i inside of this song
4           a  i kēia wā i kēia pō'aiapili hiki nō  ke 'ike 'ia   ka
            and at this time at this context     can EMP  see   PASS the
5           nīnūnē  maoli no ka wai  ma ka 'āina 'ē     ma nā nākī
            problem real for the water on the land other on the reservations
6           'ilikini ma Dakota 'ike 'ia    i kēia pae  'āina kekahi ua
            Indian  in  Dakota see PASS on this archipelago also PST
7           'ike 'ia   ka nui o nā nīnūnē  ma Maui ma nā mokupuni
            see PASS the big of the problems on Maui on the islands
8           like 'ole
            various
            "I was asked to compose a new voice, a new breath for a new
```

context as a part of this song (.) the song is filled with ancestral knowledge and Hawaiian knowledge and at this time in this context real issues can be seen concerning water in other parts of the world on the Native American reservations in the Dakotas and also can be seen here in this archipelago, issues are found on Maui and on the various different islands"

Ka'ikena begins in line 1 with the passive *noi 'ia* ("was asked") to state that he was asked to compose a song with a new "voice" and new "breath." In using this passive, he does not state the agent who made this request. Next, in lines 2 and 3 he employs the stative verb *pa'a* ("replete") to note that the song is replete with knowledge of the Hawaiian ancestors and also generally with "Hawaiian knowledge." As a stative verb, *pa'a* constructs this meaning without needing to explicitly say anything about an agent who may have put this knowledge into the song. Ka'ikena then uses the verb *'ike* ("see") three times with the passive marker *'ia* in lines 4, 6, and 7 to note the problems especially concerning water that have been "seen" on Native American reservations in the Dakotas and also in Hawai'i on Maui and the other islands.

In this eight lines of data it is possible to infer that Ka'ikena is the one who composed the song, and it is likewise possible to understand that the agents "seeing" these water issues are the general population (or perhaps a certain population of indigenous people in the United States), but the speaker Ka'ikena has managed to express his thoughts without overtly naming a doer of these actions. He is able to do this through his usage of passive constructions and stative verbs.

It is instructive to note at this point that the Hawaiian language does indeed offer resources which allow speakers to explicitly state agents. Excerpt (12) provides several examples from the same video clip used for excerpt (9) that describes the program called 'Āina Ulu that is sponsored by the Kamehameha Schools.

Excerpt (12): http://oiwi.tv/ks/huli-ka-lima-i-lalo/

```
1 Reporter: 'o  'Āina Ulu he polokolamu ia a  na kula    o Kamehameha
              'Āina Ulu a  program    it of the school of Kamehameha
2             i   ho'okumu ai no ka  ho'onauao 'ana aku i nā keiki a me
              PST create       for the education    NOM DIR O the kids and
3             ka lehulehu ākea   ma o    ka 'āina. E like me ka mau
              the public  general throughout the land like   the usual
4             ua  hui   like nā honua a pau e puni ana i kēia polokolamu
              PST meet alike the sites all   around       this program
5             'o  'Āina Ulu nō   ho'i ma ko   lākou 'aha kūmau
              'Āina Ulu EMP EMP at POS  they  event regular
```

6   'o 'Aha 'Āina Ulu. Na Papahana Kuaola a me Paepae o He'eia
               event 'Āina Ulu the program Kuaola and Paepae o He'eia
7   i   mālama i ka 'aha   i kēia makahiki ma ko lākou 'Āina
               PST hold   O the event in this year   on POS they   land
8   'o He'eia
               He'eia

"'Āina Ulu is a program that Kamehameha schools created for the education of the children and the general public throughout the land (of Hawai'i). Just like usual, all of the sites involved in this program 'Āina Ulu gathered at their regular event called the 'Āina Ulu event. The Kuaola program and Paepae o He'eia held the event this year on their land of He'eia"

The reporter begins in line 1 by identifying Kamehameha Schools as the agent who created the 'Āina Ulu program. The reporter does employ the nominalizer 'ana in line 2 with the verb "educate" (ho'ona'auao), which allows her to leave the subject of that verb unnamed. Yet, she includes the agent of the verb "meet together" (hui like) in line 4 as "all of the sites" (nā honua a pau) involved in the program. In doing so, she makes use of the fact that subjects typically follow verbs in Hawaiian by following the active form of the verb hui like with the subject, which also happens to be the agent of the action. Then, in lines 6–7 the reporter also provides an agent, but this time she employs a fronting structure with the marker na and brings the agent, the programs of Kuaola and Paepae o He'eia, to a position prior to the verb. This process of fronting highlights the fact that it was the programs of Kuaola and Paepae o He'eia that hosted the event this year on their land called He'eia. This excerpt thus contains three overt mentions of agents, demonstrating that it is very possible for speakers of Hawaiian to include the agents of actions in discourse. Moreover, there even exists at least one grammatical resource, the fronting structure, which makes it possible to emphasize agents.

Yet, despite the possibility of naming and highlighting agents, the preferred mode of expression seems to be to omit doers of actions. Excerpt (13) provides one final example to underscore this point. It comes from a clip in which the announcer is explaining the completion of a new Hawaiian Studies building on the University of Hawai'i at Hilo campus.

Excerpt (13): http://oiwi.tv/apl/haleolelo-ka-haka-ulas-home/
1 Reporter: ma hope o ke kanakolu a   'oi   makahiki o ke kōkua
               after   of the thirty   and more years   of the help
2   ma ka ho'okele 'ana i kekahi o nā aukahi   ho'ōla
               in the lead   NOM O some of the movement revitalize

3		'ōlelo	'ōiwi	ikaika loa	a puni	ka honua ua	pa'a
		language	indigenous	strong most	around	the world PST	complete
4		maila he home no ke koleke 'o Ka Haka 'Ula o Ke'elikōlani
		DIR a home for the college Ka Haka 'Ula o Ke'elikōlani
5		'o Hale'ōlelo nō ia
		Hale'ōlelo EMP it

((further talk))

6	Reporter:	he hale	piha a	pa'a	pono (1) piha i	nā lako
		a building	full and	complete	properly full	with the supplies
7		e pono ai	nā 'ano	lumi	like 'ole e pono ai a	me
		neccessary	the types	rooms	various necessary	and with
8		ka 'ohana kūpa'a	i	ka 'ōlelo	e ola maoli ai ko	kēia
		the family steadfast	with	the language	live truly PS	this
9		hale
		building

"After thirty years of helping lead one of the strongest language revitalization movements in the world, a home for the college Ka Haka 'Ula o Ke'elikōlani has been completed, it is Hale'ōlelo. It is a building filled and properly completed (1) it is filled with the necessary supplies, the necessary types of rooms, and with a family steadfast with the language that will truly give life to this building"

In lines 1–5, the reporter explains that the Hawaiian language college at the University of Hawai'i at Hilo has a new "home," which is a newly constructed bulding called *Hale'ōlelo*. In doing so, the reporter employs the marker *'ana* to nominalize the verb *ho'okele* ("lead") in line 2 and also the stative verb *pa'a* ("completed"), but there is no explicit mention of the agents of the actions of "leading" and "completing." In fact, the stative verb structure in Hawaiian is actually designed in a way that makes it difficult to express an actor who may have caused that state of being. The stative verb *pa'a* in line 3 is followed in line 4 first by the directional *maila* (as in "come to be completed") and then the subject of the completing, *home no ke koleke 'o Ka Haka 'Ula o Ke'elikolani* ("home for the college of Ka Haka 'o Ke'elikōlani"), which is preceded by the marker *he* indicating it is meant to be the subject of the stative verb. The subject of the stative verb, however, is the object that was completed, it is not the doer of the action.

Lines 6–9 are of particular interest because contained within are seven stative verbs. Line 6 begins with *pa'a* ("completed") and *piha* ("filled"), and then after a one second pause continues with a restatement of *piha* which is followed by the information that it is "filled" with *nā lako* ("supplies"). It does not, though, state the agent who did the filling. In line 7, this description continues with two uses of the stative verb *pono* ("necessary") to note first that the supplies are necessary and next that the various rooms are necessary without stating who or what may have made them necessary. Line 8 has two further stative verbs, *kupaʻa* ("steadfast") and *ola* ("life"), but it is interesting to observe that both of them have a structure that attributes agency, albeit in a slightly indirect way. The families are described as *kupaʻa* ("steadfast"), and using the particle *i,* the structure of the discourse tells us that it is the ʻōlelo ("language") that makes them steadfast. Thus, the particle *i* does make it possible to attribute a cause to the steadfastness of the families; it is the language that makes them so. Moreover, the reporter continues in line 8 with the phrase *e ola maoli ai* ("truly give life") that includes the stative verb *ola* ("life") and anaphoric *ai* that links this phrase with the ʻōlelo ("language"). This linkage attributes agency to the "language" such that it is the language that "truly gives life" to *ko kēia hale* ("those of this building"). As these last two stative verbs indicate, it is possible to add a sense of agency to stative verbs, but it requires some grammatical work through the addition of the particle *i* and also through the usage of a construction requiring the anaphoric *ai*. Stative verbs, however, do not typically take agents in the subject position following the verb, which makes it common for stative verbs to be used without any explicit expression of agency. The large number of stative verbs used in this excerpt fits with the claim of Elbert and Pukui (1979) that statives are the most common verbs used in Hawaiian, and it likewise is consistent with the idea that a preferred mode of expression in Hawaiian is to not explicitly state agents of actions.

This section has presented an analysis focusing especially on the usage of three grammatical resources, passives, nominalization, and stative verbs, that enables reporters and other Hawaiian speakers shown in video clips on ʻŌiwi TV to express actions and states of being without explicitly acknowledging agents. The suggestion was also made that the non-expression of agency is congruent with a Hawaiian perspective, particularly the idea, following Wong (2006, 2011), that indirect methods of expressing agency are preferred. Wong based his analysis on stories published in Hawaiian newspapers during a time when people grew up speaking the language in their natural environment. Although there is a growing number of families who employ Hawaiian as their home language, such an experience is still relatively rare as Hawaiian speakers have been engaging in most of their learning in a school setting. However, the earlier analysis suggests that speakers in the video clips are employing similar types of indirection in their expression of agency as the traditional speakers, an observation which suggests that current speakers of Hawaiian are preserving, at least in the expression of agency, a traditional perspective in their speech. To be sure, given the relatively brief nature of this analysis, more research is required on both traditional and current speakers in order to assess the overall degree with which the speech of modern speakers of Hawaiian matches the patterns of elder speakers. Moreover, there is a need to continue not only examining various speech patterns of traditional speakers, including repetition and agency expression, but also finding a way to incorporate that information into the educational lessons in the Hawaiian medium schools so that the younger speakers may continue learning Hawaiian through a traditional perspective.

CONCLUSION

In terms of having an indigenous language as part of its historical landscape, Hawai'i is not necessarily unique within the world. However, in possessing an indigenous language that is a contributing and even vibrant part of its multilingual society, Hawai'i is certainly quite exceptional, at least in the United States where most indigenous Native American languages are struggling to stay alive. Thanks to a strong revitalization movement, the presence of the Hawaiian language in society has grown stronger in the last forty years and, as activists and supporters continue to use and promote the language, there is optimism for an increased role of the language in Hawai'i in the future. Nontheless, there is also an awareness that, with the strength especially of English in the United States and throughout world, future progress will depend on staying steadfast in promoting the language and the continued development of a network of speakers that remains dedicated in transmitting the language to future generations.

The Hawaiian language contributes to society by first of all ensuring the spiritual (and thus physical) well-being of members of the indigenous population, but it also provides a wealth of critical knowledge about traditional ways of interacting with and sustaining the physical world. Recognition of Hawaiian as an important part of the linguistic landscape means realizing the contributions that it can make to the knowledge base upon which Hawaiian society is founded. This knowledge is embedded within Hawaiian place names, the lexicon, traditional wise sayings (*'ōlelo no'eau*), modes of expression, and also grammatical structures. This chapter focused specifically on modes of expression and grammar, offering demonstrations of the importance of repetition and agency, with an emphasis on some grammatical structures that enable speakers of Hawaiian to leave agents of actions unstated. These are modes of expression and grammatical resources that differ from those employed by speakers of other languages, particularly the dominant language of English, and therefore have the potential to be instructive in terms of understanding the diverse possibilities in terms of interacting with the social world. Future research that uses the available databases to investigate the language practices of elder Hawaiian speakers can continue to inform our understanding of Hawaiian approaches to social interaction and provide current speakers of the language with the understanding to perpetuate those traditional modes of expression.

NOTES

1. The Clinton Kanahele archive can be found at https://archive.org/details/interviewsconduc0v3kana, and the archives of the radio show developed by Larry Kimura archive is online through http://ulukau.org/kaniaina/cgi-bin/kaniaina.

2. The source listed as Schegloff (in press) is included in the list of references as Schegloff (2002).

3. The transcriptions in this chapter and in some of chapters to follow employ transcription conventions that have been adopted from conversation analysis. They are listed here. In addition, abbreviations in the interlineal gloss are also found here.

Transcription conventions:

( ) pause, with the length of the pause indicated by the number inside.
(.) micropause
(( )) information inserted by the authors to describe the context
[the start of overlapping talk
] the completion of overlapping talk
= latched utterances, that is, utterances that follow immediately without the typical pause in between
* a spate of unintelligible talk. Each * is equivalent to approximately .5 seconds

Abbreviations in interlinear gloss:

DIR: Directional marker
EP: Emphatic particle
O: Object marker
Nom: Nominalizer
Pass: Passive
PL: Plural marker
PS: Possessive
PST: Past tense marker

4. Here, it is relevant that Hawaiian is characterized as an verb-initial language with utterances frequently beginning with the predicate. This is what happens in the first sentence in line with the predicate *kama'āina* ("familiar") and then again in the

second sentence with *lō'ihi* ("long"). With this predicate at the beginning, it is possible that CK's subsequent utterance of *kēia noho* indicates that he is producing the subject of the predicate and thus projects the near conclusion of his utterance, thus prompting SK to begin speaking in line 2.

5. Tannen (1989, 54) offers the following quotation from W. H. Auden: "the notion of repetition is associated in people's minds with all that is most boring and lifeless-punching time clocks, road drills, etc."

6. The 'Ōiwi TV website is located at http://oiwi.tv.

Chapter Three

Pidgin

The Local(s) Voice

I not late, I stay on Hawaiian time (License plate frame seen in Hilo, Hawai'i)

I da maya (Words spoken by Big Island mayor, Billy Kenoi in a commencement speech at the Hawai'i Pacific University)

INTRODUCTION

The previous chapter suggested that the usage in society of the Hawaiian language, including repetitions, passive sentences, stative verbs, and nominalization constructions, contributes to a multilingual Hawai'i because it helps constitute a diversity in terms of ways of interacting with the world. The chapter also described the efforts that have been made and are continuing to be made in current society to revitalize the language, efforts that are making Hawaiian increasingly more visible and allowing it to be regarded once again with pride and dignity as an ancestral language.

Part of the revitalization movement has been increasing appreciation of Hawaiian as the indigenous language of the land, but from the perspective of multilingualism, Hawai'i is remarkable because the islands have given birth to another language, referred to locally as "Pidgin" and also known as "Hawai'i Creole English" and more recently as "Hawai'i Creole." Pidgin is reportedly spoken by nearly half of the population of Hawai'i, roughly 600,000 people (Drager 2012; Sakoda and Siegel 2003). In fact, it is considered the native language of many of the children as they grow up speaking it in the home with their family members (Tamura 2002). Yet, unlike Hawaiian, now termed "the jewel of our culture" (Kawai'ae'a, Housman, and Alencastre 2007), Pidgin's status in the hearts and minds of people in Hawai'i is not nearly so clear. It has commonly been condemned as a broken form of English, and it has been called "lazy," "faulty," "sloppy," "slothful," and "ugly" (Da Pidgin Coup 2008; Siegel 2008). At the same time, however, many people exhibit pride in the language and, despite the social stigma attached to it, continue to transmit it to subsequent generations (Drager 2012; Nordstrom 2015). This chapter attempts to explain this ambivalent attitude toward Pidgin by first describing the characteristics that distinguish Pidgin as a language and then by providing further discussion of both negative and positive views. After such discussion, two analyses are offered that probe the uses of Pidgin in society. The first analysis focuses on the speech of Billy Kenoi, a local politician on the Big Island of Hawai'i as he uses Pidgin in public, and the second examines the language of radio advertisements in order to gauge the degree with which Pidgin circulates throughout society.

PIDGIN AS A LANGUAGE

Pidgin is, as stated previously, currently classified as a creole, but it is relevant to note that language specialists have struggled throughout history to agree on a categorization in linguistic terms, particularly one that captures Pidgin's relationship to English (Sato 1985; Tsuzaki 1966, 1969, 1971). Similarities with English have resulted in characterizations of Pidgin as a regional dialect, a social dialect, a sub-standard dialect (Voegelin and Voegelin 1964), and a creolized variety of English (Hall 1966), all of which create a hierarchical relationship with Pidgin viewed in comparison to English, with English taken to be the norm. Further confounding the situation is the observation that there exists in the islands a specific variety of English that shares phonological and lexical features with Pidgin but yet is separate from Pidgin. This variety has been called "Hawai'i English" and "Hawaiian English." Higgins (2015, 149) references Drager (2012) and describes some of its distinguishing features:

> Hawai'i English is largely characterized by its phonological and lexical systems, which contrast with mainland US varieties. Words that were historically borrowed from Hawaiian, such as *keiki* (child), *ohana* (family), and *kama'aina* (resident) are commonly understood and used without translation in print advertising and in news broadcasts. Hawai'i English is distinct from mainland varieties in that reduced vowels are typical (e.g., today would be pronounced with two full vowels rather than a shwa), and because of the monophthongal nature of the vowels (and particularly /o/), which are often dipthongized in mainland varieties.

Despite these differences, it is important to emphasize that Hawai'i English is still considered a variety of English. In contrast, academics as well as activists have been taking the stance that Pidgin is its own separate, rule-governed language (Da Pidgin Coup 2008; Higgins 2010; Sakoda and Siegel 2003; Siegel 2008).

In adopting such a view of Pidgin, supporters recognize that it shares phonological and lexical features with English, but they nonetheless stress how different it is at the same time. In terms first of all of phonology, Pidgin has numerous other ways that it differs from English, for instance, the pronunciation of "th" sounds as either "t" or "d" as in *tink* for "think," *dis* and *dat* for "this" and "that," and *brudah* for "brother." Another distinction is the dropping of "r" after vowels, such as *brudah* instead of "brother" and *cheapa* instead of "cheaper." Finally, there is a tendency to drop final consonants that appear in consonant clusters, especially the clusters "pt," "ct," "ft," "st," "ld," and "nd." Hence, the word "cost" is *cos* and the word "told" appears as *tol* (see Sakoda and Siegel 2003 for further discussion).

Concerning the lexicon, Pidgin borrows vocabulary not only from English and Hawaiian but also from other languages that include Japanese and Portuguese (Sakoda and Siegel 2003). Some words from Japanese are *bocha* ("bath" or "bathe"), *habut* ("disgruntled"), and *bachi* ("punishment" or "retribution"), and some from Portuguese are *babooz* ("idiot"), *bambucha* ("huge"), and *malassada* ("Portuguese doughnut"). Some further words borrowed from Hawaiian are *wikiwiki* ("quick"), *pau* ("finished"), and *puka* ("hole"), and some from English that have become different from their English origins are *bumbai* ("later"), *choke* ("many"), and *grindz* ("food"). In addition, an article appearing in the Associated Press notes that some vocabulary items can be attributed to a combination of languages, for example, *tantaran* ("show off") from Japanese and Tagalog, *hammajang* ("messed up") from Hawaiian and English, and also *shishi* from Japanese and Portuguese ("urinate") (A list of Pidgin words 2016).

While the phonology and lexicon start to separate Pidgin from other languages, it is the grammar that has given analysts the most cause to label Pidgin as its own distinct language. The following description of the grammar owes primarily to Sakoda and Siegel (2003). It is not meant to be exhaustive but rather intends to both demonstrate some of the unique features of Pidgin grammar and also serve as a basis for understanding the analyses that follow in this chapter.

Some of the grammatical features reflect the influences of the contact languages. For example, Pidgin sometimes employs a word order that resembles the verb-subject-object organization of Hawaiian as in "Big da house" (similar to *Nui ka hale* in Hawaiian-lit. "Big the house") and also "Cute da baby"

(*Kiuke ka pēpē* in Hawaiian). Another influence of Hawaiian is the usage by Pidgin speakers of expressions such as "Oh, the pretty" which correlates with Hawaiian as in *Hō ka nani.*

Additionally, Pidgin grammar has been influenced by Cantonese, particularly the usage in Cantonese of the word *yauh* which can translate into English as "have/has" and also "there is/are," as in:[1]

    Kéuihdeih yáuh sāam go-jai   "They have three sons."
    Yáuh go haaksāang hóu síng   "There's a student who's very bright."

In Pidgin, this closely resembles the usage of the word "get," as in:[2]

    They get three sons. "They have three sons."
    Get one new building ova dea. "There's a new building over there."

Another language that has influenced the grammar of Pidgin is Portuguese, particularly in two ways. First, the usage in Pidgin of the term 'fo(r)' instead of 'to' is attributed to the Portuguese *para,* as in.

    Carlos é homem para fazer isso. "Charles is the man to do that."

In Pidgin, this would be expressed as:

    Charles is da man fo do 'um. "Charles is the man to do it."

Also, in Portuguese the word estar and its various conjugations correlates with the usage of the word 'stay' in Pidgin. The following show examples first in Portuguese and then in Pidgin.

    O livro está sobre a mesa. "The book is on the table."
    Da book stay on top da table. "The book is on the table."
    A água está fria. "The water is cold."
    Da wata stay cold. "The water is cold."
    João está escrevendo uma carta. "John is writing a letter."
    John stay writing one letter. "John is writing a letter."
    A casa está construída. "The house is finished."
    Da house stay pau already. "The house is finished."

Thus, even though the word "stay" appears to be English in origin, the usage corresponds closely with *estar* in Portuguese.

Indeed, while similarities with English might lead one to the assumption that Pidgin speakers attempted but ultimately failed to mimic "correct" usages of English, these correlations with features of Hawaiian, Cantonese, and Portuguese help debunk the notion that Pidgin is a "broken form" of English.

The previous comparisons demonstrate that these features have origins in actual languages. They have been borrowed to create a set of grammatical features that constitute a language that may at times sound similar to English but is actually quite distinct.

Indeed, there are other aspects of Pidgin grammar that further set it apart from English and other languages. These are not necessarily easily attributed to a single language, but nonetheless further highlight how the mixture of people and languages in Hawai'i gave birth to a "new" language. First, Pidgin employs both indefinite and definite articles, but they are different from the articles found in English. The indefinite article is *wan* and the definite article is *da*, as in *I had wan 1.8 GPA out of high school* ("I had a̲ 1.8 GPA in high school") and *I tol people I was goin be da̲ maya* ("I told people I was going to be the mayor").[3]

Second, the past tense in HC is not constructed through a bound morpheme in the suffix position such as "ed" but rather uses the free morpheme *wen* prior to the main verb that remains uninflected. An example from the data is *you wen learn already* ("you learned already"). HC has some irregular past tense forms, such as *sin* ("seen"), *sed* ("said"), and *tol* ("told") that are not preceded by *wen,* as in *my faddah tol me one time* ("my father one time told me"). There are reportedly far fewer of these irregular cases in HC than in English (Sakoda and Siegel 2003).

Third, Pidgin has types of sentences that would not be acceptable in English, in particular, sentences that do not require the "be" verb. Hence, sentences such as *I da maya* ("I am the mayor") and *at least you honest* ("at least you are honest") are acceptable in Pidgin.

Fourth, Pidgin has a complex negation system. Whereas English primarily uses some form of "not" after an auxiliary verb to express negation, Pidgin employs four negative markers, *nat, no, nevah,* and *nomo*. In listing the uses, I will follow Sakoda and Siegel (2003) and then provide examples—also taken from the same source—in table 3.1. According to Sakoda and Siegel (2003), *nat* is used in four grammatical contexts: 1) before a noun phrase, adjectival phrase, adverbial phrase, or prepositional phrase in a verbless sentence; 2) before the future tense marker *goin*; 3) before the -ing form of the verb when it's not preceded by the marker *ste*; 4) before the modal *sapostu*. The marker *no* is used in six contexts: 1) before the plain, unmarked verb; 2) before the future tense marker *goin*; 3) before the modals *kaen, laik, gata,* and *haeftu*; 4) before the linking verb *ste*; 5) before auxiliaries *ste, stat,* and *pau*; 6) before the serial verbs *go* and *kam*. The marker *nevah* is employed before the verb or auxiliary to indicate a past negative, and *nomo* is used before a noun in a subjectless sentence to mark negative nonpast existential forms which are expressed in English with the phrases "there is not" or "there are not."

Table 3.1. Negative Markers in Pidgin and English

	Pidgin	English
Negative marker *nat* (four grammatical contexts)		
1. Before predicates in verbless sentences	1. Mai sista <u>nat</u> wan bas jraiva	My sister is <u>not</u> a bus driver
2. before the tense marker *goin*	2. He <u>nat</u> goin broke um	He's <u>not</u> going to break it
3. before the –ing form of the verb	3. Da gaiz <u>nat</u> workin	The guys are <u>not</u> working
4. before *sapostu*	4. You <u>nat</u> sapostu do dat	You are <u>not</u> supposed to do that
Negative marker *no* (six contexts)		
1. before the unmarked verb	1. Da cat <u>no</u> eat fish	The cat does <u>not</u> eat fish
2. before tense marker *goin*	2. I <u>no</u> goin tell nobody	I am <u>not</u> going to tell anybody
3. before modals	3. I <u>no</u> laik flunk	I do <u>not</u> want to flunk
4. before linking verb *ste*	4. Da cat <u>no</u> ste in da hous	The cat is <u>not</u> in the house
5. before auxiliaries	5. Mai sistah <u>no</u> stat playin saka	My sister did <u>not</u> start playing soccer
6. before serials verbs	6. She <u>no</u> go cook rice every day	She does <u>not</u> cook rice every day
Negative marker *nevah* (negative past)	I <u>nevah</u> do em	I did <u>not</u> do it
Negative marker *nomo* (negative nonpast existential)	Now we <u>nomo</u> ka	Now we do <u>not</u> have a car

These negative markers are recognizable to English speakers as deriving from English words. Yet, they comprise a system that is arguably more complex than English negation and that speakers of Pidgin learn naturally as they grow up speaking the language.

The final grammatical difference to be noted here is the usage of the negative marker *no* to construct the negative imperative form, as in *no listen to dem* ("do not listen to them") and *no foget say thank you* ("do not forget to say thank you"). Saft, Tebow, and Santos (2018) found that negative imperatives were the most frequently employed feature of Pidgin in their data, which focused on the speeches made by Billy Kenoi at two university commencement ceremonies in Hawai'i.

This section has listed a number of grammatical features that distinguish Pidgin as a separate language that is now commonly referred to as a creole, which puts it together in that category with other languages such as Haitian Creole, Tok Pisin, and Kinubi. Yet, even the term creole brings with it complications since creole specialists have identified a creole-continua with levels such as basilect, acrolect, and mesolect. In this continua, basilect is the variety most different from the language viewed as the lexifier, acrolect the variety that is closest, and mesolect is the variety in the middle (Rickford 1985). For Pidgin, the basilect is sometimes referred to as "heavy" or "thick" Pidgin (Sakoda and Siegel 2003), which probably encompasses not only the pronunciation and lexicon but also the grammatical features just described. In this sense, then, the acrolect version of Pidgin would probably be something akin to Hawai'i English with its Pidgin pronunciations and Pidgin-influenced lexical items. The analysis presented later in this chapter, however, is not going to be concerned about placing Pidgin into one of the three creole categories. Instead, it will concentrate on describing how the features of Pidgin, namely, the phonology, lexicon, and especially grammar, are used in different contexts. Before moving to the analysis, Pidgin's status in Hawai'i is further discussed.

THE STATUS OF PIDGIN IN SOCIETY

Negative Evaluations and Social Hierarchy

Despite recent attempts to emphasize Pidgin's status as a language, it still stands that Pidgin has been and continues to be the source of considerable controversy. In order to understand Pidgin's place in current Hawaiian society, it is important to examine the different aspects of this controversy. The language has been denigrated by a variety of people, including both public officials and private citizens, but one of the interesting aspects about the Pidgin situation in Hawai'i is that, as Wong (1999b, 220) puts it, "some of the worst critics of Pidgin are Pidgin speakers themselves." For instance, it is reported that Ben Cayetano, a former governor of Hawai'i and a Pidgin speaker, once stated "I think it does the kids a disservice if you allow them to speak Pidgin" (Wong 2013). Similarly, Yokota (2008, 28), in interviewing people born and raised in Hawai'i, found references to Pidgin speakers as "acting stupid" and being "retarded sounding."

One of the reasons for these negative evaluations is a constant awareness on the part of Pidgin speakers of comparisons with English, which derives from the fact that the development of Pidgin in Hawai'i largely corresponded with the rise of English as the dominant language in the islands. Pidgin developed into a creole shortly after English became the official language of education in 1896 and after Hawai'i was annexed as a territory of the United States in 1898. As English rose to power and as more speakers of English from the mainland United States arrived in Hawai'i, it was inevitable that Pidgin would be viewed in comparison to English, especially in light of the fact that Pidgin and English share a significant amount of vocabulary. As Tamura (1996, 435) notes, Pidgin was already being degraded as "the jargon of the plantations" and "the pidgin English of the streets" (Tamura 1996, 435) even as it was just emerging as a creole in the 1920s.

One result of this early degradation of Pidgin in relation to English was the creation of a language-based social hierarchy as English came to be associated with wealth and power and Pidgin with the lower economic level of plantation laborers. Caucasians already in Hawai'i as well those moving in from the mainland expressed a desire that "Caucasian children should not be interacting with Pidgin English-speaking 'local' children" (Kawamoto 1993, 201; also quoted in Nordstrom 2003, 11), and they subsequently used their growing power within society to create a set of "English Standard Schools" that were meant to be "pidgin-free zones of education" (Roberts 2004, 343). Students were forced to pass an entrance exam and would be denied admission if features of Pidgin were found in their language. These type of tests and the existence of these schools thus reinforced this hierarchical correlation between language and economic status. Charlene Sato (1985, 266), one of the pioneers of Pidgin research and advocacy, emphasizes the disadvantage of being associated with Pidgin by writing, "being labeled a 'Pidgin' speaker was considered by many a liability in the job market, associated as it was with the plantation and with the minimal intelligence assumed necessary for manual labor." With such a connection to economic status, it is not surprising that politicians and fellow Pidgin speakers such as Ben Cayetano would encourage the younger generation to leave Pidgin behind. It also explains why a local businessman was quoted in the newspaper in 1995 as saying, "growing up in an environment where pidgin is a daily routine is like being sentenced to a life of poverty. They are doomed to struggle" (Kleinjans 1995; also quoted in Hargrove and Sakoda 1999).

Pidgin Pride and a Linguistic Divide in Society

At the same time that Pidgin was given a social stigma by those with power in society, an interesting outcome of the linguistic segregation that developed is that it promoted a sense of pride among speakers of Pidgin. The source of this pride derives largely from the construction of a distinction between two types of identities, namely, "haole" and "local." As Roberts (2004, 343) explains about "haole," "the increasingly confrontational attitude of the schools toward HCE [Hawai'i Creole English] in the 1920s reinforced the association of ASE [American Standard English] with institutional and Haole identity." From the perspective, then, of speakers of Pidgin who were denied access to the English Standard School movement, "haole" came to be viewed in a negative light as representing a person of privelege (who tended to be Caucasian). In contrast, those people not of the same privilege began to see their own life experiences, including their work on the plantations, schooling, leisure activities, eating habits, and also language as representing a typical "local" way of life. As Takaki (1983, 119) notes, it did not matter that many of them were of different ethnic backgrounds as long as they were not "haole": "on the plantations, pidgin English began to give its users a working class as well as a Hawaiian or 'local' identity, which transcended their particular ethnic identity." Those of local identity were thus aligned in language and culture, which allowed them to develop a pride among each other based on their local origins and experiences, including the Pidgin they spoke. Even though being "local" meant not having the affluence of other residents, it was nonetheless looked upon positively because it set them apart from the haoles. According to Lockwood and Saft (2016, 5), Pidgin "became a show of solidarity among those on the lower end of the hierarchy partly because they knew that it was not acceptable to the haoles." Sato (1985, 266) likewise notes that Pidgin is preferred by those with a local identity because "'Tawking laik wan haole' associated one with the economic and political exploitation practiced by such outsiders."

In sociolinguistics, the possibility that speakers take pride in a nonstandard form such as Pidgin has been discussed in terms of the idea of "covert prestige" (Trudgill 1972). In relating this concept to Hawaiian society, Furukawa (2018, 45) admits that English has "overt prestige" in Hawai'i but notes, "at the same time, Pidgin, has a covert prestige, and is therefore also associated with positive ideologies among its speakers and proponents in certain contexts." Other writers suggest that since these positive ideologies derive from Pidgin's status as an indicator of local identity, they can lead speakers to employ Pidgin as an act of resistance that signifies localness even when people are expected to conform to the English norm (Nordstrom 2015; Romaine 2005). Okamura (1994, 174; also quoted in Okamura 2008, 121) makes such a suggestion when he writes that "local identity has been maintained as an expression of resistance and opposition."

This linking of Pidgin to prestige through the notion of covert prestige thus aids in understanding the ambivalent feelings that Pidgin speakers have toward their own language (Hiramoto 2011; Lockwood and Saft 2016; Sakoda and Siegel 2003). On the one hand, they hear the negative evaluations of Pidgin in comparison to English, the language with overt prestige, and on the other hand, they learn that Pidgin also aligns themselves with other speakers of the same language, sometimes in solidarity against English and a haole identity. In terms of actual language usage, the overt-covert distinction in prestige also contributes to understanding a diglossic relationship in society, where Pidgin speakers prefer the language among themselves in more private contexts such as in the home and on the playground but at the same time are expected to employ English in more public contexts in order to meet the expectations of society. This expectation of diglossia thus results in the development of a kind of linguistic double conciousness (Young 2009; Young, Barrett, Young-Riviera, and Lovejoy 2013) on the part of Pidgin speakers; they are expected not only to know two languages but also to possess the awareness of the contexts when it is appropriate to use one and not the other.

Some researchers have employed terms such as "linguistic imperialism" (Sato 1985), "linguicism" (Higgins, Nettell, Furukawa, and Sakoda 2012), and "hegemony" (Hargrove and Sakoda 1999) to describe the imbalances that force Pidgin speakers to have to comply with such a social expectation. In employing the notion of hegemony, Hargrove and Sakoda (1999) refer to Fairclough's (1992) idea of "appropriateness" to explain that even though Pidgin speakers feel comfortable using Pidgin in private contexts, they are socialized to believe that Pidgin is not appropriate in more formal and public contexts, thus prompting them to alter their language usage.

This imbalance concerning usage of language in public sectors of Hawaiian society was on display in two events that occurred in 1987. First, the Hawaiian Board of Education for public schools attempted to ban Pidgin from being spoken in the classroom (Furukawa 2018; Higgins 2010; Tamura 1996). Although ten of the thirteen members of the board were born and raised in Hawai'i, they nonetheless, in the words of Tamura (1996, 452), "agreed with their mainland-born colleagues that Hawai'i Creole English was inferior, even if they themselves grew up speaking that language." After many members of the community, including language specialists, showed support for Pidgin, the board moved away from a complete ban and instead put forth a statement encouraging teachers, staff, and students to use English in schools. Even though public opinion was mixed on this issue, it nonetheless represented a movement to make official a policy that was already understood by much of society, namely, that Pidgin was unacceptable in a public domain such as education.

The second event was a lawsuit that occurred after two employees of the National Weather Service were not promoted to weather forecaster positions because their speech contained pronunciations that were too close to Pidgin (see Lippi-Green 1994; Matsuda 1991; Sato 1991, 1993; Tamura 1996 for detailed discussion of this case). The position was instead offered to Caucasian speakers of English who "sounded better" (Sato 1991, 655), with the weather service claiming that the two had "mispronounced words" (Tamura 1996). The employees who were denied promotion took their case to the Supreme Court, but the court ruled in favor of the weather service based on the need for the public to understand reports about the weather. As both Furukawa (2018) and Sato (1991) note, this case was presented in the newspapers as merely a case of "good" versus "bad" English, with Pidgin of course representing the "bad." Even though the two were not actually accused of speaking Pidgin per se, this event showcased a desire to keep not only Pidgin but any language sounding remotely close to Pidgin out of public sectors of Hawaiian society.

The expectation that Pidgin speakers employ English in public contexts has been especially strong in education and the media, but one public venue that seems to be an exception is standup comedy. Here, it is has been noted that comedians regularly employ Pidgin in expressing jokes, many of which poke fun of the different ethnicities and ways of speaking in Hawai'i (Furukawa 2007; Furukawa 2018; Labrador 2004). Yet, even though comedy provides an example of Pidgin being visible in public space, its usage for jokes has been viewed by some as a problem. On the one hand, a few writers have taken the perspective that such usage of Pidgin can challenge and resist the forces that have attempted to marginalize Pidgin (Furukawa 2007; Furukawa 2018), but, on the other hand, there are others who suggest that ethnic humor is demeaning to the groups who serve as the butt of the jokes. Wong (1999, 207), for example, notes that "one of the few domains outside of informal settings in which Pidgin is acceptable has been that of comedic performance; but even in this domain, the pidgin speaker is often portrayed as an ignorant buffoon." The Hawaiian journalist Lee Cataluna summed up the feeling of ambivalence in her discussion of "Portagee jokes" that put people of Portuguese ancestry, many of whom speak Pidgin, as the objects of the humor. She writes, "Portagee jokes, a genre of local humor beloved by some as integral to our culture and, I found, loathed by many as tiresome, asinine, and hurtful" (Cataluna 2000a, 2000b, quoted in Labrador 2015, 70). The ambivalence toward ethnic humor, thus, serves as a reflection of the greater ambivalence toward Pidgin in society, with the negative sentiments echoing the stigma felt toward Pidgin, particularly toward its usage in the public sphere.

Language Activism and Changing Ideologies

As noted in the previous chapter, one of the accomplishments of the Hawaiian language revitalization movement has been the transformation of some of the negative ideologies about Hawaiian into positive beliefs, which has helped propel the revitalization of the language toward success and international recognition. While Pidgin still suffers from negative ideologies that prompt speakers to monitor and alter their language usage in public contexts, there is evidence that attitudes toward Pidgin may be changing. One source of evidence comes from research of a survey nature that employs questionnaires and/or interviews to probe people's feeling toward Pidgin (Lockwood and Saft 2016; Marlow and Giles 2008; Romaine 1999; Yokota 2008). Romaine, for example, asked her students in a course titled "Pidgin and Creole Languages" at the University of Hawai'i at Hilo to conduct interviews with people in the community, and she found that slightly more than half of the respondents (53 percent) supported the usage of spoken HC in school contexts. Many of the interviewees noted that HC would allow teachers to better connect with their students and encourage participation in class. She did, however, note that some interviewees still adopted strongly negative views such as "speaking pidgin in the classroom should never be allowed because this is an English-based world where success is measured by knowledge of it" (1999, 291). Marlow and Giles (2008, 2010) found similar sentiments in their studies with some respondents suggesting that Pidgin should not be used in business settings in Hawai'i. At the same time, though, they did note that some of their respondents who had negative views of Pidgin also admitted that they sometimes used the language while conducting official settings.

Lockwood and Saft (2016) interviewed faculty members at the University of Hawai'i in Hilo from a variety of disciplines and found a growing acceptance of Pidgin. While a few faculty adopted the hardline view that only English was acceptable in a university classroom, a higher percentage of the interviewees expressed acceptance and/or support. Several faculty members who were born and raised in Hawai'i indicated that they sometimes used Pidgin with their students, and many faculty from outside of Hawai'i described how their attitudes about Pidgin became more positive over time as they came to see how articulate and capable Pidgin speakers could be. Additionally, a few of the faculty stated that they allowed their students to submit written work in Pidgin. Finally, a teacher of the Hawaiian language mentioned that Pidgin was sometimes used in class to teach Hawaiian because of the similarities between the languages, especially given that Pidgin was the first language of many of the students studying Hawaiian. Although the interviewees in this study were of an education level that may not necessarily reflect the rest of Hawaiian society, the positive results nonetheless offer optimism in terms of positive attitudes toward Pidgin, especially if we view faculty as gatekeepers who impart their knowledge and attitudes toward their material, including the languages they work with, to their students.

Another piece of evidence comes from studies finding that the usage of Pidgin is becoming more prevalent in public arenas of society. Hiramoto (2011), for one, describes Pidgin in television commercials. She finds that actors in the commercials often employ Pidgin to reach local audiences, although the Pidgin used is usually a "lighter" form of the language, not the "heavy" Pidgin associated with the basilect level. Another example is Higgins (2015), which adopts a linguistic landscape perspective to demonstrate the degree to which Pidgin can be found in public, particularly in names of businesses, written advertisements, and even political writings. In terms of local business names and advertisements, particularly for food establishments, she notes that Pidgin is "creating a link between food, place, and community," and concerning political writings, she remarks that Pidgin is "coming from people who are speaking out, often in opposition to the state or at least in opposition to the status quo. Pidgin appears to be representing a populist perspective that is demanding to be heard" (Higgins 2015, 160). That usage of Pidgin in public by members of the local community for such political purposes makes sense given the suggestion earlier that Pidgin, as the language representing a local identity, would be employed to offer resistance to the status quo of the haole. Additionally, Saft, Tebow, and Santos (2018), analyze two university commencement speeches made by Billy Kenoi on the Big Island and find that he frequently employs Pidgin especially for two purposes, to instill humor into the speeches and to emphasize important pieces of advice to the graduates. In particular, the authors find that the politician makes use of the negative imperative form in Pidgin as a means of emphasizing some of his points.

Pidgin also has entered Hawaiian society through a relatively small but consistent group of writers who produce literature in Pidgin. This list of writers includes Lee Tonouchi (2001, 2009), Eric Chock (1978, 1990), Darrell Lum (1990), and Lois Ann Yamanaka (2000, 2006), who have written books, short stories, plays, and poems that are often based on their experiences growing up locally in Hawai'i. Even though Pidgin is noted not to have its own standardized writing system, these writers have employed the English alphabet letters in various ways to express Pidgin pronunciations and identities in their work (Romaine 1994). Lum (1986, 5, also quoted in Romaine 1994, 532) nicely describes the essence of Pidgin literature when he states that it has, "a distinct sensitivity to ethnicity, environment (in particular that valuable commodity, the land), a sense of personal lineage and family history, and the use of the sound, the languages and vocabulary of island people." With this emphasis on the connection among, ethnicity, land, and language, it is not a surprise that these authors often choose Pidgin as their language of expression. Moreover, although from a very different tradition of literature, it is noteworthy that the Bible has also been translated into Pidgin and is available under the title of *Da Jesus Book* (http://www.pidginbible.org).

Emerging research is thus suggesting that besides a connection between Pidgin and humor in public (Furukawa 2007; Furukawa 2018; Saft, Tebow, and Santos, 2018), the usage of Pidgin extends beyond comedy and is currently employed for the purposes of business, politics, and emphasizing key points in some public venues as well. Credit for the change in attitudes that has allowed Pidgin to become part of the public landscape in Hawai'i is largely due to language activism (Florey 2008) that has created a critical language awareness (Fairclough 1992) in Hawaiian society. Language activism has been especially spurred by the activities of a group at the University of Hawai'i at Mānoa known as "Da Pidgin Coup" (Da Pidgin 2008; Higgins 2010), which has resulted in programs, lectures, and books devoted to raising awareness about Pidgin. Da Pidgin Coup was instrumental in establishing an undergraduate certificate at the University Hawai'i Mānoa in Pidgin and Creole studies (Higgins 2010). In addition, the work of writers and activists such as Lee Tonouchi, Eric Chock, Darrell Lum, and Eileen Tamura who have been speaking, teaching, writing, and even establishing publishing presses featuring Pidgin writers have been crucial in promoting Pidgin for numerous years. These increased efforts of Pidgin activists recently resulted in a decision in 2015 by the Census Bureau to recognize Pidgin as an official language choice in Hawai'i.

With this language activism as one contextual backdrop, the remainder of this chapter further explores the uses of Pidgin in society through two analysis, beginning with an analysis of a Pidgin-speaking politician who uses Pidgin to accomplish a variety of actions and also for political purposes. The second analysis focuses on Pidgin in radio advertisements.

Analysis 1: The Versatility of Pidgin in the Public Sphere

Supporters of Pidgin suggest that one reason for the general lack of appreciation of Pidgin in society is the dearth of understanding of how Pidgin functions in actual discourse (Drager 2012; Watson-Gegeo 1994; Wong 1999). Wong (1999) makes this point in his analysis of Pidgin discourse that focuses on a process referred to as "false reference," in which a speaker of Pidgin attributes to her/his interlocutor "a relationship with a third party that is not otherwise true" (1999, 209). In his explication of how false reference works, Wong emphasizes that it demonstrates a "a complexity and depth that rivals that of SE (Standard English)" (1999, 209). He subsequently argues for the need to engage in similar types of analyses because they allow Pidgin speakers to "recognize the complexity inherent in their own language" and "celebrate the poetics of their language and honor those who use it well, in the same way that SE speakers and writers are honored for their proficiency" (1999, 220). The analyses in this section is meant to contribute to this line of argument by showing some of the complexities involved in employing Pidgin.

This first analysis centers on the speech of Billy Kenoi, a politician on the Big Island of Hawai'i who is known for being an entertaining speaker who regular uses Pidgin in his public speeches and who was accordingly dubbed "the Shakespeare of Pidgin" (Laitinen 2012). This analysis examines his speech in two contexts, a television program broadcasted in Hawai'i called "In the Car with Andy Bumatai" and a community meeting about an access road to Waipi'o Valley on the Big Island that was recorded and posted on YouTube.[4]

The program "In the Car with Andy Bumatai" typically features an interview of a well-known person in Hawai'i by Andy Bumutai, a local comedian and TV personality, as they drive around in a car driven by Bumatai. In the episode with Kenoi, they drive around the city of Hilo, beginning in the parking lot of the county building which houses Kenoi's main office. One of the interesting aspects of the interaction between the host Bumutai and Kenoi is that it begins with some joking around by Kenoi, with Pidgin featuring prominently in the jokes. Excerpt (1) offers an example. It begins as they are leaving the parking lot and as Kenoi sees and waves to someone on the street.

Excerpt (1): In the Car
1 Kenoi: Ya know local style eh brah ya gotta wave at anybody just
2   in case brah you neva like miss anybody
3 AB: haha [haha
4 Kenoi: [ya know it's costly dat one auntie one uncle one
5   former classmate
6 AB: aw da buggah [wen snub me
7 Kenoi: [(*) you wen foget where you was from
8   you use to be one good brudah before growin up
9   take a right over hiya (1) check um out

10	AB:	[(*) wave back]	
11	Kenoi:	[(* *] neva even wave back brah and I wen sign	
12		wave fo him	
13	AB:	((laughter))	

Kenoi begins explaining his action of waving in lines 1–2 by stating that you have to always wave to make sure you do not miss anyone. In doing so, he calls this "local style" and employs the word *brah* twice, a common term of address in Pidgin. He also makes use of the Pidgin negative marker *neva*. This elicits laughter from Bumatai in line 3 and Kenoi continues in lines 4–5 to note that not waving could be "costly," suggesting that it could have political ramifications. He refers to some of the people he might miss as "dat one auntie" and "one uncle," commonly used terms of reference for older people in Hawaiʻi. Although not necessarily specific to Pidgin, these are considered respectful terms of reference/address in local culture in Hawaiʻi. Next, in line 6 Bumatai makes a statement in which he uses Pidgin to give voice to an imaginary person who was snubbed by Kenoi. He uses the Pidgin word *buggah*, a derogatory term to refer to Kenoi and then the Pidgin past tense marker *wen*. Kenoi then in lines 7–8 also adopts this third-party perspective and addresses himself directly through the pronoun "you" and through Pidgin. He uses the past tense marker *wen*, the indefinite article *wan* and the referential term *brudah* to construct an imaginary complaint toward himself. Kenoi then takes a brief break from this frame in line 9 to give Bumatai driving directions. In doing so, his pronunciation is still Pidgin-like, but it is noticeable that he uses the English indefinite article "a" ("a right over hiya") and not the Pidgin equivalent *wan*. This is seemingly just a quick break as both participants in lines 10–12 move back to the imagined third-person complaint. Unfortunately, the beginning portion is inaudible due to overlap, but it is apparent from the rest of Kenoi's utterance in lines 11–12 that he is employing Pidgin to continue this embodiment. With the utterance "neva even wave back brah and I wen sign wave fo him," he uses the negative *neva*, the term *brah*, and the past tense marker *wen* to complain that Kenoi did not wave back even though the imagined complainer had campaigned for Kenoi by holding signs on the side of the road prior to the election. This elicits laughter from Bumatai (line 13), indicating that this short exchange serves as a source of humor.

There are two points of interest from this excerpt. First, Pidgin plays an integral role in the construction of an action that has been discussed under various names such as "reported speech," "constructed dialogue" (Tannen 1995), and "ventriloquism" (Cooren 2012, 2013), all of which have ties to the work of Bakhtin on the notion of "voicing" (Bakhtin 1981, 1986). As indicated by the attention given to this phenomenon, it is considered to be an intricate action requiring considerable cognitive skills. It requires a speaker, or in this case speakers, to coordinate their actions such that they can create a third party, who in this case is not even an actual person but instead an imagined one, and then give this imagined person a voice that will contribute to the entertainment value of the program. Moreover, Kenoi and Bumatai do not just give this imagined third party any voice; they make her/him a Pidgin speaker. Through Pidgin, then, Kenoi and Bumatai co-construct this imaginary complainer as someone with a local identity, which has political relevance because many, if not the majority, of the voters in Hawai'i county are Pidgin speakers. For Kenoi, as a politician known for employing Pidgin, the possibility of a disgruntled local Pidgin speaker complaining about Kenoi's actions could be detrimental to his political status. It is a potential problem that can be avoided, as Kenoi states in the excerpt, by making sure he waves "at anybody just in case."

This usage of Pidgin to give voice to this "constructed speech," therefore, provides another example of Pidgin used in actual discourse in a way that has the complexity and depth of any other language. In fact, this usage of constructed speech is even more complex when we consider that the two participants not only construct the speech of an imagined Pidgin speaker but they do it to create humor. This is the second interesting aspect of this excerpt, that is, Pidgin is employed to add comedic value to the program. As noted previously, a connection has been made between Pidgin and humor, a connection that has been both praised by some (Furukawa 2007; Furukawa 2018) and also criticized for sometimes reinforcing stereotypes of Pidgin speakers as "ignorant buffoons" (Wong 1999). The interesting aspect of the connection between Pidgin and humor on the program is that the usage of Pidgin noticeably decreases as the participants begin discussing "serious" topics. Excerpt (2), taken shortly after excerpt (1), provides an example.

Excerpt (2): In the Car
```
1   AB:     It must be difficult you know with all the people there
2           are you know and how different they are I mean
3   Kenoi:  Especially Hawai'i I think more so than anyplace else
4           you know you get people who've lived here for
5           generations and people who moved here last week
6           (.) and ah you know people talk about race or ethnicity
7           you know it's more than that you know it's also class right
8   AB:     yeah=
9   Kenoi:  =so da plantation days when you listen to the kupunas talk
10          story it's always one cool story because everybody was poor
11          so whether you was Japani Filipino Portuguese Hawaiian
12          everybody lived together everybody played together
```

13		everybody was raised together ya, all da values was da same
14	AB:	But but Hilo especially Big Island in general
15	Kenoi:	yah
16	AB:	it's another kind of mentality isn't it=
17	Kenoi:	=well I- I- I look at it well you know lookin at all da islands
18		I think Maui and Oahu share a lot of similarities I think
19		Kaua'i you know and and Hawai'i Island or da Big Island
20		kind of like Molokai you know small towns everybody know
21		each otha when the kupunas tell you hi they ask you who
22		your parents where you from you know
23	AB:	they look at your hands
24	Kenoi:	yah yah where you wen high school ya know
25		I think it's you know you know and you go to the mainland
26		everybody asks you where did you get your degree you know
27		where did you get your graduate degree from

Bumatai initiates this excerpt in lines 1–2 with a statement in English that prompts Kenoi in line 3 to begin talking about the different people in Hawai'i and the need to reach out to all of them. In doing so, he brings into the discussion topics such as race and ethnicity in line 6 and values in line 13. In contrast to excerpt (1), there is little or no laughter, and likewise, there is much less Pidgin. Kenoi does employ terms such as *kupunas* (from the Hawaiian *kupuna* for "elder") in lines 9 and 21 and *Japani* (a Pidgin term for "Japanese") in line 11, and he also uses pronunciations of Hawai'i and Kaua'i with the glottal stop (*'okina*), both of which signal his local connection. In addition, he does use the indefinite article *wan* in line 10 and also the definite article *da* in line 13, and he also employs the term *wen* in line 24 as the past tense for went. This usage of *wen* serves as a Pidgin utterance because it does not use the preposition 'to.' However, on the overall, the speech in this excerpt is predominantly English. In particular, Bumatai uses only English.

This indeed marks a pattern that is seen in this episode. Although both Bumatai and Kenoi are Pidgin speakers and use Pidgin terms and Pidgin pronunciations throughout the program, the heaviest usage of Pidgin, that is when they use a Pidgin grammar, occurs as a part of making jokes, as shown in excerpt (1). When they are discussing so-called serious points, they use English, or what is probably better termed Hawai'i English since it does contain vocabulary and pronunciations that are shared with Pidgin. In that sense, then, the two parties mark themselves as local through the usage of Pidgin, and in doing so, are reproducing a commonly seen relationship between Pidgin and English in society, namely, that Pidgin is used for joking around and English for discussing serious issues. As discussed earlier, this fits with the division of labor often seen in public sectors of society where English and not Pidgin is accepted as the medium of education in public discussions that, unlike standup comedy, call for a serious approach.

Yet, while this division of labor may still exist to a certain extent, it is important to note that it does not prevent the usage of Pidgin for purposes other than comedy. The next three excerpts once again feature Billy Kenoi but they show him putting Pidgin to use for a different purpose, namely, for engaging in local politics. These excerpts are taken from a short YouTube clip of about seven minutes in which Kenoi, during his time as mayor, addresses a group of people in a gynamsium to talk about a road termed "the Waipio access road," which serves as the main road that allows people to go from a tourist lookout down into an area next to the ocean known as Waipiʻo Valley.[5] It is known to be a treacherous road, but it is an important road because people still live and work down in the valley. Excerpt (3) is taken from near the beginning of the episode, after Kenoi has introduced himself and some others from the county who have accompanied him to the meeting.

Excerpt (3): Waipiʻo Valley
1   Kenoi: So us guyz yeah county whether you maya, council person
2   department heads you gotta listen yah cuz you not from hiya
3   so when you walk into wan community you ask the people
4   who live dea what cha guyz tink how can we do good
5   how can we do betta how can we do da right ting
6   cuz at da end of da day it's nevah about credit us it's about
7   our kids and the community dey gonna live in tomorrow
8   so dats what we gotta be mindful of when we make one every
9   decision

In this excerpt, Kenoi employs Pidgin pronunciations as well as a Pidgin grammar in the first line when he constructs the verbless sentence *whether you maya, council person, department heads*. He continues to use Pidgin in line 2 when he utters the negative *cuz you not from hiya*, in line 3 with the indefinite article *wan* to state *when you walk into wan community*, in lines 5 and 6 with the definite article *da*, and then again in line 7 with the future marker *gonna* in stating *the community dey gonna live in tomorrow*. On the surface, Kenoi uses these Pidgin utterances to portray himself as an outsider who is aware of the delicate nature of his job since it requires him to enter other people's communities. Accordingly, he states in line 2 that *you gotta listen yah cuz you not from hiya* and in line 3 that *so when you walk into one community you ask the people*.

On the other hand, though, Kenoi's usage of Pidgin expresses his status as an insider. Although he is a politician not from that specific community, he is a fellow local person who, like the members of that community, speaks

Pidgin. Put another way, his usage of Pidgin aligns himself with those in the community, many—if not most—of whom are Pidgin speakers. Even for those who may not have been born and bred in Hawaiʻi (i.e., not Pidgin speakers), his Pidgin usage marks him as local and thus as someone who has grown up in a local community like the one he is currently addressing. Excerpt (4) provides a further example of how the speaker Kenoi progresses through the meeting by using Pidgin.

Excerpt (4): Waipiʻo Valley
1   Kenoi: And I not- I not gonna stand hea as da mayor and say I
2   understand or know Waipio (.) Waipio is dat kine place
3   you always jus listen (.) try not fo talk too much not ask
4   too many questions (.) if you pay attention listen you gonna
5   learn (.) and um you know everybody get manaʻo (.) everyone
6   get wan view (.) but all we like do is da right ting

Here, Kenoi utters in line 1 the Pidgin negative future form *not gonna* to emphasize that he may not know or understand Waipiʻo. He then uses the Pidgin expression *dat kine place* ("that kind of place") in line 2 and the Pidgin grammar in line 3 and 4 with *try not fo talk too much* and *you gonna learn* to further stress that his job is to listen and learn about the topic. Next, in the last two lines he employs more Pidgin, including the term *manaʻo* which is the Hawaiian word for "idea" or "thought" and the term *get* in lines 5 and 6. He also employs the word *like*, which according to Sakoda and Siegel (2003) serves as a modal in Pidgin, in order to assure the audience that despite the different opinions about the topic the goal is to do *da right ting*.

Kenoi thus is being quite careful to construct himself as a "sensitive outsider" who is there not to tell the community what to do but rather to listen to the people and to do the right thing. At the same time, though, he is employing Pidgin and thus constructing himself as an insider, that is, as a local. The next excerpt, the final one of this section, occurs immediately after excerpt (4) and demonstrates how Kenoi, once again using Pidgin, moves to set the agenda of the meeting.

Excerpt (5): Waipiʻo Valley
1   Kenoi: But we goin talk about da road today cuz I know everybody
2   get- and we hiya fo listen about everything (.) but we like
3   do something (.) about da road how we gon do da road
4   what are our options yah da buggah- cuz we can improve
5   dat road (.) you know (.) dangerous (.) um (.) spooky (.) ah
6   for those of you no maʻa driving down Waipio if you don't

7	know no go (.) right (.) um (.) but the question becomes (.)
8	what can we do (.) what do we have the resources to do when
9	can we do it by (.) and what is the best option you know becuz
10	it would be nice fo have dis two lane road both sides you know
11	but we get wan cliff (.) and we get wan mountain (.) and we
12	no like do anything dat da valley no like happen

Kenoi employs the Pidgin future marker *goin* in line 1 to state clearly that the purpose of the meeting is to *talk about da road*. He uses the Pidgin *fo* in line 2 as part of the verbless sentence *we hiya fo listen about everything* to emphasize again their willingness to listen, but he once again stresses his desire in lines 2–3 to set a course of action with the Pidgin modal *like* in *we like do something about da road* and with the Pidgin future marker and definite article in *how we gon do da road*. Here, his usage of the first person plural pronoun "we" is interesting because it suggests that he is speaking not only on behalf of himself but instead on behalf of his mayoral staff and even possibly the entire community. After that, he continues in lines 5–6 to use Pidgin expressions such as *da buggah* and *dat*, in addition to the English terms "dangerous" and "spooky." He also employs the Hawaiian word *maʻa* ("used to") with the Pidgin negative marker *no* in line 6 to assert through line 7, *if you no maʻa driving down Waipio if you don't know no go*, ending this with the Pidgin negative imperative *no go*.

Interestingly, though, Kenoi next employs primarily an English grammar as he announces in line 7 what "the question becomes," which he follows with four questions in English through line 9. He next switches back to a Pidgin grammar in line 10 to offer a possible solution with *it would be nice fo have dis two lane road both sides*, but he then quickly notes the problems with such a solution, again using Pidgin grammar and specifically *get* sentences in stating *but we get one cliff (.) and we get one mountain*, before ending in Pidgin with *and we no like do anything dat da valley no like happen*. It is impossible to get inside Kenoi's head and know precisely why he switches to English in lines 7–9 and then back again to Pidgin in lines 10–12, but this switch seems to mark a change in "voice." More specifically, the four English questions in lines 7–9 may embody the voice of the government officials who are asking questions about what can realistically be done, and the response in lines 10–12 represents, through the usage of Pidgin, the voice of the community, who might want a nice, two lane road on both sides (even there are obstacles and other considerations that would make such a solution difficult). Here, Kenoi's usage of the plural pronoun "we" three times in line 11 suggests that he is embodying the community and even possibly including himself in that community.

These last three excerpts of Kenoi's speech at the community meeting thus suggest a very skillful and delicate deployment of Pidgin for political purposes. Although Kenoi addresses the crowd as someone very aware that he is coming from outside of the community, his usage of Pidgin nonetheless portrays him as someone who is local and therefore an "insider." By aligning himself with his audience in such a way, he is able to employ a rather "thick," basilect level of Pidgin to set the agenda and begin the meeting, sometimes even using the ambiguous pronoun "we" (ambiguous because it is often unclear as to precisely who is included in his usage) to possibly include himself as part of the community. Moreover, his skillful language usage allows him in excerpt (5) to switch from English to Pidgin to lay out the "official" questions about the Waipio access road through English and then change back to Pidgin to construct a possible community response that includes some of the problems with the road. In that sense, there is a corollary here with excerpt (1), where Kenoi and Bumutai employed Pidgin to embody the speech of an imagined third party. In this case, Kenoi has used English and Pidgin to embody official questions and a possible response by the community. The big difference, though, is in contrast to the humor created in excerpt (1), Kenoi does this embodiment in excerpt (5) as a part of serious political discourse.

With a still fairly limited amount of research available on Pidgin, it is difficult to know the extent to which Pidgin is employed in political discourse in Hawaiian society, but these last three excerpts certainly show how Pidgin could serve as an advantage in local politics. It allows the politician Kenoi to construct himself as an insider and begin working with a local community on a solution to a specific community problem. Likewise, switching between Pidgin and English enables the speaker to construct an "us," embodied by Pidgin, versus a "them," embodied by English, that makes it possible to lay out some of the official questions in English and begin working toward a response with the local community in Pidgin. On the overall, then, the skillful usage of Pidgin by Kenoi in these last three excerpts, together with the usage by Kenoi and Bumutai in the first two (especially the first), provides a further glimpse of the potential of Pidgin within society. With Pidgin employed to construct reported speech that adds humor to a TV show (excerpt 1) and with Pidgin serving as a primary resource for leading a local community meeting, it is apparent that Pidgin exhibits in its usage in society "a complexity and depth that rivals that of SE (Standard English)" (Wong 1999, 209).

Analysis 2: More Pidgin in Public: Radio Advertisements

The previous section focused primarily on the speech of a local politician, Billy Kenoi. Since he has been recognized as a speaker unafraid of using Pidgin in public, questions still may be linger about the extent to which Pidgin is employed generally in public space. In order to investigate further, I examine radio advertisements in Hilo, Hawai'i. The basic premise of the analysis is that if advertisers hope to attract people from the community to their businesses, events, and the like, they may use Pidgin in their advertisements as a way of connecting with the local population.

This analysis follows from a study by Hiramoto (2011) that examined television commercials in Hawai'i. In lieu of the increased advocacy for Pidgin within Hawaiian, she set out to observe the degree to which Pidgin was employed in the commercials, which she described as a "relatively new" context of usage (Hiramoto 2011, 252). From a corpus of 26 locally produced commercials, Hiramoto did find that Pidgin was employed in commercials, but she also found it to be a fairly "light" version of Pidgin, one that would fall within the acrolect level on the pidgin continuum. This usage was described as "the right touch" for appealing to an eclectic audience. A heavy basilect variety was viewed as "as possibly detrimental to brand image" and thus avoided (Hiramoto 2011, 247). Given that the Big Island of Hawai'i is composed of many rural communities with a fairly large population of Pidgin speakers who had elected a Pidgin-speaking mayor, I felt there was a chance of hearing more Pidgin in the public sphere on the radio.

The analysis is also motivated by my own informal observations as someone who has lived in Hilo and listened daily to the radio for over 10 years now. During this time, I found that Pidgin is indeed sometimes used in radio advertisements, but I also developed a sense that the frequency with which it is used paled greatly in comparison to English. Here, I attempt a systematic study of the language in advertisements in order to probe more deeply the relationship among Pidgin, English, and Hawaiian society.

The analysis centers on advertisements found on four FM radio stations heard regularly in Hilo, Hawai'i, The Wave (92.7), KWXX (94.7), The Beat (95.9), and KBig (97.9). These four were chosen because they are popular stations not only in Hilo but also throughout the Big Island. KWXX is available at 101.5 in Kona, The Beat is heard on 93.9 in Kona, and KBig appears at 106.1 in Kona. Although none of the stations limit themselves to one brand of music, both The Wave and The Beat seem to be known for contemporary popular and hip-hop music, KWXX for local music, including Hawaiian music, and KBig for easy listening. They are all administered locally with offices in both Hilo and Kona, and the advertisements are primarily for businesses, events, services pertaining to the Big Island. Accordingly, if advertisers are trying to appeal to the local community, we might expect Pidgin to play a role in the advertisements.

In order to gather data, I recorded each radio station for two one-hour periods of time per day for five consecutive weekdays, from Monday through

Friday. I did this twice, once from October 16–20, 2017 and once more from January 29–February 2, 2018. More specifically in terms of procedures, during those two five-day periods, I recorded one station from 6:00–6:59 a.m., then changed to a different station from 7:00–7:59 a.m., next switched again from 8:00–8:59 a.m., and finally to a fourth from 9:00–9:59 a.m. I then repeated the same process again in the afternoon in one-hour intervals beginning at 3:00 p.m. and continuing until 7:00 p.m. I started the same process again the following day, but I switched the order in which the radio stations were recorded. This way I would not be recording programming from the radio stations at the same hour each day. In total, then, across 10 days, 20 hours from each station were recorded. Typically, each hour consisted of a variety of programming, most of it focusing on music. In addition, there were news and weather reports, various announcements and other types of talk from disc jockeys, and there were always at the least a few advertisements within each hour. For the purposes of this analysis, I focus only on the advertisements. Table 3.2 shows the total number and average per hour of advertisements for each station.

The shortest advertisement was just over 10 seconds and the longest was approximately 90 seconds. On average, they were about 30–40 seconds in length. Furthermore, it should be noted that many of the advertisements were repeated frequently on the same radio station and also across stations. Accordingly, included in the total number of advertisements in table 3.2 are ads that were repeated commonly throughout the data.

In general, there were three types of advertisements: ads for larger, national companies that had connections in Hawai'i (i.e., Seven Eleven, Geico); ads for businesses and services located specifically on the Big Island; and announcements/ads for upcoming events such as concerts and sports for which tickets could be purchased. While the expectation would be that ads specifically for local businesses and services would employ the most Pidgin, this was not necessarily the case. In fact, one of my most general findings fits with the basic impression I expressed earlier, namely, the amount of Pidgin in the advertisements is, relative to English, quite minimal. The first excerpt shows one of the

Table 3.2. Advertisements on Hawaiian Radio

Station	Number of Hours	Number of Advertisements	Avg. Advertisements per Hour
The Wave	20	264	13.2
KWXX	20	276	13.8
The Beat	20	281	14.05
KBig	20	287	14.35

ads in the recordings that featured the most Pidgin as it begins with two men having a short dialogue about a local business called Tax Advantage.

Excerpt (6): 2-1-2018: Tax Advantage

1	Man 1:	Did ya hiya?
2	Man 2:	Hiya what?
3	Man 1:	Tax Advantage is back
4	Man 2:	Fo real?
5	Woman:	yup guys that's right Tax Advantage is back in Hilo still
6		on hualalai street and ready to assist you in all your tax
7		preparation needs call our office today to set up your
8		appointment at 969-7979 or just drop off your paperwork
9		and we'll take care a of the rest our tax professionals will set
10		you at ease with our their knowledge of the new tax laws
11		including tax credit and health reforms and whether you are
12		a single filer or a business Tax Advantage will work towards
13		your largest refund or smallest tax (*) call tax advantage today
14		at 969-7979 and know that your taxes will be handled
15		professionally honestly and quickly so come in today to get
16		your tax advantage on hualalai street in Hilo at 969-7979
17	Man 3:	It's tax time at Tax Advantage

The two men in the dialogue at the beginning employ pronunciations that are recognizably Pidgin. Man 1 in line 1 uses *"ya"* and also *"hiya"* ("hear"), with Man 2 repeating *"hiya"* in line 2. Man 2 then in line 4 utters the common Pidgin expression *"fo real"* ("really?") in line 4 to express his surprise at the news that Tax Advantage is back. Next, it is a woman who responds in line 5 with the phrase "yup that's right guys," and this response then leads to the start of an explanation through line 16 about the benefits of Tax Advantage, which is done soley in English. Finally, a third man's voice is used in line 17 to briefly highlight, once again in English, that "it's tax time at Tax Advantage," thus ending the advertisement.

This ad does feature Pidgin pronunciations and the expression *"Fo real,"* but it is not a heavy version of Pidgin as it does not employ any grammatical structures specific to Pidgin. Excerpt (7) shows a similar phenomenon in an advertisement for Seven Eleven.

Excerpt (7): 10-17-2017: Seven Eleven

1	Man 1:	I already grabbed the musubi
2	Man 2:	But the sign says to choose snacks and drinks labeled
3		"choose healthy now" I think I am goin to chance em
4	Woman:	aloha I see you found one of our new healthy options all seven

5		eleven and Aloha Island Mart Stores are now selling healthy
6		and tasty snacks and drinks labeled "choose healthy now"
7		there's a full list of locations at choosehealthynow.com
8	Man 2:	Hey dis is ono. I gotta go tell all my friends "choose healthy
9		now"

Like the ad for Tax Advantage in excerpt (6), this one also begins with a dialogue between two men. After Man 1 announces in line 1 that he already "grabbed the musubi," referring to a common food item in Hawai'i that consists of rice with some kind of meat and wrapped in nori (seaweed paper), Man 2 points out in lines 2–3 that "the sign says to choose snacks and drinks labeled 'choose healthy now.'" He subsequently announces at the end of line 3 that he is going to *"chance em,"* indicating that he going to try one of the healthy options. *"Chance em"* is a Pidgin phrase that is marked by the pronounciation "em" ("them"), but it is used here as part of a longer grammatical construction, "I think I am goin to chance em," that is English. He does employ the pronunciation "goin," but this is an English grammar that contains the auxiliary verb "am" and also the infinitive "to." It is not a Pidgin grammar even though it contains a Pidgin phrase.

Later in the ad in line 8, Man 2 returns to describe his food choice as "Hey dis is ono," using the Pidgin term *"ono"* and also the Pidgin pronunciation *"dis."* Yet, the grammar is still essentially English with the usage of the predicate "is." Man 2 does continue with the nonstandard "gotta" in line 8, but this is also primarily an English construction "I gotta go tell all my friends 'choose healthy now.'"

It is also noteworthy that Man 2's description of the taste in line 8 is preceded by a woman's voice that explains in lines 4–7 the details about this promotion. In doing so, she does utter in line 4 the word "aloha" as a greeting to the two men, but she does not use any Pidgin terms or Pidgin pronunciations in her explanation. In fact, this advertisement in excerpt (7) shares with excerpt (6) the trait that Pidgin features are only employed in the dialogues but not in the part of the ads that describes the details of the products and services. This observations supports Hiramoto's (2011) finding that Pidgin is used to add some localness to the ads but the descriptions are primarily accomplished in English. Moreover, when Pidgin does appear in the ads, it is a fairly conservative form of Pidgin that centers on pronunciations and expressions but not grammar. This adds "the right touch" to the local ads.

In fact, the usage of small bits of Pidgin is a very common trend in the commercials that I recorded. The next four excerpts exhibit such a phenomenon.

Excerpt (8): 1-31-2018: Dr. Melissa Hernandez

1	Woman:	You want the very best for your keiki and so do I as the newest
2		children's doctor in the community of Kona and with the team

3		at Paniolo pediatrics I want to express my thanks for
4		welcoming me into your community moving my family to
5		beautiful Hawai'i island and being able to practice children's
6		medicine at Paniolo pediatrics is a dream come true when your
7		keiki aren't feeling well know that I will be here to help
8		with same day accessibility my name is Doctor Melissa
9		Hernandez and I am the newest pediatrician at Paniolo
10		pediatrics here in Kona

Excerpt (9): 10-19-2017: Kona Coffee and Tea

1	Man:	Ever had a hard time finding a place to go meet up with
2		friends just hang out someplace during the day where you
3		can sit outside enjoy the weather I'll let you in on a secret
4		go to Kona coffee and tea I was there the other day and ran
5		into choke friends it's a great atmosphere and the best coffee
6		in fact they won best cup of coffee west Hawai'i for the second
7		year and did you also know they serve kambucha, beer and
8		wine at Kona coffee and Tea yup beer and wine at Kona Coffee
9		and Tea it's on Palani by KTA Kona Coffee and Tea open from
10		6:00 am to 6:30 pm daily meet your friends there today

Excerpt (10): 1-30-2018: Aloha Plus Storage

1	Woman:	It could happen to you or your loved ones it starts off
2		innocent enough but before you know it bam your garage
3		your guest bedroom maybe even your entire home can
4		become (.) filled with clutter bring your overflow to Aloha
5		Plus Storage and regain your space park in your garage
6		or make it your pauhana palace and frolick around the house
7		naked if you want to because you've got your space back
8		in the new industrial area below Costco
9	Man:	Visit Alohaplusstorage.com

Excerpt (11): 1-29-2018: Bowman Termite and Pest Management

1	Woman:	This is Jill from Bowman termite and pest management our
2		family owned business has been serving the Big Island for
3		over eleven years we're the pest and termite specialists that
4	Kids' voices:	get them buggahs out
5	Woman:	big or small we get them all from tent fumigation to centipedes
6		cockroaches, little fire ants, and rodents we will
7	Kids' voices:	get them buggahs out
8	Woman:	call Bowman termite to schedule a free estimate 935-8510
9		Remember that Bowman Termite
10	Kids' voices:	get them buggahs out

The language of these four advertisements is English, except for one linguistic term in each that is Pidgin. In Excerpt (8), the doctor twice uses the word "*keiki*" ("children"), which is originally a Hawaiian term that is also employed by Pidgin speakers. Excerpt (9) is all English except for the term "*choke*" in line 5, which serves as a modifier meaning "many." Excerpt (10) makes usage in line 6 of the Pidgin term "*pauhana*," which is derived from two Hawaiian words "*pau*" ("finish") and "*hana*" ("work") to mean a point in time when work is completed. Excerpt (11) features the refrain voiced by a group of children "get them buggahs out" that contains the term "*buggah*," a derogatory term for a person or something that is a nuisance or a pest.

In all of these excerpts, this brief smattering of Pidgin marks these commercials as "local," that is, as services provided to the local communities of the Big Island. As noted earlier in this chapter, speaking Pidgin became associated with a local identity, and thus it is possible to suggest that even the small amount of Pidgin in these ads is just enough for advertisers to connect their products and services to the idea of "local." In some cases, the advertisements also contain other linguistic clues that signify "localness." In excerpt (8), the doctor doing the speaking is part of Paniolo Pediatrics, where the Hawaiian term "*paniolo*," which is actually the Hawaiian term for "cowboy," marks the clinic as a local establishment. In excerpt (9), not only does the name of the business use the place name "Kona," but the speaker also describes the location as "on Palani," the name of a well-known street in the town of Kona. Additionally, the name of the company doing the advertising in excerpt (10) features the Hawaiian term "aloha," also used by Pidgin speakers.

Even though this marking as local is sometimes very minimal, it can nonetheless be argued that it is important to the businesses. For example, the doctor in excerpt (8) has neither a name, Melissa Hernandez, nor an accent that suggests she is "local." In fact, she even begins her ad in lines 1–2 by saying she is "the newest children's doctor," suggesting that she may be viewed as an outsider. Her inclusion of the term "*keiki*" and the name "*Paniolo* Pediatrics" shows her attempts to connect with the local community through an understanding of local terminology.

In some cases, though, when local connections are more apparent, some businesses may not need to include Pidgin in their ads. Excerpt (12) is for a car dealership with the Hawaiian name "*Pono*."

Excerpt (12): 1-31-2018: Pono's Used Cars The Wave
1   Women: It is time to move forward with a new vehicle for yourself
2   made easy with online financing options available at
3   Pono'susedcars.com and with a huge selection of cars, trucks,
4   and vans on the lot you'll be able to find the right fit for your

5	needs to keep you going on adventures and rides around the
6	island come as a customer leave as a friend stop in at Pono's
7	used cars today just passed the airport on Kanoelehua avenue
8	Pono's used cars 934-pono

In addition to the name of "*Pono*," this ad lists the place of business to be on "*Kanoelehua*" Avenue, which is both a Hawaiian name and one of the main roads in Hilo.

As I noted earlier, during my time living in Hilo, I have heard advertisements on the radio that use more Pidgin than the ads recorded in this study. That such ads did not show up in my data of 80 hours primarily in English suggests a discrepancy in this particular context of radio advertising between Pidgin and English. This difference is not just about the percentage of usage but also the functions of the language within the ads. Pidgin was sometimes added through dialogues and also through expressions and pronunciations in a way that provided hints of localness for the ads, but, in contrast, English was the primary language through which information about the products and services was imparted to the audience.

One possible way of explaining this difference may be in terms of intelligibility. In other words, it may be argued that even though a large percentage of the people on the Big Island speak or at least understand Pidgin, there are some newcomers or some living in isolated communities that may not. However, due to the linguistic double consciousness that was discussed earlier, Pidgin speakers also understand English, and therefore, it makes sense to employ primarily English in radio advertising in order to ensure that the "correct" information about products and services is delivered to as far-reaching of an audience as possible. This would also help explain the employment of a light touch of Pidgin and not a heavy or basilect version of the language, which would not be understood of some portion of the population.

Yet, while intelligibility may be a factor, it is difficult to imagine the longtime stigma attached to Pidgin not figuring (perhaps subconsciously) into the decision to use English to do the majority of the product and service descriptions. Although efforts of Pidgin advocates in Hawai'i have promoted critical language awareness about Pidgin, it still remains that for a majority of the population for a long period of time, Pidgin has not been deemed acceptable in most public contexts, except for possibly standup comedy. Moreover, as noted before, some of the worst critics of Pidgin can be Pidgin speakers themselves, which means that besides for Pidgin advocates, many users of Pidgin may support the usage of English over Pidgin in local radio advertisements. This is part of what Hargrove and Sakada (1999) meant by the "hegemony of English," in which speakers of minority languages are led to believe that their own way of speaking is inadequate. Pidgin speakers have been taught throughout history not only that Pidgin is appropriate in certain contexts, but also that it is "marginal and even irrelevant" (Hargrove and Sakada 1999, 51). Pidgin thus might have a place in radio advertisements to impart a sense of "localness," but it is not appropriate for describing the important content of the ads. Just like the notions of hegemony and appropriateness, the language usage in advertisements reflect a hierarchy in terms of language, with English above Pidgin.

CONCLUSION

This chapter has attempted to understand the place of Pidgin in Hawai'i's multilingual society through discussion of the stigma attached to Pidgin as well as its importance for a local identity, and also through two analyses of Pidgin used in public. Based on the discussion and analyses, it is possible to see that Pidgin occupies a dynamic, yet still controversial role in Hawai'i. It is dynamic in that Pidgin is found in a variety of contexts not limited to the casual confines of people's homes. The analyses shows the use of Pidgin on television, in local politics, and also in radio advertisements. Increased efforts, such as those of the Pidgin Coup, to raise critical language awareness about Pidgin suggest the possibility of an expanded role for Pidgin in society. As Higgins (2015) notes based on her study of the linguistic landscape in Hawai'i, Pidgin is "earning capital" in society and "has arguably grown in visibility and acceptability across domains over the past decade" (Higgins 2015, 148). Even though Pidgin was comparatively sparse in the radio commercials, it was indeed employed regularly and served a role in terms of appealing to a local audience. As Higgins (2015, 160) further states, "no matter what studies on language attitudes in Hawai'i might indicate, Pidgin clearly has a place in Hawai'i's symbolic economy, as illustrated in its linguistic landscape."

At the same time, though, the analysis of radio advertisements suggests that Pidgin remains stigmatized in society, at least concerning its usage in public. Although the discussion early in the chapter attempted to emphasize Pidgin's status as a language, the analysis of radio advertisements showed that Pidgin was not employed to communicate referential meanings to the audience. In that sense, it still remains in an unequal relationship with English, which was the language of choice for explanations and for imparting information to the radio listeners. As discussed, this imbalance is indicative of the lingering beliefs that Pidgin is not appropriate in certain sectors of society.

In pursuing an understanding of the role of Pidgin in Hawai'i, this chapter speaks to the importance of examining Pidgin as it is used in specific social domains. Based on the analyses here and in previous studies (i.e., Furukawa 2007; Furukawa 2018; Higgins 2015; Hiramoto 2011; Lockwood and Saft 2016; Wong 1999), it is apparent that sweeping generalizations about the inappropriateness of Pidgin in public domains in Hawai'i are no longer sufficient. There may be certain situations, such as some educational contexts, where Pidgin is still deemed inappropriate, but there may also be an expanding public space for Pidgin that includes local politics, comedy, and possibly advertising. In addition, further analyses of language usage in specific situations will enhance knowledge not just about the usage of Pidgin but also about the relationship between English and Pidgin (and possibly other languages). In general, then, an increased focus on situations of language use will be key to attaining a heightened understanding of the role of Pidgin, and it will also be a point that I return to in subsequent chapters as critical for attainment of the larger goal of this book, namely, understanding multilingualism in Hawai'i.

NOTES

1. All of the examples in this section are taken directly from Sakoda and Siegel (2003).

2. A system for writing Pidgin in a way that preserved actual pronunciations was developed in the 1970s by Carol Odo (Bickerton and Odo 1976; Odo 1975, 1977). For the purposes of this and remaining chapters, I am going to write Pidgin in a way that does not fully follow the Odo system but does try to represent some of the pronunciations used in the language. I do this in order to make data comprehensible to readers of English while at the same time still present it as different from English.

3. The examples in this and the next two paragraphs come from the corpus of university commencement speeches made by Billy Kenoi (see Saft, Tebow, and Santos 2018).

4. The clip from "In the Car with Andy Bumutai" was most recently available at https://www.facebook.com/AndyBumatai/videos/1526666907616174/, and the clip featuring the local community meeting was found at https://www.youtube.com/watch?v=UtRbyM4Zr2A. Both were accessed on July 18, 2018.

5. Although the Hawaiian pronunciation features a glottal stop between the last "i" and "o," it is most commonly pronounced without the glottal stop, and therefore, I am going to follow in the data excerpts the way it was pronounced in the video clip.

Chapter Four

Heteroglossic Language Practice in Hawaiian Society

No dump opala here (sign on rural road in Hilo)
Keiki swim lessons (sign in a local business establishment in Hilo)
Hele mai your butt over here (uttered by a parent at a youth basketball game in Hilo)

INTRODUCTION

The previous chapter focused on Pidgin, but it is evident that most of the data excerpts contain examples in which Pidgin was mixed together with other languages, especially English but also some Hawaiian phrases as well. Indeed, arguably one of the most underappreciated aspects of language usage in Hawai'i is the tendency for languages to be used together in everyday contexts, including both written and spoken forms of communication. The three examples are a case in point. The first one is taken from a handwritten sign posted on the side of a rural road in Hilo. It employs the Pidgin negative imperative marker *"no"* combined with the term *"opala,"* which is Pidgin but comes from the Hawaiian word *"'ōpala"* for garbage. In the sign it is spelled without the modern conventions of the *"'okina"* and the *"kahakō"* ("macron"), suggesting that it is Pidgin and not Hawaiian. The word "here," especially with the English spelling (as opposed to *"hea"* or *"hiya,"* which might mark a Pidgin usage), seems to be drawing from English, meaning that there are at least three voices in the language of this sign, Pidgin, English, and also Hawaiian (the Hawaiian usage has transferred to Pidgin but the connection to Hawaiian is still obvious to those who know Hawaiian). The second example combines the English idea of "swim lessons" with the term *"keiki,"* which is the Hawaiian word for child/children but is also used in

Pidgin for the same meaning. The third example is a spoken discourse that begins with the term "*hele mai*," the Hawaiian expression for "come here," and concludes with English. It is not an exaggeration to say that the majority of people in Hawai'i see, hear, and even use this type of language mixing on a daily basis.

Moreover, it is possible to make the case that Pidgin, with its origins in a variety of languages as first a pidgin and now a creole, is the embodiment of the propensity in Hawai'i to mix languages. As noted in the last chapter, the vocabulary of Pidgin is a combination of terms from languages that include English, Hawaiian, Japanese, Portuguese, and Tagalog, and aspects of the grammar can be attributed to other languages such as Hawaiian, Portuguese, and Cantonese (and also English). Even the variety of English in Hawai'i referred to as Hawai'i English is described as a combination of English and Pidgin pronunciations and lexical items (Drager 2012; Higgins 2015). Sociolinguistic research sometimes suggests that hybridity in language and culture is largely a recent phenomenon spurred by technological advances and the process of globalization (Blommaert 2003; Chouliaraki and Fairclough 1999; Rubdy and Alsagoff 2013), but language mixing in Hawai'i is hardly a new phenomenon with origins reaching back to the arrival of the missionaries in 1820 and the establishment of the sugar plantations in the 1830s. Perhaps it is this history that has rendered the mixing of languages common within the Hawaiian linguistic landscape.

The purpose of this chapter is to explore this penchant for language mixing in Hawai'i. To do so, a central concept is heteroglossia, a term that derives from the work of the Russian writer Mikhail Bakhtin (1981, 1986). As Bailey (2012) notes, heteroglossia is translated from the Russian term *raznorechie* and consists of two main components:

> the simultaneous use of different kinds of forms or signs; and (2) the tensions and conflicts among those signs, based on the sociohistorical associations they carry with them. (Bailey 2012, 499; Ivanov 2001, 95–97)

Heteroglossia is one of a number of terms employed by academics to discuss the phenomenon of mixing languages; other terms include translanguaging, pluralingualism, metrolingualism, translingual language practices, codemeshing, and also codeswitching. Codeswitching has perhaps been the term most extensively used, but I choose heteroglossia here because of the second component listed, namely, heteroglossia acknowledges conflicting "sociohistorical associations" and attempts to understand the significance of these conflicts for communicative practice. Although there are studies of codeswitching that consider ideological and political aspects of language usage (Gal

1988; Woolard 2004), codeswitching research, as noted by Bailey (2012), has tended to treat the mixed languages as separate autonomous systems and to proceed by examining the functions of each individual language within the discourse. This chapter does discuss the functions of languages appearing in the data, but a focus is given to description of how the mixing of languages brings together sociohistorical meanings thought to clash with one another.

In order to consider the sociohistorical relationships of the languages that are employed together, the notion of indexicality will also be instrumental in this chapter. Indexicality is a term that has been employed to understand that languages are imbued with meanings that are not just referential but rather social and even ideological in nature (Ochs 1992, 2012; Silverstein 2003). While these indexical meanings can be attached to languages on the overall, they also can be derived from the individual features of languages. As Johnstone and Kiesling (2008, 7) explain, "repeated use of different variants in different self-presentation styles associated with locally relevant social groupings can cause particular variants to become semiotically associated with particular ways of being and acting." In their own work, Johnstone and Kiesling (2008) describe how the repeated usage of the pronunciation of the monophthongal /aw/ in the areas surrounding Pittsburgh have led residents there to associate that linguistic feature with a local identity and local ways of acting and being. Although not explicitly invoked in the last chapter, we can apply this idea of indexicality to understand that the phonological, lexical, and grammatical features of Pidgin Billy Kenoi's speech in political meetings function as indexes of "localness" that enable him to connect with the community at a level that goes beyond just the referential meaning of his words. The same is true in the radio advertisements. The inclusion of Pidgin words and phrases such as *choke* and *keiki* is an advertising strategy that makes indexical connections with the local community of listeners.

Another important concept that relates to both heteroglossia and indexicality is "multivocality," which is also derived from the ideas of Bakhtin (Bakhtin 1981; also see Higgins 2009; and Holquist 2002). As described by Higgins (2009, 7), "multivocality refers to the different 'voices' or polyphony that single utterances can yield due to their syncretic nature." Multivocality is a very relevant aspect of heteroglossia for the analyses in this chapter because it underscores the various "voices" that are indexed through heteroglossic language practice in Hawai'i. It will make it possible to see how even one utterance or sentence can carry with it multiple voices. In particular, this chapter will focus particularly on the conflicting voices that are merged through the simultaneous usage of Hawaiian, Pidgin, and English.

I proceed in this chapter by first offering an analysis of two university commencement speeches made in the public sphere by Billy Kenoi. The speeches are very heteroglossic in nature and feature a mixing of Hawaiian, Pidgin, and English. The analysis of the speeches will be followed by an examination of written materials appearing on the website for Kamehameha Schools, the largest private school system in Hawai'i. The schools were created for students of Hawaiian ancestry who are not necessarily proficient in the Hawaiian language, and the analysis focuses especially on the blending of Hawaiian and English voices on the website. Those two analyses lead into a discussion of the ramifications of heteroglossic language practice for our conception of language. More specifically, I will address the ideas of theorists such as Makoni and Pennycook (2005, 2006) and Blommaert (2005, 2010), who question the existence of autonomous languages. To such critics, languages are ideological inventions not supported by the reality of heteroglossia. Then, in order to explore how heteroglossia coexists in a Hawaiian society that regularly employs language categories and advocates for individual languages such as Hawaiian, Pidgin, and English, I present an analysis of language categories as they occur in a database of newspapers in Hawai'i. The analysis, which adopts insights from membership category analysis, describes the common-sense knowledge involved in deploying and comprehending the names of languages in the newspapers.

HETEROGLOSSIA IN COMMENCEMENT SPEECHES

The data for this first analysis once again comes from the speech of the politician Billy Kenoi. This time, the data are taken from two university commencement speeches made by Kenoi in Hawai'i, which were also analyzed in Saft, Tebow, and Santos (2018). One of the speeches was made at the University of Hawai'i at Hilo in 2010 and the other at Hawai'i Pacific University in 2014, and both contain features of English, Pidgin, and Hawaiian.[1] Excerpt (1) is reproduced as an example of language mixing (Saft, Tebow, and Santos, 2018).

Excerpt (1): Commencement at UH-Hilo
67 you know somebody said one time and it made sense you know
68 success is just getting up and dusting yourself off (.) one more time than you
69 fell (.) ya know (.) it's that simple (.) no get confused ya guyz people make life
70 out to be chess when it's really just checkaz okay (.) so no let it be any more
71 confusing than it needs to be (.) it's not that hard (.5) ya know all of you (.)
72 um (.) owe so much to so many um who have helped you get here (.) mom and
73 dad (.) grandmah granpah sistah brudah (.) husband wife (.) professahs librarians

74 people in the community (.) pastor at church (.) no foget say thank you (.)
75 no foget say mahalo (.) my faddah tol me one time and I agree neva (.) no
76 such ting as saying mahalo too much

This excerpt begins with Kenoi employing English as he refers to a general "somebody" in line 67 who offered a definition through line 69 of success. He switches, however, in line 69 to utilize the Pidgin negative imperative form that begins with *no* as a part of giving advice to the audience. He states "*no get confused ya guyz,*" and continues in line 70 with another Pidgin negative imperative, "*so no let it be any more confusing than it needs to be.*" He moves back to an English grammar in lines 71–74 even though he employs Pidgin pronunciations for words such as "*sistah,*" "*brudah,*" and "*professahs*" in line 73. He next switches once again in lines 74 and 75 to express two more negative imperatives, "*no foget say thank you*" and "*no foget say mahalo.*" These last two negative imperatives are identical except for a change from the English term "thank you" in line 74 to the term "*mahalo*" in line 75. "*Mahalo*" is originally a Hawaiian word that is translated into English as "thank you," but it has been adopted by Pidgin speakers as well as English speakers. Woolard (1998) uses the term "bivalent" to refer to words like "*mahalo*" that have crossed languages.

It is interesting that Kenoi's switch in language in line 69 from English to Pidgin seemingly corresponds to a change in voice as he moves from embodying a general "somebody" in English in lines 67–69 in order to define success to offering his own advice through a series of Pidgin negative imperative constructions that begin in line 69. In shifting voice from English to Pidgin, this multivoicedness plays on the nonreferential meanings attached to each language, thus allowing Kenoi to highlight his advice because it is stated through Pidgin negative imperative forms. More specifically, with English imbued with meanings associated with formality, appropriateness, and also a "haole" identity and Pidgin with the opposite meanings of informality, inappropriateness, and a local identity, Kenoi is able use this switch from English to Pidgin first in line 69 and then again in line 74 to emphasize his *no*-prefaced points because of the contrast in the nonreferential meanings.

Moreover, although the change from English "thank you" to the Hawaiian term "*mahalo*" in line 75 seems like a simple change, the usage of "*mahalo*" brings with it a different ideological orientation than the English "thank you."[2] Its origins in the Hawaiian language invoke a traditional voice that, through its bivalency, also resonates with Pidgin speakers. Through the usage of symmetrical constructions that vary only in "thank you" and "*mahalo,*" Kenoi's speech places the voices of Hawaiian and Pidgin on the same level as English. Furthermore, not only is Kenoi aligning "*mahalo*" with an English term but he is also using both as part of a Pidgin grammatical construction,

130   Chapter Four

namely, the negative imperative. He has thus mixed three voices, including a local voice represented by Pidgin that has also been part of an ideological struggle in Hawai'i, particularly with English. Kenoi's heteroglossic practice of integrating these voices makes use of the indexical meanings associated with each language in at least two different yet related ways. On the one hand, his language mixing plays on the contrasting ideologies to switch languages so that pieces of advice may be expressed more emphatically. On the other hand, his heteroglossia conveys the idea that, despite conflicting ideologies, these three languages can stand together in a public space.

Kenoi is not noted to be a fluent speaker of Hawaiian but he made an effort to place Hawaiian at a level equivalent to English and Pidgin, and in the process insert different voices into his speech. Excerpt (2) provides an example. It occurs as he moves to the conclusion of one of his speeches.[3]

Excerpt (2): University of Hawai'i at Hilo
82 that's my little um (.) last words of wisdom (.) kay finally (.) hey guys (.)
83 I know I gotta get off da stage (.) somebody told me one time hey brudah
84 Billy you give pleny speeches you brah ya get any words of advice ya brah keep
85 em shaut (.) ya know no such ting as one bad shaut speech (.) bottom line
86 is ya know here (.) as mayor (.) this island of Hawai'i this beautiful
87 Moku o Keawe ya know I feel da kuleana and responsibility everyday you wake
88 up early every day you stay up late just like all of you will in your careers and
89 your professions but always be proud that every one of you are an alumni from
90 the university of Hawai'i at Hilo (.) be proud of that

In line 82, Kenoi seems to move toward the end of his speech by uttering in English "that's my little um (.) last words of wisdom," but soon thereafter, he begins to employ Pidgin pronunciations and expressions, including *"brudah," "pleny," "brah*, and *"shaut"* in lines 83–85, as he makes a joke related to short speeches. In doing so, he also uses the Pidgin negative form *"no"* and the indefinite article in line 85 when he says *"ya know no such ting as one bad shaut speech."* His switch from English to Pidgin here is consistent with the findings of previous research on codeswitching that has found humor to be a common reason for changing languages (Garcia Vizcaino 2011; Siegel 1995; Woolard 1987). After that, though, he moves toward the conclusion with the phrase "bottom line" in line 85 as he starts talking about his responsibility as mayor in lines 86–87. As a part of doing so, he employs more English pronunciations and he also uses the Hawaiian phrase *"Moku o Keawe,"* which is another name for the Island of Hawai'i that literally means "the island of Keawe." *Keawe* is the shortened name of a Hawaiian chief who ruled peacefully over the island in the 1700s and who was also the great-grandfather of King Kamehameha I, the first king of the Hawaiian Islands and the man credited with uniting all of the islands. Shortly thereafter, Kenoi utters another Hawaiian term *"kuleana,"* which is usually translated as "responsibility."

By uttering these terms, Kenoi demonstrates, first of all, that he has the knowledge of the Hawaiian language and culture to employ these terms. Second, in displaying this knowledge, he also accesses the positive ideologies now associated with the Hawaiian language. In particular, his employment of the name *"Moku o Keawe"* invokes a connection to a figure who is respected in Hawaiian history. Moreover, although it appears that his usage in line 87 of the terms *"kuleana"* and responsibility is repetitive since they have the same meaning, the indexical meanings of the two are quite different. *Kuleana* invokes a traditional voice that, although once considered unequal to English, is now associated with dignity and pride. By aligning these two terms one after another, Kenoi situates the Hawaiian voice on the same level as English. One final excerpt from the conclusion of the speech at Hawai'i Pacific University underscores the degree to which Kenoi's speeches are heteroglossic.

Excerpt (3): Commencement at Hawai'i Pacific University
85 so all of you all of you I jus like leave you with a couple
86 tings one from this great Hawaiian American storyteller (.) named
87 Ralph Waldo Kamakawiwo'ole Emerson (.) I trew in da
88 Kamakawiwo'ole cuz anybody who dat smart and dat cool gotta be
89 Hawaiian (.) But he said (.) what lies behind us and what lies before
90 us (.) are tiny matters compared to what lies within us (.) remember
91 dat you guyz (.) what lies behind us (.) and what lies before us
92 tiny matters compared to what lies within us say what you mean and
93 mean what you say (.) you know my fadda told me ey boy (.)
94 don't just think before you talk (.) tink and feel before you talk (.)
95 that way everything you say come from your heart (.) whether people
96 agree or disagree with what you say (.) at least you honest (.) you
97 know so you guys one oddah Shakespearean Pidgin English brudah
98 sed no skaed em go get em okay shall I leave you guys with that
99 and finally from a great Hawaiian scholar Kamehameha the Great
100 (.) before the valley of io valley in the face of overwhelming odds
101 and numbers (.) he looked at all of his warriors and yelled i mua
102 e na poki'i a inu i ka wai 'awa'awa that meant go forward my
103 brothers and sisters until you drink the bitter waters of battle for
104 there is no turning back congratulations class of 2014
105 Hawaii Pacific University you earned it you deserve it aloha

This is a rich and rather lengthy excerpt with significant language mixing. As Kenoi lets his audience know in lines 85–86 that he is moving to the end of his speech, he employs a Pidgin grammatical construction in line 85 in uttering

"*I jus like leave you with a couple tings*," which features "*like leave*" without the infinitive marker "to" (Sakoda and Siegel 2003). He then states the name "Ralph Waldo Emerson," except he inserts "*Kamakawiwo'ole*," a recognizably Hawaiian name, between the Waldo and Emerson. He does not, I believe, have a specific Hawaiian person in mind with the uttering of "*Kamakawiwo'ole*," but instead chooses a name that is very obvious in its Hawaiianness. He explains in lines 87–88 using Pidgin pronunciations "*trew*," "*cuz*," and "*dat*" that he put the Hawaiian name in there because he equates being smart with being Hawaiian. His ability to make this connection is aided by the fact that ideological beliefs about Hawaiian identities and the Hawaiian language have shifted since the Hawaiian Renaissance of the 1960s and 1970s. His insertion of the Hawaiian name "*Kamakawiwo'ole*" both draws on these positive ideologies and further reinforces that a Hawaiian identity can be associated with pride and intelligence.

In reinforcing the positive nature of a Hawaiian name, the role of the English name Ralph Waldo Emerson needs to emphasized. The Poetry Foundation (https://www.poetryfoundation.org/poets/ralph-waldo-emerson) calls Emerson "one of the most influential writers and thinkers of the nineteenth century in the United States," and his name is generally associated with high-level literary skills. Hence, the insertion of Emerson's name invokes this positive imagery and attaches it to the Hawaiian name "*Kamakawiwo'ole*." For speakers of English in the audience not very familiar with Hawaiian names and identities, this connection may create a strongly positive link with being Hawaiian. For those who are familiar with Hawaiian, this combination of names may be a surprise but especially with Kenoi's explanation that "anybody who dat smart and dat cool gotta be Hawaiian," it is a mixture that will make sense since it fits with the positive evaluations of Hawaiian identities in current society.

It is interesting to note that Kenoi's insertion of "*Kamakawiwo'ole*" draws laughter from the audience, which may be a result of the fact that he is smiling as he says it and also because it comes as a surprise to the audience. As already noted, prior research has made a connection among Pidgin, humor, and also a local identity (Furukawa 2018; Labrador 2004; Saft, Tebow, and Santos, 2018), and thus it is possible that Kenoi's usage of Pidgin terms and pronunciations in lines 87–89 serves as an indication that he intends this combination of names to be a humorous event. This does not necessarily detract from the status of a Hawaiian name next to a revered writer, but it does suggest the possibility that such a connection, due to its unexpected nature, may also be a source of laughter. It is impossible to know exactly why Kenoi decides to combine these names at this particular time of his speech, but it is notable as a heteroglossic practice that does not just blend names but also aligns the indexical meanings attached to those names and, in the process, adds to the creative and entertainment value of the speech. These five lines of data alone (lines 85–89) thus display a fairly remarkable sequence of heteroglossia as the speaker's multivoicedness draws on the voice of a respected American writer through Ralph Waldo Emerson, a Hawaiian voice represented by the name "*Kamakawiwo'ole*," and also a Pidgin voice that helps frame this sequence as a source of localness and humor.

The mixing of languages continues in lines 89–90 as Kenoi employs English to quote Emerson. He marks the end of the quotation in lines 90–91 by employing a Pidgin pronunciation with "*remember dat ya guyz*," but he switches back to English as he repeats the quotation in lines 91–92 and adds his own piece of advice with "say what you mean and mean what you say" through line 93. He then moves back into Pidgin pronunciations in lines 93–95 as he quotes his father "*you know my fadda told me ey boy (.) don't just think before you talk (.) tink and feel before you talk (.)*." He elaborates on this in lines 95–96 using a Pidgin verbless sentence "*at least you honest*" before starting to quote himself in lines 97–98 with "*you guys one oddah Shakespearean Pidgin English brudah sed no skaed em go get em*" ("another Pidgin English speaker, [who has been likened to Shakespeare] said don't be afraid, go out there and get them"). This includes a reference to himself as he shows awareness that he has been called the "Shakespeare of Pidgin." Second, it is a reference to the commencement speech he made at the University of Hawai'i at Hilo in 2010 when he ended his speech with the line "*no skaed em go get em*" that begins with the Pidgin negative imperative marker "*no*." This line was featured in news stories about that speech in 2010 (http://www.bigislandvideonews.com/2010/05/16/video-kenois-uh-hilo-commencement-address/).

Lines 89–98 thus add more voices to what is already a heteroglossic speech. They are mostly local Pidgin voices, but this Pidgin voice is actually itself multivoiced as it is used to invoke the words of his father and also of Kenoi himself. It adds further layers to the multivoicedness of his speech through the voices of authority represented by his father "don't just think before you talk (.) tink and feel before you talk (.) that way everything you say come from your heart (.) whether people agree or disagree with what you say (.) at least you honest" and himself with "no skaed em go get em" in order to impart advice to the graduating students. Pidgin is responsible for adding a local voice to his speeches and also creating humor, but these few lines indicate that Pidgin can also be a source of authority and advice. And beyond that, he includes yet another voice in these lines with his invocation of the name Shakespeare. It is a move that is somewhat similar to his construction of the name "Ralph Waldo *Kamakawiwo'ole* Emerson" as he employs the name of a another literary figure but this time combines the name with the Pidgin reference, "Pidgin English *Brudah*." This combination creates an indexical conflict as Shakespeare is aligned with Pidgin English, which has at times been stigmatized as a form of broken English. Like the combination "Ralph Waldo *Kamakawiwoʻole* Emerson," this mixture is met with some laughter, but it does not prevent Kenoi from being able to state his main points and distribute advice. In fact, we can say that the humor adds to the entertainment value of the speech which may in turn even strengthen the force of his advice since people are demonstrating their engagement with the speech through laughter. This is largely done through a very creative form of heteroglossia.

The remainder of Kenoi's speech continues to be heteroglossic as he switches to English in lines 98–99 to introduce one last quotation, which inserts still another voice into his speech. He introduces the source of this voice in English as "a great Hawaiian scholar Kamehameha the Great." As just noted, Kamehameha the Great is recognized as the man who united the Hawaiian Islands as a kingdom and served as the first king. After providing information about the context of the quotation in English, he performs it in Hawaiian as he states "*i mua e na pokiʻi a inu i ka wai ʻawaʻawa*" in lines 101–102. He then offers translation in English through line 104 before expressing his congratulations to the graduates and ending his speech with the word "*aloha*." Through the naming of Kamehameha as a "Hawaiian scholar" and "Kamehameha the Great," this language change constructs and thus creates a bond between a Hawaiian identity as well as the language and a sense of pride and dignity. By employing not just this quotation from Kamehameha the Great but also a Hawaiian name with Ralph Waldo Emerson, Kenoi's heteroglossia has instilled his speech with voices that reinforce the positive ideologies attached to the Hawaiian language. The same can also be said about his usage of Pidgin. In addition to placing himself on the level of Shakespeare, Kenoi uses the connection between Pidgin and humor to construct an entertaining speech that imparts serious advice to the graduates. In doing so, his integration of Pidgin with Hawaiian and English put all three on equal footing as resources for a public speech. Moreover, as one last contribution to the heteroglossic quality of his speech, Kenoi chooses the word "*aloha*" as his final word. "*Aloha*" is another bivalent term that is a good example of the multivocality of language in Hawaiʻi as it has its origins in Hawaiian but is used by Pidgin speakers and also by English speakers as well. It allows Kenoi one final chance to connect with all members of his audience, including parents of graduates whose only connection to Hawaiian language and culture may be prior knowledge of the word "*aloha*," and it also enables him to conclude in a way that summons the various voices that had already been included in his speech.

HETEROGLOSSIA ON THE KAMEHAMEHA SCHOOLS WEBSITE

As noted earlier, Billy Kenoi is still regarded as a bit special in Hawai'i due to his willingness to employ Pidgin in the public sphere. Nonetheless, I would stress that the frequency with which he mixes languages is not necessarily unusual in Hawaiian society. The analysis in this section examines a different domain of language usage in order to further explore heteroglossic language practice. The focus here is a website and, more specifically, the website of Kamehameha Schools (http://www.ksbe.edu). This website (http://www.ksbe.edu) provides an interesting opportunity to investigate heteroglossia because Kamehameha Schools is a well-known system of schools specifically for students of Hawaiian ancestry with education primarily through the medium of English. There are certainly students who speak Hawaiian attending their schools and there are requirements and opportunities to take language courses and be actively involved in cultural activities, but there are no entrance requirements concerning Hawaiian. The following analysis is based on the content of the website on two days, March 15, 2018 and February 11, 2019.

Much of the website is in English, but as figure 4.1 indicates, Hawaiian also occupies a significant place. This screenshot shows the very top of the website.

Following the top line, which offers viewers a choice to search employment opportunities or to get access to resources for people already employed with Kamehameha Schools, the website provides a brief explanation on the left side of the founding of the schools through the will of Bernice Pauahi Bishop. The Kamehameha Schools logo can be seen in the middle and a search engine to the right. Except for the names Kamehameha and Pauahi, all of this is in English. At the bottom of this screenshot, the website offers five clickable items, with the first one being in Hawaiian, "*Nā Kula 'o Kamehameha*" (lit. "the schools, Kamehameha"). With the plural marker "*nā*" preceding the word "*kula*" ("the schools"), this option links viewers to websites for the different schools that constitute the Kamehameha Schools system.

Figure 4.1.   Screenshot 1

Figure 4.2. Screenshot 2

Figure 4.2 above, taken from a different day, offers another opportunity in the menu items on the left to click on the category "*Nā Kula ʻo Kamehameha*."

This time, though, viewers of the website are offered a chance to choose one of the three campuses and/or the preschools, all of which are marked by the abbreviation KS and spelled using contemporary orthographic conventions. Next, just below the link for KS preschools, there is another link that begins with the Hawaiian phrase "*Mālama Ola*" (lit. "preserve health"). This is then followed by the English "Student health, safety, and well-being" that clarifies the meaning of the Hawaiian phrase.

The Hawaiian headings in the meno on the left side can be understood, more or less, without knowing the language by looking at the words that follow them. Yet, the expression in large font in the middle, "*I Mua* Newsroom," should be appreciated as a blended Hawaiian and English phrase. "*I Mua*" translates to "go forward" and has become a slogan for Kamehameha Schools. Although it is difficult to see because of its small size, it is included at the bottom of the Kamehameha Schools logo that is pictured in the middle of figure 4.1. This expression has its roots in the famous words of King Kamehameha I that were used by Billy Kenoi in excerpt (3): "*I mua e nā pokiʻi a inu i ka wai ʻawaʻawa*" ("Go forward my brothers and sisters and drink the bitter waters [of battle]"). With the combination of "*I Mua*" plus the English term "Newsroom," this is a good example of

Heteroglossic Language Practice in Hawaiian Society 137

Figure 4.3. Screenshot 3

heteroglossia as the two language are mixed to create one rather large and general category that contains news stories pertaining to Kamehameha Schools. As shown in figure 4.2, the news begins with two stories concerning the Kamehameha schools. The next screen shot, figure 4.3, shows further entries listed under "*I Mua* Newsroom" and contains more mixing of Hawaiian and English.

In addition to the menu items on the left "*Hiʻikua* Helpline" that blends the two language, the first headline under "Top Stories" reads "Manaola shares manaʻo with KS ʻohana." The name Manaola is recognizably a Hawaiian name and it is followed by other words, "*manaʻo*" and "*ʻohana*" that are marked as Hawaiian words by syllable structure and orthographic conventions. These are also fairly common Hawaiian terms that would arguably be understood by a large portion of the non-Hawaiian speaking population, particularly those born and raised in Hawaiʻi. The mixing of languages does not stop there. In the smaller print used to start the story, the first sentence reads, "In an interactive session with KS staff at Kawaiahaʻo Plaza appropriately dubbed 'Naʻau or Never,' Native Hawaiian fashion designer Manaola Yap implored attendees to look for answers within." In particular, the phrase "naʻau or never" is a clever blend of Hawaiian and English that plays on the similarity of the sound of the word "*naʻau*" with the English word "now." "*Naʻau*" is a Hawaiian word that refers to a person's guts or intestines but also is used to represent feelings or affections, in much the same way that English speakers refer to their "heart" or "mind" to express their feelings.

At a basic level, this mixing of languages on the Kamehameha Schools website seems easily explained. On the one hand, the mission of Kamehameha Schools is to serve people of Hawaiian ancestry and thus it makes sense that the website would demonstrate this connection to Hawaiian culture and a Hawaiian identity through the employment of the Hawaiian language. On the other hand, with no Hawaiian language requirement for admittance into its schools and with a relatively small percentage of Hawaiian speakers in the islands, it can be assumed that the majority of those viewing the website will be speakers of English who are not fluent in Hawaiian, although many will know some basic expressions and terminology. It therefore would seemingly follow that the best linguistic strategy for the website would be to adopt predominantly English but add Hawaiian terminology that reminds viewers of the schools' connection to Hawaiian ancestry and to a Hawaiian identity.

The notion of heteroglossia, however, enables a deeper understanding of the mixing of these two languages. In particular, heteroglossia requires consideration of the historical context of the two languages in Hawai'i, especially the contrasting ideologies that left the Hawaiian language as a source of anguish for people of Hawaiian blood. Although the language helped bind them to their ancestral identity, Hawaiians were physically punished for employing their language in a school setting, which in turn resulted in Hawaiian speakers not transmitting their language to younger generation. In short, then, through contact between the two languages, the Hawaiian language became burdened with the ideological belief that it was a "useless" language of a people who, as discussed in chapter 2, were given labels such as "lazy" and "undependable." In contrast, English became an index of "intelligence" and "affluence." This contrast was so strong that even Kamehameha Schools, upon its creation in 1887, a time when Hawaiian was still a widely spoken language, chose English as its medium of education (Eyre 2004).

However, as noted in chapter 3, due to the Hawaiian Renassaince of the 1960s and 1970s and the Hawaiian language revitalization movement beginning in the 1980s, language ideologies concerning Hawaiian have changed to the extent that people of Hawaiian ancestry once again view the language with pride and dignity. Hawaiian has thus become an index of a proud connection to a traditional Hawaiian ancestry. Therefore, the aligning of Hawaiian with English on the Kamehameha Schools' website stands as a symbol of the strength of and pride in the language. Note again that this does not mean that ideological beliefs about the strength of English have diminished; it still serves as an index of power and affluence in Hawai'i. Instead, the placement of the two languages side-by-side, sometimes in the same sentence and even the same expression (as in *I Mua* Newsroom), suggests just how far the ideological meanings of Hawaiian have risen to stand with English on the website. In doing so, it imparts just such a message to viewers of the website, which certainly includes prospective students and their parents.

This, of course, does not mean that the indexical meanings of Hawaiian and English are fully equivalent. At the same time that it reflects pride and dignity, Hawaiian also represents the traditional voice of the islands, something known by most non-Hawaiian speakers in Hawai'i. Hence, English and Hawaiian still conflict in their ideological underpinnings, and this conflict allows for the nonreferential meanings of Hawaiian to be accessed and emphasized through heteroglossia on the website.

Here, it is of interest to note that one of the languages considered thus far, Pidgin, is absent from the website. This may not be a surprise given that Kamehameha Schools was established for people of Hawaiian ancestry, but it is worthy of consideration if we acknowledge that many, if not most, of the students who attend Kamehameha Schools come from a Pidgin speaking background. From the perspective of indexicality, Pidgin's absence makes sense given the mixed ideologies about Pidgin in society. While beliefs may be shifting in a positive direction (Furukawa 2018; Higgins 2015), Pidgin is not associated with the power and affluence of English nor is it considered as traditionally and spiritually important as Hawaiian. Inclusion of Pidgin on the website, thus, could make indexical connections between Pidgin and localness that may detract from the symbolic linkage drawn on the website between the power of English and the traditional status of Hawaiian that would be attractive to current and prospective students, their parents, as well as current and future employees.

Yet, even without the usage of Pidgin on the website, it still stands as a good example of the heteroglossia that is regularly found in modern Hawaiian society. The excerpts of Billy Kenoi's commencement speeches together with examples of phrases such as "*I Mua* Newsroom" and "Na'au or Never" in the website screenshots provide glimpses of the degree to which people are willing to mix languages. Moreover, this language mixing also highlights the creative abilities of people to employ languages in ways that do not merely follow the boundaries of single languages. These creative abilities as well as language boundaries are discussed in further depth in the next section, which brings into question the custom in contemporary linguistics of considering languages as autonomous systems.

HETEROGLOSSIA AND THE STATUS OF LANGUAGES

Thus far in this chapter, and in previous chapters as well, I have employed language categories such as "Hawaiian," "Pidgin," and "English" as though they were autonomous languages that existed separately in the minds of people in Hawai'i and in the minds of the readers as well. However, the willingness of Billy Kenoi and also those who maintain the website for Kamehameha Schools to fuse pronunciations, vocabulary, and sometimes even grammatical structures seems to fly in the face of traditional conceptions of how languages work. What, for instance, is the approach toward language of people who create phrases such as "Na'au or never" and "I Mua Newsroom" and names like "Ralph Waldo Kamakawiwo'ole Emerson" and "Shakespearean Pidgin Brudah"? They are seemingly engaging in actions that contradict the traditional understanding in linguistics of a language system. The degree of language mixing in Hawaiian society suggests that people may not fully buy into the notion that languages are supposed to be closed systems that are kept separate from one another.

Indeed, scholars have used heteroglossic language practice to suggest that prior linguistic research has erred by treating languages as autonomous systems that are best examined in and of themselves (Makoni and Pennycook 2005, 2006). In such a view, languages, instead of constituting individual systems, should be conceived of as sets of semiotic resources from which speakers can pick and choose when constructing their speech in various contexts that include formal as well as everyday speech and also genres of written communication. This fits with Bakhtin's explanation of heteroglossia, "language is not an abstract system of normative forms but rather a concrete heteroglot conception of the world" (Bakhtin 1981, 293; also quoted in Higgins 2009).

Some writers have, in fact, taken this even further and expressed doubts concerning the existence of individual languages. Reagan (2004, 42), for example, states:

> There is, or at least there may well be, no such thing as English. Indeed, my claim is even a bit stronger than this—not only is there no such thing as English, but there is arguably no such thing as Russian, French, Spanish, Chinese, Hindi, or any other language. (Also quoted in Makoni and Pennycook 2005: 137)

Part of such a claim is that the very notion of "separate languages" is a historical invention, often a result of process of colonization that would privilege the colonizers and their "language." This critique is most recently found in the work of Makoni and Pennycook (2005, 2006), Blommaert (2005, 2010), and Blommaert and Rampton (2016) but it is also linked to the ideas of Harris (1980, 1981, 1998), Muhlhausler (1996, 2000), Toolan (2003), and Bauman and Briggs (2003), some of whom have referred to the notion of a language as an autonomous system as a "myth." They further note that the creation of this "myth" has allowed the creators to construct languages as a scientific study and also themselves as those with the analytic expertise to understand those languages. This invention of languages, then, enables them to control and use this knowledge for their benefit by doing such things as creating scientific fields and educational curricula that center on so-called standard languages, also inventions.

For these critics, the appropriate question is not how does a specific feature of a language fit into the whole of a language but how is it used in communication within a specific speech community that itself might be undergirded by different social beliefs about community, humanity, or language. Such a question is thus a very apt one for multilingual societies constituted by people of various backgrounds. In outlining an approach to the studying multilingualism as a "multivoiced multilingualism," Higgins (2009) argues for a need to understand "multilingual repertoires" that are employed in and across domains of language usage in a society. In such a view, language is recast as one of many "mobile resources" that can be employed across different contexts, genres and the like (Blommaert 2010; Blommaert and Backus 2012; Pennycook 2011). Likewise, people are not viewed as individual possessors of languages but rather "as social actors using heteroglossic sets of linguistic resources to negotiate the social word" (Bailey 2012, 504, referring to the work of Bakhtin). Hence, it does not necessarily matter whether Billy Kenoi is a fluent speaker of Pidgin, English, and or Hawaiian, but what matters is that he has access to the resources that allow him to mix in words such as "*kuleana*" and sentences like "*I mua nā* poki'i a inu i ka *wai 'awa'awa*" ("Go forward my brothers and sisters and drink the bitter waters (of battle)") into speeches that otherwise consists mostly of Pidgin and English. Similarly, it allows Kenoi to combine the name "Ralph Waldo Emerson" with the Hawaiian name "*Kamakawiwo'ole*" to produce an entirely new name that communicates a unique message to his audience. The same is true in the language usage on the Kamehameha Schools website. Hawaiian and English provide resources for language users in a multilingual society to mix together to create novel expressions, such as "I Mua Newsroom" and "Na'au or Never" that convey not just referential messages to viewers but also align Hawaiian and English, with their different social histories, together at the same level on the same webpage.

In such a perspective, whether someone is fluent in a particular language becomes a strange and/or mute question that derives from an assumption of the existence of autonomous language systems. What becomes important is their ability to construct language according to communicative needs of the domain, or context, at hand. Billy Kenoi is considered a good communicator not because of his command of individual languages but because of his ability to mix resources to fit the context. He is dubbed "the Shakespeare of Pidgin," but it is probably rare that he employs only Pidgin when speaking in public contexts. He has developed this reputation because of his ability to integrate

Pidgin effectively into speeches that might also include English and Hawaiian. The Kamehameha Schools website communicates effectively with its perceived audience not because it employs a language believed to be formal English but because of its creative amalgamation of Hawaiian and English voices into one website that appeals to people looking for a specific type of education that itself might cross typical educational borders (mixing English and Hawaiian worlds).

Blommaert (2003, 610) discusses this language amalgamation in terms of "semiotic opportunity," a concept that readily applies to the heteroglossia found in Hawai'i. Each domain such as a university commencement speech or a website is a "semiotic opportunity" that allows for the display of "fantastic semiotic creativity" (Blommaert 2003, 611) through deployment of the various linguistic (and nonlinguistic) resources that are available. The addition of the adjective "fantastic" may seem to border on exaggeration, but it must be remembered that this semiotic creativity enables speakers to mix not just words and grammar but also various indexical meanings, some of which may seemingly be in direct contrast. For Billy Kenoi, the commencement speeches served as an opportunity for semiotic creativity that is realized through the blending of multiple voices to construct entertaining speeches that provided advice to the audience. The same is true of the website, where words like "*na'au*" and phrases such as "now or never" were resources that could be merged for particular communicative effects including an aligning of English and Hawaiian together in the same context.

This view that questions the status of languages as autonomous entities is attractive because it aids in appreciating the linguistic talents of many people who are raised in Hawai'i's multilingual environment. Billy Kenoi is one person who has received some notoreity due to his public presence but there are surely many other residents who also mix languages on a daily basis and move between languages based on the domain in which they are speaking. A heteroglossia that does not worry about defining fluency in terms of the mind's control of autonomous languages has the potential to focus specifically on uncovering the vast semiotic creativity of language users and hence understand the linguistic and communicative potential of people in multilingual communities such as Hawai'i.

At the same time, however, this emphasis on heteroglossic language practice reveals an apparent contradiction within Hawaiian society. While embracing heteroglossia may be a key to understanding Hawai'i as a multilingual society, there are many people in Hawai'i who believe in and actively promote the existence of autonomous languages. A very basic example is education in Hawai'i, in which educators in most schools expect students to focus on developing English. In fact, it is conceivable that some of the same people who claim to appreciate Kenoi's heteroglossic language practice may also be the ones insisting on English only in the schools. Are such educators referring merely to an invented language that is an ideological abstraction? Or is English a reality? We may pose a similar question about Pidgin. Although most of the data offered thus far shows him mixing Pidgin with other languages, Kenoi's reputation as a fearless speaker of Pidgin presumes the existence of an autonomous language called Pidgin. How does "Pidgin" exist separately if it is frequently used in combination with other languages? Finally, we have already noted the place of the Hawaiian language revitalization movement in Hawai'i's linguistic landscape. For those involved in that movement, the continued existence of the Hawaiian language is extremely important. Would supporters of Hawaiian agree that language categories are mere historical inventions? In order to explore these questions and probe the degree to which languages exist as separate entities in Hawaiian society, the next section examines references to languages in newspapers published in Hawai'i.

HETEROGLOSSIA AND LANGUAGE CATEGORIES IN NEWSPAPERS IN HAWAI'I

I hope to shed light on some of the questions just raised about the status of languages in Hawai'i in this section through an analysis of references to languages in Hawaiian newspapers. To do so, I use a database of newspapers available through the library at the University of Hawai'i at Hilo. The database is called "America's News," and it has a filter that enables searches of the following 11 publications: Associated Press State Wire: *Hawaii* (HI), *Big Island Weekly* (Hilo, HI), *The Garden Island* (Lihue, HI), *Hawaii Tribune-Herald* (Hilo, HI), *The Honolulu Advertiser* (HI), *Honolulu Examiner* (HI), *Honolulu Star-Advertiser* (HI), *Honolulu Star-Advertiser: Blogs* (HI), *Honolulu Star-Bulletin* (HI), *North Hawaii News* (Waimea, HI), *West Hawaii Today* (Kailua-Kona, HI). For the purposes of this analysis, I did a search for the keywords, "Hawaiian language," "Pidgin," and "Japanese language." Even though Japanese has yet to be a focus of analysis, I include it here to add a different perspective; Hawaiian as the indigenous language, Pidgin as the creole language, and Japanese as an immigrant language. I engaged in this search on March 18, 2018.

The analysis primarily draws on the ideas of membership category analysis (MCA), a perspective with origins in the work of Harvey Sacks, Emanuel Schegloff and their colleagues (Sacks 1992; Sacks and Schegloff 1979; Schegloff 2007) in their attempts to explicate the common-sense reasoning behind the deployment of categories such as "teacher," "hotrodder," "baby," and "gambler." MCA has most frequently been applied to spoken interaction, but I find that it can assist in the elucidation of the inferences involved in the usage of language categories in the newspaper columns.

The first result of my searches for the language names "Hawaiian," "Pidgin," and "Japanese" is that they were all used frequently in the newspapers. The first two excerpts, excerpts (4) and (5), show references to the Hawaiian language. Excerpt (4) is from the events calendar of the *Hawai'i Tribune Herald* on March 18, which is based in Hilo and serves the Big Island of Hawai'i. Excerpt (5) is from a story in the *Honolulu Star-Advertiser*, based in Honolulu, that is titled "Strength in language: Hawaiian usage gains momentum." This story ran on March 11, 2018. For all of the excerpts in this section, references to the relevant languages have been bolded.

Excerpt (4): *Hawai'i Tribune Herald*, March 18
PERFORMANCE BY UNIVERSITY OF HAWAII AT HILO'S THEATER 'AUANA PROGRAM
Where: Hilo Public Library, 300 Waianuenue Ave., Hilo
When: 4 p.m. today
Details: Tutu, a grandmotherly narrator, tells three familiar tales local-style: "Three Billygoats Gruff," "The Three Little Pigs" and "Three Blind Mice." As she narrates, the characters perform the action using **Hawaiian language** dialogue. Free and suitable for all ages. Children ages 5 and younger must be accompanied by an adult.

Excerpt (5): *Honolulu Star-Advertiser*, March 11
The state of the **Hawaiian language** renaissance, said Na'alehu Anthony, can be gauged by a visit to the drug store, or some similar community stomping grounds. He's done that, and the conclusion he's drawn: **Hawaiian** is gaining in strength.

"What you have now is a metric of the numbers game starting to play in your favor," said Anthony, filmmaker and chief executive director of 'Oiwi TV. "You started with one or two able to speak **Hawaiian** fluently, and now there are many more.

"Before, if you heard someone else speaking **Hawaiian** in Longs, guarantee you knew them, because there weren't that many of us," he added. "Now you hear someone speaking Hawaiian, you look up—and you have no idea who they are."

The reference to the Hawaiian language in excerpt (4) points out that some of the dialogues from three children's books will be performed through Hawaiian. Here, it is considered noteworthy that the books are going to be acted out in Hawaiian. Excerpt (5) features four mentions of the Hawaiian language in the first three paragraphs of the story, as the article writer refers to the experiences and thoughts of Naʻalehu Anthony, filmmaker and chief executive director of ʻŌiwi TV. Anthony is quoted as he describes measuring the progress of Hawaiian language renaissance through the frequency with which Hawaiian can be heard at Longs, a popular chain of drugstores throughout Hawaiʻi.

For those who believe that languages are historical inventions, one possible argument is that people employing these language names have merely adopted the categories that were created and passed down by their English-speaking predecessors. Accordingly, the usage of categories such as "Hawaiian language" would not necessarily prove their existence. Instead, the newspaper writers and those quoted within are merely adhering to linguistic conventions without reflecting on the heteroglossic reality of actual language use in society. Putting this another way, the claim could be made that the belief in the existence of these languages constitutes an ideology that undergirds at least part of Hawaiian society and its approach to languages.

There may indeed be some truth to the connection of language categories to ideological beliefs, but I want to pursue further the usage of such categories in the database of newspapers from the perspective of MCA because MCA, without necessarily worrying about the notion of ideology, has the potential to highlight just how important these categories are to the common-sense knowledge of members of Hawaiian society. As Schegloff (2007, 469) emphasizes, categories "are the store house and the filing system for the common-sense knowledge that ordinary people . . . have." Thus, when the writer in excerpt (4) notes that Hawaiian language dialogue will be featured, the category "Hawaiian language" is understandable to readers without further explanation because of their common-sense knowledge that there is indeed such a category. If this category was not a part of the shared common-sense knowledge of readers of the newspaper, then it would not be possible for readers to make sense of this announcement in excerpt (4).

Moreover, Sacks (1992, 236) stresses that categories are "inference rich," which essentially means that members who share this common-sense knowledge of a category are able to draw larger inferences about that category based on its usage in context. Hence, people who understand the category "Hawaiian language" will be able to infer why it is noteworthy in excerpt (4) that the books are to be read in Hawaiian. That is, it is noteworthy because it is quite rare still in Hawaiʻi for Hawaiian to be employed in public readings, thus making it necessary to explicitly state that the books at this event will be performed in such a way. If the books were to be read in English, this would not be so remarkable and probably go unstated. The common-sense knowledge of people about the category "Hawaiian language" makes it possible for them to infer the reason that there is a need to mention explicitly the Hawaiian language in this announcement.

One further related point about categories is that there are certain activities that our common-sense knowledge associates with categories. In one of Sacks's most famous examples, the "The baby cried. The mommy picked it up," our common-sense knowledge tells us that the baby was picked up by her/his own mother because picking up their own babies is something we know mommies to do. Such activities have been called category-bound activities (Sacks 1992; Schegloff 2007) because of their close attachment to the categories themselves. In excerpt (5), many of the connections drawn in the article, including a Hawaiian language "renaissance" and the Hawaiian language "gaining in strength" fit this characterization of category-bound activities because they become part of people's knowledge about the Hawaiian language, namely, that it is in the midst of a strong revitalization movement. The connection made by the article writer and Na'ahelu Anthony simultaneously draws on and reinforces this common-sense knowledge.

These notions of "inference rich" and "category-bound activities" thus emphasize the extent to which knowledge about language categories pervades the minds of people in Hawai'i. This knowledge makes it possible not only to draw general inferences about this knowledge but also, more specifcally, to connect these categories unproblematically to certain activities. Based on the importance of these categories to the knowledge base in Hawai'i, it is difficult to argue against the reality of their existence in the minds of people. Pidgin presents a rather telling example because the category of "Pidgin" itself represents an amalgam of languages that has been very dynamic and has at times baffled language specialists in terms of categorization. Nonetheless, the category "Pidgin" is employed in a way in newspapers that suggests it is very meaningful to people in Hawaiian society. Excerpt (6) is from the section "Hawaiian News" of the newspaper *The Garden Island* on Kauai. It was printed on February 26, 2018, and uses the term "Pidgin" in the title: "EKK offers Pidgin humour, Hawaiian music."

> Excerpt (6): *The Garden Island*, February 26
> Da Tita Aunties lead off with a hilarious hour of teaching **Pidgin** English, Kauai-style.
> They'll headline tonight's session of E Kanikapila Kakou, a Hawaiian music-focused program held at the Aqua Kauai Beach Resort.
> Arrive early for a good seat.

The content makes it clear that the abbreviation EKK in the title stands for "*E Kanikapila Kakou*" and suggests that this is a regular session at the Aqua Kauai Beach Resort.[4] According to the announcement, the session on that particular day begins with "a hilarious hour of teaching Pidgin English." This statement as well as the usage of the category "Pidgin" in the title construct a link between Pidgin and humor, which constitutes a category-bound activity that makes sense because it draws on common-sense knowledge held by members of people in Hawai'i, namely that Pidgin can be used to create comedy. Here, the further linkage of Pidgin to the activity of teaching might seem to contradict commonly held beliefs about Pidgin not belonging in education, but the connection of this action of teaching Pidgin to "a hilarious hour" recontextualizes this activity as a humorous one, hence reinforcing the common-sense connection between Pidgin and humor. Likewise, the listing of Pidgin as "Pidgin English" also fits with another common-sense understanding about Pidgin, that it is a form of English (even despite attempts by advocates to accentuate Pidgin's status as a separate language). Moreover, the inclusion of the descriptor "Kauai-style" suggests that there is something unique about this event that relates to the island of Kaua'i. Here, it can be surmised that the addition of this description resonates with another aspect of the common-sense understanding of Pidgin, namely, that there may be special styles involved in the speaking and teaching (humorously) of Pidgin on different islands. Through these associations with humor, English, and Kauai-style, these references to Pidgin in this article simultaneously draws on the fact that their exists a language category "Pidgin" in the minds of people in Hawai'i and reinforces the importance of that category.

Excerpt (7) demonstrates a similar point, but it segues into an article that is actually written in Pidgin. The excerpt shows the lead-in to the article and also the very ending of the article, both of which employ Pidgin. The title of the article "Da Kine 5 Tings We Love: Valentine's Day" sets the tone with its usage of the Pidgin phrase "*Da kine*" and also the spelling of "*tings*." The article appeared in the *Honolulu Star-Advertiser* in the section titled "Features" on February 11, 2018. The date is relevant because the article itself offers, in Pidgin, suggestions for presents to give on Valentine's Day (February 14).

Excerpt (7): *Honolulu Star-Advertiser*, February 11
You still dunno what for buy your sweetheart for Valentine's Day on Wednesday? Author and playwright Lee A. Tonouchi, aka "Da **Pidgin** Guerrilla," offers his thoughtful suggestions:
((Followed by a listing of five things to purchase for your sweetheart—not included in the excerpt))
Try tell us what you stay loving this week by emailing features@staradvertiser. com. No forget da featured products might stay in short supply and maybe no more 'em available at da store locations; prices may stay varying, too.

The article begins with linguistic features, including the spelling "*dunno*" and the Pidgin grammar "*what for buy*," which will make sense to many readers when put together with the name of the author, Lee Tonouchi, and the term

148   Chapter Four

"Pidgin Guerilla." Pidgin Guerilla is recognizable because Lee Tonouchi is known in Hawai'i through this nickname and because he is a regular contributor to the newspaper. The combination of Pidgin with the term "Guerilla" will also make sense to readers because of the common-sense understanding that newspaper articles are typically written in English and not Pidgin. As someone bold enough to go against this expectation and write in Pidgin, Tonouchi fits with the understanding of what a "Pidgin Guerilla" would be, which allows this nickname to further reinforce Pidgin's existence as well as its status in society.

Moreover, the inclusion of Tonouchi's name with "Pidgin Guerilla" at the outset of the article raises the expectation that the rest of the article will feature Pidgin. Indeed, this is what happens as Tonouchi offers his five suggestions of *"tings for"* buy using a Pidgin grammar. Additionally, as shown in the excerpt, the article concludes with a solicitation of feedback that is also highly marked by Pidgin. This conclusion contains several usages of the Pidgin grammatical feature *"stay,"* and it also features the negative imperative *"no"* and the definite article *"da"* in *"no foget da featured products might stay in short supply."* Usage of the language category "Pidgin" at the outset as a part of "Pidgin Guerilla" is thus meaningful to the readers because it contextualizes the article as consisting of language that fits readers' common-sense understanding of what Pidgin is.

The four excerpts offered thus far in this section have underscored how meaningful the language categories of "Hawaiian" and "Pidgin" are to people in Hawai'i. In order to further emphasize how language categories are both pervasive and meaningful, I present two excerpts that make reference to the category "Japanese language." Excerpt (8) is from an article in the *Hawai'i Tribune Herald* on March 12, 2018, titled "A century of learning: Chiefess Kapiolani Elementary celebrates 100th anniversary." The article is not about the Japanese language but this category adds meaning to the context of the story.

Excerpt (8): *Hawai'i Tribune-Herald*, March 12
Kapiolani opened in 1917 as the Piopio School, according to research compiled by teachers Jackie Kubo Luna and Jonette Fujitake.

It is believed to have initially operated inside a **Japanese language** school building in the basement of a Buddhist temple. There were reportedly 144 students enrolled that first year and the school served primarily families in plantation camps, house lots and homesteads in the area.

After the second paragraph notes that the school opened in 1917 under the name Pi'opi'o School, the article reports that "it is believed to have initially operated inside a Japanese language school building." In doing so, it draws on the common-sense knowledge of readers not only that there exists an understandable category of "Japanese language," but also that there would have been "Japanese language schools" and "Japanese language school buildings." As noted in chapter 2, Japanese language schools were a relevant part of the linguistic history in Hawai'i, and even if current readers are unfamiliar with these schools, their familiarity with the category "Japanese language" and also with the possibility that there were would have been "Japanese language schools" in Hawai'i help them understand this part of the historical context of the Chiefess Kapiolani School. Excerpt (9), the final one of this section, invokes a very similar type of knowledge on a part of the readers of newspapers in Hawai'i. It is also from the *Hawai'i Tribune Herald*, this time an article published on March 1, 2018. Like excerpt (8), it comes from an article that does not focus on the Japanese language. The article is titled: "Kailua-Kona Lions collecting instruments for school."

> Excerpt (9): *Hawai'i Tribune Herald*, March 1
> Bernaldo Evangelista, Kealakehe Intermediate's band, orchestra and **Japanese language** teacher, said this year he has 200 students and just 100 working instruments. He's looking for any brass, woodwind and percussion instruments, as well as violins and cellos.

As part of an article that discusses attempts by the school to acquire instruments for their band, the article describes one of the leaders of the initiatives as "Kealakehe Intermediate's band, orchestra and Japanese language teacher." The category Japanese language is thus used as a part of a description of another category, teacher. In this sense, teaching works as an activity that can be attached to Japanese in a way that matches the common-sense knowledge in Hawai'i that the Japanese language is a subject taught in schools. Moreover, the inclusion of Japanese language with the descriptors of band and orchestra may seem to be a bit of an odd combination of subjects for a teacher, but it nonetheless related to another piece of accepted knowledge about teachers in Hawai'i, that they sometimes have to work in different capacities and teach various courses. In short, then, "Japanese language" serves as an easily understood category of language in both this excerpt and the previous one (excerpt 8). Language categories such as "Hawaiian," "Pidgin," and "Japanese" seem to be an integral part of the common-sense knowledge upon which people in Hawai'i rely in order to make sense of their social world. Accordingly, while such an analysis does not dispute the possibility that language categories may have begun as inventions, it is difficult to deny, as evidenced by their usage in newspapers, that they have become an essential part of everyday experience in Hawaiian society.

DRAWING CONCLUSIONS: HETEROGLOSSIA, LANGUAGE IDEOLOGIES, AND ENDANGERED LANGUAGES

The last section has attempted to show that despite frequent language mixing in Hawaiian society, language categories remain very meaningful to people. Even for those who want to declare languages as historical inventions that live on as ideogical constructions in the minds of people, it is impossible to dismiss the role that they play in the inferential processes of everyday members of society. The question becomes, then, what is the role of these language categories in a multilingual society where language mixing is so frequent that it seems to challenge our understanding of languages as separate, autonomous systems?

To attempt to answer this question, we must first emphasize the complexity of a multilingual society such as Hawai'i, where language mixing occurs frequently and where language (and other) ideologies abound. In fact, heteroglossia is still an apt term to apply here to this complexity because it emphasizes the sociohistorical associations involved in language mixing. It is thus difficult to employ a Hawaiian term or even the language category "Hawaiian" without indexing the various historical, nonreferential meanings that are attached. This is why it immediately becomes relevant to the newspaper excerpts (4) and (5) that Hawaiian is an endangered language that is in the midst of revitalization process. Such nonreferential meanings play an important role in the inferences made by speakers, writers, listeners, and readers of language in Hawai'i. The same is true of Pidgin, which indexes localness and often humor. It is thus nearly impossible in Hawaiian society to hear Pidgin mixed with other languages or to hear the category "Pidgin" and not draw inferences based on Pidgin's place in local culture. As shown previously, Pidgin is not always used for humor, but this indexical connection between humor, Pidgin, and localness is often part of the inferential process involved in understanding references to Pidgin in the newspapers observed in excerpts (6) and (7).

Explaining this complexity in multilingual Hawai'i also requires what I will refer to for the moment, following some of the ideas of Higgins (2009), as a "situational approach" to multilingualism that appreciates the dynamic role that context plays in a multilingual society. Here, it is not just that the use of language might vary from context to context but more importantly that ideological associations also depend greatly on contexts of language use. This would help explain why the same people in Hawaiian society might enjoy and support Billy Kenoi's heteroglossic mixture of Hawaiian, Pidgin, and English in a university commencement speech but also frown upon such language mixture in a regular high school classroom in Hawai'i where English is supposed to serve as the medium of education. On the surface, this seems like an internal contradiction, but it makes sense if we recognize that the inferences made by people vary from situation to situation.

Likewise, this would aid in undestanding why Kenoi's usage of Pidgin in the community meetings described in chapter 4 did not index humor while much of his usage of Pidgin in the commencement speeches in this chapter did. The inferential processes of people in multilingual Hawai'i allow them to see humor in Pidgin but, at the same time, to distinguish the contexts of language usage in which such an association is relevant.

This situational approach to multilingualism also works with language categories. Beliefs in language categories are relevant in some educational domains, for instance in promoting English in the classroom, but they are especially pertinent in the realms of language advocacy and language revitalization. A member of the Hawaiian language revitalization movement may be able to appreciate Billy Kenoi's inclusion of Hawaiian words and phrases in his heteroglossic speeches because it aligns Hawaiian with English in a public domain, but that same person would likely not be pleased at all if her/his student began mixing the Hawaiian language with English and Pidgin in speeches at a Hawaiian medium school in front of a group of Hawaiian speakers. A belief in the existence of the Hawaiian language and a fairly strict policy in terms of using Hawaiian is essential to the Hawaiian revitalization movement, even though members of the movement recognize that usage of Hawaiian, as well as the indexical meanings of Hawaiian, varies from domain to domain in Hawaiian society.

In fact, this is the place where those researchers who want to unmask languages as historical inventions risk doing a disservice to multilingual societies with indigenous languages. Blommaert (2003, 608), for instance, in his discussion of the effects of globalization on language, quotes both Hymes (1996) and Silverstein (1998) and writes that "we need to *move from Languages to language varieties and repertoires*. What is globalized is not an abstract Language but specific speech forms, genres, and forms of literacy practice" (emphasis in original). While this chapter has certainly shown that there is a need to understand heteroglossia in Hawai'i by viewing repertoires, speech forms, and the like, as resources separate from autonomous languages, the idea of "Language" is still important to understanding the multilingualism in Hawai'i. In fact, we can say that members of both the Hawaiian revitalization movement and Pidgin advocacy are attempting to use the idea of "Language" as a resource to support their causes as they lobby for the recognition of their languages. For the Hawaiians especially, who were victims of the English-speaking colonizers' belief in English and their eventual belief that

English should replace Hawaiian, it seems cruel to suggest now, as supporters fight to revitalize the role of Hawaiian in society, that we not focus on "Language" because it is a mere invention.

To be sure, it could be suggested that the Hawaiian language still lives on in the frequent heterolgossia that exists in society, as evidenced by the Hawaiian used in Kenoi's speeches and on the Kamehameha website. Blommaert (2003, 609), in fact, seems to refer to this possibility in discussing the effects of globalization on localized speech varieties and also the development of "international speech varieties" (see also, House 2003; Meyerhoff and Niedzielski 2003):

> We see that (American) English does not eliminate what was around, it does not bury the local languages, but it enters the repertoire of language users as a resource that fulfills both pragmatic functions, lingua franca functions, a certain degree of vernaculization.

Indeed, this is very much what happens in certain contexts, such as Kenoi's speeches. In being mixed with other languages, Hawaiian fulfills important pragmatics roles, namely, it imparts a traditional voice to the audience and it also enables Kenoi to situate that traditional voice on equal footing with English (and Pidgin) in the public sphere.

However, the growing number of Hawaiian language advocates would surely object to any suggestion that it is currently acceptable for Hawaiian speakers to mix English (and other languages) in their speech. This certainly happens in many domains in society and it is acceptable in some of those domains, but there are still contexts in Hawaiian society, particularly in institutions where Hawaiian is the medium of communication, where such mixture is viewed with disapproval.

The answer, therefore, seems to lie in a willingness to understand both how heteroglossia works in society and also how autonomous languages remain important to the social practices and inferential processes of members of that society. To do so, it is crucial to examine not just language usage but also "spaces of multilingualism" (Blommaert, Collins, and Slembrouck 2005). As Blommaert, Collins, and Slembrouck (2005, 197) emphasize, "multilingualism is not what individuals have and don't have, but what the environment, as structured determinations and interactional emergence, enables and disables." Accordingly, an ethnographic approach that examines language usage in spaces of multilingualism will aid in observing the extensive language mixing of heteroglossia in some situations and in appreciating the usage and even reliance on strict beliefs in language categories in other situations. The next chapter builds on this idea of a domain approach to multilingualism by investigating the place of the Japanese language in Hawai'i's multilingual landscape.

NOTES

1. The speech made at Hawai'i Pacific University is available at https://www.youtube.com/watch?v=p_7bqrzFYj4&t=464s. It was last accessed on June 19, 2018. The speech at UH-Hilo was previously available at http://www.bigislandvideonews.com/2010/05/16/video-kenois-uh-hilo-commencement-address/. Although it is no longer posted there, the website does feature a summary of the speech as well as further information about Kenoi (last accessed on June 19, 2018).

2. According to the Hawaiian dictionary at wehewehe.org, in addition to thank you, "*mahalo*" also conveys a sense of admiration and respect.

3. This and the next excerpt of data from the commencement speeches have not been presented previously in any publication.

4. The name of the session "*E Kanikapila Kākou*" is meant to be Hawaiian that basically means "Let's play music." The usage of this phrase adapted from Hawaiian is interesting because it makes this newspaper announcement an example of heteroglossia. However, I will not discuss the heteroglossic aspect of this excerpt at this time.

Chapter Five

The Many Japanese Voices in Hawai'i

INTRODUCTION

This chapter examines Japanese as an example of an immigrant language, a category used here merely to highlight the fact that the Japanese language, unlike Hawaiian and Pidgin, did not originate in Hawai'i.[1] It was brought here originally with the first Japanese immigrants in 1868 and has remained and grown in relevance since that time. Although Japanese is arguably more prevalent in current Hawaiian society than some of the other immigrant languages, including Chinese, Portugese, and Korean, many of the points made in this chapter are also meant to apply to other languages that have arrived in the islands throughout the course of history. In particular, this chapter intends to emphasize the diversity that exists within the Japanese language and also Japanese identities in modern Hawai'i.

In fact, even though the Japanese language has been an integral part of the linguistic landscape of Hawaiian society, one question that may be asked in a chapter attempting to understand the role of Japanese is: which Japanese language? Is it the language that first came over with the immigrant laborers from Japan, most of whom came from the countryside and spoke rural dialects? For many ancestors of these immigrants, this is the Japanese language that has been the most relevant in their lives.

Or, is it the Japanese of those most recently arriving from Japan either to visit as tourists or to live and work in commerce or in the tourism industry. These are the people who make the Japanese language highly visible in tourist areas such as Waikīkī, where it is possible to dine, shop, and find accomodations all through the medium of Japanese.

Or, is it the Japanese spoken by people in engaged in the learning of Japanese as a foreign language. Japanese language study is popular in Hawai'i, with some looking to employ Japanese in business sectors of Hawaiian society, particularly tourism. Others choose to study Japanese to connect with their cultural heritage. Still other learners without an ancestral connection may be inspired by an interest in the culture as a well a desire to connect with current fashions, foods, games, and technologies offered in Japan. Japanese is considered a very difficult language to learn for speakers of English, a point which suggests that the Hawaiian linguistic landscape may consist of speakers of Japanese with various levels of proficiency.[2]

And what about the people from Okinawa who also came over as plantation laborers beginning in 1900? These people, often referred to as Uchinanchu, speak languages that are related to Japanese but yet are known to be different. Despite longstanding attempts by the Japanese to assimilate the Uchinanchu into Japanese society and ensure that they learn only Japanese in school, there is now a growing movement to revitalize the cultures and languages of the islands of Okinawa (Yuuji 2018). Are the Uchinanchu people and their languages also to be included in a discussion of the "Japanese language" in Hawai'i?

These questions suggest that any attempt to ascertain the role of Japanese in Hawai'i's multilingual society will be incomplete if it is approached with a conception of the Japanese language as a single, stable entity. The Japanese language in Hawai'i is penetrated by different voices, including the old and the new, the rural and the urban, the standard and the nonstandard, and the formal and the informal. This chapter follows the focus in chapter 4 on heteroglossia in considering diverse Japanese voices in an attempt to understand some of the roles played by the Japanese language in the lives of people in Hawai'i. In order to do so, I begin with sections that elaborate on the questions raised earlier. Following that, the chapter presents analyses of four different sets of interviews involving people of different ages and backgrounds in Hawai'i.

The analysis in this chapter follows the work of Suzuki (2009), who asked similar questions about a Japanese identity in Hawai'i. Suzuki (2009) offers an analysis of how participants in a panel presentation titled "Japanese American Contemporary Experiences in Hawai'i" used categories such as "Japanese American" and "local Japanese" to construct different Japanese identities through the discourse. Her basic question, "Who is 'Japanese' in Hawai'i?" (Suzuki 2009, 148) stems from some of the same observations and questions raised in this chapter. This chapter contributes to the same line of inquiry as Suzuki's study by employing a discursive analysis that relies on an MCA perspective on categories as well as indexical approaches to identity in which identity construction is conceived of as an emergent process mediated by the ideological beliefs of the participants (Bucholtz and Hall 2005; Inoue 2004; Ochs 1992). The analysis in this chapter will focus on how the participants in the group discussions position themselves and others in discourse and thus construct discursive identities according to their beliefs concerning their relationships with the Japanese language.

THE JAPANESE LANGUAGE OF THE EARLY IMMIGRANTS

The first Japanese immigrants in 1868, called *gannenmono* because it was the first year of the Meiji Period in Japan, were from the urban area of Yokohama. However, the influence of their language in Hawai'i was minimal given that they were few in number and given that immigration from that location was discontinued shortly thereafter. The next wave of Japanese immigrants began again 1885, this time with workers from the countryside, particularly from the areas of Hiroshima and Yamaguchi (Hiramoto 2010). These workers spoke a dialect of Japanese known as *Chuugokuben* (the Chuugoku dialect); they spoke neither English nor standard Japanese (Hiramoto 2010). Later Japanese immigrants came from different parts of Japan, including Fukuoka, Okinawa, Fukushima, and Niigata, and thus spoke different dialects, but statistics offered by Hiramoto (2010; credit given to Nagara 1972) suggest that in the year 1929, nearly 65 percent of the Japanese immigrants were speakers of *Chuugokuben*.

The first immigrants were primarily young, male bachelors, but unlike Chinese immigrant workers before them who often found brides from within the local population in Hawai'i, many Japanese arranged for "picture brides" to come over from their hometowns in Japan. This helped maintain the Japanese dialects in Hawai'i. Further statistics offered by Hiramoto (2010; credit given to Nagara 1972) indicate that nearly 58 percent of the Japanese speakers in Hawai'i in 1960 spoke *Chuugokuben*. In this respect, little had changed in the interim thirty-one years.

With a large portion of the immigrants speaking *Chuugokuben*, it became the "standard Japanese" of Hawai'i. As Kimura (1988, 32) writes, "words that were peculiar to *Chuugokuben* became part of Hawaii's standard Japanese language or 'Hawaii no Hyojun Nihongo,' as it was described by the late Hoover Tateishi, a veteran broadcaster on Honolulu's KZOO Japanese language radio station." Its status as the Japanese language of power in Hawai'i prompted later immigrants to learn *Chuugokuben* in order to assimilate into the Japanese community (Hiramoto 2010). Those who did not do so risked being ridiculed and left out of the often close-knit communities. Kimura writes the following about the relationship of *Chuugokuben* to other dialects in Hawai'i:

> [CD] became the prevailing Japanese language in Hawaii. Those who spoke non-Chūgoku-ben were not readily accepted and were often ridiculed. The Tohoku dialects of northern Honshu were referred to by the derogatory nickname "Zuuzuu-ben," an onomatopoeic name for what the Tohoku dialect supposedly sounds like to non-Tohoku ears—"Zuu-zuu-zuu-zuu." Many of the immigrants who did not speak the Chūgoku-ben when they came to Hawaii eventually learned to do so. . . . The children of non-Chūgoku immigrants were also subjected to ostracism because of their dialects. (Kimura 1988, 30–31)

These observations were corroborated by both Hiramoto (2010) and Kimura (1988) through interviews with elder first generation Japanese, who are commonly referred to through the Japanese term *issei*. Kimura (1988, 31) reports an interview with an *issei* woman who came from Wakayama prefecture in 1923 as a child to join her parents who were already in Hawai'i:

> Since I could not understand what the other young people were saying I was Terribly lonesome. They teased me constantly, called me "Japan bobura," and "You Okinawan! You speak Okinawan!" They did not understand either my dialect [Kansai-ben] or Okinawa-ben. But I could not talk back because I could not speak their dialect.
>
> In those days all the children and young people who joined their parents after they finished elementary school [sixth to eighth grades] in Japan were treated by the other children and called "Japan bobura" [idiots from Japan], because they could not understand English or Chūgoku-ben.

This passage shows that it did not matter to the speakers of *Chuugokuben* that Wakayama prefecture is not in Okinawa and that Wakayama-ben is not spoken in Okinawa. What mattered is that any child not speaking *Chuugokuben* was different and thus the subject of ridicule.

Hiramoto includes in her study a woman named Rie, who was interviewed in 1975 at the age of 80. Rie was an immigrant from the Tohoku area who arrived in Hawai'i 58 years prior in 1917 and who described her efforts to assimilate to *Chuugokuben*. The translation is from Hiramoto (2010, 242):[3]

> *Sokoni hachinen orimashita. Sonotokini, ma, hazukashii koto ni ne, . . . chotto wakarinikukatta desu ne. Maa, onnashi nihonjin dakara sugu naraimashitanga ne . . . , Yamaguchi-ken no kotoba sokkuri naraimashitano yo. Aaja kooja warawarerukara narawannya ikemasen ne? . . . teakano tsukezô tokanantokatte waraimasun. Ee kusootto omotte ne, soo bakani saretewa komaruu yuute.*

I stayed there for eight years. At that time, well, I was ashamed but, . . . I had a hard time understanding [their dialect]. Well, because they are Japanese, too, I learned [their dialect] in no time. I became fluent in Yamaguchi dialect. Because they mock me for this and that [about my dialect], it had to be learned. . . . Country bumpkin or something, they laughed at me. Oh, shit, I said, don't tease me so much.

Of interest here is that the interviewee Rie was mocked for being a "country bumpkin" for speaking the Tohoku dialect and not *Chuugokuben* even though *Chuugokuben* has its origins in an area of Japan considered to be in the countryside.

Due to the relative insulation of the Japanese community in these early years of immigration, it was suggested that the Japanese language would persevere in Hawai'i for a long period of time, even despite the growing strength of English and the development of Pidgin. Indeed, as the *issei* immigrants gave birth to *nisei* ("second generation"), efforts were made to maintain the language ability of the children, including the creation of Japanese language schools. Matsuo Takabuki (1998, 27), one such *nisei*, writes in his memoirs:

While much of my Japanese language and values were passed on to me by my parents, Japanese language school also played a major role. Children of immigrant Japanese families were required to attend Japanese language school after English school from first grade through high school. Our language school was held at the Buddhist church in Haleiwa.

Takabuki's Japanese school on O'ahu was one of over 200 such schools which existed at some point throughout the islands between the years 1893–1940 (Menton and Tamura 1999). Asato (2006) reports that in 1920, 20,196 of the 20,651 children of Japanese ancestry in Hawai'i attended these schools, a percentage of 97.8. Menton and Tamura (1999) similarly note that these schools persisted until just prior to World War II, when approximately 80 percent of all Japanese children in Hawai'i were counted as attendees.

The influence of the language schools, as well as the arrival of immigrants from various parts of Japan speaking different dialects, including the standard language of Tokyo, meant that the speech of second (*nisei*) and third generation (*sansei*) Japanese in Hawai'i consisted of a mixture of Japanese voices. The following is taken from an interview by Yoshida (2008) of an elder *nisei* in Hawai'i referred to only as Mr. Inoue.

Washiga, yoo, Sakana demo chiisaino toru,
yeah? Uchino house motteittara, mendokusai tte okorukara,
ano house ittene. Ano obasanga, ryourishite, soide, tofuuya
dakara, aburaga aru, yeah? Asukode, soijake, washi, natsuyasumi
no tokide, uchinoieni ite tabetakoto nai.

As Yoshida points out, this is a rich piece of linguistic data that consists of the voices of different dialects and languages. Mr. Inoue makes use of English terms "house" and "yeah," standard (Tokyo) Japanese vocabulary and grammar such as *mendokusai tte okorukara* and *tabetakoto nai*, words from other dialects such as *soide* and *asukode*, which according to Yoshida (2008) were used in western and southern Japan, and also *Chuugokuben* with the term *soijake*. Just in this one passage alone then, there are at least four different voices, with three of them being "Japanese."

Unfortunately, the advent of World War II created an atmosphere of paranoia that led to the closing of the Japanese language schools (Menton and Tamura 1999). Fear of the Japanese and the Japanese language had actually begun many years prior to the war as relations between Japan and the United States worsened and as the United States promoted an agenda of Americanization in Hawai'i (Okihiro 1991). Japanese were branded a "menace," and in order to prove their willingness to follow the Americanization movement, many people of Japanese ancestry felt it necessary to abandon their language and began passing only English and/or Pidgin down to future generations of Hawaiian-born Japanese Americans.

Yet, even with fewer people acquiring fluent Japanese, remnants of the Japanese language, specifically the so-called Hawaiian Japanese (Kimura 1988), were left in Pidgin, especially in the lexical items adopted into Pidgin due to the influence of the early Japanese immigrants. Since the early Japanese immigrants were largely speakers of *Chuugokuben*, this meant that many of the adopted terms were from *Chuugokuben*. As Fukazawa and Hiramoto (2005, 164) point out, this "Hawaiian Japanese became a major donor language of HCE along with the Hawaiian language at the lexical level." Fukazawa and Hiramoto (2005) offer a list of some terms borrowed from *Chuugokuben* into Pidgin that include *bocha* ("bath or bathe"), *habut* ("pout or sulk"), *monku* or *monkutare* ("complaint") or ("complainer"), *bobora* or *bobura* ("pumpkin") or ("fresh-off-the-boat Japanese") and *baban* or *obaban* ("grandmother").

In an interesting study, Fukazawa and Hiramoto (2005) asked 38 Hawaiian-born Japanese Americans if they were familiar with these and several other words adopted from *Chuugokuben* into Pidgin. The 38 respondents were of various ages ranging from 20s through 80s, but all had ancestors who arrived in Hawai'i prior to 1924, which was the last year of official plantation immigration from Japan. The data collection was done in Honolulu in 2001, with Fukazawa and Hiramoto finding that the participants were familiar with many of the terms. In particular, they found that 37 out of 38 knew *bocha*, 36 were familiar with *habut*, 33 with *monku* and/or *monkutare*, 29 with *bobora/ bobura*, and 25 with *baban* or *obaban*.

Further observing their data for generational differences, Fukazawa and Hiramoto (2005) indicate that the elder *nisei* were more likely than the younger *sansei* and *yonsei* to know these words, and they thus suggest that with the passage of time, fewer people of Japanese ancestry in Hawai'i will remember these terms of *Chuugokuben* origin. While this may be true, I would also posit that in some rural communities, such as Hilo, which had a large immigration of Japanese in the plantation era, there may be more of a tendency for younger generations to retain these terms. For example, in one of the classes that I teach every spring semester called "Languages in Hawai'i," I ask my students whether they know these *Chuugokuben* terms and typically have at least several students of Japanese ancestry born in Hawai'i who exhibit familiarity. One male student told me that his grandmother called him "my little *bobura*," and many others explained that their families still use terms like "*bocha*" and "*habut*" regularly. I also had a colleague of Japanese ancestry who was born and raised on the Big Island inform me that he called his grandmother "*baban*." Interestingly, the response of the Japanese students born in Hawai'i contrast sharply with exchange students from Japan who take my class. When I ask them if they are familiar with the same terms, they almost always state they are not. Hence, it may be true that with the passing of time fewer people in Hawai'i are employing these *Chuugokuben* terms, but it still stands that for many families of Japanese ancestry, this is the Japanese that is the most meaningful to them because it offers a direct connection to their ancestors.

THE JAPANESE BOOM

Yaguchi and Yoshihara (2004) note that the Japanese interest in Hawai'i as a tourist destination began in the 1920s, even amidst poor relations between Japan and the United States. Yet, due to the war and also due to Japan's financial difficulties immediately following World War II, tourism from Japan to Hawai'i was relatively minimal prior to the 1970s. This began changing in the 70s as the Japanese economy gained strength and as Hawai'i turned into a "paradise" not just as a tourist destination but also because of the economic opportunities it presented for Japanese investors. In the words of Yaguchi and Yoshihara (2004, 89):

> During the seventies, more and more Japanese tourists sought a temporary escape into "paradise," thanks to such factors as the growing affluence of Japanese society, the introduction of the jumbo jet (Boeing 747) in March of 1970 for flights over the Pacific, and bulk-discount tickets. By 1978, more than 500,000 people were traveling annually to Hawai'i. Japanese corporations also began investing heavily in Hawai'i during the 1970s—purchasing hotels, condominiums, golf courses, and shopping complexes.

According to Yaguchi and Yoshihara (2004:89), "the number of Japanese visitors to Hawai'i reached one million in 1987" and currently "of sixteen million Japanese who now travel abroad every year, about two million are bound for Hawai'i, making by far their most popular foreign destination."

With the Japanese spending large sums of money in Hawai'i, there has been an impact on the economy in Hawai'i, which had gone from being dependent on sugar plantations to focusing on tourism. Former Governor Cayetano has made the public statement that "'it would be difficult to refute the notion that much of what Hawaii is today' would not have been possible 'were it not for the huge economic impact of Japanese investment in Hawai'i'" (Yaguchi and Yoshihara 2004, 82). The increase in Japanese tourism and Japanese investment has resulted in an increase in not just tourists speaking Japanese in Hawai'i but also people in the service business who speak the language in order to attract Japanese customers and promote spending. This includes people already living in Hawai'i who speak Japanese, but it also has led to an upsurge in Japanese speakers from Japan who come to Hawaii'i to live and work in businesses related to the tourist industry. The 2010 census showed that 15.7 percent of the population of O'ahu, which houses Waikīkī beach and other popular tourist destinations, identified as only Japanese (not of mixed race). This is significantly higher than the other Hawaiian islands. Hawai'i county on the Big Island of Hawai'i was the second highest with 9.8 who identified only as Japanese. This indicates then that O'ahu is the Hawaiian island most densely populated with Japanese. While this does not mean all 15.7 on O'ahu work in the tourist industry or are fluent speakers of Japanese, it does suggest a correlation with a need to provide service to Japanese visitors.

Some writers have made a distinction between these current Japanese nationals who live in Hawai'i to work in the service industry and the *issei* who came 100 or more years ago. The more recent arrivals have been called *shin issei* (Kameyama 2012; Komai 2015; Muromoto 1992; Suzuki 2009), and their children have been referred to as *shin nisei* (Kondo 1998). Both categories are a bit problematic since they are meant to cover diverse sets of people (Komai 2015); for example, *shin issei* is supposed to refer to arrivals post–World War II even though those who came soon after the war were not nearly as affluent as those Japanese who arrived in the 1970s. Nonetheless, this distinction has been made as a way of discerning between the two not only in terms of timing but also in terms of motivation and available resources for residing in Hawai'i. While the first *issei* started as poor plantation workers, the *shin issei*, especially those who arrived after the 1960s, tended to have more wealth and a higher education level with the ability to buy land and send their children to private schools.

The *shin issei* also differ in terms of language. Although they represent a wide range of residents in Japan with different dialect backgrounds, most, if not all of them, are capable of speaking "standard Japanese," considered to be based on the language spoken in Tokyo. Indeed, informal discussions with two acquaintances born and raised in Japan but now living in Honolulu seem to confirm this. Both of them are from the Osaka area and speak a dialect of Japanese known as *Oosakaben*, but they both note that they speak mostly standard Japanese in their workplaces in Honolulu, where they deal with other Japanese and also sometimes with tourists.

The upshot of the observations in this section is that the Japanese spoken in the areas of Hawai'i that cater to Japanese speakers is considerably different from the Japanese that was dominant during the plantation era in the late 1800s and early 1900s. The previous section suggested that the Japanese of the plantation era is still relevant to the relatives of the original *issei*, but the enormity of the tourist industry in Hawai'i makes it clear that modern standard Japanese must also be considered as a major part of the linguistic landscape of Hawai'i.

JAPANESE LANGUAGE LEARNING

Given the large number of Japanese immigrants who came to Hawai'i, and also given Hawai'i's location as the closest point in the United States to Japan, it is not surprising that the Japanese language has been one of the most popular languages chosen by students to study as a foreign language. As Kondo-Brown (2015, 164) states about the University of Hawai'i at Mānoa (UHM):

> UHM offers one of the largest Japanese language programs in North America; every semester, there are over 1,200 enrollees in various Japanese language, linguistics, and literature courses.

Additionally, Japanese language courses are offered at all other universities and community colleges in Hawai'i. Japanese is also offered at the high school and junior high school levels, and there are numerous adult education courses in Japanese throughout the different communities on the Hawaiian islands. Moreover, although few in number, there are still some Japanese language schools for school-aged children operating throughout Hawai'i. The largest of these schools, known as Rainbow School (*Reinboo Gakuen* in Japanese), states that has over 500 students, all at the elementary and junior high school level, who engage in a course of study through Japanese every Saturday (http://www.hjschl.org). With so many people of various ages studying the Japanese language in Hawai'i, it is difficult not to consider this aspect of the language in any attempt to describe the role of Japanese in Hawai'i.

Focusing on the teaching and learning of Japanese in Hawai'i is important because other than speaking to how popular the language is, it also aids our understanding in especially two ways of the varieties of Japanese that are prominent in Hawai'i. First, although there are various textbooks and materials employed in the different courses and levels of Japanese language study throughout, there seems to be an assumption that students of the language in Hawai'i are learning "standard Japanese." This, however, usually remains implicit in Japanese courses. For example, Kondo-Brown's (Kondo 1998, 1999; Kondo-Brown 2015) research on heritage language learners of Japanese in Hawai'i is informative because of a discussion of the influences of other languages in Hawai'i, especially Pidgin and Standard English, on the study of Japanese. Yet, there is rarely any discussion of the variety of Japanese studied by these learners nor is there mention of the varieties they may been exposed to. The following passage from Kondo-Brown (2015, 155–156) is a case in point that describes the desires of *issei* parents in Hawai to have their children grow up as speakers of Japanese:

> Japanese parents, especially Japanese mothers, who want their children to become bilingual, not only use the language at home, but also make various efforts to enhance children's linguistic networks in Japanese outside of the formal educational system (e.g., by sending children to Japan regularly, signing them up in Japanese language afterschool programs).

Despite the reference to Japanese mothers and language at home, there is no suggestion that learners may have been exposed to different varieties of Japanese. The purpose here is not to criticize this previous research but rather, on the hand, to point out that terms such as Japanese and Japanese language are often employed without reflection on the type of Japanese in question and, on the other hand, to suggest an implicit understanding that learners focus on modern standard Japanese.

Second, while the focus of learning may be standard Japanese, the learners themselves may be acquiring different proficiencies in the language. As some researchers (Kondo 1999; Sugita 2000; see also Crookes and Schmidt 1991 for general discussion about motivation) indicate, students in Hawai'i have various motivations for studying Japanese, including pleasing parents and grandparents who want them to maintain their cultural heritage, communicating with relatives, studying abroad in Japan, wanting to become bilingual, learning more about Japanese culture, succeeding in business, and fulfilling curricular requirements. With different motivations for studying Japanese and also with different access to educational resources, it also follows that learners will have varying levels of proficiency in the language. This goes for not just students in programs in English-medium schools in Hawai'i but for students in the Japanese language schools as well. Tamura (1993b) remarks that traditionally these schools were often unsuccessful in producing fluent speakers of Japanese because of indifference on the part of some of the *nisei* students who felt they were being forced against their will to learn the language (also see discussion in Sugita 2000).

There may be a tendency to overlook the possible effects of Japanese language learning on the status of Japanese in society since learners may typically only be attempting to use Japanese in class while employing primarily English or maybe Pidgin outside. Yet, in the case of Hawai'i, where the Japanese language serves an important role in the tourism business that undergirds much of Hawai'i's economy, it is common to find people of various Japanese proficiency levels working in tourism. As noted earlier, the Japanese constitute a majority of the tourists who visit Hawai'i, thus necessitating Japanese-speaking workers to meet the needs of the Japanese tourists. To be certain, this type of Japanese, which we might term language learners' Japanese, is not heard in all or even most regions of Hawai'i, but it is certainly relevant in places such as Waikīkī, parts of Hilo and Kona, and also Maui and Kaua'i, where the Japanese tend to visit.

THE UCHINANCHU AND THE RYUKYUAN LANGUAGES

The inclusion of the Uchinanchu and the languages of the Okinawan Islands in this chapter may seem slightly odd because the islands were originally an independent kingdom with its own government (Heinrich 2012). Although the languages are known to be related to Japanese, they have been classified as separate languages by several scholars. Heinrich (2012, 85), for one, asserts that "the Ryukyuan languages and Japanese are two distinct branches of the Japonic language family."[4] As Heinrich (2012) also notes, UNESCO (2009) lists six different languages in the Ryukyuan Archipelago, Amami, Kunigami, Uchinaaguchi, Miyako, Yaeyama, and Yonaguni. These languages are reportedly not mutually intelligible with Japanese (Heinrich 2012). Moreover, the immigration of the Uchnanchu to Hawai'i occurred separately from that of Japan. They began immigrating in 1900 to work in the plantation fields, and they distinguished themselves from immigrants from Japan, who were referred to by the people from Ryukyu as "Naichi" (Higa 2009). There is also documented discrimination of the Naichi toward the Uchinanchu (Higa 2009; Kimura 1988, 2009).

The Uchinanchu were, in other words, treated as different and as outsiders by the immigrants from Japan.

At the same time, though, the Japanese government has engaged in an exhaustive process of assimilating Okinawa into Japan. Soon after the beginning of the Meiji era in 1868, the Meiji government "openly claimed the Ryukyu Kingdom for Japan, and forcibly annexed it to the Meiji state, as Okinawa Prefecture, in 1879" (Heinrich 2012, 84). As part of this forced annexation, the king, King Shō Tai, was exiled to Tokyo. Hence, at the time of the Uchinanchu immigration in 1900, Okinawa was a prefecture of Japan.

In terms of language, the Japanese language gradually grew in prominence due to this annexation, but the Japanese government, in order to promote Japanese in the Ryukyu Islands, helped spur what is termed "the great dialect debate," *hōgen ronsō* in Japanese (Heinrich 2012, 124–132). As Heinrich notes, intense debate really began in 1940 and focused not really on the place of the Japanese language in Okinawa but rather on the status of the Ryukyuan languages within the Japanese state. Although there were supporters of the Ryukyuan languages, the position being pushed was that the Ryukyuan languages were not actual languages but instead dialects of Japanese. As Heinrich (2012, 129) notes, the position adopted "was essentially the position taken by dialectologist Tōjō, that the Ryukyuan languages were effectively dialects (*dai-hōgen*) of the national language." This view was all but a death sentence for Ryukyuan languages because it "led administrators to argue that any dialect unintelligible to speakers in the rest of Japan could not be maintained and should therefore be suppressed" (Heinrich 2012, 129). The adoption of such a position resulted in the usage of the Japanese language across the Ryukyuan Islands for most written and spoken forms of communication and the ultimate endangerment of the Ryukyuan languages, even though Ryukyuan continued to be used in private domains (Heinrich 2012). There has, therefore, been a government-promoted language shift in the islands with two of the languages, Yaeyama and Yonaguni, classified as "severely endangered" and the other four as "definitely endangered" by UNESCO (2009; Heinrich 2012).

Despite these processes of linguistic and cultural assimilation, people of Okinawan ancestry in Hawai'i maintain a sense of separateness and distinctness. Hawai'i has a set of what are referred to as *kenjinkai*, groups of prefectural associations that were created to allow the immigrants to gather and assist each other and also to engage in cultural activities. *Ken* is the word for prefecture in Japanese and emphasizes that these associations were created according to the prefectures from where the immigrants came. Hawai'i has several *kenjinkai*, including ones devoted to Fukuoka, Fukushima, and Hiroshima. There is also a separate one for Okinawa that is called the Hawaii

United Okinawa Association and *Okinawa jin rengo kai* in Japanese. Neither the English nor the Japanese names employ the word "prefecture." According to Higa (2009), the Japanese name originally was *Okinawa kenjin rengo kai* but they later dropped the *ken,* thus eliminating the part that emphasized it was a prefecture. There is a branch on the Big Island that uses the Hawaiian term *hui* ("association") in its name *Hui Okinawa*, and there is also a branch in Maui that, according to the website still uses the term *ken* in its Japanese name, *Maui Okinawa Kenjinkai.*

Higa (2009) notes that in response to the Okinawa Reversion Agreement of 1971, in which the United States relinquished to Japan the rights to Okinawa it had taken as a result of the Second World War, there were Uchinanchu in Hawai'i who were opposed to the return of Okinawa to the Japanese. This opposition stemmed from the discrimination the Uchinanchu endured from the Japanese not just in Japan but also in Hawai'i. Higa (2009, 39) writes in a passage that supposedly speaks on behalf of people in Hawai'i who are from Okinawa:

> When the Okinawans are subjected to such humiliation, there is no reason for Okinawa to become part of Japan. Okinawa should become an independent nation or it should part of the United States. . . . As long as they are willing to remain in the position of second-class Japanese, they will not be able to have a clear and sound identity. They should establish their identity as Uchinanchu immediately, assert the Uchinanchu in Hawaii.

Moreover, in another move that suggests a distinctiveness from the Japanese, some people of Ryukyuan descent in Hawai'i have begun not just to emphasize Okinawan culture but also to re-learn Ryukyuan languages. There is, for example, a group in Hilo on the Big Island who gather once a month to engage in Okinawan cultural practices as well as language lessons (Yuuji 2018). Also, beginning in 2015, there have been yearly summits on different Hawaiian islands to promote Ryukyuan languages and culture. These summits are sponsored by a group named Ukwanshin Kabudan and have thus far been held on Maui, O'ahu, and also the Big Island.[5] In addition, the University of Hawai'i at Mānoa features the Center for Okinawan Studies that sponsors linguistic and cutural events and also promotes courses at the university in the languages and cultures of Okinawa. These activities demonstrate attempts by people of Okinawan ancestry to practice their own languages and cultures. In terms of this chapter, it is still not clear whether Okinawa and the Ryukyuan languages should be included as part of a discussion of the Japanese language in Hawai'i, but as the analysis shows, the relationship between Okinawan and Japanese was relevant to two of the participants in the interviews.

ANALYSIS: JAPANESE IDENTITIES AND LANGUAGE VARIETIES IN HAWAI'I

The analysis in this section is based on data from four interviews, three that were conducted by myself, and one from YouTube. The four interviews are employed as a means of investigating the diversity of Japanese identities and the Japanese language in Hawai'i. Of the three interviews I conducted, one was with a third generation Japanese female aged 50 who grew up in a plantation village on the Big Island of Hawai'i. She will be referred to as LG. The second interview featured two female students at the University of Hawai'i at Hilo who both identify as bilingual speakers of Japanese and English. One of them was born and raised in Okinawa and the other on the main Japanese island of *Honshu*. The former will be referred to in the data as MC and the latter VC. The third interview involved myself and three students at the University of Hawai'i at Hilo who were in the beginning stages of Japanese language study. Two are male, referred to as DU and AA in the data, and the third, SO, is female. The two males are both born and raised in Hawai'i, DU in Honolulu and AA in Hilo, and have Japanese ancestry that can be traced to the plantation immigrants. SO is from Los Angeles and is not of Japanese ancestry. She came to Hilo approximately three years prior to the interview to attend college and focus on Japanese. The fourth interview, which I discovered on YouTube as part of my research, was conducted by a digital nonprofit media group known as ThinkTech that, according to its founder Jay Fidel, posts material concerning "tech, energy, diversification, globalism, and progress for . . . the state of Hawai'i" (https://www.youtube.com/user/ThinkTechHawaii). This particular episode features the host Hong Jian (referred to as Host in the excerpts) who interviews two male guests from the Japanese Cultural Center in Honolulu, John Okutani (JO) and Derrick Iwata (DI).[6] Table 5.1 provides a brief summary of the data.

Table 5.1. ThinkTech Hawaii Interviewees

Interview	Participants	Date Conducted
Third Generation Plantation Immigrant	LG (50- born on Big Island)	April 17, 2016
Bilingual Japanese-English Students	MC (48- born in Okinawa) VC (24- born in Okinawa)	May 16, 2017
Japanese Learners	DU (21- born in Honolulu) AA (22- born in Hilo) SO (22- born in Los Angeles)	September 14, 2017
Japanese Culture Center	JO (approx. 65 from Honolulu) DI (approx. 35 from Honolulu)	Posted March 3, 2013

The primary research method upon which the analysis is based can be described as "the ethnographic interview," a recognized technique in anthropology and linguistics in which the researcher takes a central role in probing the knowledge and understandings of their informants (Briggs 1986; Spradley 1979). There has been some debate in the literature about the usage of interviews to gather information concerning language usage (Speer 2002). Some critics argue that interviews involving the researcher should not be considered as "objective" data because interviews are unnatural, contrived situations that can be affected by the biases of the interviewer (Potter and Hepburn 2005; Suchman and Jordan 1990). In particular, researchers of social interaction point out that the interview "is a piece of interaction, not a neutral resource for a social science investigation" (Speer 2002, 512, referring to Mishler 1986). In a sense, these critiques seem readily applicable to the data in this chapter because I participated in three of the interviews in order to make sure the interview interaction focused on topics related to the Japanese language and Japanese identities.

On the other hand, it has also been suggested that as long as the interviewer is upfront about how her/his presence may influence results, "interviews are a valuable research tool which can provide interpretation and opinion that might not be available from observation alone" (Copland et al. 2015, 37). Copland et al. additionally note (2015, 27) that interviews can aid researchers "in gaining an *emic* perspective on research, that is, understanding from the participant's persesptive." Accordingly, in presenting the data, I will make sure that my own voice in the interviews is visible in the data excerpts (SS in the excerpts) in the form of questions that prompt the participants to elaborate on issues of language, identity, and culture. The information in the interviews in this chapter should not be treated as the final word on Japanese in Hawai'i but is meant to be appreciated for the efforts made by the participants to explain and understand their own relationship to Japanese identities and varieties of language.

As indicated earlier in the chapter, the analysis relies at times on insights from MCA in explicating how participants invoke and negotiate categories such as "Japanese" and "typical Japanese" in the interview discourse. Insights from MCA will contribute to a discursive approach to identity that treats categories and other features of language as resources "whereby interactants indexically position self and other in discourse" (Bucholtz and Hall 2005, 587).

The analysis is divided into four sections according to the interviews, beginning first with the YouTube interview of two representatives from the Japanese Cultural Center. After that, I will discuss the results of the interview with the third generation Japanese woman from the countryside of the Big Island,

170   *Chapter Five*

next I will focus on the discussion with bilinguals from Japan, and then I will conclude with the group interview of the Japanese language learners.

Diversity in Japanese Identities in the Interview of Two Representatives from the Japanese Cultural Center

The first excerpt is from the YouTube interview of two workers from the Japanese Cultural Center. The excerpt is from the beginning of the video as the host asks for statistics about the number of Japanese people in Hawai'i.

Excerpt (1): Cultural Center
```
 1  Host:   Let's hear (from) the current state of Japanese in Hawai'i uh first
 2          in terms of numbers how many are there or is there a way to tell
 3          how many Japanese are there in Hawai'i
 4          (.5)
 5  JO:     I think uh (.5) I guess you have to go back to the 2010 census
 6          to look at that although aa I'm not too sure (.) you know a lot of
 7          the classifications are different than before (.) Asian Americans
 8          Asian Pacific Islanders I mean that's another classification but
 9          aa (.) roughly I think aa percentage is about 23 percent Japanese
10          out of 1.3 million here in Hawai'i
11  Host:   mm-hmm
12  JO:     So[:
13  Host:      [that will come up to about 3[00
14  JO:                                     [300,000 and some[thing
15  Host:                                                    [10,000
16  JO:     Yeah somewhere around there but then aa (.) that also includes
17          th- (.) people who are mixed because as you know Hawai'i is very
18          multi-ethnic and aa a lot of aa in fact a lot of people who come
19          through the Japanese Culture Center a lot of them are not pure
20          Japanese but a mixture and you know we have a lot of different
21          ethnic groups and all combined and so I'm not so sure that figure
22          is a very solid figure as far as the number of only Japanese people
23          in Hawai'i that live here
```

The host asks in lines 1–3 for a number but, with the wording "or is there a way to tell how many Japanese are there in Hawai'i," also orients to the possibility that it might not be an easy question to answer. After a short pause (line 4), JO starts to respond in line 5 by referring to the 2010 census, but also employs the term "although" shortly thereafter in line 6, which signals a possible problem in responding. He does continue but does so by invoking the categories "Asian Americans" and "Asian Pacific Islands" in lines 7 and

8 in order to note that the classification system is different now. He does not pursue these two categories at that particular moment but instead goes back to the category of "Japanese" in line 9 to offer a statistic from the census, 23 percent. JO has thus provided an answer to the question, and seems in line 12 to make a move to continue speaking, but the host starts an utterance in overlap in line 13 with "that will come up to about 300." Yet, before she can finish her number, her talk is overlapped by JO in line 14 to confirm that it is 300,000 and something. The host overlaps again in line 15 to add the 10,000, which represents her calculaion of 23 percent of 1.3 million. JO agrees in line 16 but he adds the contrastive conjunction "but" that once again indicates a possible problem. He elaborates in lines 17 and 18 to say that the number includes people of "mixed" ethnicity because Hawai'i is "multi-ethnic." He then employs the adjective "pure" in line 19 to invoke another category, "pure Japanese," in lines 19 and 20. He has thereby explicitly invoked a pair of categories, "pure Japanese" and "mixed Japanese," that together might constitute some larger category "Japanese." Yet, he uses the contrast in the two to suggest that the number of 310,000 might not be a "very solid figure" if the goal was to focus on the category of "pure Japanese." The implication is that the presence of "mixed Japanese" in the category of "Japanese" might result in an inflated representation of Japanese in Hawai'i.

One of the points Sacks (1992) made when he developed membership categorization analysis is that people may have different ways of describing their own identity, for example, an individual can simultaneously be a "father," "teacher," "Christian," or "gambler," but not all of these categories are going to be relevant at all times. In the case of a census, this could become a practical problem because a resident may fall into the categories "Japanese," "Caucasian," "Asian American," and "Asian Pacific Islander" but not choose all of them when responding on a census. This seems to be the point JO starts to make when he invokes the categories of "Asian Americans" and "Asian Pacific Islanders" in lines 7 and 8. He is, in other words, suggesting that the identity classifications for the Japanese in Hawai'i could be quite diverse and that it might be difficult to know just which category (or categories) people may choose. Furthermore, by employing the term "multi-ethnic" and invoking the categories "pure Japanese" and "mixed Japanese," he is emphasizing the various types of Japanese identities that could exist in Hawai'i. In fact, as excerpt (2) demonstrates, JO continues in the interaction to stress the diversity of Japanese identities in Hawai'i.

Excerpt (2): Cultural Center
1 Host: Um talk a little bit of about the kind of origin of the Japanese (*)
            here in Hawai'i and also their relationships you know the
3   relationships between people coming from different areas in Japan

172   Chapter Five

```
 4  JO:    in terms of today you are [talking about
 5  Host:                             [aa first talk about the origin about where
 6          they came from
 7  JO:    (.) most of the Japanese immigrants came from hmm the southern
 8          part of aa Honshuu the main island of Japan and Kyushu mainly
 9          Hiroshima prefecture Yamaguchi prefecture and um (.) Fukuoka
10          and a Kumamoto (.) and also Okinawa also and these were um the
11          main groups that came came from Japan I think
```

The host puts forth a request in lines 1–3 for information about the category "Japanese," which leads JO to initiate repair in line 4. His utterance of repair in line 4 "in terms of today you are talking about" indicates that the category "Japanese" is too general and in need of further clarification between two possibilities, the Japanese of today and the Japanese of an earlier time. The host clarifies in lines 5–6 that she is requesting information about the "origin about where they came from." JO indicates his understanding in line 7 by invoking the category "Japanese immigrants" and by explaining through line 11 that they came from different places. He includes Okinawa in line 10 as one of the "main groups" (line 11), thus suggesting his view that the people from Okinawa be placed in the category of "Japanese immigrant."

JO demonstrates an orientation to the diverse nature of the category of "Japanese" in Hawai'i in two respects. First, his repair initiation that leads him to employ the category "Japanese immigrants" creates a distinction between this group and other more recent groups of Japanese in Hawai'i. Second, his listing of the different immigrant groups, including Okinawa, indicates that "Japanese immigrant" is itself a diverse category. The next excerpt, which shows the continuation of this discussion, further speaks to this diversity. It begins shortly after the end of excerpt (2).

Excerpt (3): Cultural Center
```
 1  Host:  One thing that I found out in um among the different kind of
 2          groups the Chinese, Japanese, the Filipinos is um a a lot of people
 3          come here to Hawai'i and they still identify pretty much with their
 4          origin they're not just from Japan they are from this particular area
 5          of Japan for example for example there is this a Okinawan
 6          Okinawan festivals um and clearly people who still very much
 7          identify with the origin of their immigration um that is that the case
 8          for the Japanese immigrant immigrants here after this um long time
 9          that have past
10  JO:    well again if you look at um when 18- from 1885 when the first
11          immigrants come came until now you are looking at 5 generations
```

12	basically so a lot of that uh continuity has uh uh sort of been
13	stretched and I wouldn't say it's been broken but you know it it's
14	been diluted based on Americanization but again Derrick can talk
15	to as far as some of the cultural things that we still kind of retain
16	here you know in the islands as far as the connection

In a move that seemingly builds on JO's reference in excerpt (2) to the various groups of Japanese immigrants, the host in lines 1–9 expresses her observation that people in Hawai'i tend to identify not just with the larger categories of "Chinese," "Japanese," and "Filipino," but also with the specific places from which they come. As an example, she offers Okinawan festivals, although she does not entertain the possibility that the Okinawans might put on such festivals to emphasize that they are separate from the Japanese. In fact, she invokes the category "Japanese immigrants" in line 8 in a way that indicates she is including the Okinawans within this larger category. In response to the host's statements, JO begins in line 10 by uttering "well again," which indicates that he will be referring back to something he already mentioned. Indeed, he goes on to stress through line 14 what may be generally referred to as the diversity of the Japanese in Hawai'i. He emphasizes in lines 11–12 that five generations have passed since the first immigrants, and he uses metaphorical language such as the "stretching of continuity" and "dilution" as well as the process of "Americanization" to state that the connections to the origins of Japanese immigration are not so clear. He does refer in line 14 to Derrick, the other participant in this interview, as someone who can speak to some of the traditions that have been retained, but for the most part, he has used his response to once again emphasize the difficulty in attributing specific Japanese identities to the people (more specifically, the descendants of the immigrants) who may be categorized as "Japanese immigrants."

Excerpt (4) provides one final excerpt from this discussion that highlights the problem with category labels such as "Japanese"and "Japanese immigrants." It follows shortly after the conclusion of excerpt (3).

Excerpt (4): Cultural Center

1	Host:	Just in terms of the relationships between the different Japanese
2		immigrant groups coming here to Hawaii were there you know
3		can you dete- detect any difference a conflicts in terms of the
4		relationships between the Japanese immigrants
5		(.5)
6	Host:	Or are they all identifying themselves just as Japanese immigrants
7		and what about the differences within
8		(.5)

```
 9  JO:    well you know I thin- I don't think there's um I mean we have
10         become so multi-ethnic here I mean (.) it's hard for us to just
11         identify with one group you know basically because a lot of I
12         guess you (.) would call it more identification with being local
13         as opposed to being from Japan, Korea or China
```

Even though JO had in excerpt (3) attempted to problematize the "continuity" of Japanese immigrants' identification with their places of origin, the host in lines 1–4 of this excerpt pursues the category "Japanese immigrants" and asks about "differences" and "conflicts" between the groups. Her initial yes-no question that begins in line 3 with "can you detect" is met with a .5 second pause in line 5, which prompts the host to attempt to clarify in lines 6–7 with another yes-no question that once again employs the category "Japanese immigrants." This second yes-no question is met with another .5 second pause and then an attempt by JO in line 9 to respond. His response, however, begins with "well you know" and contains some disfluencies that indicate trouble in responding. Then in line 10 he once again employs the term "multi-ethnic" to state through line 11 that it is "hard for us to just identify with one group," which serves as an explanation for why it is difficult for him to answer the question. If it is hard to identify with one group, it is difficult to judge how the groups that would fall into the category "Japanese immigrants" would have been in conflict. Finally, he invokes another category label, "local" in lines 12–13 to suggest that "local" is a more fitting category than "Japanese," "Korean," or "Chinese."

In invoking the category of "local," JO agrees with academics suggesting that, over the course of time, the identity of local became more relevant to the immigrants who came to work on the plantations than individual ethnic labels that include Japanese, Chinese, and the like (Okamura 1994; Takaki 1983). As discussed in chapter 3, it was through this identity of local that the families of the plantation workers eventually bonded together, largely through the language of Pidgin, in a working class identity that contrasted with the privileges and language associated with a haole identity. By choosing "local," JO is, for all intents and purposes, problematizing the host's attempts to divide the Japanese immigrants into groups according to their places of origin in order to ask her question about conflict among the groups.

These first four excerpts thus demonstrate the problems with labels such as "Japanese" and even "Japanese immigrant" in current Hawaiian society. "Japanese" begs the question as to whether it is "pure Japanese" or "mixed Japanese" while "Japanese immigrant" stands as a category that, due to the multi-ethnic character of Hawai'i, may not be as relevant in current society as the category "local." It is, in sum, difficult to explain a category such as "Japanese" in the current makeup of Hawai'i society.

The Many Japanese Voices in Hawai'i 175

However, at the same time that the category "Japanese" remains difficult to define in Hawai'i, it still remains relevant to many people in current society. The next section focuses on the interview with a granddaughter of a Japanese plantation immigrant and shows how she applies the category of Japanese to describe herself and others like her in Hawai'i.

Third-Generation Plantation Immigrant

This interview was conducted by myself and two research assistants, one who appears as RS and one who was present but not involved in the interaction. Excerpt (5) begins as RS asks the interviewee, LG, about the place where she was raised.

Excerpt (5): LG: Third-generation plantation
```
1   RS:   So, um tell (.) tell us about, uh where you grew up
2   LG:   Um, I grew up in a plantation community Hamakua sugar we
3         lived in a camp um it was mostly Filipino and Japanese and
4         plantation life it was very um fun time
5   RS:   Um, what did you guys used to do for fun as kids
6   LG:   oh we used to do all kinds of stuff, like of course there was the
7         bikes. We used to ride skateboard we used to fish a lot
8         we used to fly kites shoot BB gun play slingshot that kind
9         stuff go hiking and uh, go to the cane fields and stuff.
10  SS:   oh who's who's we? who'd ya hang out with?
11  LG:   oh my brudda guyz. my sista. yeah ((laughs))
12  RS:   So, um, in your neighborhood, um, what was it was it like an
13        even mix of everything or more Filipino or Japanese?
14  LG:   more Filipino. especially um, right next to us um we, had a
15        neighbor, (*) and (*) and their garage was like a
16        casino where they're playing poker and all of the Filipino guys
17        with their chickens used to come so, that was one of the major
18        hangouts so we used to always, there was always some kind of
19        action at their house.
```

LG employs the categories "Filipino" and "Japanese" as she explains in lines 2–4 that she grew up in a plantation community. RS pursues these categories further in lines 12–13 as he asks about the mixture of "Filipino" and "Japanese" in her community. LG responds in line 14 by saying "more Filipino" and she then goes on to explain about her neighbors and the activities that went on in their garage. She concludes in lines 18–19 by noting that there was always "some kind of action at their house."

176   *Chapter Five*

Unlike the first four excerpts, where the host and the participant JO had difficulty negotiating the category "Japanese," LG in this excerpt employs it without problem. Even though she lived among a group of people that were unified as a "plantation community," the category "Japanese" is still relevant to her because it distinguished her and her family from another category, "Filipino." The next excerpt, excerpt (6), further shows how meaningful the category of "Japanese" is to her. This excerpt begins shortly after excerpt (5) as LG is explaining how her mother would clean and prepare the chickens that died after the chicken fights in which her father participated in with the Filipino neighbors.

Excerpt (6): LG: Third-generation plantation
1 LG: then she use to clean 'em and show us the heart, cut open the
2   stomach show us all the feed (.) show us the balls and all dat kine
3   stuff so it was like
4 RS: like anatomy class
5 LG: Ya ya ya and then make chicken sabao after that
6 RS: ya sabao so you know you-you do like the Filipino recipes
7 LG: Ya ya ya I like Filipino food
8 RS: Did your mom make mostly Japanese food
9 LG: She made some but she made many kinds of food- some
10   Filipino food, American, everything
11 SS: But your family was Japanese yah
12 LG: Oh yeah, we're Japanese but we just mixed all the food together
13   with our neighbors

After RS likens the mother's preparation of the chicken to anatomy class in line 4, LG agrees and states that her mom would make a dish called chicken sabao. This next leads RS in line 6 to invoke the category of "Filipino" to ask whether she likes Filipino food. LG confirms in line 7 that she does and RS follows in line 8 with another question that specifically asks whether her mother made mostly Japanese food. LG notes in her response in line 9 that her mom made some but also made various foods that include Filipino, American, and everything. SS, the researcher, interjects in line 11 to confirm that LG's family was Japanese, to which LG strong confirms with "Oh yeah," before stating explicitly "we're Japanese" in line 12. She then adds "but" to stress that food was not only Japanese but instead was mixed together with the foods of the neighbors.

LG's quick and assertive response that her family is "Japanese" suggests that this category has meaning to her. At the same time, though, it is difficult to gauge based on this excerpt why it is so meaningful. This category is apparently not derived from the types of food that her mother made and her family consumed. As she states, her mother made "everything" and the family mixed their food with their neighbors. Excerpt (7), from the same interview, speaks to both the meaningfulness of the category as well as the difficulty in pinpointing the source of such meaning. It focuses on language and is taken from a point in the interview following excerpt (6).

Excerpt (7): LG: Third-generation plantation

```
1   SS:   so your parents (.) you said your parents spoke (.) Japanese ya?
2         Did they ever try to speak- teach you Japanese?
3   LG:   No they never did.
4   SS:   Never?
5   LG:   Never.
6   SS:   But how abo-ya (.) you lived with your grandparents too or did
7         they-they [were?
8   LG:            [My grandparents lived in Ookala
9   SS:   Oh
10  LG:   So they spoke English with us but when they conversed with my-
11        my parents (.) sometimes they had more of a tendency to talk
12        Japanese. (.) Over the years they spoke more English.
13  SS:   Oh okay
14  LG:   Ya
15  RS:   Um. Did they ever explain why they (.) they never wanted to teach
16        you (.) how to speak Japanese or
17  LG:   No we never questioned it.
18  SS:   Did that make you feel strange to see your close relatives speak
19        Japanese but not understand what they were saying
20  LG:   No we were just typical Japanese kids on the plantations (.) my
21        Japanese friends at school all spoke English (.) or I guess Pidgin
```

The excerpt begins as the researcher SS employs the term Japanese to ask in lines 1–2 about LG's language background. Following up on the fact that LG had previously noted in the interview that her grandparents and parents spoke Japanese, he asks whether they taught her the language. She replies that "they never did" in line 3, and confirms this in line 5 after being asked further by SS in line 4. SS then asks another question in line 6 about LG's grandparents that prompts LG to explain in line 8 that her grandparents lived in a place called 'Ō'ōkala, which is different from the plantation camp where LG lived.[7] Following an "oh" token from SS in line 9, LG describes in more detail in lines 10–12 the usage of Japanese and English by her grandparents. Shortly thereafter, RS further probes the issue by asking in lines 15 and 16 if her grandparents explained why "they never wanted to teach you." LG responds in line 17, just like she did in lines 3 and 5 with a direct negative statement.

This leads to a yes-no question from SS in lines 18–19 asking if this made her feel "strange," to which LG once again replies with a direct "no" in line 20. The only difference in her response here is that she adds an account to her negative response as she invokes a category, "typical Japanese kids" and links that category to a specific language behavior, speaking English and Pidgin, but not Japanese.

Just as LG employed the category "Japanese" at the end of excerpt (6) to describe herself and her family, so too does she apply a related category "typical Japanese kids" to herself at the end of this excerpt. Note, though, that in both excerpts (6) and (7), her invocation of these categories comes as a result of a line of questioning from the researcher that, in a sense, pushes LG to define herself. In excerpt (6), SS asked her a tag question in 11 that employed the category "Japanese" and in excerpt (7), SS once again pushed the issue in lines 18–19 with the yes-no question that asks her if she felt strange. Without these two utterances from the researcher, it is probable that LG would not have invoked those two categories. Here, it is relevant that in his discussion of categories, Sacks (1992; also see Kitzinger 2000) sometimes pointed to details of interaction that were not stated explicity. By not noting them explicitly, participants can orient to them as "normal" or "accepted" aspects of their lives. Hence, the fact that LG only employs the category "Japanese" when specifically asked suggests that it is in general an accepted (yet often unmentioned) aspect of her identity. In excerpt (6), she only invoked "Japanese" when the connection between food and identity was question, and in excerpt (7), she responded with "typical Japanese kids" only when pressed about the relationship of language to her ethnicity.

Nonetheless, it is of interest that LG employs the term "typical Japanese kids" when pressed to categorize herself. It is interesting because it seems to contradict a belief in a direct relationship between ethnicity and language. Here, it does not matter that LG is not a speaker of Japanese for her main identity to be "Japanese." In fact, she seems to be specifically "typical Japanese" because she does not speak Japanese but instead speaks English and also Pidgin. It is also important that she adds the plural term "kids" to this category because it emphasizes her belief that she is not unique in possessing such a relationship between language and ethnicity. This categorization, at least according to LG, fits many in a situation similar to hers. In other words, this identity category may not apply to all people with a Japanese background in Hawai'i, especially those recently coming from Japan and living and working in tourist areas such as Waikīkī, but it certainly seems to be applicable to those like LG that were "typical Japanese kids" growing up in the plantation camps.

In our interview with her, LG did not express an ideological belief that a person had to speak a particular language to claim that identity, but there were some interviewees that adopted a stronger view concerning the connection between language and identity. The next subsection focuses on the interview involving the two Japanese-English bilingual women and provides examples of such a stance.

Bilinguals from Japan

Excerpt (8) shows how one of the participants, MC, associates language ability with her identity as a "halfbreed." Prior to this excerpt, MC had described herself as someone born in Okinawa and possessing a mixture of three ethnicities, Japanese, Okinawan, and Hawaiian.

Excerpt (8): Bilinguals from Japan
```
 1  MC:   And then my Japanese and Okinawan are self taught
 2  SS:   oh=
 3  MC:   =yah because I have never been to a Japanese school
 4        I am [still teaching myself ah Japane[se
 5  SS:        [that is pretty (*              [(*)
 6  VC:                                        [naah
 7  MC:   ye[s
 8  VC:     [she- she knows everything
 9        ((laughter from all three))
10  MC:   no no
11        ((further laughter))
12        I really have to (.) um because a lot of my friends are bilingual
13  SS:   un
14  MC:   but mostly they are trilingual because most of my friends speak
15        Okinawan too
16  SS:   cool [oh
17  MC:        [ah they do not read and write and Japanese
18  SS:   ah o[kay
19  MC:       [and that is pretty typical
20  SS:   yeah sure
21  MC:   we call ourselves halfbreeds
22  SS:   hmm
23  MC:   haafu ne
```

This excerpt focuses on MC's language abilities as she states in line 1 that her Japanese and Okinawan are self-taught and in line 3 that she did not attend a Japanese school. After MC comments in line 4 that she is still teaching herself Japanese, VC overlaps to reject this assessment with "naah" in line 6 and "she knows everything" in line 8. This elicits laughter from all participants, but MC utters "no no" in line 10 and then follows in line 12 with "I really have to (.) um because a lot of my friends are bilingual." She then upgrades her statement in line 14 to say that her friends are trilingual with Okinawan included. She does note in line 17 that they do not read and write, which seems to be referring especially to the Japanese language given that MC had earlier stated that she had been educated at an American school. She further notes in line 18 that "that is pretty typical" before putting herself together with her friends in line 21 in the category of "halfbreed." Finally, she employs in line 23 the Japanese term "haafu" which is used for people like herself, who are half-Japanese and half-Western. Yoshida (2014) in fact defines "haafu" as half-Japanese and half-white. It does not matter, though, that MC has already claimed to be a mix of three ethnicities, none of which are actually Caucasian; she and her Okinawan speaking friends are in the category of "haafu."

This excerpt speaks to especially two points. First, it is of interest that MC constructs Okinawan as a separate language and also ethnicity. In fact, her upgrade in lines 12 and 14 from bilingual to trilingual indicates an attempt to emphasize Okinawan as she includes the phrase "because most of my friends speak Okinawan too" in lines 14–15. Second, it shows a belief in the connection between language and identity, although it is not necessarily a direct correlation. Like LG in excerpt (7), MC uses the descriptor "typical" to formulate a specific relationship of language to identity. In MC's case, it is typical that her friends do not read or write Japanese, although they are trilingual in Japanese, Okinawan, and English. This lack of writing ability, in fact, seems to be what motivated MC to teach herself Japanese even though she already knows it and even though it also seems to be a part of constituting the identity of *haafu*, at least according to MC.

MC in excerpt (8) describes the situation in Okinawa, but the same two participants negotiate a similar type of language-identity relationship when the discussion turns to their experiences in Hawai'i. Excerpt (9) focuses on their participation in the association *Hui Okinawa*, which as mentioned in this chapter, is devoted to people of Okinawan descent to promote their ancestral culture and language(s).

Excerpt (9)
1   MC: And then of course being away from Okinawa and not being
2   able to speak Okinawan on a regular basis
3   SS: yeah=
4   VC: =yeah cause the community here even though they say they're
5   Okinawan [they're

```
 6  SS:              [un
 7  VC:  they're generations (far) and I feel like they don't know actual
 8       like speak fluent Okinawan
 9  SS:  yeah right right
10  VC:  they're just familiar with their own culture
```

This excerpts begins as MC suggests in lines 1–2 that is difficult for people in the *Hui Okinawa* to speak Okinawan since they are not there. After a short response token from SS in line 3, VC enters the discussion in lines 4–5 and then again in lines 7–8 to note that even though the community in Hawai'i categorizes themselves as "Okinawan," they do not speak the language fluently. She further adds in line 10 that "they're just familiar with their own culture."

The way VC constructs her comment in lines 4–5, with the term "even though" adds a bit of an evaluative tone to her utterance. The expectation would be that since they say they are Okinawan, they would speak the language. Yet, she comments that they do not "speak fluent Okinawan," thus constructing them as somehow odd, or at least notable for their lack of fluency. Indeed, the next excerpt, excerpt (10), further demonstrates how the language usage in the *Hui Okinawa* did not necessarily fit with the expectations of VC and MC based on ethnic background. This excerpt begins as VC employs the Japanese term *kenjinkai*, which, as discussed earlier, refers to the associations in Hawai'i for people of Japanese ancestry. In line 1, VC begins to liken most of the *kenjinkai* to the *Hui Okinawa* in terms of language usage, namely that they do not use the language of their ancestral homeland.

Excerpt (10):
```
 1  VC:  Like most of the kenjinkais are like that
 2  MC:  But I think the other kenjinkais um because a lot of the
 3       new first generations come in
 4  SS:  yeah yeah
 5  MC:  and it's part of the club that aa a lot of them do speak
 6       Japanese
 7  VC:  Japanese [yeah  (*)
 8  SS:           [Japanese (*)
 9  MC:  in their whatever Hiroshima-ben or [(*)
10  VC:                                     [dialects yeah
11  MC:  yeah the hui Okinawa itself it's it's not you don't hear it
12  VC:  no no [(*)
13  SS:        [but how about how about Japanese then is Japanese
14       kind of the same way you know
```

15	VC:	I was in the Hui Okinawa [but we counted we counted in=
16	MC:	[(**)
17	VC:	=Okinawan but everything else was like Otsukaresama desu
18		and it was like just common phrases in Japanese
19	SS:	oh so you guys spoke in=
20	VC:	=oh we spoke in English=
21	SS:	=you spoke in English=
22	VC:	=yeah there are some Japanese people who jus- who's been living
23		here maybe six years who speak Japanese of course but that's
24		about it

MC leads in 2 with "but" in order to offer a counter viewpoint. She invokes the category "first generations" to maintain through line 6 that a lot of them do use Japanese. Both VC and MC seem to recognize this in lines 7 and 8 before MC elaborates in line 9, using the Japanese term *Hiroshimaben* ("Hiroshima dialect"), that the "first generations" will be speaking the dialect of their Japanese prefecture. VC seems to offer agreement in line 10 with "dialects yeah" which leads MC to suggest in line 11 with the double negative "it's not you don't hear it" that Okinawan is heard in the *Hui Okinawa*. VC begins to express in line 12 express another opposing view with "no no" before the researcher SS overlaps her to ask a question in lines 13 and 14. Yet, before he can finish, VC enters in line 15 to note her point of opposition. She explains through line 18 that the *Hui Okinawa* counted in Okinawan but also used Japanese phrases such as "*Otsukaresama desu*" ("Thank you for your work"). This observation seemingly serves as evidence that Okinawan was actually not used that much. SS begins in line 19 with an utterance that begins to pose a question about language usage within the *Hui Okinawa*, but VC quickly emphasizes in line 20 that they spoke mostly in English. After a repeat from SS in line 21, VC notes in lines 22 and 23 that there are some people who recently came from Japan who speak in Japanese, but she ends with the contrastive statement "but that's about it" that points back to her original assessment that English is most commonly used.

VC's description in this excerpt suggests that, at least to her, there is something odd about the language usage in the "kenjinkais." Although these are groups that are organized based on their ancestral connections to places in Japan and Okinawa, they employ mostly English in their meetings, except for some who have arrived relatively recently from Japan. Membership in *kenjinkai* does not depend on speaking a specific form of Japanese and does not, in fact, require much, if any, Japanese at all. This more or less fits with LG's category of "typical Japanese." LG did not affiliate herself with a specific place of origin in Japan in her interview, but it was clear that membership in her category "typical Japanese" did not require Japanese ability. This is undoubtedly the case for many members of *kenjinkai* in Hawai'i, as the name *kenjinkai* itself, at least as it is used in Hawai'i, suggests that members will have a Japanese identity but does not necessarily speak the ancestral language.

It is also noteworthy that there seems to be a kind of negative evaluation expressed in this excerpt toward heteroglossia. VC notes that the members of the *Hui Okinawa* counted in Okinawan, used Japanese phrases, but otherwise spoke mostly of English. Yet, even though chapter 5 attempted to emphasize how common such language mixing is in Hawai'i, VC still in this excerpt as well as excerpt (9) appears to consider such as language behavior as odd since the members claim affiliation with a specific place, namely, Okinawa that does have its own language. Here, it is interesting that VC does show some language mixing in her own speech with the use of the term "kenjinkais," which adds the English plural "s" to the Japanese term *kenjinkai*.[8]

The three excerpts in this subsection thus reveal that people may possess different approaches to the relationship between language and identity. For some like MC and VC who grew up outside of Hawai'i, there seems to be a belief that people claiming membership in a specific group speak that language. In particular, VC seemed to hold this view more strongly than MC as she interpreted the lack of Japanese and Okinawan in the *kenjinkai* as strange. Such an approach seems to stand in contrast with LG's categorization of herself and her family as "Japanese" regardless of Japanese ability. For LG, in fact, her lack of proficiency in Japanese made her a "typical Japanese kid."

The analysis thus far has focused on the usage of identity categories and how they are or are not connected to languages such as Japanese and Okinawan in Hawai'i, but little has been said about the actual varieties of Japanese spoken in Hawai'i. Here, it is notable in the last excerpt, excerpt (10), that MC does try to emphasize that some members of *kenjinkai* speak dialects of Japanese, a point that VC initially agrees with in line 10. Her attribution of dialects to a specific membership category, first generation, is interesting because it creates a kind of contrastive pair that centers on the activity of speaking Japanese dialects. First generations are those who were born in Japan and are also those speaking varieties of Japanese. They contrast with second generations, who are not born in Japan and are probably speaking English. While such a contrastive pair suggests that varieties of Japanese were somewhat limited, the interview with learners of Japanese was more focused on diversity within the Japanese language in Hawai'i.

Learners of Japanese

The first excerpt in this subsection focuses on the experience of the one learner who grew up in O'ahu, DU. As evidenced by line 1, he is describing Japanese usage in his own family. As a point of reference, it can be noted that it was his great grandparents that originally came to O'ahu to work in the plantation fields.

Excerpt (11): Japanese learners
```
 1  DU:  My family has what's like clashing Japanese dialects
 2  SS:  oh (.) what do you mean clashing dialects
 3  DU:  My grandma we call her baba (.) her parents were born in Japan
 4       but she grew up on Oahu and learned Japanese and English
 5  SS:  aa okay
 6  DU:  and her Japanese was a very informal way of speaking but my
 7       Aunty Fumi was born in Japan and knew formal Japanese
 8  SS:  oh yeah
 9  DU:  And so they both speak Japanese in a different way and they
10       sometimes have some misunderstandings
11  SS:  Like what happens
12  DU:  well I asked my mom and she thinks it's because my grandma's
13       Japanese is from the plantations and maybe has Pidgin in it
14  SS:  Do you think that makes your grandma's Japanese any lesser than
15       your aunty's
16  DU:  Nah they are both good it's just that my grandma's is easier for me
17       to understand since it has Pidgin words
18       ((laughter))
```

DU asserts in line 1 that his family has "clashing Japanese dialects," and after SS asks for clarification in line 2, DU explains in lines 3–4 that his grandmother learned her Japanese on O'ahu at the same time as English. He then describes her in line 6 as having "a very informal way of speaking." He continues in line 7 to suggest that this contrasts with his Aunty Fumi who was born in Japan and speaks formal Japanese. After a short response from SS in line 8, DU elaborates in lines 9–10 to stress that they speak "in a different way" and that they "sometimes have misunderstandings." SS asks for more information in line 11, which prompts DU in lines 12–13 to report that his mom attributes this difference to the place where the two were raised. More specifically, his grandma was raised in Hawai'i on the plantations and thus has Pidgin in it. SS poses a follow-up questions that asks DU to pass judgment on the grandma's Japanese, but he states in lines 16–17 that "they are both good" and that his grandma's Japanese is easier for him to understand "since it has Pidgin words."

Despite the different origins of the languages spoken by DU's grandma and aunt, they are both categorized by him and by the researcher SS as Japanese. This categorization suggests that in addition to the Japanese dialects that might be spoken by *kenjinkai* members, the Japanese learned by second generation speakers serves as another variety of Japanese in Hawai'i. As was the case for DU's grandmother, many of the children born to the plantation immigrants grew up speaking a Japanese that was learned in Hawai'i, with possible influences from Japanese dialects such as *Chuugokuben* and from the creole language of Pidgin. As discussed earlier, Pidgin itself was affected by several languages that included Hawaiian, Chinese, Portuguese, and English. Despite these possible influences, this language also falls under the category of Japanese, as evidenced by DU's calling it so, but it may have been considerably different from the Japanese dialects employed in the various areas of Japan.

Concerning this possibility that a variety of Japanese spoken in Hawai'i may diverge significantly from varieties spoken in Japan, I offer one final excerpt from the discussion with the Japanese learners. Excerpt (12) demonstrates some of the creativity that can affect the repertoire of learners of Japanese.

Excerpt (12): Japanese learners
1 SS: What do you do if you know you can't say something fully
2   in Japanese?
3 AA: I ask my Japanese friends
4 SS: okay but aa=
5 SO: =I have a friend learning Japanese who always says half English
6   half Japanese she is not afraid to put them together
7 SS: Do you have any examples
8 SO: Yeah she always say owari as in are you owari
9 AA: I always use wakaru like Can you wakaru and I wakarued that
10 SS: really? That's quite=
11 AA: =oh and also are you daijoubu
12 SS: Do you think that kind of mixing is bad
13 AA: My teacher does not like it
14   ((laughter))
15 SO: I think it is okay and fun with friends and I know the Japanese
16   students do it too when they don't know English words
17 AA: Yeah, codeswitching is a part of communication anyway so
18   why not ya know

In response to SS's question about what the learners do if they are unable to say something in Japanese, AA responds in line 3 that he asks his Japanese friends. As SS starts to formulate a response, SO offers the information in lines 5–6 that she has a friend learning Japanese who is not afraid to mix the languages. SS asks for examples in line 7, and two of the learners answer unhesitatingly with the examples "are you *owari*" ("finished") in line 8, "can you *wakaru*" ("understand") and "I *wakaru*ed" in line 9, and "are you *daijoobu*" ("okay") in line 11. In particular, "I *wakaru*ed" is striking because it is not just the insertion of Japanese words into an English grammar but instead adds the English past "ed" morpheme to a Japanese word, thus creating a hybrid that is neither English nor Japanese. SS follows up with a question in line 12 that asks the learners if they think that this kind of mixing is bad. AA offers a first response in line 13 that draws laughter from the other participants, but SO follows in lines 15–16 with the remark that it is "okay and fun," which leads AA to re-enter the discussion in lines 17–18 and, using the term codeswitching, states that it is a part of communication. AA and SO thus seem to have a tolerant approach to the mixing of Japanese and English in speech.

The examples given by the learners in the above excerpt would probably be characterized as an English grammar that is mixed with Japanese words, something which may be attributed to the fact that both AA and SO are at the beginning stages of their Japanese study and thus are not yet comfortable with a Japanese grammar. It does nonetheless demonstrate the ability of learners of Japanese as well as their willingness to mix the two languages and even create new forms.

Based on this one excerpt involving two of the Japanese learners, it is difficult to gauge the extent of this type of language mixing in Hawai'i, but if we note again the popularity of Japanese study in Hawai'i, we can imagine that the usage of forms of Japanese with English (and possibly other languages) would not be uncommon in situations in Hawai'i involving people who are studying or have studied Japanese. Moreover, for learners at more advanced stages of Japanese study, it is a possibility that they would be producing a Japanese grammar with innovate uses of English within. I discuss this and other varieties of Japanese in more depth next.

CONCLUSIONS: STRESSING THE HETEROGENEITY OF THE JAPANESE LANGUAGE

Although this chapter presented excerpts from four interviews, the analysis is incomplete in terms of the possibilities of Japanese identities and varieties of Japanese found in Hawai'i. For instance, it would be interesting in future studies to consider the voices of first generation speakers of Japanese who came more recent to Hawai'i to work in the tourist industry. Likewise, it would be informative to interview the children of first generation speakers who were born in Hawai'i and grew up speaking both Japanese and English. As Kondo (1998, 1999, 2015) shows in her research, their experiences with the language and their sense of their own identities can be very diverse.

That having been said, the four interviews do suggest the heterogeniety of Japanese in Hawai'i. First, in terms of identities, the interviewees exhibited a diverse understanding of the category of "Japanese" in Hawai'i, with at least some of the views contrasting with one another. The four excerpts from the interview with members of the Japanese Cultural Center problematized a Japanese identity as JO invoked the multi-ethnic character of people in Hawai'i to question the host's uncritical employment of categories such as "Japanese" and "Japanese immigrants." To JO, the identity label that was more relevant was "local" as the development of Hawaiian society since the time of the plantations made it difficult to apply specific categories to a Japanese identity. In contrast, though, the label "Japanese" seemed very relevant to the third generation plantation immigrant LG, even though it did not correlate directly with aspects of culture such as food and to Japanese language ability. In fact, we may note that her lack of Japanese language ability did contribute to her identity because she grew up as a "typical Japanese kid" in Hawai'i speaking English and Pidgin but not Japanese. Hence, for LG there was a connection between language and identity, but it was not the language that we might ordinarily associate with the category of "Japanese." As expressed by LG, the evolution of Hawaiian society made it more "typical" for those with a Japanese immigrant background to speak English and Pidgin.

The two bilingual learners also conveyed a relationship between language and identity but they seemed to take the more conventional position that assigns an already assumed language to an ethnic origin. Thus, VC relayed a feeling of strangeness at seeing the people in the Hui Okinawa employ not Okinawan but Japanese and English. Even MC's labeling of herself as the identity "halfbreed" seems to have a heavily linguistic component. Being from Okinawan, "halfbreed" means speaking the three languages of Japanese, Okinawan, and English, but it also typically comes with an inability to read and write Japanese. Gal and Woolard (1995, 2001) and Woolard (2008) have discussed this assumed connection between language and place in terms of the ideology of authenticity, which "locates the value of a language in its relationship to a particular community" (Woolard 2008, 2). MC and VC did not necessarily pass judgment on the value of particular languages but they did seem to evaluate the authenticity of specific identities based on how strongly those groups were attached to languages expected to be spoken in those places.

MC and VC also employed the term "dialect" to refer to the languages spoken by "first generation" members of *kenjinkai* in Hawai'i, but it was probably the discussion among the Japanese learners that was most suggestive of diversity in the Japanese language employed in Hawai'i. Not only did DU describe the "clashing dialects" between his O'ahu-born grandmother and

Japan-born aunt, but AA and SO both indicated the possibility that learners may be using the language in some creative ways. It is apparent that it would be a mistake to expect the Japanese language in Hawai'i to conform to one particular style or variety.

On the overall, then, the findings of this chapter fit with the basic characterization of multilingualism that is emerging in this book. Although this chapter did not focus on heteroglossic language practice per se, it does suggest the multivoiced quality of the Japanese language and a Japanese identity in Hawai'i. To understanding what the Japanese language means to people in Hawai'i, we must consider the many voices that currently exist. There were "Japanese immigrants" who spoke a rural dialect of Japanese that is still relevant to some in Hawai'i because of the remnants of the dialect in Pidgin. We must also embrace the possibility that the category "Japanese" may apply to some in Hawai'i who do not speak the language. Likewise, we also need to know that there are new "first generation" Japanese in Hawai'i who may speak "Standard Japanese" in their work in business but who also may speak "dialects" as part of their membership in *kenjinkai*. And then there are learners of Japanese who are employing Japanese in innovative ways that consists of mixings with English. Finally, Hawai'i's approach to the category "Japanese" also features a negotiation involving the identity of "Okinawan." There are, on the one hand, those who place "Okinawan" within the larger category of "Japanese," and there are, on the other hand, those who are working to keep "Okinawan" separate from "Japanese."

The findings, therefore, suggest once again the need to promote an approach to the study of multilingualism that focuses on domains and spaces of multilingualism. The type of Japanese being employed and the meaning of a Japanese identity is bound to vary from situation to situation in Hawai'i. At the same time, though, we need to acknowledge that our conception of domain and space must be expanded to go beyond the actual physical space in which an interaction occurs given that the interviews themselves could have been performed anywhere. Instead, since the meaning of a Japanese identity and the interpretation of the Japanese language seem to vary from individual to invidual based on their own experiences, the ideas of domain and space need to include the life experiences of individuals and groups of individuals. For some, like LG, a Japanese identity is not tied to the speaking of a language or the consumption of Japanese food but rather is tied to the experience of growing up on a plantation community in a particular way with a specific familial background. For others, like MC and VC, who were raised outside of Hawai'i in parts of Japan, a Japanese identity is more closely tied to the speaking of the language. Similarly, for some, such as DU, who grew up in a family with different forms of Japanese, including forms probably not heard in Japan, there is no single Japanese language that is better than others. It is these life experiences that social actors carry with them to and across social spaces. Hence, while attempts to understand the role of Japanese in Hawai'i must certainly probe spaces in which the language it is used, this chapter suggests that we must also consider the experiences of people in Hawai'i, including especially the ways that they themselves invoke categories related to Japanese in their speech.

Finally, I would note that although this chapter focused on Japanese, any further exploration of multilingualism in Hawai'i must include similar types of observations of the ways that categories such as "Chinese," "Portuguese," "Korean," or "Samoan" are used in society and how they relate to the life experiences of people in actual communities. The next chapter continues along such a line of inquiry by concentrating particularly on usages of "Filipino" and "Micronesian" in newspaper articles.

NOTES

1. I choose to refer to Japanese here as an "immigrant language" even though it is most commonly known in applied linguistics as a heritage language (see Kondo-Brown 2015). The category "immigrant language" is meant to distinguish Japanese from Hawaiian and also Pidgin based on the fact that Japanese was first brought to Hawai'i from an outside source of origin.

2. The Foreign Service Institute lists Japanese together with Arabic, Cantonese, Mandarin, and Korean as Category V languages, described as "exceptionally difficult for native English speakers." This information is according to the website at http://www.effectivelanguagelearning.com/language-guide/language-difficulty, last accessed on June 22, 2018.

3. I have slightly altered the Romanization symbols in representing the Japanese in this passage so that double vowels are used to indicate long vowel sounds.

4. Following Heinrich (2012), I use the terms Ryukyu and Ryukyuan to refer to the languages and also the group of islands considered to constitute Okinawa.

5. Ukwanshin Kabudan is a group devoted to the preservation of Okinawan music and dance. Information can be found at http://www.ukwanshin.org.

6. Derrick Iwata (DI) will not actually appear in any of the excerpts of data presented below, but he was present during the entire interview.

7. The data excerpt represents the fact that she pronounced the name of the town 'Ō'ōkala without the 'okina and the kahakō. The way she pronounced 'it is the most common way that it is pronounced in Hawai'i.

8. To be fair, VC does demonstrate later in the interview (not shown in the data excerpts) a more flexible attitude toward heteroglossia when she discusses her own tendency to mix languages as an advantage stemming from her bilingualism. Her slightly critical feelings in these excerpts toward heteroglossia in the *Hui Okinawa* meetings seems to be derived from her observation that little Okinawan is employed despite the fact that many in the group say that they are interested in preserving their ancestral language(s).

Chapter Six

Ideology and the Latest Arrivals

The Construction of "Filipino" and "Micronesian" in Newspaper Discourse

INTRODUCTION

Included in chapter 2 is a discussion of the ideological beliefs attached to the immigrants that came to Hawai'i to work on the plantations, and the intent of this chapter is to focus again on the concept of ideology in order to explore the complexities of multilingualism in current Hawaiian society. More specifically, I compare the ideologies expressed in public discourse concerning two of the more recent groups that have arrived in Hawai'i, "Filipinos" and "Micronesians."[1] These are, to be sure, very different groups that began arriving in Hawai'i at separate points in history. Filipino immigration began in the early 1900s while Hawai'i was still largely agricultural based whereas people from Micronesia began arriving steadily in the 1980s, when the economy had shifted its focus to tourism. Also, it is true that both groups are, in actuality, diverse groups. "Filipino" is a cover term for people who speak a variety of languages across a set of islands known as the Philippines. Likewise, Micronesia comprises approximately 2,000 islands that stretch across 3,000 miles in the western Pacific and consist of fifteen languages that are not mutually intelligible (Palafox et al. 2011). Nevertheless, I propose here that these two groups will make for an interesting comparison because, at their respective times of arrival, both faced the challenge of integrating into a society that was already very diverse and multilingual. Since the Filipinos came first by approximately eighty years, their experience should be informative in terms of understanding the situation of the Micronesians, who currently are struggling to find acceptance in Hawaiian society.

In order to investigate the ideological beliefs that have affected each group, this chapter presents an analysis of the usage of category terms such as "Filipino" and "Micronesian" in recent newspaper articles in Hawai'i. By examining newspaper articles, the analysis will make it possible to assess the perceptions of these groups of people that are being disseminated throughout society. Before describing the analytic procedures in more detail, I proceed in the next two sections by providing further background information related to the categories of "Filipino" and "Micronesian" in Hawai'i.

"FILIPINO" IN HAWAI'I

As noted in chapter 2, Filipino immigration to Hawai'i began in 1906 with the arrival of fifteen workers from Tagalog-speaking areas of the Philippines. As is also described in chapter 2, the Filipino workers faced discrimination from not just the haole planters but also the other immigrants who saw the Filipinos as a threat to their livelihood because they worked for low wages and accepted substandard living conditions. Moreover, the Filipinos were viewed as inferior because they were unfamiliar with the language and customs of Hawai'i (Jung 2006). Accordingly, they were likened to children and stereotyped as knife-wielding hotheads and sexual aggressors who could not be trusted (Jung 2006; Teodoro 1981).

Despite these stereotypes, many Filipino plantations workers persevered and carved out niches for themselves within the developing twentieth-century Hawaiian society. And even though plantation work helped define the early Filipinos, several scholars have pointed out that the Filipino experience in Hawai'i is actually quite complex and has resulted in multiple Filipino identities within current Hawaiian society (Labrador 2015; Revilla 1996; San Buenaventura 1996). After 125,000 Filipinos came to Hawai'i between 1906–1935 to work as contract workers, the recruitment of Filipino workers ceased for ten years until the Hawaiian Sugar Planters Association (HSPA) recruited an additional 6,000 in 1946 (Revilla 1996; San Buenaventura 1996) to fill a need for workers on the plantations just after the conclusion of World War II. Immigration ceased again shortly thereafter due to strict immigration laws in the United States that placed quotas on the number of people who could enter the United States.

However, subsequent changes to US immigration laws in 1965 ended the quotas and made it possible for Filipinos to come to Hawai'i to be reunited with their family members and also for occupational preferences. As Labrador (2015) and Espiritu (1995) note, this change in laws had a significant impact on Filipino immigration not only in Hawai'i but also throughout the United States as Filipinos comprised about one-quarter of the total number of Asian immigrants. San Buenaventura (1995, 452; also quoted in Labrador 2015, 10) describes the effects of such large-scale immigration:

Post-1965 immigration has had an empowering, replenishing effect on the Filipino American community, providing the numerical strength needed to push for minority rights. However, the dual chain migration has also begun to highlight the diversity of the Filipino community, reflecting conflicting values and concerns based on the differing perspectives and interests of the American-born and immigrant Filipinos.

Labrador (2015) further notes that the uptick in Filipino immigration starting in 1965 also corresponded with the change in emphasis in the Hawaiian economy from plantations to tourism, further creating a division between the original Filipino immigrants and the new immigrants. Summarizing the work of others, Labrador writes that these post-1965 immigrants have been referred to as "postwar Filipinos" (Teodoro 1981), "new breed" Filipinos (Dionisio 1981), and even "educated Filipinos" (Labrador 2015, 11). Hence, while the history of Filipino contact with Hawai'i starts in 1906, "Filipino labor history and the plantation experience no longer serve as the primary of Filipino experience in Hawai'i; it is only one of the available resources in the repertoire of identification" (Labrador 2015, 11).

In fact, Labrador (2015) points to three types of identities, local, immigrant, and mainland, among Filipinos in Hawai'i. Local signifies the families of the plantation workers who have grown up in Hawai'i, immigrant refers to those who come from the Philippines, and mainland Filipinos are those who moved to Hawai'i from the parts of the mainland United States Statistics show that Filipinos on the mainland United States tend to achieve a higher level of education and income than those in Hawai'i, hence terms such as "new breed" and "educated Filipinos" (Labrador 2015). One outcome of this combination of identities in Hawai'i is that Filipino identities are not unified and also sometimes contested in terms of authenticity, which has led some to declare an "identity crisis" (see discussion in Labrador 2015).

Within the three types of identities, the distinction between local and nonlocal is particularly meaningful as Filipinos in Hawai'i have tried to dissociate themselves from the newer immigrants by eschewing a Filipino identity in favor of a local identity (Labrador 2015; San Buenaventura 1996). Terming these processes "localization" and "ethnic disidentification," Labrador (2015) notes that local Filipinos express shame in their Filipino background. Such shame is partly due to the legacy of the plantation era when Filipinos were denigrated and stereotyped as sexual aggressors and as dog-eaters (Labrador 2015; Okamura 1996), but it is also a result of a desire not to be seen as "outsiders" in Hawai'i, like the new Filipino immigrants and those from the mainland.

Understanding attempts by the Filipino community to adopt a local identity requires going beyond the local/haole dichotomy employed in earlier chapters.

Immigrant and mainland Filipinos are neither "local" nor are they "haole." In addition to "haole," the labels "immigrant," "mainland," and also possibly "tourist" and "military" must be added to categories that constitute the nonlocal side of the distinction (Labrador 2015). Although "local" has its origins in the plantation communities, it is a category that now more generally denotes "those residents who claim a natural and rightful belonging to Hawai'i" and is marked by a "loyalty and attachment to the peoples, cultures, and lands of Hawai'i" (Labrador 2015, 9). Given the possibility of being placed in a nonlocal category, many relatives of the Filipino plantation immigrants have chosen to emphasize their localness, thus distancing themselves from the descriptors "immigrant" and "mainland" that can be attached to the category "Filipino."

Language has been a central factor in the negotiation and adoption of identities. Although the original Filipino immigrants were a diverse mix of speakers of Filipino languages such as Ilocano, Tagalog, and Visayan, Pidgin has been the language that allows the local Filipinos to claim a local identity. Pidgin differentiates them from the accented English of the newer immigrants and also from the "haole-sounding" English spoken by Filipinos born and reared on the mainland. As Teodoro (1981, 58; also quoted in Labrador 2015, 11–12) writes, "for many local Filipinos speaking English that is not Pidgin is interpreted as wanting to be considered better than the locals; speaking with a nonpidgin Filipino accent means that a person is a 'noninsider' Filipino." At the same time, speaking with a Filipino English accent not only distinguishes Filipinos as immigrants but also can become a source of discrimination and harassment. This harassment frequently comes from the local Filipino population—Revilla (1996, 10) states that "immigrant Filipinos will say that they hate local Filipinos because the locals were the ones who were the most notorious for harassing the immigrants in school." And it also comes from the general local population at large as a Filipino accent is famously used in local comedy to poke fun at Filipinos (Labrador 2004, 2015).

Labrador (2004, 2015) describes the language employed by local comedians to make fun of Filipino immigrants as Mock Filipino, which is characterized mostly by using English, with possibly some recognizable words from a Filipino language such as Tagalog or Ilocano, with a Filipino accent. Labrador, in fact, describes Mock Filipino as "a strategy often employed by Local comedians to differentiate the speakers of Philippine languages from speakers of Pidgin," and he continues by noting that "Mock Filipino produces stigmatizing discourses of immigrant Filipinos, which in turn work to stigmatize Locals as immigrants" (Labrador 2015, 50–51). In short, then, this type of language reinforces the fact that Filipino immigrants are not local to Hawai'i and it also poses problems for local Filipinos who, because of appearance and Filipino ethnic background, may be lumped together as nonlocal and thus denigrated by association. This fear, then, of being grouped together with immigrant Filipinos as outsiders may then prompt local Filipinos to prove that they are different by demonstrating their own disdain for the immigrants.

Understanding the intricacies of the Filipino situation is important to the development of this chapter for at least four reasons. First, it raises questions as to whether the attributes historically associated with stereotypical depictions of the category of "Filipino," such as dog-eating, criminal, and sexual aggression, have a place in newspaper discourse in current society. Second, we may be interested in observing the degree to which the diversity of Filipino identities is represented in public discourse. Do, for example, newspaper writers demonstrate a recognition of the fluidity in Filipino identities or is the Filipino community treated as one static entity? Third, the fact that the length of the Filipino presence in Hawai'i has resulted in the construction of multiple identities that consist of generational as well as regional differences raises questions about the Micronesian presence in Hawai'i, which is of a much shorter period of time. For instance, given that Micronesian parents are raising families in Hawai'i, questions can be asked about whether children are following the Filipinos and identifying more as local rather than Micronesian? Finally, observation of how the Filipinos were stigmatized from their point of arrival 1906 begs questions about the degree to which the more recently arrived Micronesians have been similarly stigmatized and what roles public discourse plays in either provoking or allaying this stigmatization. I move toward further examination of these four concerns with additional information about the Micronesian situation in Hawai'i.

"MICRONESIAN" IN HAWAI'I

The year commonly given as a start date for the steady arrival of Micronesians to Hawai'i is 1986, but their relationship to Hawai'i and more generally to the United States begins before that. Following World War II, the United States took over administration of several of the islands in Micronesia, thus allowing the United States to use the islands according to their own needs. The United States subsequently detonated 67 nuclear weapons in the Marshall Islands between 1946 and 1958 as part of their weapons testing program, and the effects of the bombings, considered equal to 7,200 Hiroshima nuclear bombs (Palafox et al. 2011), made large portions uninhabitable and led to a sharp increase in disease. Due to pressure from external forces like the United Nations, the United States signed a series of treaties in 1986 known collectively as the Compact of Free Association (COFA). The COFA gave independence first to the Marshall Islands and the Federated States of Micronesia (which includes

Yap, Chuuk, Pohnpei, and Kosrae) in 1986 and then later in 1994 to Palau. The COFA still gave the United States control of the foreign affairs, airspace, and waters of COFA nations, but in return the United States is required not only to aid the economic development of COFA nations and provide for their national security but also to allow citizens of those islands to migrate to and work in the United States without visas or green cards. They are therefore referred to as migrants and not as immigrants, since the term immigrant is reserved for people who settle in the countries not freely associated with the United States (Palafox et al. 2011). With poverty widespread and a growing need of health care due to the nuclear testings, many people from these Pacific islands made the decision to leave their homes for the United States. As Blair (2015) notes, since 1986 "it's estimated that at least 30 percent of Micronesians have fled their far-flung island communities in search of economic opportunity, better education and . . . crucial health care." Weiner (2016) also reports that migration to Hawai'i picked up after 2003, and recent estimations indicate that there could be as many as 20,000 COFA migrants in Hawai'i, with the largest groups coming from the Marshall Islands and from Chuuk (Palafox et al. 2011).

As migrants to Hawai'i, they have had to adjust to a new linguistic situation. Talmy (2006) notes that in Hawai'i one of the fastest growing groups of limited-English proficiency students in schools has been children from Micronesia. Language barriers have also made it difficult for Micronesians to figure out how to obtain public services, even though Hawai'i is recently making an effort to offer services such as driver's license tests and court interpreting in languages such as Marshallese and Chuukese.

Micronesians also have been the victims of housing discrimination, which together with economic hardship has led to a high rate of homelessness (Weiner 2016). Hawai'i is already noted to have the highest rate of homelessness in the United States, and a growing portion of the homeless population comes from Micronesia (Blair 2015; Weiner 2016). Blair (2015) offers statistics from the University of Hawaii at Manoa Department of Urban and Regional Planning showing that the category "Micronesians" constitutes about one-fifth of the homeless populations in Kakaako and Kapalama. Only the "Hawaiian/Part Hawaiian" category has a higher percentage.

Homelessness is not the only reason for the development of a negative public image toward Micronesians. Due to the belief that the American government's generosity enabled the Micronesians to come to Hawai'i, there is the misconception that they do not work and merely live off the government. As Wiener (2016) writes:

> Micronesians have become the present-day Hawaiian version of the welfare queens of Readan-era American. Many locals, a rung or two up the economic ladder from the new Micronesian arrivals, view them as lazy, unmotivated, and

entitled-common stereotypes for any new migrant group—and they they've come to the United States to live regally on public largesse.

Such beliefs exist despite the fact that Micronesians work, pay taxes and regularly serve in the American military. These beliefs also do not consider that they are unable to vote and often have difficulty gaining access to cheap health care, the very reason that many of them came to Hawai'i.

These misconceptions have led to stereotyping as well as tensions between the Micronesian and the local population. In his ethnography of a school in Hawai'i that is populated by many Micronesian students, Talmy (2006, 37) describes some of the negative comments made by non-Micronesian youth:

> There were also more overt expressions of non-Micronesian students' racism, mostly manifest in comments about Micronesians' appearance, intelligence, hygiene, classroom behavior, and motivations for being in the U.S. As one 9th grader from Hong Kong noted about his Micronesian classmates: "They disgust me. They spit, they dig their nose in the middle of the class, they talk so ((loud screeching voice)) wa ya wa wa ya! They don't do their work. They're thieves. I can't work with people like that." Said another, "They talk too much. They so loud. They don't even work. They lazy." A Taiwanese boy said he was "embarrassed" being in the same class as Micronesians, while a Korean refused to touch them because he believed they had *Uku*, or lice. These comments are similar to those made by a number of teachers as well.

These quotations from children speak to the prevalence of stereotypes about Micronesians, including laziness and thievery. A separate article by Blair (2015) reports a teacher describing how even fourth graders are concerned about "Micronesian people coming here and taking our stuff." Likewise, Palafox et al. (2011, 307) reports "a stereotype that has now been assigned to the Chuukese by some in the Honolulu Police Department is that they are troublemakers and violent."

Tensions between the Micronesians and local residents culminated in a brawl at Kealakehe High School on the Big Island in 2012, which resulted in eight students being arrested. The state's Department of Education cited "a misunderstanding between local, Micronesian and Marshallese cultures" as the cause of the fighting (cited in Blair 2015). According to Blair, tensions have since subsided, but the stereotypes that helped create these tensions persist. Even though the history of immigration in Hawai'i is very much a story of immigrant groups being treated as "others," such prejudice suggests that the Micronesians are currently positioned as outsiders in a society in which the ancestors of many current residents were once viewed as "others." Accordingly, Talmy (2006) aptly refers to the Micronesians in Hawai'i as the "the other *Other*," thus capturing their status in the current sociopolitical landscape.

Although the Micronesians are attempting to survive in Hawai'i at a different point in history than the early Filipinos, there are definite parallels in the discrimination and prejudices that both had to endure. Another similarity between the two groups may be emerging in the experience of young Micronesians. Blair (2015) presents thoughts from Vidalino Raatior, director of UH-Hilo's Pacific Islands Student Center, who states "the young people growing up are beginning to disclaim their roots and heritage. If they were proud Micronesians, they are hiding it now because of possible negative impact. They start hearing negative jokes and begin doubting the label 'Micronesian' and begin to disclaim that." Talmy (2006) also reports a comment from a fifteen-year-old-girl, who was born in Chuuk but only educated there until the second grade before coming to Hawai'i. As Talmy (2006, 28) writes, she "admitted that she did not miss Chuuk much, since she had not lived there for a long time, and claimed with a halting laugh that she had 'no idea' when asked where she felt 'home' was." It is perhaps too early in the history of the Micronesians to pinpoint trends of identity choice by younger generations, but comparison with the Filipino experience suggests several options, including a local identity, a traditional Micronesian one, or something else altogether. In order to better compare and assess the status of both groups in current Hawaiian society, the rest of this chapter focuses on the analysis of newspaper discourse. The next section begins to do so by describing the analytic framework and procedures.

THE ANALYSIS: THEORETICAL APPROACH

Like parts of the analyses in chapters 4 and 5, the analysis in this chapter focuses on the usage of category terms. While the previous chapters drew on insights from membership category analysis (MCA), the analysis here relies primarily on the perspective of critical discourse analysis (CDA). By doing so, the analysis intends to complement the prior analyses as CDA will be used here to probe the ideological beliefs attached to categories and consider the effects of those beliefs on some of the people in Hawaiian society. With origins in the work of critical linguistics (e.g., Fowler 1991; Fowler et al. 1979; Kress and Hodge 1979) and also Halliday's functional approach to grammar (Halliday 1985; Halliday and Hasan 1989), CDA elucidates structural features of language in actual discourse and considers how those features contribute to the creation and reinforcement of unequal power relations in society (Fairclough 1989, 1995; van Dijk 1993, 2015). CDA does not give analytic primacy only to ideology, but discourse is viewed as a central location for the expression of ideologies that can disadvantage certain groups of people and at the same advantage others (Fowler 1996; Verschueren 2012). As Fowler (1996, 3) writes about the contributions of critical linguistics to CDA "we formulated an analysis of public discourse, an analysis designed to get at the ideology coded implicitly behind the overt propositions, to examine it particularly in the context of social formations." CDA thus provides a theoretical basis for examining how ideological beliefs may be expressed through an aspect of language such as category terms in public discourse in Hawai'i.

CDA is known to be a highly interdisciplinary approach. In the words of Garrett and Bell (1998, 6), "CDA is best viewed as a shared perspective encompassing a range of approaches rather than just one school." Accordingly, at the same time that the analysis in this chapter utilizes ideas from within CDA, it also looks to research in other disciplines as well, particularly the work of Altheide (Altheide 1997; Altheide and Michalowski 1999), who works in the field of communication studies and examines how the media constructs "problem frames" that shape the public's perceptions of critical issues in the news.

Proponents of CDA note that a large percentage of CDA research investigates language in the media. Garrett and Bell (1998, 6), for example, estimated in 1998 that 40 percent of the publications in the journal *Discourse and Society*, which was originated by Teun van Dijk to promote CDA research, employ data from the media. For scholars like Fairclough (1995, 2), such a focus makes sense given "the substantively linguistic and discoursal nature of the power of the media" and given the role of the media in the "contemporary processes of social and cultural change." More specifically, Richardson (2007, 7) promotes CDA as a perspective for investigating newspaper discourse by asserting "journalism exists to enable citizens to better understand their lives and their position(s) in the world." The analysis to follow attempts to uncover the ideologies employed in newspapers in Hawai'i that help define the current social positions of the categories "Filipino" and "Micronesian."

The Analysis: Procedures

The analysis focuses on six category terms, "Filipino," "Ilocano," "Tagalog," "Micronesian," "Marshallese," and "Chuukese." "Filipino" and "Micronesian" were selected for the reason that these are the two most common terms employed currently in Hawai'i to refer to the groups being examined in this chapter. The other four terms were chosen because they refer mostly to languages besides English (and possibly Pidgin) spoken by people in the categories "Filipino" and "Micronesian." As noted earlier, the two largest groups of people who fall into the category of Micronesian are from the Marshall Islands and Chuuk.

Table 6.1. Language Mentions in Hawaiian Newspapers

Categories	First Date Found	Last Date Found
Filipino	February 11, 2018	January 1, 2018
Ilocano	February 13, 2018	February 18, 2016
Tagalog	February 13, 2018	February 18, 2016
Micronesian	January 18, 2018	November 24, 2016
Marshallese	January 20, 2018	May 8, 2016
Chuukese	February 1, 2018	November 18, 2014

In order to examine these categories, I employ the same database of Hawaiian newspapers that I used in chapter 4, namely, "Newsbank." For this chapter, I did a search of the database for the six key categories, and then chose the first thirty articles that appeared in the results as my corpus. In some cases, the same or almost identical articles were shared across newspapers, and these were therefore only counted once as part of the corpus.[2] Sometimes, a category term appeared several times in a single article. In such instances, it was still counted as just one of the thirty results. The searches produced results from different sections of the newspapers, including the main news stories, sports, short community announcements, as well as obituaries. For the purposes here, I included articles in all sections of the newspapers included in "Newsbank." I engaged in the search on February 15, 2018, and continued to go back in the database as far as necessary to produce thirty results for each category term. Table 6.1 summarizes the spans of time needed to find thirty mentions of each category.

Of interest here is that the category "Filipino" occurred far more frequently in the newspapers than any of the others. It was employed in thirty articles in a span of forty-one days. The other categories were fairly similar in terms of frequency, except that mentions of "Chuukese" were less common than the others. It took nearly eighteen additional months for "Chuukese" to appear in thirty newspaper articles. The next section focuses on a qualitative analysis of the usage of these categories. The analysis begins with a focus on categories related to Filipino and subsequently compares the usage of those terms to that of the Micronesian categories.

Analysis: Filipino and Related Categories

Given the relative frequency with which it appeared, I begin the analysis with the category "Filipino." The two most common usages of "Filipino" in my corpus are as modifiers for cuisine and for community groups. Altogether, these two usages combined to constitute sixteen of the thirty articles in the corpus. Excerpts (1) and (2) provide examples related to cuisine. Excerpt (1) is from the food section of the Honolulu Star Advertiser, based in Honolulu, and Excerpt (2) is from the "News" section of *West Hawai'i Today*, a publication for the Kona side of the Big Island.[3]

Excerpt (1): *Honolulu Star Advertiser*, February 7, 2018
WINE DINNER HIGHLIGHTS FILIPINO MENU
The Third Thursday wine-pairing dinner this month at Bread & Butter focuses on Filipino cuisine. Chef Arnaldo "Masa" Gushiken's five course menu Feb. 15 centers on an entree of lamb adobo with pomegranate pearls, artichoke frito and calamansi, served with a 2013 Hartford Russian River Zinfandel. Dessert will be a deconstructed banana lumpia with cinnamon cookies and ice cream.

Excerpt (2): *West Hawai'i Today*, February 5, 2018
The tropical specialty bowl is Ignacio's version of halo halo—a Filipino "shaved ice sundae" made with boba tapioca balls in a slushy cream base, topped with fruit, sweet potato pieces, a scoop of ube ice cream made from purple yams and a condensed milk drizzle. The Snowball and Cookie Butter acai bowls are other dessert-like treats.
((Skip a few lines of the article))
"I decided to add modern Filipino cuisine to the menu after looking at other restaurants' menus in town so we could be different, but not take business away from them," Ignacio said. "I'm proud of where I'm from and my culture. I wanted to do a play on pork belly. Growing up, I always had a banana with my adobo and everybody seems to be loving it."

In excerpt (1), the capital letters at the top mark this first line as the headline of the article, where it can be seen that "Filipino" is used to highlight the type of menu to be offered. The category "Filipino" is also used again in the first line of the article to note that dinner on the third Thursday of the month will focus on "Filipino cuisine." In excerpt (2) Filipino is used first by the writer of the article to describe a type of "shaved ice sundae" called *halo halo* and then later by Ignacio, the owner of the establishment, to describe the general type of "cuisine" served at the restaurant.

There is a kind of "othering" occurring in these excerpts in that the category Filipino is used to set restaurants and types of cuisine apart as different based on their ethnic status. They are distinguished from other types of foods because they are Filipino. Interestingly, though, this is done not just by the writers of the newspaper articles but also by the people themselves as exemplified by Ignacio's usage of "Filipino" to describe his own food. In some sociological research on identity, a distinction has been made between an "ethnic category," defined as the identity assigned to a group by those outside the group, and an "ethnic group," explained as an identity that is established from within the group itself (Jenkins 1994; see Kang 2004 for discussion). Cornell and Hartman (1998) suggests a sequence in which those in power in a society first assign "ethnic categories" to "outsiders" who subsequently accept that as their "ethnic group." Such a process may indeed capture the sequential turn of events in Hawai'i as workers, despite coming from diverse areas of the Philippines, including places that were Ilocano, Tagalog, and Visayan-speaking, were assigned the category of "Filipino" once they arrived to work on the plantations. Then, as the immigrants started to assimilate into society they adopted this categorization as their ethnic group. Ignacio's description of his food as "Filipino cuisine" and his subsequent statement that he is proud of his culture and where he comes from indicates that he has embraced the category "Filipino." Excerpt (3) provides another example also related to food. It is from an article reporting the victory of a Hawaiian resident named Edward Ramos on the Food Network's television series "Bakers vs. Fakers."

> Excerpt (3): *Honolulu Star-Advertiser*, January 31, 2018
> Ramos razzle-dazzled judges in the first round—assignment: lava cake, secret ingredient: lavender—with an ube lavender lava cake with a lavender tea and lavender honey granita, plus a banana lumpia brushed with lavender honey. "I was trying to pay homage to my Filipino heritage and my mom's desserts," he said.

Ramos's reference to his desire to "pay homage to my Filipino heritage and my mom's desserts" indicates not only a willingness to assign the label of Filipino to himself but also an assertion of pride in doing so. Excerpt (4) exhibits a similar phenomenon.

> Excerpt (4): *Honolulu Star Advertiser*, February 7, 2018
> Ron Dalmacio bought a 1995 Chevy for $6,505 to expand the customer base of Shay's Filipino Cafe, the restaurant he opened in the Waipio Shopping Center in 2016.
> He opened the food truck in late January in Mililani. Originally black, the truck is now a royal blue, with a new battery, generator and propane tank.

Here, there is no direct quotation from the owner, but the name of the restaurant is given as "Shay's Filipino Café," suggesting the owner willingly included the category "Filipino" in the name as something that would attract people to the restaurant.

A possible concern of this ethnic labeling is that even if an ethnic group willingly adopts the label for themselves, it still may carry with it the remnants of oppression since it was originally assigned by the dominant group (Pyke and Dang 2003). Indeed, in the case of Filipinos in Hawai'i, this could seemingly be worrisome given the history of discrimination that caused immigrants from the Philippines to struggle when they first arrived. Yet, in light of such a concern, it is interesting that the category "Filipino" is often employed in my corpus in a way that creates the appearance of an accepted and unified community. Excerpts (5) and (6) begin to speak to this point. Excerpt (5) is taken from an obituary in the West Hawai'i today and excerpt (6) from an announcement in the *The Garden Isle*, the newspaper that serves the island of Kaua'i.

> Excerpt (5): *West Hawai'i Today*, February 4, 2018
> Alfredo Cortez Madriaga, 74, of Na'alehu, Hawaii, died Jan. 16, 2018, at Hospice of Kona's Nakamaru Hale. Born in Bantay, Ilocos Sur, Philippines on Oct. 24, 1943, he was a planter for Kau Agribusiness, a member of the Ka'ū Filipino Community Club and the Sacred Heart Catholic Church in Na'alehu.

> Excerpt (6): *The Garden Isle*, February 2, 2018
> The Kaua'i Filipino Chamber of Commerce formally inducted its 2018 board and leaders, and presented recognition awards to community individuals and organizations for their respective efforts Saturday during the gala at the Koloa Landing Resort.
> Laurie Yoshida was sworn in as the new KFCC president, taking over from Bobby Ayonon who led the group since 2015.

Excerpt (5) emphasizes that the man who passed away was a member of the Ka'ū Filipino Community Club and excerpt (6) refers to the activities of the Kaua'i Filipino Chamber of Commerce. Filipino is in fact a category that is attached to various different groups as well as places in the community. In addition to the two organizations in these last two excerpts, there is reference in the corpus to a "Filipino club" in Kohala, a "Filipino Community Center" in Waipahu, a "Filipino Chamber of Commerce of Hawai'i" on O'ahu, a "Filipino Catholic Church" in Honolulu, a "Miss Kaua'i Filipina Pageant," and also a place called the "Filipino Clubhouse" on the island of Lāna'i.

Morever, there were some community groups in my corpus that employed the term Ilocano, including an "Ilocano Ancestry Club" on the Big Island of Hawai'i and also a "Big Island Ilocano Club." This usage of either Filipino or Ilocano may seem rather mundane, but it is this mundane usage through which the newspapers depict these categories as accepted features of Hawaiian society. These community groups are not treated as problematic or even remarkable. Much like the language categories discussed in chapter 5, these community groups are listed in the newspapers as though they are just regular features of the landscape of Hawaiian society. This mundane usage is slightly different from the references to food in excerpts (1)–(4), which treated Filipino cuisine as remarkable, but this was for positive reasons as a source of pride.

These uses depicting "Filipino" as an accepted category that is attached to a unified community conflict with the earlier discussion in this chapter of the disjointed sense of identity among the Filipino population in Hawai'i. As outlined earlier in this chapter, Filipino immigration occurred in different waves and from various parts of not just the Philippines but also the United States (the "mainland" or "educated" Filipinos). Yet, despite this history and despite a sense of an identity crisis, the tendency of the newspaper articles in my corpus is to link the category "Filipino" to aspects of society such as types of food and community organizations that constructs for readers a sense of an accepted and unified Filipino community in Hawai'i.

While this construction of a cohesive community may provide an oversimplified picture of the actual situation in Hawai'i for people of Filipino ethnicity, it is in general suggestive of a positive place in current society that includes few, if any, references to the stigma that were attached to the Filipino immigrants that came over 100 years ago. At the same time, though, the corpus contains some uses of the category "Ilocano" in reference to activities that would be evaluated negatively. To develop this point, I first note that both "Tagalog" and "Ilocano" were almost exclusively employed to describe language services and other opportunities in Hawai'i. Excerpts (7), (8), and (9) speak to this point.

> Excerpt (7): Associated Press State Wire, Hawai'i, March 24, 2016
> English and Hawaiian are the state's official languages, and lawmakers are pushing a bill to offer both on ballots. Right now, English, Japanese, Cantonese and Ilocano must be offered on ballots in some counties.

> Excerpt (8): *The Garden Isle*, February 13, 2018
> Syngenta must also develop compliance kits for use at these trainings and for wider distribution in the agricultural community in English and four other languages commonly spoken by growers and farm workers in the training locations—Mandarin, Korean, Tagalog, and Ilocano.

> Excerpt (9): *Honolulu Star Advertiser*, August 7, 2017
> Students who apply for the seal need to successfully complete English requirements for high school graduation with a minimum 3.0 grade point average, and meet scoring benchmarks for world languages that include French, German, Ilocano, Italian, Japanese, Korean, Latin, Mandarin, Spanish, Tagalog or Vietnamese.

Excerpt (7) is taken from an article that discusses the fact that Hawaiian, despite being an official language of the state, is not included on state voting ballots. As part of this discussion it notes that Ilocano, along with English, Japanese, and Cantonese, "must be offered on ballots in some counties." Excerpt (8) describes the requirements made by the Environmental Protection Agency of a seed company called Syngenta to resolve pesticide violations on its farm on the island of Kauaʻi. One of the requirements is to develop compliance kits that are available in four other languages that include Tagalog and Ilocano. Excerpt (9) is slightly different in that it describes an award termed the "biliteracy award" offered by the Department of Education for students demonstrating proficiency in two or more languages. Ilocano and Tagalog are listed as examples of the languages for which students can be awarded.

While this connection to languages is generally not made in a negative way, there were some references to language services in "Ilocano" in the context of accusations of crimes and appearances in court. Excerpt (10) shows an example. The excerpt begins with the initial description of the crime and then later utilizes the category of "Ilocano."

> Excerpt (10): *Hawaii Tribune Herald*, July 3, 2017
> A 46-year-old Kurtistown man is alleged to have intentionally set his car on fire early Wednesday morning while it was inside an open-air carport, setting off a destructive and potentially deadly chain reaction that brought firefighters and police to his mother's home. According to court documents filed by police, Hermundo Tagalicud told officers responding to a 2 a.m. call to the family's Iwasaki Camp home that he used a lighter and brown paper bag to torch his car "because I didn't like it anymore."
> At Tagalicud's initial court appearance Friday, Deputy Public Defender Patrick Munoz asked Hilo District Judge Harry Freitas to grant Tagalicud supervised release or to order an updated bail study using an Ilocano interpreter.

Notice here that the initial description, "A 46-year old Kurtistown man" does not include any information about the ethnicity of the accused. The article does provide his name in the second sentence, which may lead some readers familiar with names in Hawaiʻi to speculate about his ethnicity, but the most obvious clue concerning his ethnicity comes in the reference to an "Ilocano interpreter" at the end of the excerpt. Without explicitly listing an ethnic category, this reference makes his identity as "Filipino" quite clear. Since the accused requires an interpreter, this reference suggests that he is a Filipino immigrant as opposed to a local Filipino or a mainland Filipino. However, it is difficult to know for certain the number of everyday readers who would actively consider this distinction in Filipino identities in their reading of this piece of information.

The mention of "Ilocano interpreter" may seem like a very indirect way of providing information about ethnicity, but Teodoro (1981) notes that prior to the 1970s, newspapers frequently included the ethnic identities of people accused of crimes. Although this practice is no longer employed, the inclusion of information about the languages of interpretation offers readers an opportunity to infer this information. Including excerpt (10), there were three articles that employed the term "Ilocano" (there were none that focused on Tagalog interpreting in court) in the context of crime and court interpreting, with all three following the same pattern of indirectly referencing the ethnicity of the accused. Excerpt (11) provides one further example.

> Excerpt (11): *The Garden Isle*, May 10, 2017
> A man police believe stabbed his wife was arraigned Tuesday on attempted murder and assault charges. Wendell Badua, 37, appeared before District Court Judge Michael Soong on charges stemming from a Friday arrest after police say he attacked his wife with a knife. Badua, who lives in Hanamaulu, enlisted the help of an Ilocano translator for the proceedings.

Like excerpt (10), this excerpt begins with a description of the crime, next reveals the name of the accused, and then, without assigning an ethnicity directly to the accused, notes that he "enlisted the help of an Ilocano translator." Although indirect, this does make information about the accused available to readers, enabling inferences that the accused is Filipino and also a recent immigrant.

The three articles that employed these indirect practices of revealing ethnic identity all described violent crimes that included arson and attempted murder. However, these articles were only a small percentage of the ninety articles found in the database in relation to people and languages. In contrast, the vast majority of the articles treated these categories as accepted and established aspects of Hawaiian society. Moreover, in doing so the articles made little or no reference to the diversity of Filipino identities in current Hawaiian society. The closest that the articles in my corpus came to doing so were the last three cases that suggested that the violent crimes described were committed by Filipino immigrants. The next section presents the analysis of the usage of Micronesian categories in the newspaper articles and demonstrates that the treatment of the Micronesians is considerably different from that of the Filipinos.

Analysis: "Micronesian"

To begin, it should be noted that, like the term "Filipino," categories that refer to people from Micronesia were sometimes used in a way that suggests acceptance in the community. Excerpt (12) shows an example of the category "Micronesian" and excerpt (13) focuses on "Marshallese."

> Excerpt (12): *Hawaii Tribune-Herald*, February 20, 2017
> A Senate bill introduced in this year's legislative session would provide funding for 'ulu research and cultivation, noting that ulu has reached a point where it

could be a "major commercial crop, even while remaining closely connected to traditional Hawaiian, Polynesian, Micronesian and Melanesian values."

Excerpt (13): *West Hawaii Today*, December 25, 2017
As of last week, Honokaa Seventh-day Adventist Church became Blue Zones Project—North Hawaii's fifth church to become approved, and Waimea Marshallese Full Gospel is the first Marshallese church registered in the state.

Excerpt (12) centers on the 'ulu, a fruit that has been a staple for many groups of people in the Pacific. The excerpt contains a quotation stating that 'ulu could become a "major commercial crop," but the person is also quoted as adding "even while remaining closely connected to traditional Hawaiian, Polynesian, Micronesian, and Melanesian values." One of the interesting points about this statement is that "Micronesian" is grouped together with the categories of "Hawaiian" and "Polynesian," both of which are generally viewed favorably in current Hawaiian society. Furthermore, all of the categorical terms are attached to the two words "traditional" and "value," both of which also suggest positive evaluations. In excerpt (13), the reference to the church "Waimea Marshallese Full Gospel" as the first "Marshallese church register in the state" also appears to be positive as it indicates progress on the part of the "Marshallese" in terms of becoming accepted in Hawai'i.

However, the majority of the articles, while often sounding supportive and sympathetic, include some form of a negative statement that underscores the problems faced by migrants from Micronesia. Excerpt (14) begins to speak to this point.

Excerpt (14): *Honolulu Star-Advertiser*, July 24, 2017
A fledgling nonprofit in Kalihi-Palama is trying to help Micronesians in Hawaii hold on to the cultural values that mean the most to them. Micronesians value family relationships above most things, but their communal lifestyle can clash with the Western value of individuality, said We Are Oceania Director Josie Howard.

This article attaches the label "Micronesian" to "values" to describe a nonprofit group that is trying to aid Micronesians in Hawai'i. The article includes the statement that "Micronesians value family relationships," which seems to highlight a positive attribute. Yet, at the same time, the article also employs the contradictory conjunction "but" to point out that this cultural value poses a problem for Micronesians. It "can clash with the Western value of individuality." While this in and of itself may not seem negative, the remainder of this article continues to point out three problems, discrimination, homelessness, and health care, that are commonly associated with people described as "Micronesian." Excerpt (15), which is taken from a point later in the same article, exemplifies this.

> Excerpt (15): *Honolulu Star-Advertiser*, July 24, 2017
> We Are Oceania aims to help Micronesians retain communal values and succeed in a modernized world. Being successful, she said, means "to be able to navigate both worlds . . . find that safe place for what works for you." Howard, who moved here from Chuuk to study in 1989, said Micronesians in Hawaii often face discrimination. "We feel very unwelcome," she said. Her three Hawaii-born children are "bullied at school because they're Micronesian," she said. Many newcomers are homeless, without job skills and in dire need of health care—which places a major strain on social services and has led to some resentment.

The writer of this excerpt notes that the organization "We Are Oceania" is trying to help people from Micronesia retain their "communal values," but in doing, the article quotes a person from Chuuk who states that they face discrimination and bullying. The article then continues by mentioning homelessness and health care as problems that lead to resentment from other people in Hawai'i. Note here that the usage of the term "resentment" changes the focus of the problem being discussed. Homelessness and health care are problems that directly affect Micronesians, but by adding the term "resentment," this extends the scope of the problem to society in general. It suggests that there are those in society who are unhappy due to the actions of people from Micronesia.

In inspecting the thirty articles that employ the category "Micronesian," it is striking that twenty-one of them mention, either directly or indirectly, the problems faced by the Micronesian population. I will provide further discussion of indirect mentions shortly, but I first want to focus on how the articles construct "Micronesian" problems as greater problems for society through the process of "generalization." CDA researchers have been wary of generalizations in discourse because they can extend the focus of problems from a specific population to a larger one and thus construct a much greater sense of a problem (Billig 2008; Khoirunisa and Indah 2017; Van Dijk 1995; Van Leeuwen 1996). In the process, a generalization can also redirect the focus of a problem in a way that frames a group not as the victims but as the cause of the greater social ill. Excerpt (16) shows how the challenges faced by Micronesians are "generalized" and recast as social problems caused by the Micronesian population. This excerpt is from an article that discusses possible budget cuts to COFA funding given to the Hawaiian governement to assist people from Micronesia.

> Excerpt (16): *Honolulu Star-Advertiser*, August 22, 2017
> It's hard to see the rationale for such cuts. The administration acknowledges that some of the discretionary funding has been used to cover job training and

other social services. The growing numbers of Micronesians among Hawaii's homeless should bolster the argument to keep such support to encourage their self-sufficiency. According to recent state reports, the total fiscal impact of the Micronesian population on the state is about three times what Hawaii receives in federal funds. The largest costs fall under the state Department of Education for public schooling, with the Department of Human Services running up nearly as much in social program assistance. And if recent statistics maintain their current trajectory, the costs are rising.

The noun phrase "the growing numbers of Micronesians among Hawaii's homeless" could potentially serve as the subject of a sentence describing homelessness as a problem of homelessness for Micronesians. Yet, this phrase is just a part of emphasizing the effects of this problem on the state of Hawai'i. The article notes first that "the total fiscal impact of the Micronesian population on the state is about three times what Hawaii receives in federal funds," and then applies this specifically to the Department of Education, which bears the burden of "the largest costs." The excerpt concludes by highlighting the problem with the statement "the costs are rising." The category "Micronesian" is invoked here not to discuss the situation of a specific group of people but rather to extend the problem to other aspects of Hawaiian society. In doing so, the Micronesians are constructed as the cause of the "total fiscal impact ... on the state," thus creating a situation of resentment in which the Micronesians may be blamed for fiscal problems in Hawai'i.

Excerpt (17) provides a different example of how this process of "generalization" is accomplished in the articles. This excerpt is taken from the beginning of an article that focuses more generally on the problem of health care in Hawai'i and the role of community health centers. The excerpt shows the only instance of the label "Micronesian" employed in the article.

Excerpt (17): *Honolulu Star-Advertiser*, December 11, 2016
More than three years ago, an elderly Micronesian couple first visited Honolulu's Kalihi-Palama Health Center (KPHC). Experiencing homelessness, they were seeking help to manage their challenges with diabetes and high blood pressure. Teko Gabriel, a KPHC community health worker, became the couple's frontline advocate, providing them with assistance in their native Chuukese language.

This excerpt refers to a "Micronesian couple" that visited the Kalihi-Palama Health Center. It describes the couple as "experiencing homelessness" and as having health "challenges." The tone is quite sympathetic as it notes a health care worker who became their advocate and provided "assistance in their native Chuukese language," but it should be emphasized that this is the only concrete example given in the article of people seeking and receiving health care assistance. In choosing the descriptors "Micronesian" and "homelessness" as the lone example, this article helps reinforce the stereotypical portrayal of people labeled as "Micronesian." They are homeless and require health care assistance. Later, as excerpt (18) demonstrates, the same article generalizes the problem of health care to society in general.

> Excerpt (18): *Honolulu Star-Advertiser*, December 11, 2016
> Community health centers save billions of dollars in health care costs each year but themselves struggle for funding and resources. This includes payment or reimbursement for in-language assistance—required of but often insufficiently met by federally funded health plans—and critical enabling services such as transportation and those addressing social determinants of health, such as housing. Community health centers need support to sustain the progress they have achieved. Elected officials and all policymakers must continue to invest in health centers, and health plans must partner with community health centers to effectively serve the most vulnerable patients.

This excerpt cites at the beginning that community health centers help save money but quickly points out that they "struggle for funding and resources." The excerpt continues to list some of the ways that the centers struggle financially, and even though the label "Micronesian" is not employed, it is indexed in at least two ways. First, the mention of "payment or reimbursement for in-language assistance" is a reference to people like the "elderly Micronesian couple" who received assistance in Chuukese. Second, the reference to services such as "those addressing social determinants of health, such as housing" also reaches back to the "elderly Micronesian couple" because they were "experiencing homelessness." By employing the Micronesian couple as an example and continuing to index their situation in a discussion of finanical challenges of health care centers, this article uses "generalization" to reinforce the role played by Micronesians in contributing to the larger problem of providing health care in Hawaiʻi.

Given this tendency to frame problems faced by Micronesians as "general" social problems in Hawaiʻi, I would like to invoke the concept of "problem frame" to suggest that the linking of Micronesians to social problems constructs a version of reality for readers such that they view Micronesians in a negative way. "Problem frame" is employed by Altheide (Altheide 1997; Altheide and Michalowski 1999) in order to explain the media's role in structuring the social world for media consumers. According to Altheide (1997, 651), "frames are the focus, a parameter or boundary, for discussing a particular event. Frames focus on what will be discussed, how it will be discussed, and above all, how it will not be discussed." A common example offered is the framing of illegal drug use as a "public health issue" or as a "criminal justice issue." As Altheide notes (1997, 651), "these are two different frames that entail a way of discussing the problem, or the kind of discourse that will follow." He also continues to state that "what we call things, the themes and discourses we employ, and how we 'frame' and allude to experience is crucial for what we take for granted and assume to be true" (Altheide 1997, 652).

Altheide concentrates much of his work on how problem frames in media discourse help instill a sense of fear in the minds of the general public, but the idea can be applied here to see how the newspapers help control discussion of the category of "Micronesian" in Hawaiʻi. By framing the experience of Micronesians in terms of the "problems" of discrimination, homelessness, and health care, the newspaper discourse creates a social reality that leads the public to view Micronesians in this way. Moreover, by utilizing the process of "generalization," the newspaper discourse, despite a tone of sympathy, pushes readers toward resentment of Micronesians because their specific problems cause larger social problems that impact society in negative ways.

In fact, I would suggest that implicit acceptance of this problem frame concerning Micronesians in public discourse in Hawaiʻi has reached the point that even without mentioning these problems directly, writers can invoke this frame by merely referring to the "experience" of Micronesians. This problem frame, in other words, has become a kind of default for understanding references in the newspapers. Excerpt (19) speaks to this point.

> Excerpt (19): *Honolulu Star-Advertiser*, July 7, 2017
> Honolulu's 2017–2018 theater season is a fresh cornucopia of diversity that includes revival productions of Broadway classics and recent Broadway and off-Broadway hits that are being presented by Honolulu theater groups for the first time. The schedule also contains new works by island playwrights and addresses subjects ranging from the music of Cole Porter to the experiences of Micronesian immigrants in Hawaii.

In describing the lineup of plays for the upcoming theater season, this excerpt refers only to "the experiences Micronesian immigrants in Hawaii," but if viewed through the usual problem frame employed to discuss "the Micronesian experience," it is possible to see how just this reference could incite negative perceptions in readers. That this is indeed the case is supported by an article appearing approximately three months later that discusses the content of the play in more depth. As excerpt (20) shows, the article again refers to the "experiences" of Micronesians in Hawaiʻi. The excerpt offers quotations from one of the authors of the play.

> Excerpt (20): *Honolulu Star-Advertiser*, October 20, 2017
> He describes the play as an introduction to the experiences of Micronesians in Hawaii.

"We've tried to be as inclusive as possible, but there have been waves of people coming here from Micronesia, going back to the '80s," Saopeng said. "Some come here to get an education, some for economic reasons, some to get health care that isn't available there, and some because as the ocean level rises their islands are becoming uninhabitable. We can't tell everybody's story but this is a start." What it's about: The experiences of children and teens from the Micronesian nations of Yap, Chuuk, Pohnpei, Kosrae, the Marshall Islands and Palau in adjusting to life in Hawaii without losing touch with the cultures of their homelands and while also serving as a bridge between "America" and their immigrant parents.

This excerpt does refer to health care, as well as education and economic reasons, but besides a reference to "the experiences of Micronesians in Hawai'i" at the beginning of the article and a later mention of "the experiences of children and teens," this portion of the article is not necessarily negative. However, the article also includes the following statement, shown as excerpt (21).

Excerpt (21): *Honolulu Star-Advertiser*, October 20, 2017
In recent years the most visible group of immigrants in Hawaii has been the Micronesians. Some have had trouble adjusting to Hawaii's laws and social customs. Some of their practices regarding dress and behavior have made them the subject of unfavorable stereotypes. The fact that "Micros" can come to Hawaii in unlimited numbers under the Compact of Free Association between the United States and the nations of Micronesia (established in exchange for U.S. defense operations in this part of the Pacific), and that some newcomers to the islands are unprepared to enter the workforce or need expensive medical care, has fueled negative perceptions.

Here, the article makes reference to the visibility of Micronesians, and then proceeds to note that they have "trouble adjusting," have become the subject of "unfavorable stereotypes," and fuel "negative perceptions" because they "are unprepared to enter the workforce or need expensive medical care." This is basically a reiteration of the "Micronesian experience in Hawai'i" that constitutes the problem frame through which they are viewed by the public. It is noteworthy that this article began by discussing a play focusing on "the Micronesian experience," a specific topic that segued into a more general discussion of stereotypes and the view of Micronesians as a social problem.

Moreover, there is evidence from the articles in the corpus that the people in the category "Micronesian" have come to believe this problem frame. The next excerpt is from an article intended to honor a particular high school student for his achievements in the sport of basketball.

Excerpt (22): *Honolulu Star-Advertiser*, December 13, 2016
"It was a great experience for me to see a whole new perspective of basketball and life," he wrote via text. "Those guys can really ball. Having that label of

being a 'Micronesian' ball player is something that most wouldn't be proud of. However, I am proud to tell everyone that I AM a Mirconesian ball player and I don't care about the label or anything attached to that title. I want to inspire more athletes like me who grew up playing ball at Crane Park and Makiki Park because without those experiences of playing with the men at those parks, I would never be where I am today."

This excerpt focuses on the words texted by the basketball player himself, including his mention of the label "Micronesian" and his declaration that it is a label "most wouldn't be proud of." He does go on to assert his pride in being a "Micronesian ball player," but his words show his own understanding of the public image attached to Micronesians in Hawai'i. Like many of the other articles, there is an attempt to be sympathetic and even express positivitity toward Micronesians, but it still contains a reference to the problem frame. Even though the subject of the article does not explain the negative image, readers will understand because of the frequency with which newspaper and other public discourse has reinforced the problem frame. The problem frame, in short, has constructed a version of social reality in which the category of "Micronesian" is viewed negatively in Hawaiian society.

At this point of the analysis, it is of value to step back and point out the degree to which this problem frame and the newspaper discourse concerning Micronesians contrast with depictions of Filipinos in the corpus. Except for three articles that pointed to the use of the Ilocano language in criminal court cases, "Filipino" was not treated as a problematic category. There was not an identifiable problem frame that attempted to steer public discourse toward aspects of the label "Filipino" that harmed general Hawaiian society. Instead, "Filipino" was by and large constructed as an accepted category that was established in the community. Furthermore, in contrast to the basketball player who showed awareness of the negative perceptions of the label "Micronesian," the corpus showed that the category "Filipino" was embraced by people in that category. This was evidenced by the addition of "Filipino" to restaurants and types of foods as well as to community groups.

Yet, there is one similarility between the two groups in the corpus. Like the category Ilocano, there is a connection made in the newspapers between the languages Marshallese and Chuukese and crime through the mention of language interpreters in court. Excerpt (23) offers an example.

Excerpt (23): *Honolulu Star-Advertiser*, February 1, 2018
A 22-year-old man has been charged with murder in connection with the fatal stabbing of a 23-year-old man in Waipahu. Aiven Angei appeared in District Court today after he was charged Wednesday with second-degree murder in the death of the victim identified in court records and by the Honolulu Medical Examiner's Office as Jonathan Makana Kanui-Flores. Deputy Public Defender

John Foster pleaded not guilty to the charge on Angei's behalf. A court-appointed Chuukese interpreter assisted Angei during his arraignment.

This excerpt is taken from the beginning of the article and it starts with a description of both the accused and the victim that provides their genders and ages. The name of the accused is given in the second sentence, but there is not any reference to the ethnicity of either man until the last sentence notes that the accused received assistance from a Chuukese interpreter. This pattern is the same as the excerpts shown earlier concerning Ilocano. The newspapers refrain from assigning an ethnic label to the accused, but the language category of the interpreter makes it easy to infer ethnicity (even though there is the possibility that the inference could be incorrect).

On the overall, articles employing the language names "Chuukese" and "Marshallese" for court-related cases did not constitute a large percentage of the articles found in the corpus. Of the thirty articles using Chuukese from November 18, 2014, to February 1, 2018, four of them employed Chuukese to describe actual usages in a court situation. For Marshallese, there were three articles for a period covering May 8, 2016, through January 20, 2018. These numbers suggest that the frequency with which crime was linked to people from Micronesia is not nearly as high as other social problems.

Nonetheless, there were a couple of tendencies in the discourse that, in terms of reinforcing stereotypes, are notable. Excerpt (24) provides an example from an article describing an accusation of sexual assault.

Excerpt (24): *Hawaii Tribune-Herald*, July 4, 2017
Sardis also allegedly admitted to police, after being advised of his rights, that he had sexually penetrated the alleged victim. At Sardis' initial appearance Monday in Hilo District Court, Deputy Public Defender Austin Hsu told Judge Michael Udovic there had been "a potential request for a Chuukese interpreter in this matter." "I did speak to Mr. Sardis previously about that, and he does not need a translator. . . . He was a court interpreter," Hsu said.

Following the general pattern, no explicit ethnic labels are attached to the accused, but the article quotes the deputy public defender as stating that there was "a potential request for a Chuukese interpreter." However, the same defender notes that there was no need for a translator because the accused "was a court interpreter." The outcome, then, is that there ultimately was no need for a court interpreter, hence raising the question as to why this information was even necessary in the first place. In general, when speakers of English are accused of crimes, newspapers do not take the time to note that an interpreter is not necessary. The only thing that this information in excerpt (24) accomplishes is that it emphasizes the language spoken by the accused as Chuukese, thus revealing his ethnicity. This disclosure of his ethnicity, therefore, brings with it the potential that this added information could reinforce ideological beliefs about people from Micronesia as violent.

Excerpt (25) offers a related yet different example where the addition of information feeds negative public perceptions. This excerpt is taken from the start of the article.

> Excerpt (25): Hawaii Associated Press Wire, July 25, 2015
> A recent case involving a man accused of shooting a woman and a police officer on the Big Island highlights a growing challenge in Hawaii: finding people who can translate court hearings in other languages. The man speaks Marshallese, and his right to hear his proceedings in the Marshall Islands tongue has led to delays in his case.

The article begins by describing court translation as a "growing challenge in Hawaii." In doing so, it refers to a specific case in which a man speaks Marshallese, and it notes that his right to hear the case in Marshallese has become an impediment in moving forward. The accused has not been explicitly assigned an ethnic label, but his Marshallese ethnicity is accessible from the discourse.

Thus, much like the article described in excerpts (17) and (18) in which an elderly Micronesian couple was used to exemplify problems in health care in Hawaiʻi, the writer of this article employs the process of generalization to take a specific problem involving one court case and characterize it as a general problem in society. Moreover, by adding that the accused's "right to hear his proceedings in the Marshall Islands tongue has led to delays in his case," the writer extends the reach of the problem. It is not just a problem of finding interpreters but it more generally affects the prompt execution of court cases.

In fact, this same article goes on to draw an even more direct connection betweens migrants from Micronesia and the problem of court interpretation, as shown in excerpt (26).

> Excerpt (26): Hawaii Associated Press Wire, July 25, 2015
> Meanwhile, requests for their services have soared, fueled by an influx of migrants from certain Pacific island nations who come to Hawaii under an agreement with the federal government. The deal, known as the Compact of Free Association, lets citizens from the Federated States of Micronesia, the Republic of the Marshall Islands and the Republic of Palau live and work freely in the United States in exchange for allowing the U.S. military to control strategic land and water areas in the region."

"Requests for services" at the outset of this excerpt refers to requests for court interpretation, which is attributed to "an influx of migrants." The excerpt then mentions the Compact of Free Association (COFA) in order to explain why there has been an "influx." Through the process of generalization, the writer of this article has employed one singular example of a request for Marshallese court interpretation to identify the COFA migrants as the source of a social problem. This process of generalization, then, represents a difference in the way court cases related to Micronesians were treated in the corpus in comparison to that of Filipinos. The three articles that noted the necessity of Ilocano interpreters did not use generalization to construct court interpretation as a social problem. The articles that framed court interpretation requests as a social issue tended to focus on either Chuukese or Marshallese. In doing so, these articles fit the basic the pattern found in the corpus of attributing some social problems in Hawai'i to the recent migration of people from Micronesia.

Furthermore, it could be argued that the usage of court interpretation to reveal the ethnic origins of alleged criminals is especially noteworthy because the court cases often center on violent crimes such as murder and sexual assault. By choosing to publish accounts of these crimes and by highlighting the growing need for interpretation services of languages spoken by the COFA migrants, these types of articles, although not as frequent as articles that focus on other social problems, help reinforce public perception of the migrants as potential perpetrators of violent crime.

DISCUSSION

The analysis focused on a corpus of recent articles in newspapers in an attempt to highlight differences in the treatment of two groups of people in Hawai'i referred to simply as "Filipinos" and "Micronesians." In contrast to the category of "Filipino," which was constructed as an accepted and established category, "Micronesian" was viewed as the cause of several social problems. Here, it should be emphasized that the "tenor" of most of the articles employing the term "Micronesian" was not necessarily negative. The articles were, in fact, often sympathetic to the problems related to their recent arrival in Hawai'i. Nonetheless, even when adopting a sympathetic stance, the articles still reinforced ideological perceptions about Micronesians in Hawai'i, particularly that they are homeless, they put a strain on public finances and social services, and they even may commit violent crimes.

The analysis showed that the discourse promoted these beliefs first through a process of generalization, whereby specific instances involving people from Micronesia were generalized to the societal level. This was apparent in the example given in excerpts (17) and (18) of a Chuukese couple who attempted to obtain health care services and also in the request discussed in excerpts (25) and (26) by a Marshallese speaker for interpretation services. Furthermore, the frequency with which social problems are attributed to the "influx" of migrants from Micronesian is indicative of a "problem frame" that constructs for readers a version of reality in Hawaiian society such that Micronesians are perceived negatively as contributors to social and financial problems. This problem frame thus leads consumers of the articles to read references to the "Micronesian experience" in Hawai'i in relation to the existing social stigma, and it also prompts people from Micronesia to show an awareness of negative public perceptions when quoted in the newspapers.

Even though the usage of "Filipino" constrasted significantly with the negative perceptions attributed to "Micronesian," it is worthwhile to note that references to "Filipino" may also be problematic since they do not demonstrate awareness of the complexities of the category of "Filipino" in Hawai'i. These complexities were outlined prior to the analysis as consisting of various Filipino identities in Hawai'i, including "local Filipino," "immigrant Filipino," "mainland Filipino," and possibly "educated Filipino." Despite the fact that identity has been an issue within the Filipino community in Hawai'i, the newspaper articles tended to treat "Filipino" as a unified entity, thus presenting an oversimplified view. In particular, articles such as those presented in excerpts (1)–(4) that showed people of Filipino ethnicity promoting Filipino restaurants and foods suggest a united sense of Filipino pride. Likewise, the usage of "Filipino" as a modifier of community organizations in excerpts (5) and (6) intimates that these are places to be accessed by members of the Filipino community. Such representation of "Filipino" in the newspapers may not constitute a negative perception of Filipinos, but images of unification may be problematic for some members of the community who consider themselves "Filipino" but who may not agree with this image and who may not have access to as many aspects of the Filipino community as Filipinos of other identities.

This is not to suggest that all newspaper articles in Hawai'i treat the category of "Filipino" so straightforwardly. The analysis in this chapter limited itself to the most recent thirty articles. Given the extensive changes in the Filipino community since 1906, it would be interesting to observe newspaper references at different points of time over the last 100 years in order to examine how the perceptions of "Filipino" developed throughout the course of modern Hawaiian history.

The suggestion that perceptions of Filipinos in Hawai'i may have changed throughout history makes it possible to speculate about the future of Micronesian communities in Hawai'i. Discussion prior to the analysis indicated that younger generations of Micronesians may already be attempting to distance themselves from traditional Micronesian identities. Given the negative perceptions and the ideologies expressed in newspaper discourse, we may posit that some children born in Hawai'i to Micronesian parents will desire to separate themselves from such stigmatized views, raising the possibility of an identity crisis similar to the one described by researchers of the Filipino experience in Hawai'i. Relatedly, we can also posit that younger generations of Micronesians will move away from their ancestral languages in order to adopt English and possibly Pidgin, languages that could be key to gaining acceptance into local Hawaiian society. Finally, another point of speculation concerns the negative ideologies expressed in newspapers. In particular, we may ask, as the history of Micronesians in Hawai'i extends in length and as the community becomes more complex in identities, will the newspapers start to treat them as a more accepted and established like the Filipinos? Will there be discussion about types of Micronesian cuisine and restaurants and will the newspapers include more references to churches and community organizations modified by the category "Micronesian?" While depiction in the newspapers of the category "Filipino," with many positive references to cuisine and community, provides much food for thought, these are questions that only time and further research will be able to answer.

CONCLUSION

This chapter focused on ideological beliefs expressed in newspapers in Hawai'i concerning the categories "Filipino" and "Micronesian" in order to highlight some further complexities in Hawai'i as a multilingual society. Multilingual societies are complex linguistic ecologies due to the various points in which languages intersect, with these intersections constituted by ideologies about not only languages but also speakers of languages. As noted previously, efforts are being made to offer more official services in Hawai'i in Micronesian languages such as Marshallese and Chuukese, but the ideological beliefs expressed and reinforced in newspapers suggest that struggles of people from Micronesia concerning the degree of social stigmatization may require more than interpreting services. As Verschueren (2012, 7) asserts, "*ideology* is associated with *underlying patterns of meaning, frames of interpretation, world views*, or *forms of everyday thinking and explanation*."[4] It thus seems, based on the data presented in this chapter, that beliefs about the Micronesian migrants, namely, that their existence in Hawai'i puts on a strain on social and economic services, have become part of the underlying patterns of meaning and frames of interpretation in Hawaiian public discourse.

This chapter employed media discourse to probe general public beliefs about the categories "Filipino" and "Micronesian," but it should be noted, in keeping with the conclusions of the previous two chapters, that together with language usage itself, ideologies may also vary depending on the situation. Accordingly, there is a strong chance of finding social situations as well as communities in Hawai'i that are undergirded by different beliefs.[5] The next chapter, the conclusion, addresses the relationship between the expression of ideologies in specific social spaces and the general beliefs that may exist at a general, societal level.

NOTES

1. These terms are written with quotation marks to indicate that they are abstract category names applied to diverse groups of people. This point is discussed in more detail as a part of this chapter.

2. One example would be obituaries that were the same in different newspapers. However, in the case where two articles had similar topics but differed in content, these were counted as two separate articles.

3. In the newspaper articles appearing in the database, it was sometimes not clear whether modern orthographic conventions (the *'okina* and the *kahakō*) were used for spelling Hawaiian words. For example, sometimes the word "Hawai'i" appeared as Hawaii without the 'okina. For the purposes of presenting the data, I am going to include these conventions to be consistent.

4. Italics are included in the original.

5. See, for example, a study by Marshall Carucci (2012) about Marshallese identities in Kona, a town on the Big Island of Hawai'i. This study discusses some of the negative beliefs toward the Marshallese but also describes the intricate interplay of different beliefs in that specific community.

Conclusion

Linguistic Ethnography and Multilingualism in Hawai'i

INTRODUCTION

The chapters in this book have presented a linguistic ethnography intended to promote understanding of Hawai'i as a multilingual society. Linguistic ethnography was chosen as the basic mode of inquiry because it facilitates the employment of a variety of research and analytic procedures toward the ultimate goal of gaining insight into the linguistic situation of a complex and dynamic society. Whereas concepts utilized previously to study bilingual and multilingual situations, for instance, territorial bilingualism and diglossia, tend to present relationships between and among languages as quite stable, linguistic ethnography, with its focus on situated language usage, enables a heightened ability to appreciate multilingualism as a negotiated and sometimes contested social phenomenon. Language ecology, as described by Haugen (1972), moved attention away from individual languages and toward the intersection of languages in society, but it is linguistic ethnography's commitment to examining the details of such intersections, including the social histories and ideological beliefs of the participants, that allows for insights into the language ecologies that constitute a modern society.

The linguistic ethnography presented here examined spoken and written data from various sources. The spoken data included archived interviews of elder speakers of Hawaiian, interviews conducted by the researcher, radio advertisements, university commencement speeches, and video clips available on social media of television programs and also community meetings involving politicians. The written materials concentrated particularly on newspaper articles but also featured websites as well as a few observations of signage in the town of Hilo. Each individual source of data in and of itself offers a glimpse of situated language usage in Hawai'i, and, when put together as a linguistic ethnography that considers the historical and ideological context, the collective observations begin to piece together a larger picture of how Hawai'i is constituted by multiple languages.

Linguistic ethnography also makes it possible to draw from a diverse set of analytic methods and concepts. The chapters in this book employed at times the perspectives of conversation analysis, membership category analysis, and critical discourse analysis, and it also adapted ideas from Lakoff's metaphor theory, ethnopoetics, indexicality, heteroglossia, and functional approaches to grammar and the expression of agency. Regardless of differences in theoretical orientation, these frameworks and ideas served as more or less equal resources toward a common goal of elucidating the relationship between language and society in Hawai'i. A line-by-line sequential analysis associated with CA helped explicate the basic organization of repetitions employed by elder speakers of Hawaiian, which subsequently made it possible to appreciate repetition as part of the ethnopoetics of a traditional Hawaiian approach to speaking. The concept of indexicality allowed for understanding of the nonreferential meanings that became attached throughout history to languages such as Hawaiian, Pidgin, and English, and the notion of heteroglossia made it possible to see how these nonreferential meanings could be mixed and contrasted in instances of discourse that accomplished various social actions such as joking around, giving advice, and setting agendas in political meetings. Membership category analysis was employed to emphasize, on the one hand, how meaningful language categories such as "Hawaiian," "Pidgin," "English," and "Japanese" are to people in Hawai'i, and, on the other hand, how an ethnic category such as "Japanese" can have many meanings within the same society. CDA's focus on inequality and ideology allowed for insight into the newspaper's role in perpetuating negative perceptions about the Micronesian population in Hawai'i. The combination of these analytic perspectives highlights the complexity of Hawaiian society, and in the process, provides resources for making sense of such complexity.

The chapters in this book therefore employed linguistic ethnography not to produce a singular model of multilingualism per se but instead as a way of describing how multiple languages come together in a specific society by producing both broad generalizations about language in Hawai'i as well as elucidating specific details of actual instances of language usage. Based on the findings, it is possible to go back and locate four key points that facilitated comprehension of both general and specific aspects of multilingualism in Hawai'i, recognition, heteroglossia, situational understandings, and ideology. The remainder of this concluding chapter focuses on these key ideas.

RECOGNITION

Recognition here is meant to refer simply to the act of "seeing" and "accepting" the importance of languages in a society. In order to study and appreciate multilingualism, there has to be recognition that a society is constituted by several languages. In some cases, for example, English, it is easy to see the place of a language in a society, but in other cases, either due to a lack of visibility or to ideological concerns that prompt people to overlook languages, recognition is not necessarily so simple. In this study, recognition was important to the inclusion of languages such as Hawaiian and Pidgin in the study. As noted in chapter 2, questions have been raised about the relevancy of the Hawaiian language to current society despite recent efforts to revitalize the language as the medium of education in some schools and programs. Similarly, Pidgin has struggled to gain recognition in Hawai'i due to its marginalized status as a form of broken English.

Recognition, it should be noted, is not just a concern in Hawai'i but is a problem in situations throughout the world where languages have been the objects of marginalization. According to De Mejia (2006, 2017), Colombia struggles to recognize its multilingualism, particularly Amerindian and creole language as well as the usage of Portuguese in border areas. Relatedly, Ndhlovu (2006, 2008) describes the marginalization of minority languages in Zimbabwe, where only the languages of the ruling elite, Shona and Ndebele, receive recognition. Likewise, Mohanty (2010) has linked linguistic problems in India to a hierarchically structured multilingualism that leaves languages at the bottom unrecognized.

Fortunately, both Hawaiian and Pidgin have been gaining in recognition not just in academic studies but also in society itself. The language revitalization movement continues to produce more young speakers of Hawaiian, and as more students enter and complete Hawaiian language schools and programs, the presence of the language is expected to continue to expand, bringing with it more chances to be heard not only in educational settings but also at shopping malls, grocery stores, restaurants, as well as in the media. Although Pidgin still remains stigmatized, it has been recognized as a language of Hawai'i on the census and it has likewise benefited from efforts of advocates to promote critical awareness throughout the general population.

In some respects, however, progress in recognizing multilingualism in Hawai'i has been relatively slow. Despite a growing Micronesian presence since the mid-1980s, it has been difficult to access services in Hawai'i such as driver's examinations in languages such as Marshallese and Chuukese until fairly recently. The same is true of court interpretation, something that has also affected the Hawaiian language. Although Hawaiian has been an official language in 1978, the denial of requests to use Hawaiian in court has continued to be an issue (Hofschneider 2018).

The notion of recognition also highlights the fact that this study is strikingly incomplete. While I chose some of the languages I considered to be important in the current social landscape in Hawai'i, there are numerous other languages that could have been selected. These include some obvious choices such as Mandarin, Cantonese, Sāmoan, and Korean as well as others that may not be so transparent. One example is Russian, which I raise here because of the admonishment I received from a student, who, after taking a course of mine that focuses on a survey of the various languages in Hawai'i, criticized my lack of attention to her native tongue. According to her, not only did she use it among her family and friends on a daily basis but she also attended a church where Russian was the primary language. Spanish is another language that students have brought up as being relevant to them in Hawai'i. Then, of course, there are other Asian languages that are important in parts of Hawai'i, including Thai and Vietnamese, and there are also additional Polynesian languages like Tahitian and Fijian and even more Micronesian languages such as Kosraen and Pohnpeian that are growing in visibility. Some of these languages may be majority languages in other countries, but they are all minority languages in Hawai'i that have varying degrees of influence on the linguistic landscape. From the perspective of recognition, then, this study should be considered only a beginning attempt to understand multilingualism in Hawai'i.

HETEROLGOSSIA

Recognition concerns not just languages but also language practices, which leads to the next important key to understanding multilingualism in Hawai'i, heteroglossia. As noted in chapter 4, heteroglossic language practices have rarely been a topic of study in a Hawaiian context, even though there is a multitude of evidence suggesting how pervasive such practices are. The mixing of languages was prevalent in many, if not most, of the excerpts of language data presented in this study. All of the excerpts with politician Billy Kenoi, including his speech on television programs, university commencement speeches, and community meetings exhibited heteroglossia involving at least English and Pidgin and sometimes Hawaiian. Additionally, radio advertisements, websites, and signs around town all employ heteroglossic language practices that mix combinations of English, Pidgin, and Hawaiian to varying degrees. The interviews in chapter 5 concerning the Japanese language and identities also contained a significant amount of language mixing, especially the interviews with the bilingual speakers and the learners of Japanese. Even the newspaper data, which mostly used English, presented at least one example of an article written primarily in Pidgin. Any attempt to consider multilingualism in Hawai'i would be grossly incomplete without significant discussion devoted to heteroglossia.

As noted in chapter 4, other terms—most notably codeswitching—have been used to consider this phenomenon, but the concept of heteroglossia is particularly attractive because of Bakhtin's (1981) desire to attend to the contrasting sociohistorical meanings that have become attached to languages. Given Pidgin's ties to the plantation immigrants and given its development at the basically same time that English emerged as a dominant language, the mixing of these two language indexes voices that were historically in conflict with one another. Moreover, the addition of Hawaiian, the indigenous language of the land that is now a source of pride for many people of Hawaiian ethnicity, brings to the discourse a very different voice that contrasts with both Pidgin and English. The data showed that the politician Billy Kenoi was particularly adept at accessing the meanings associated with these languages as he employed Pidgin not only to makes jokes but also to connect with the local community, English to add a sense of formality to some of his speeches, and Hawaiian to access traditional sayings and values.

The concept of heteroglossia moves us away from a "monolingual mindset" approach (Clyne 2005; Hajek and Slaughter 2015, Ndhovlu 2015) to appreciate the creative potential in a multilingual society of speakers to employ language in a way that goes beyond the boundaries of individual languages. Again here, the speech of the politician Kenoi is the most obvious example as his mixing of Hawaiian, Pidgin, and English embodied the "fantastic semiotic creativity" (Blommaert 2003, 611) that is possible when speakers employ the linguistic resources that are available in a society constituted by multiple languages. Kenoi's heteroglossia in commencement speeches allowed him to construct entertaining speeches that also provided serious advice, and his speech in community meetings enabled a connection with an audience presumed to be mostly local. Creativity was also on display in the Kamehamemeha Schools website, with unique mixtures of Hawaiian and English meant to promote a school system that offers both English and Hawaiian language and cultural education. This creativity was also visible in the radio advertisements described in chapter 3. Even the excerpts where advertisements mixed only single Pidgin words into speech that was otherwise English-dominant serve as examples of people crossing languages to make usage of available multilingual resources.

The basic idea of heteroglossia also applies to the attempt in chapter 5 to understanding the role of the Japanese language in Hawai'i. Such an attempt made it apparent that there were multiple voices in not only the Japanese language but also in the construction of Japanese identities in Hawaiian society. These different Japanese languages and identities stem from the simultaneous existence in society of relatives of the early plantation worker immigrants, some of whom do not speak Japanese, the *shin issei* who often came to work in the tourist industry, learners of Japanese who may be employing various forms of the language, and the ambiguous relationship of the people from Okinawa to a Japanese identity. The interviews in chapter 5 suggest a complex relationship in Hawai'i between the Japanese language and a Japanese identity that varies depending on the experiences of individuals. While chapter 6 focused on "Japanese," an approach that is prepared to recognize the various voices that constitute language usage will be critical to understanding the place of other immigrant languages and identities, for example, Chinese, Portuguese, Korean, or Puerto Rican.

As discussed in detail in chapter 4, an interesting aspect of the notion heteroglossia is the possibility it brings in terms of advancing the postmodern critique of language and ethnic categories. In its strongest form, this critique questions whether languages such as Japanese, English, Hawaiian actually exist. These language categories are considered to be ideological constructions that have "played a major role in the development of the European nation state as in the expansion and organization of empires" (Blommaert and Rampton 2016, 25). In the further words of Blommaert and Rampton (2016, 25), "the traditional idea of a 'a language,' then, is an ideological artefact with very considerable power—it operates as a major ingredient in the apparatus of modern governmentality, it is played out in a wide variety of domains (education, immigration, education, high and popular culture, etc.), and it can serve as an object of passionate personal attachment." Indeed, the analysis of newspaper discourse included in chapter 4 demonstrated just how much language categories pervade the everyday common sense of people in Hawai'i, and it even suggested that a postmodern critique of language categories may not appreciate the importance of those categories to movements that advocate for marginalized and endangered languages. Nonetheless, without pursuing this argument further here, we can suggest that this heteroglossic approach is important as an analytic mindset so that researchers, instead of taking for granted categories of language and identity in a society, set out to examine the occasioned practices used to constitute them as everyday matters of relevance. Thus, in addition to noting the general importance of the category of "Hawaiian" to the Hawaiian language revitalization, an interesting research tact would be to examine how the category "Hawaiian" is invoked in written and spoken discourse in ways that contribute to the revitalization movement. An interesting example is currently occurring in the town of Hilo involving plans to build a new Portuguese Cultural and Education Center (Cultural and Education Center 2017). Portuguese is considered an immigrant language due to the plantation history, but while many people identify as Portuguese in Hawai'i, the Portuguese language is rarely seen or heard in everyday society. As part of this project to honor the Portuguese heritage, it would be interesting to examine how people constitute themselves and others as Portuguese, and also how they invoke the category of "Portuguese" in discourse in society as a part of making sure that such a category gets maintained as a part of the cultural history of Hawai'i.

One final point about the potential of heteroglossia to aid in our understanding of multilingualism concerns the uniqueness of linguistic practices in society. Although I suggested that the heteroglossic practices used by Billy Kenoi as well as those appearing on the Kamehameha Schools website were all unique mixtures created by the people in those particular contexts, heteroglossia does not necessarily consist of only novel linguistic practices. Blommaert and Rampton (2016, 29–30) make such a point when they note:

> understanding the relationship between conventionality and innovation in these practices is difficult and there are a variety of traps that researchers have to navigate. It is easy for a practice's novelty to the outside analyst to mislead him/her into thinking that it is a creative innovation for the local participants as well.

In fact, the data presented throughout is full of possible examples of conventionality in heteroglossia, for example, terms such as "*aloha*" and "*mahalo*" that have become bivalent and cross two and even three languages. Due to a history in Hawai'i of heteroglossia that goes back 200 years, usage of "*aloha*" and "*mahalo*" in Pidgin or in English is no longer unique or very creative. Heteroglossic language practice in Hawaiian society consists of both the conventional and the creative. Not only did Kenoi regularly employ "*aloha*" and "*mahalo*" in his speeches, but he likewise incorporated words such as "*kuleana*," which is not necessarily creative given that it is a Hawaiian word commonly used by people who do not speak Hawaiian. Even Kenoi's quotation from King Kamehameha I draws on words that have been reproduced frequently in Hawaiian society. Accordingly, it is hoped that as future research begins to focus more on heteroglossic language practice in Hawaiian society, we will gain more knowledge about how multilingual speech practices in Hawai'i make use of both conventionality and innovation.

A SITUATIONAL APPROACH TO MULTILINGUALISM

Another key to understanding heteroglossic language practice is the examination of situations or spaces of language usage in society. As Blommaert et al.

(2005) suggest, space plays an important role in organizing multilingualism in a society. In their words (Blommaert et al. 2005, 203), "context (including space) does something to people when it comes to communicating. It organizes and defines sociolinguistic regimes in which spaces are characterized by sets of norms and expectations about communicative behavior." This is evidenced in a relatively straightforward way in educational domains in Hawai'i, where students capable of speaking multiple languages that include Pidgin are expected to employ only English in the classroom. However, in other situations, the same students (and possibly teachers) may exhibit heteroglossic tendencies. This was apparent to a certain degree in the speech of Billy Kenoi. When given the floor in the commencement speeches, he filled his formal speeches with Hawaiian, Pidgin, and English, but in other situations, for instance, the community meetings, he employed much more Pidgin (even though there was still considerable language mixing) as a part of displaying his status as a local insider. Observance of people in one situation will not serve as an accurate measure of their multilingual abilities.

There is in fact a close relationship between a situational approach and recognition in that the notion of space shows us the danger of trying to assess the overall overall position of languages within a society. As noted in chapter 2, the casual observer (Hale 2013) may conclude that Hawaiian has little or no place in Hawai'i. Yet, such a conclusion is undoubtedly a product of the particular spaces inhabited by the observer. Similarly, I have heard colleagues of mine say that they almost never hear Pidgin on the Big Island even though Pidgin seems to exist in various domains (including politics). However, such statements make sense when you consider that many university faculty and administrators find themselves in social spaces, for instance, the university, where Pidgin may not be common. An approach that considers specific spaces of language usage is important to understanding the roles occupied by Hawaiian and Pidgin in society.

The same is certainly true of other languages, particularly languages such as Japanese that are penetrated by different voices in Hawai'i. A tourist area such as Waikīkī expects a certain type of Japanese (a modern standard one) while a rural (former) plantation village on the Big Island calls for insiders to be familiar with certain Japanese terms such as "*bocha*," "*baban*," and "*habut*" that are associated with the *Chuugokuben* dialect of Japanese. One of these voices might represent a "modern" voice and the other an "old-fashioned" or "country" voice, but their appropriateness is shaped by context. It would be just as strange to call out to someone in a rural part of the Big Island in standard Japanese as it would be to address random Japanese tourists in Waikīkī in *Chuugokuben*.

A situational approach takes emphasis away from the individual as the possessors of language abilities. As Higgins (2009, 4) writes in the introduction to her book that examines the place of English in multilingual situations, "a focus on context deemphasizes multilingualism or fluency in English as a property of the individual and reestablishes it more firmly as a property of situation." With the focus on situations, we are able to facilitate understanding of why certain spaces remain basically English-only while others have now become essentially Hawaiian-only zones. Likewise, we could enhance our ability to look for instances of heteroglossia and analyze how the meanings and even functions of heteroglossic language practice might work in particular social spaces. Language is, in fact, largely connected to the situation through the process of indexicality whereby participants' language to point to aspects of the context, including ideological beliefs. Even though radio advertisements analyzed in chapter 3 employed primarily English, Pidgin was inserted in order to index Pidgin's connection to the context, namely that it has a close connection to a local identity.

At the same time, the notion of indexicality also reminds us that even though multilingualism is greatly conditioned by social space, the study of individual and groups of participants is still important because it is through language that people relate to context and construct and reinforce identities. Billy Kenoi's desire to connect with the participants in a specific social space of the community meeting led him to employ Pidgin, but his usage of Pidgin enabled him to index a certain aspect of his identity, that is, that he is a Pidgin speaker and thus "local." In fact, this is what I meant at the end of chapter 5 when I suggested that a situational approach to multilingualism also must consider the diverse experiences of people who act in those situations. Although it is relatively easy to conceive of Hawai'i as a single society because it is an isolated island chain in the Pacific, it is a society constituted by a diverse group of people and languages. People bring with them to social spaces a vast history of experiences and a long list of potential identity labels, and it is through language (as well as other semiotic resources) that they draw on those experiences and construct identities in instances of interaction. Thus, in chapter 5, the granddaughter of Japanese immigrants (LG) voiced her experience of growing up Japanese in a plantation village without speaking Japanese, which she construed to be "typical Japanese," a label that applied to her and other children in the village. Such an experience differs from other Japanese identities in Hawai'i, through which people may assume a more direct relationship between speaking a language and the development of identity. The point here is that any study of multilingualism in a society must consider not just how social space influences multilingual practices but also how people use linguistic resources to invoke their own experiences in relation to the social spaces that they inhabit.

IDEOLOGY

The final key notion in the attempts to understand multilingualism in this book is ideology. Recognition that language and language usage can be saturated with ideological beliefs is partly what makes it difficult to accept the "Hawai'i as multicultural melting pot model." Even in the absence of explicit expressions of hostility there may be negative beliefs that underlie relationships among people in society. As indicated in chapter 6, newspaper articles that seemed sympathetic to the struggles of Micronesian migrants nonetheless reinforced perceptions that serve as the basis of feelings of resentment.

The concept of ideology was applied to both languages and people. The chapters that focused on Hawaiian, Pidgin, and also heteroglossia mostly considered language ideologies, detailing how negative beliefs developed toward both Hawaiian and Pidgin through contact with English, which came to be the language of power and control in Hawai'i. At the same time, it was noted that ideological beliefs can change over the course of time, with Hawaiian serving as a good example. Due to changes in society resulting from the Hawaiian Renaissance and also the Hawaiian language revitalization movement, Hawaiian went from being a language that parents did not want to pass on to their children to a language representing the dignity and pride associated with a Hawaiian identity. And while negative attitudes about Pidgin have proven to be more persistent, efforts to promote critical language awareness have helped Pidgin become more well received in some public domains.

The analyses demonstrated that ideological beliefs about language factor into spaces of language usage through the concept of indexicality. Through indexicality, we can see how Pidgin, Hawaiian, and English may be mixed so that ideologies serve as resources for the accomplishment of actions such as making jokes and emphasizing points of advice. Billy Kenoi was shown to be especially adept at this as he used heteroglossic language practices to contrast the formality of English with the localness indexed by Pidgin and the traditional voices represented by Hawaiian. Ideological beliefs also underpinned the usage of language in radio advertisements, as Pidgin enabled the creators of the ads to align briefly with a local audience while otherwise maintaining a general sense of formality through English.

The notion of ideology was also used in this study to discuss the attitudes about people that developed in a society that changed drastically since Cook's arrival in 1778. With an influx of not just Europeans and Americans but also people from various parts of Asia, Polynesia, and other Pacific Islands, the swift transformation into an immigrant society brought with it belief systems that, when expressed, have served as a means for exerting control over groups of people. Chapter 1 provided discussion of the negative perceptions expressed by the haole plantation owners toward both the native Hawaiian population as well as the immigrants that arrived to work on the plantations. These ideologies often took the form of metaphors that placed the Hawaiians and the immigrants in the role of children, hence rationalizing the haole owners' usurpation of power in society. Ideologies about people were revisited in chapter 6 with a particular focus on the categories of "Filipino" and "Micronesian." A critical discourse analysis of newspaper discourse indicated that public discourse about "Micronesian" was dominated by beliefs that stirred resentment toward this recent group of migrants among the larger population of people in Hawai'i. More specifically, the analysis showed the reinforcement of the beliefs that Micronesians served as a source of resentment and generally were a strain on the economy because of their need for social services because of health and homelessness issues.

The analysis underscored processes such as "generalization" and also frameworks such as "problem frames" that contributed to the construction of these ideologies in the discourse, and it likewise pointed to an indexical aspect to the expression of ideologies in the newspaper discourse. More specifically, it suggested that due to the pervasiveness of these ideologies in discourse, the mere reference to the "Micronesian experience" served to index the negative perceptions that made adaptation to life in Hawai'i difficult for these new migrants.

Exploration of ideologies and their expression in discourse has the potential to inform our understanding of the links between specific social spaces and general beliefs that undergird society. Ideologies develop because of their pervasiveness as "underlying patterns of meaning" and "frames of interpretation" (Verschueren 2012, 7), and they therefore serve as the basis for the semiotic expression of ideas in specific episodes of interaction. At the same time, their expression in specific instances reinforces their status as general ideological beliefs in society. A good example is the mixture of Pidgin and English in the radio advertisements presented in chapter 3. As discussed, the usage of Pidgin to express a sense of localness in this particular space draws on and reinforces the connection between Pidgin and a local voice in general society. Likewise, the usage of English to emit a sense of formality relies on the underlying belief about English, namely, that it is the "proper" language to be used in formal settings. And, by employing only English to explain products and Pidgin to express localness through a few words and/or dialogues, the organization of language in this particular space is reproducing the general ideological belief that English is more appropriate in public domains.

To be sure, specific spaces of interaction can counter the dominant ideologies of a society. This is undoubtedly what happened with the Hawaiian language as both the Hawaiian Renaissance and the Hawaiian language revitalization were grassroots movements that started with spaces of activism that eventually helped reverse ideological beliefs toward a Hawaiian identity and the Hawaiian language at a general, societal level. The same may be happening for Pidgin, and it may have already happened for some people of Filipino ancestry. Even though the immigrant workers from the Philippines in the early 1900s were socially stigmatized, the analysis presented in chapter 6 indicated that Filipino was used in the newspapers to emphasize community and also pride in a Filipino culinary heritage. Continued research should be able to further probe the ideologies that underlie language usage in specific social spaces and how they interact with ideological beliefs at a more macro level.

FINAL COMMENTS

Aronin et al. (2013, 4) makes a case for the importance of pursuing research on multilingualism with the statement, "multilingualism has developed to a stage where it is no longer just one of the characteristics of human society; it has become an inherent and, arguably, in many ways, the most salient property of postmodern human society as a whole and of large numbers of specific communities, whatever their size." In an attempt to further understanding of multilingualism, this book focused on a particularly society, Hawai'i, and selected a methodological approach, linguistic ethnography, that was flexible enough to allow for a diverse set of analyses of situated language usage. Through the four key notions of recognition, heteroglossia, situational approach, and ideology, the analyses drew connections between specific sites of language usage and general tendencies at the societal level in Hawai'i. Of course, no claim can be made that this is the only or best way to examine the intersection of language in complex societies. In the words of Aronin and Jessner (2014, 57), "research methodology on multilingualism is remarkably open in that it allows for a wide range of approaches." Accordingly, there are undoubtedly other methodological orientations that may be able to add knowledge about the uses of various languages in a society such as Hawai'i. Nevertheless, it is hoped that within the details of the analyses and points of discussion in this book lie insights that will assist in future endeavors to understand language in Hawai'i as well as the organization of multilingualism in other societies.

Bibliography

A list of Pidgin Words. 2016. Associated Press. https://www.seattletimes.com/nation-world/a-list-of-pidgin-words-the-languages-that-influenced-them/. Last accessed on June 19, 2018.

Abbi, Anvita. 1975. *Reduplication in Hindi: A generative semantic study*. Dissertation, Cornell University.

Adams, Romanzo. 1926. "Hawaii as a racial melting pot." *The Mid-Pacific Magazine* 32(3): 213–216.

Allen, Riley. 1921. "Education and race problems in Hawai'i." *The American Review of Reviews* 613–624.

Altheide, David. 1997. "The news media, the problem frame, and the production of fear." *The Sociological Quarterly* 38(4): 647–668.

Altheide, David, and R. Sam Michalowski. 1999. "Fear in the news: A discourse of control." *The Sociological Quarterly* 40(3): 475–503.

Anderson, Benedict. 1983. *Imagined Communities*. London: Verso.

Andrade, Naleen Naupaka, and Stephanie Nishimura. 2011. "The Portuguese." In *People and cultures of Hawai'i: The evolution of culture and ethnicity*, ed. John McDermott, John Andrade, and Naleen Naupaka, pp. 81–106. Honolulu: University of Hawai'i Press.

Ansaldo, Umberto. 2015. "Review of Vandenbussche, Hakon Jahr, and Trudgill, eds., Language Ecology for the 21st Century: Linguistic Conflicts and Social Environments." *Journal of Sociolinguistics* 19(2): 257–260.

Arnaut, Karel, Jan Blommaert, Ben Rampton, and Massimiliano Spotti. 2016. *Language and superdiversity*. New York: Routledge.

Aronin, Larissa, and Ulrike Jessner. 2014. "Methodology in bi- and multilingual studies." *AILA Review* 27: 56–79.

Aronin, Larissa, Joshua Fishman, David Singleton, and Muiris O Laoire. 2013. "Current multilingualism: A new linguistic dispensation." In *Current Multilingualism: A New Linguistic Dispensation*, ed. David Singleton, Joshua Fishman, Larissa Aronin, and Muiris O Laoire, pp. 3–23. De Gruyter Mouton.

Asato, Noriko. 2006. *Teaching Mikadoism: The attack on Japanese language schools in Hawaii, California, and Washington*. Honolulu: University of Hawai'i Press.
Aspinwall, Dorothy. 1960. "Languages in Hawai'i." *PMLA* 75(4 Supplement): 7–13.
Auden, W. H. 2009. "Introduction: Navajo poetry and poetics." In *Explorations in Navajo Poetry and Poetics*, ed. Anthony Webster, pp. 1–15. University of New Mexico.
Auer, Peter, and Li Wei. 2008. "Introduction: Multilingualism as a problem? Monolingualism as a problem?" In *Handbook of multilingualism and multilingual communication*, ed. Peter Auer and Li Wei, pp. 1–12. De Gruyter Mouton.
Bakhtin, Mikhail. 1981. *The dialogic imagination*. Austin: Texas University Press.
Bakhtin, Mikhail. 1986. *Speech genres and other late essays*. Austin: University of Texas Press.
Bailey, Benjamin. 2012. "Heteroglossia." In *The Routledge Handbook of Multilingualism*, ed. Amrilyn Martin-Jones, Adrian Blackledge, and Angela Creese, pp. 499–507. New York: Routledge.
Baker, Colin, and Sylvia Prys Jones. 1998. *Encyclopedia of bilingualism and bilingual education*. Multilingual Matters.
Barron, Colin, Nigel Bruce, and David Nunan. 2002. *Knowledge and discourse: Towards an ecology of language*. London: Longman.
Bauman, Richard, and Charles Briggs. 2003. *Voices of modernity: Language ideologies and the politics of inequality*. Cambridge: Cambridge University Press.
Bayer, Ann Shea. 2009. *Going against the grain: When professionals in Hawai'i choose public schools instead of private schools*. Honolulu: University of Hawai'i Press.
Beaglehole, Ernest. 1937. "Some modern Hawaiians." *University of Hawai'i Research Publications*, no. 19. University of Hawai'i, Honolulu.
Becker, Alton. 1984. "The linguistics of particularity: Interpreting subordination in a Javanese text." *Berkeley Linguistics Society* 10: 425–436.
Beechart, Edward. 1985. *Working in Hawai'i: A Labor History*. Honolulu: University of Hawai'i Press.
Benham, Maenette, and Ronald Heck. 1998. *Culture and educational policy in Hawai'i: The silencing of native voices*. Mahwah, NJ: Lawrence Erlbaum.
Benton, Richard. 1981. *The flight of the Amokura: Oceanic languages and formal education in the South Pacific*. Wellington: New Zealand Council for Educational Research.
Berman, Eliza. 2015. "The beautiful half-truth of the Hawaiian melting pot." *Time.com*. August. Accessed on June 18, 2018, http://time.com/3985733/hawaii-melting-pot/
Bhatia, Tej, and William Ritchie, eds. 2013. *The handbook of bilingualism and multilingualism*, 2nd ed. London: Blackwell.
Bickerton, Derek. 1998. "Language and language contact." In *Multicultural Hawai'i: The fabric of a multiethnic society*, ed. Michael Haas, pp. 53–64. New York: Garland Publishing.
Bickerton, Derek, and Carol Odo. 1976. *Change and variation in Hawaiian English. Volume 1. General phonology and Pidgin syntax*. Honolulu: Social Sciences and Linguistics Institute, University of Hawai'i at Mānoa.

Bickerton, Derek, and William Wilson. 1987. "Pidgin Hawaiian." In *Pidgin and Creole languages: Essays in memory of John E. Reinecke*, ed. Glenn Gilbert, pp. 61–76. Honolulu: University of Hawai'i Press.

Billig, Michael. 1999. "Whose terms? Whose ordinariness? Rhetoric and ideology in conversation analysis." *Discourse & Society* 10(4): 543–582.

Billig, Michael. 2008. "The language of critical discourse analysis: The case of nominalization." *Discourse & Society* 19(6): 783–800.

Bingham, Hiram. 1969. *A residence of twenty-one years in the Sandwich Islands*. Praeger Pub.

Blair, Chad. 2015. "An untold story of American immigration." *Honolulu Civil Beat*. Accessed June 10, 2018. http://www.civilbeat.org/2015/10/an-untold-story-of-american-immigration/

Blommaert, Jan. 2003. "Commentary: A sociolinguistics of globalization." *Journal of Sociolinguistics* 7(4): 607–623.

Blommaert, Jan. 2005. *Discourse: A Critical Introduction*. Cambridge: Cambridge University Press.

Blommaert, Jan. 2006. "Ethnopoetics as functional reconstruction: Dell Hymes' narrative view of the world." *Functions of Language* 13(2): 255–275.

Blommaert, Jan. 2010. *The sociolinguistics of globalization*. Cambridge: Cambridge University Press.

Blommaert, Jan. 2012. "Chronicles of complexity: Ethnography, superdiversity, and linguistic landscapes." *Tilburg Papers in Culture Studies* 29.

Blommaert, Jan. 2015. "Commentary: Superdiversity old and new." *Language & Communication* 44: 82–88.

Blommaert, Jan, and Ad Backus. 2012. "Superdiverse repertoires and the individual." In *Multimodality and multilingualism: Current challenges for educational studies*, ed. Ingrid de Saint-Jacques and Jean-Jacques Weber, pp. 11–32. Rotterdam: Sense Publishers.

Blommaert, Jan, and Ben Rampton. 2011. "Language and superdiversity." *Diversities* 13(2): 1–21.

Blommaert, Jan, and Ben Rampton. 2016. "Language and superdiversity." In *Language and superdiversity*, ed. Karel Arnaut, Jan Blommaert, Ben Rampton, and Massimiliano Spotti, pp. 21–48. New York: Routledge.

Blommaert, Jan, James Collins, and Stef Slembrouck. 2005. "Spaces of multilingualism." *Language and Communication* 25(3): 197–216.

Blommaert, Jan, Sirpa Leppanen, and Massamiliano Spotti. 2012. "Endangering multilingualism." In *Dangerous multilingualism: Northern perspectives on order, purity, and normality*, ed. Jan Blommaert, Sirpa Leppanen, Paivi Pahta and Tiina Raisanen, pp. 1–24. New York: Palgrave MacMillan.

Bond, John, and Faapisa Soli. 2011. "The Samoans." In *People and cultures of Hawai'i: The evolution of culture and ethnicity*, ed. John McDermott, John Andrade, and Naleen Naupaka, pp. 240–259. Honolulu: University of Hawai'i Press.

Bowman, Sally-jo Kealaoanuenue, Tamara Leiokanoe Moan, and Moses Elwood Kalauokalani. 2005. *Lua: Art of the Hawaiian warrior*. Honolulu: Bishop Museum.

Braunmuller, Kurt, and Christoph Gabriel, ed. 2012. *Multilingual individuals and multilingual societies.* Amsterdam: Benjamins.
Brenzinger, Matthias, and Patrick Heinrich. 2013. "The return of Hawaiian: Language networks of the revival movement." *Current Issues in Language Planning* 14(2): 300–316.
Briggs, Charles. 1986. *Learning how to ask: A sociolinguistic appraisal of the role of the interview in social science research.* Cambridge: Cambridge University Press.
Brown, Marie Alohalani. 2016. *Facing the spears of change: The life and legacy of John Papa Ii.* Honolulu: University of Hawai'i Press.
Bucholtz, Mary, and Kira Hall. 2005. "Identity and interaction: A sociocultural linguistic approach." *Discourse Studies* 7(4–5): 585–614.
Buck, Elizabeth. 1993. *Paradise remade: The politics of culture and history in Hawai'i.* Philadelphia: Temple University Press.
Camacho Souza, Blasé. 1984. "Trabajo y Tristeza—'Work and Sorrow': The Puerto Ricans of Hawaii 1900–1902." *The Hawaiian Journal of History* 18: 156–173.
Carr, Elizabeth. 1972. *Da Kine Talk: From Pidgin to Standard English in Hawaii.* Honolulu: University of Hawai'i Press.
Cataluna, L. 2000a, November 21. "'Portagee' jokes born of cruelty." *Honolulu Advertiser*, Hawai'i B1.
Cataluna, L. 2000b, November 28. "Readers, too, hate 'Portagee' jokes." *Honolulu Advertiser*, Hawai'i B1.
Char, Tin-Yuke. 1974. "Chinese merchants, adventurers, and sugar masters in Hawai'i: 1802–1852." *Hawaii Journal of History* 8: 3–9.
Char, Tin-Yuke. 1975. *The Sandalwood Mountains: Readings and stories of the early Chinese in Hawaii.* Honolulu: University of Hawai'i Press.
Char, Tin-Yuke and Wai Jane Char. 1975. "The first Chinese contract laborers in Hawaii, 1852." *The Hawaiian Journal of History* 9: 128–134.
Charlot, John. 1998. "Pele and Hi'iaka: The Hawaiian language series." *Anhtropos* 93: 55–75.
Chock, Eric, ed. 1978. *Talk story: An anthology of Hawaii's local writers.* Honolulu: Petronium.
Chock, Eric. 1990. *Last days here.* Honolulu: Bamboo Ridge.
Chouliaraki, Lilie, and Norman Fairclough. 1999. *Discourse in late modernity: Rethinking critical discourse analysis.* Edinburgh: Edinburgh University Press.
Chun, Malcolm Nāea. 2006. *Kapu: Gender roles in traditional society.* Honolulu: University of Hawai'i at Mānoa Curriculum and Research Development Group.
Chung-Do, Jane, John Huh, and Mark Kang. 2011. "The Koreans." In *People and cultures of Hawai'i: The evolution of culture and ethnicity*, ed. John McDermott, John Andrade, and Naleen Naupaka, pp. 176–200. Honolulu: University of Hawai'i Press.
Clyne, Michael. 2005. *Australia's language potential.* University of New South Wales Press.
Copland, Fiona, and Angela Creese. 2015. *Linguistic Ethnography: Collecting, Analysing, and Presenting Data.* London: Sage.
Copland, Fiona, Sara Shaw, and Julia Snell, eds. 2015. *Linguistic ethnography: Interdisciplinary explorations.* London: Palgrave.

Cook, Katherine. 1938. "Coordinator's statement." In *Successful practices in the teaching of English to bilingual children*: Bulletin 1937, No 14, compiled by Willis Coale and Madorah Smith, p. ix, US Department of the Interior: US Government Printing Office.

Cooren, Francis. 2012. "Communication theory at the center: Ventriloquism and the communicative constitution of reality." *Journal of Communication* 62(1): 1–20.

Cooren, Francis. 2013. "Incarnation, sensation and ventriloquism: For a sensitive and constitutive view of pragmatics." *Journal of Pragmatics* 58: 42–45.

Cowell, Andrew. 2012. "The Hawaiian model of language revitalization: Problems of extension to mainland native America." *International Journal of the Sociology of Language* 218: 167–193.

Creese, Angela, Peter Martin, and Nancy Hornberger. 2008. "Introduction to volume 9: Ecology of language." In *Encyclopedia of Language and Education*, 2nd ed., ed. Angela Creese, Peter Martin, and Nancy Hornberger, pp. i–vi. Springer Science.

Crookes, Graham, and Richard Schmidt. 1991. "Motivation: Reopening the research agenda." *Language Learning* 41(4): 469–512.

Cultural and Educational Center. 2017. Accessed June 26, 2018, http://hipcc.org/cultural-and-education-center/

Da Pidgin Coup. 2008. "Pidgin and education: A position paper." *Educational Perspectives* 40: 30–39.

Daws, Gavan. 1968. *Shoal of time: A history of the Hawaiian Islands*. Honolulu: University of Hawai'i Press.

De Mejia, Anne-Marie. 2006. "Bilingual education in Colombia: Towards a recognition of languages, cultures, and identities." *Colombian Applied Linguistics Journal* 8: 153–168.

De Mejia, Anne-Marie. 2017. "Language education and multilingualism in Colombia: Crossing the divide." *Language and Education* 31(3): 449–262.

Dekneef, Matthew. 2016. "Why Martin Luther King Jr. wore a Hawaiian lei on Selma march." *Hawaiian Magazine*, January 18. Accessed on April 27, 2017, http://www.hawaiimagazine.com/content/why-martin-luther-king-jr-wore-hawaiian-lei-selma-march

Dervin, Fred. 2015. "Discourses of Othering." In *The international encyclopedia of language and social interaction*. https://onlinelibrary.wiley.com/doi/pdf/10.1002/9781118611463.wbielsi027.

Desmond, Jane. 1999. *Staging tourism: Bodies on display from Waikiki to Sea World*. Chicago: University of Chicago Press.

Diamond, Heather. 2008. *American Aloha: Cultural tourism and the negotiation of tradition*. Honolulu: University of Hawai'i Press.

Dionisio, Juan. 1981. *The Filipinos in Hawaii: The first 75 years, 1906–1981*. Honolulu: Filipino News Specialty Publication.

Donne, M. A. 1866. *The Sandwich Islands and their people*. London: Society for Promoting Christian Knowledge.

Dorian, Nancy. 1994. "Purism vs. compromise in language revitalization and language revival." *Language in Society* 23: 479–494.

Drager, Katie. 2012. "Pidgin and Hawai'i English: An overview." *IJLTIC* 1(1): 61–73.
Duarte, Joana, and Ingrid Gogolin, ed. 2013. *Linguistic superdiversity in urban areas.* Amsterdam: Benjamins.
Duranti, Alessandro. 1994. *From grammar to politics: Linguistic anthropology in a western Samoan village.* Berkeley, CA: University of Berkeley Press.
Duranti, Alessandro. 2003. "Language as culture in U.S. anthropology (including comments from Laura Ahearn, Jenny Cook-Gumperz and John Gumperz, Regina Darnell, Dell Hymes, Alan Rumsey, Debra Spitulnik, Teun van Dijk)." *Current Anthropology* 44(3): 323–347.
Duranti, Alessandro, and Elinor Ochs. 1979. "Left-dislocation in Italian conversation." In *Discourse and syntax*, ed. Talmy Givon, pp. 377–416. New York: Academic Press.
Elbert, Samuel. 1951. "Hawaiian literary style and culture." *American Anthropologist* 53(3): 345–354.
Elbert, Samuel, and Mary Kawena Pukui. 1979. *Hawaiian grammar*. Honolulu: University of Hawai'i Press.
Elbert, Samuel, and Noelani Mahoe. 1970. *Nā Mele o Hawai'i Nei: 101 Hawaiian songs*. Honolulu: University of Hawai'i Press.
Elbert, Samuel, Mary Kawena Pukui, and Esther Mo'okini. 1974. *Place names of Hawai'i*. Honolulu: University of Hawai'i Press.
Enninger, Werner, and Lilith Haynes, eds. 1984. *Studies in language ecology*. Wiesbaden, Germany: Steiner.
Epstein, Jennifer. 2011. "Obama: Hawaii a 'melting pot.'" *Politico* 44. November 13. Accessed on July 2, 2018, http://www.politico.com/politico44/perm/1111/from_honolulu_65e89b1a-2db6-4122-a5c0-d1d18ba7e368.html
Espiritu, Yen Le. 1995. *Filipino American lives*. Philadelphia: Temple University Press.
Eyre, Kawika. 2004. "Suppression of Hawaiian culture at Kamehameha Schools." *Makali'i: An eclectic array*. Accessed on June 8, 2018, https://apps.ksbe.edu/kaiwakiloumoku/makalii/feature-stories/suppression_of_hawaiian_culture
Fairclough, Norman. 1989. *Language and Power*. London: Longman.
Fairclough, Norman. 1992. "The appropriacy of appropriateness." In *Critical language awareness*, ed. Norman Fairclough, pp. 33–56. London: Longman.
Fairclough, Norman. 1995. *Critical discourse analysis: The critical study of language*. New York: Routledge.
Ferguson, Charles. 1959. "Diglossia." *Word* 15(2): 325–340.
Field, Margaret, and Paul Kroskrity. 2009. "Introduction: Revealing Native American language ideologies." In *Native American language ideologies: Beliefs, practices, and struggles in Indian country*, ed. Paul Kroskrity and Margaret Field, pp. 3–28. Tucson: University of Arizona Press.
Finney, Joseph. 1961–1962. "Attitudes of others toward Hawaiians." *Social Process* 25.
Fishman, Joshua. 1967. "Bilingualism with and without diglossia." *Journal of Social Issues* 23(2): 29–38.
Fishman, Joshua. 1980. "Bilingualism and biculturalism as individual and as societal phenomena." *Journal of Multilingual and Multicultural Development* 1(1): 3–15.
Fishman, Joshua. 1991. *Reversing language shift*. Clevedon, England: Multilingual Matters.

Fishman, Joshua. 2001. *Can threatened languages be saved: Reversing language shift, revisited*. Clevedon: Multilingual Matters.
Florey, Margaret. 2008. "Language activism and the 'new linguistics': Expanding opportunities for documenting endangered languages in Indonesia." In *Language Documentation and Description* (Vol. 5), ed. Peter Austen, (pp. 120–135). London: SOAS.
Foucalt, Michel. 1972. *The archaeology of knowledge*. London: Tavistock Publications.
Fowler, Roger. 1991. *Language in the news: Discourse and ideology in the press*. London: Routledge.
Fowler, Roger. 1996. "On critical linguistics." In *Texts and practices: Readings in critical discourse analysis*, ed. Carmen Rosa Caldas-Coulthard and Malcolm Coulthard, pp. 3–14. London: Routledge.
Fowler, Roger, Bob Hodge, Gunter Kress, and Tony Trew. 1979. *Language and control*. London: Routledge and Kegan Paul.
Franceschini, Rita. 2011. "Multilingualism and multicompetence: A conceptual view." *Modern Language Journal* 95(3): 344–355.
Fuchs, Lawrence. 1961. *Hawaii Pono*. New York: Harcourt, Brace, and World.
Fukuda, Michael, and Anongnart "Mickie" Carriker. 2011. "The Thais." In *People and cultures of Hawai'i: The evolution of culture and ethnicity*, ed. John McDermott, John Andrade, and Naleen Naupaka, pp. 262–269. Honolulu: University of Hawai'i Press.
Fukazawa, Seiji, and Mie Hiramoto. 2005. "Chuugoku dialect terms that remain in Hawaii Creole English." *Hiroshima University Educational Bulletin* 53(2): 163–171.
Furukawa, Gavin. 2018. "Stylization and language ideologies in Pidgin comedic skits." *Discourse, Context and Media* 23: 41–52.
Furukawa, Toshi. 2007. "No flips in the pool: Discursive practice in Hawai'i Creole." *Pragmatics* 17(3): 371–386.
Gal, Susan. 1988. "The political economy of code choice." In *Codeswitching: Anthropological and sociolinguistic perspectives*, ed. Monica Heller, pp. 245–264. Berlin: Mouton de Gruyter.
Gal, Susan, and Kathryn A. Woolard. 1995. "Constructing languages and publics: Authority and representation." *Pragmatics* 5(2): 129–138.
Gal, Susan, and Kathryn A. Woolard, eds. 2001. *Languages and publics: The making of authority*. Manchester: St. Jerome Publishing.
Garcia Vizcaino, Maria Jose. 2011. "Humor in code-mixed airline advertising." *Pragmatics* 21(1): 145–170.
Garner, Mark. 2005. "Language ecology as linguistic theory." *Kajian Linguistik dan Sastra* 17(3): 91–99.
Garrett, Peter, and Allan Bell. 1998. "Media and discourse: A critical overview." In *Approaches to media discourse*, ed. Allan Bell and Peter Garrett, pp. 1–20. Oxford. Blackwell.
Geracimos-Chapin, Helen. 1998. "The media." In *Multicultural Hawai'i: The fabric of a multiethnic society*, ed. Michael Haas, pp. 67–82. New York: Garland Publishing.

Geschwender, James, Rita Carroll-Seguin, and Howard Brill. 1988. "The Portuguese and Haoles of Hawaii: Implications for the origin of ethnicity." *American Sociological Review* 53(4): 515–527.

Glick, Clarence. 1938. *The Chinese migrant in Hawaiʻi*. PhD Dissertation, University of Chicago.

Goodwin, Charles. 2000. "Action and embodiment within situated human interaction." *Journal of Pragmatics* 32(10): 1489–1522.

Goodwin, Charles, and Marjorie Goodwin. 2004. "Participation." In *A companion to linguistic anthropology*, ed. Alessandro Duranti, pp. 222–244. Oxford: Basil Blackwell.

Goodyear-Kaʻōpua, Noelani. 2017. "Protectors of the future, not protestors of the past: Indigenous Pacific activism and Mauna a Wākea." *South Atlantic Quarterly* 116(1): 184–194.

Goodyear-Kaʻōpua, Noelani, Ikaika Hussey, and Erin Kahunawaikaʻala Wright, eds. 2014. *A nation rising: Hawaiian movements for life, land, and sovereignty*. Durham: Duke University Press.

Gorter, Durk. 2013. "Linguistic landscapes in a multilingual world." *Annual Review of Applied Linguistics* 33: 190–212.

Grenoble, Lenore, and Lindsay Whaley. 2006. *Saving languages: An introduction to language revitalization*. Cambridge: Cambridge University Press.

Grimes, Joseph. 1972. "Outlines and overlays." *Language* 48: 513–524.

Grosjean, Francois. 2010. *"Bilingual" life and reality*. Cambridge, MA: Harvard University Press.

Gumperz, John. 1982. *Discourse strategies*. Cambridge, U.K.: Cambridge University Press.

Gumperz, John. 1986. "Interactional sociolinguistics in the study of schooling." In *The social construction of literacy*, ed. Jenny Cook-Gumperz, pp. 45–68. Cambridge: Cambridge University Press.

Haas, Michael. 1998. "A brief history." In *Multicultural Hawaiʻi: The fabric of a multiethnic society*, ed. Michael Haas, pp. 23–52. New York: Garland Publishing.

Hajet, John, and Yvette Slaughter, eds. 2015. *Challenging the monolingual mindset*. Bristol/Buffalo/Toronto: Multilingual Matters.

Hale, Constance. 2013. "Is the Hawaiian language dead or alive." *The Honolulu Magazine*. Accessed on June 12, 2018, http://www.honolulumagazine.com/Honolulu-Magazine/November-2013/Hawaiian-Dead-or-Alive/

Hall Robert. 1966. *Pidgin and Creole languages*. Ithaca, NY: Cornell University Press.

Halliday, M. A. K. 1985. *An introduction to functional grammar*. London: Edward Arnold.

Halliday, M. A. K. 2003. *On language and linguistics*. London: Continuum.

Halliday, M. A. K., and Ruqaiya Hasan. 1989. *Language, context, and text: Aspects of language in a social-semiotic perspective*. Oxford: Oxford University Press.

Hamers, Josiane, and Michel Blanc. 2000. *Biliguality and bilingualism*. Cambridge: Cambridge University Press.

Hanks, William. 1996. *Language and communicative practices*. Boulder, CO: Westview Press.

Hargrove, Emile, and Kent Sakoda.1999. "The hegemony of English or Hau kam yu wen kawl wat ai spik ingglish wen you no no waz." *Bamboo Ridge* 75: 48–70.
Harris, Roy. 1980. *The language-makers*. Ithaca, NY: Cornell University Press.
Harris, Roy. 1981. *The language myth*. London: Duckworth.
Harris, Roy. 1998. *Introduction to integrational linguistics*. London: Pergamon.
Harrison, K. David. 2007. *When languages die: The extinction of the world's language and the erosion of human knowledge*. Oxford: Oxford University Press.
Harrison, K. David. 2010. *The last speakers: The quest to save the world's most endangered languages*. National Geographic.
Haugen, Einar. 1972. *The ecology of language: Essays by Einar Haugen*. Stanford, CA: Stanford University Press.
Hawaii's English Standard Schools. 1948. Report #3. Accessed June 18, 2018, http://lrbhawaii.info/lrbrpts/48/engstan.pdf
Hawai'i Language Roadmap Initiative. 2013. Final report. Available at http://nflrc.hawaii.edu/languageroadmap/. Accessed June 10, 2018.
Hawai'i Tourism Authority. 2015. A record 8.3 million visitors came to Hawai'i in 2014; total visitor expenditures grew to 14.7 billion. http://www.hawaiitourismauthority.org/default/assets/File/research/monthly-visitors/December%202014%20Visitor%20Stats%20Press%20Release%20(final).pdf.
Hawai'i Tourism Authority. 2016. Annual Report to the State Legislature. http://www.hawaiitourismauthority.org/research/. Accessed on June 10, 2018.
Hawaii Economic Issues. 2011. Available at http://files.hawaii.gov/dbedt/census/acs/Report/Data-Report-Non-English-Speaking-Profile-Hawaii.pdf
Helot, Christine, and Monica Barni. 2013. *Linguistic landscapes, multilingualism and social change*. Peter Lang.
Heinrich, Patrick. 2012. *The making of monolingual Japan: Language ideology and Japanese modernity*. Bristol: Multilingual Matters.
Henze, Rosemary, and Kathryn Davis. 1999. "Authenticity and identity: Lessons from indigenous language education." *Anthropology and Education Quarterly* 30(1): 3–21.
Higa, Masanori. 2009. "Okinawa in Hawaii." In *Uchinanchu: A history of Okinawans in Hawaii*, ed. Center for Oral History, pp. 37–47. University of Hawai'i at Mānoa. Honolulu: University of Hawai'i at Mānoa.
Higashionna, Ryokichi, Gilbert Ikehara, and Leslie Matsukawa. 2011. "The Okinawans." In *People and cultures of Hawai'i: The evolution of culture and ethnicity*, ed. John McDermott, John Andrade, and Naleen Naupaka, pp. 131–151. Honolulu: University of Hawai'i Press.
Higgins, Christina. 2009. *English as a local language: Post-colonial identities and multilingual practices*. Bristol: Multilingual Matters.
Higgins, Christina. 2010. "Raising critical language awareness in Hawai'i at Da Pidgin Coup." In *Creoles in education: An appraisal of current programs and projects*, ed. Bettina Migge, Isabelle Leglise, and Angela Bartens, pp. 31–54. Amsterdam: John Benjamins.
Higgins, Christine. 2015. "Earning capital in Hawai'i's linguistic landscape." In *Unequal Englishes across multilingual spaces*, ed. Ruanni Tupas, pp. 145–162. New York: Palgrave Macmillan.

Higgins, Christine, Richard Nettell, Gavin Furukawa, and Kent Sakoda. 2012. "Beyond contrastive analysis and codeswitching: Student documentary filmmaking as a challenge to linguicism in Hawai'i." *Linguistics and Education*, 23: 49–61.

Hinton, Leanne. 2013. *Bringing our languages home: Language revitalization for families*. Heyday.

Hinton, Leanne, and Jocelyn Ahlers. 1999. "The issue of 'authenticity' in California language restoration." *Anthropology and Education Quarterly* 30(1): 56–67.

Hiramoto, Mie. 2010. "Dialect contact and change of the northern Japanese plantation immigrants in Hawai'i." *Journal of Pidgin and Creole Languages* 25(2): 229–262.

Hiramoto, Mie. 2011. "Consuming the consumers: Semiotics of Hawai'i Creole in advertisements." *Journal of Pidgin and Creole Languages* 26(2): 247–275.

Hofschneider, Anita. 2018. "Hawaiian is an official language so why isn't it used more?" *Honolulu Civil Beat*. Accessed June 7, 2018, http://www.civilbeat.org/2018/02/hawaiian-is-an-official-language-so-why-isnt-it-used-more/

Hoganson, Kristin. 2000. *Fighting for American manhood: How gender politics provoked the Spanish-American and Philippine-American wars*. New Haven, CT: Yale University Press.

Holmes, Leilani, Russell Leong, and David Yoo. 2012. *Ancestry of experience: A journey into Hawaiian ways of knowing*. Honolulu: University of Hawai'i Press.

Holquist, Michael. 2002. *Dialogism: Bakhtin and his world*. London and New York: Routledge.

Hopper, Robert. 1990/1991. "Ethnography and conversation analysis after talking culture." *Research on Language and Social Interaction* 24: 161–170.

House, Juliane. 2003. "English as a lingua franca: A threat to multilingualism?" *Journal of Sociolinguistics* 7(4): 556–578.

Huebner, Thom. 1984. "Language education policy in Hawai'i: Two case studies and some current issues." *International Journal of the Sociology of Language* 56: 29–50.

Huffines, Marion Lois. 1989. "Case usage among the Pennsylvania German secretarians and non-secretarians." In *Investigating obsolescence*, ed. Nancy Dorian, pp. 211–216. Cambridge: Cambridge University Press.

Hughes, Judith. 1993. "The demise of the English Standard School system in Hawai'i." *Hawaiian Journal of History* 27: 65–89.

Huot, Suzanne, Andrea Bobadilla, Antoine Bailliard, and Debbie Laliberte Rudman. 2016. "Constructing undesirables: A critical discourse analysis of 'othering' within the protecting Canada's immigration system act." *International Migration* 54(2): 131–143.

Hutchby, Ian, and Robin Wooffitt. 1998. *Conversation analysis: Principles, practices and applications*. New York: Wiley.

Hymes, Dell, ed. 1964. *Language in culture and society: A reader in linguistics and anthropology*. New York: Harper & Row.

Hymes, Dell. 1996. *Ethnography, linguistics, narrative inequality: Toward an understanding of voice*. London: Routledge.

Hymes, Dell. 2003. *Now I know only so far: Essays in ethnopoetics*. University of Nebraska Press.

Inoue, Miyako. 2004. "What does language remember?: Indexical inversion and the naturalized history of Japanese women." *Journal of Linguistic Anthropology* 14(1): 39–56.

Ivanov, Vyacheslav. 2001. "Heteroglossia." In *Key Terms in Language and Culture*, ed. Alessandro Duranti, pp. 95–97. Oxford: Blackwell.

'Iwalani, Else, Naleen Andrade, and Earl Hishinuma. 2007. "The role of Native Hawaiian mothers and fathers in conveying traditional Hawaiian beliefs and practices to children." *Hūlili: Multidisciplinary Research on Hawaiian Well-Being* 4(1): 93–106.

Jakobson, Roman 1960. "Closing statement: Linguistics and poetics." In *Style in Language*, ed. T. A. Sebeok, pp. 350–377. Boston: MIT Press.

Jakobsen, Roman 1966. "Grammatical parallelism and its Russian facet." *Language* 42(2): 399–429. DOI: http://dx.doi.org/10.2307/411699

Jespersen, Otto. 1905. *Growth and structure of the English language*. Garden City, NY: Doubleday Anchor Books.

Jenkins, Richard. 1994. "Rethinking ethnicity: Identity, categorization, and power." *Ethnic and Racial Studies* 17: 197–223.

Jessner, Ulrike, and Claire Kramsch. 2015. "Introduction: The multilingual challenge." In *The multilingual challenge: Cross-disciplinary perspectives*, ed. Ulrike Jessner and Claire Kramsch, pp. 1–20. Berlin: De Gruyter Mouton.

Johnstone, Barbara, ed. 1994. *Repetition in discourse: Interdisciplinary perspectives*. Norwood, NJ: Ablex Publishing.

Johnstone, Barbara, and Scott Kiesling. 2008. "Indexicality and experience: Exploring the meanings of /aw/-monopththongization in Pittsburgh." *Journal of Sociolinguistics* 12(1): 5–33.

Jourdan, Christine, and Johanne Angeli. 2014. "Pijin and shifting ideologies in urban Solomon Islands." *Language in Society* 43(3): 265–285.

Jung, Moon-Kie. 2006. *Reworking race: The making of Hawaii's interracial labor movement*. Colombia: Columbia University Press.

Kai, Peggy. 1974. "Chinese settlers in the village of Hilo." *Hawaiian Journal of History* 8: 39–75.

Kamakau, Samuel. 1992. *Ka Po'e Kahiko: The people of old*. Honolulu: Bishop Museum Press.

Kamakau, Samuel. 2001. *Ke Aupuni Mō'ī*. Honolulu: Kamehamemeha Schools.

Kamanā, Kauanoe, and William Wilson. 2014. "Beyond P-20: Reviving a dying language." YouTube Video, accessed on June 12, 2018. https://www.youtube.com/watch?v=6Uhmj7jRvCA.

Kame'eleihiwa, Lilikalā. 1992. *Native land and foreign desires: Pehea lā e Pono ai*. Honolulu: Bishop Museum Press.

Kameyama, Eri. 2012. *Acts of being and belonging: Shin-Issei transnational identity negotiations*. PhD Dissertation, University of California, Los Angeles.

Kanahele, George. 1982. *Hawaiian renaissance*. Honolulu: Project WAIAHA.

Kanahele, George. 1986. *Kū Kanaka stand tall: A search for Hawaiian values*. Honolulu: University of Hawai'i Press.

Kanahele, Pualani. 2011. *Ka Honua Ola: 'Eli'eli Kau Mai*. Honolulu: Kamehameha Publishing.

Kang, M. Agnes. 2004. "Co-constructing ethnic identity through discourse: Self-categorization among Korean American camp counselors." *Pragmatics* 14: 217–233.

Kawai'ae'a, Keiki, Housman, Alohalani, and Alencastre, Makalapua. 2007. "Pū'ā i ka 'ōlelo, ola ka 'ohana: Three generations of Hawaiian language revitalization." *Hūlili: Multidisciplinary Research on Hawaiian Well-Being* 4, 183–237.

Kawamoto, Kevin. 1993. "Hegemony and language politics in Hawai'i." *World Englishes* 12(2): 193–207.

Kelleher, Jennifer Sinco. 2014a. "Feds support Hawaii's driver's license lawsuit." *Associated Press*, March 28, 2014. Accessed on July 12, 2017, http://www.sandiegouniontribune.com/sdut-feds-support-hawaii-drivers-license-lawsuit-2014mar28-story.html.

Kelleher, Jennifer Sinco. 2014b. "Driver's test in new languages." *Associated Press*. Reported in the *Hawai'i Tribune Herald*, February 15.

Khoirunisa, Andini, and Rohmani Nur Indah. 2017. "Argumentative statements in the 2016 presidential debates of the U.S.: A critical discourse analysis." *JEELS* 4(2): 155–173.

Kikiloi, Kekuewa. 2010. "Rebirth of an archipelago: Sustaining a Hawaiian cultural identity for people and homeland." *Hūlili: Multidisciplinary Research on Hawaiian Well-Being* 6, 73–115.

Kim, Haeyeon. 2002. "The form and function of next-turn repetition in English conversation." *Language Research* 38(1), 51–81.

Kimura, Larry. 2002. *Nā mele kau o ka māhele mua o ka mo 'olelo 'o Hi 'iakaikapoliopele na Joseph M. Poepoe: He kālailaina me ke kālele ma luna i nā ku 'inaiwi kaulua.* Master's Thesis, University of Hawai'i at Hilo.

Kimura, Larry. 2012. *He kālailaina i ka panina 'ōlelo a ka mānaleo Hawai'i: Ka ho'ohālikelike 'ana i ka 'ōlelo manaleo a nā hanauna 'elua, 'o ka 'ōlelo kūmau a ka makua a me ka 'ōlelo kūpaka a ke keiki.* PhD Dissertation, University of Hawai'i at Hilo.

Kimura, Larry, and April G. L. Counceller. 2009. "Indigenous new words creation: Perspectives from Alaska and Hawai'i." In *Indigenous language revitalization: Encouragement, guidance, and lessons learned*, ed. Jon Reyhner and Louise Lockard, pp. 121–139. Flagstaff: Northern Arizona University.

Kimura, Larry, Kamanā, Kauanoe, and William Wilson. 2003. "Hawaiian: Back from the brink." *Honolulu Advertiser*, posted April 23. Retrieved from http://the.honoluluadvertiser.com/article/2003/Apr/24/op/op04a.html.

Kimura, Yukiko. 1988. *Issei: Japanese immigrants in Hawaii.* Honolulu: University of Hawai'i Press.

Kimura, Yukiko. 2009. "Social-historical background of the Okinawans in Hawaii." In *Uchinanchu: A history of Okinawans in Hawaii*, ed. Center for Oral History, pp. 51–71. Honolulu: University of Hawai'i at Mānoa.

Kitzinger, Celia. 2000. "Doing feminist conversation analysis." *Feminism and Psychology* 10(2): 163–193.

Kleinjans, Edith. (1995, January 29). "Standard English critical in classroom." *The Honolulu Advertiser*, B-1.

Kloss, Heinz. 1977. *The American bilingual tradition.* Rowley, MA: Newbury House.

Komai, Chris. 2015. "Who's more Japanese?" *Discover Nikkei*. Accessed June 22, 2018, http://www.discovernikkei.org/en/journal/2015/1/8/5618/
Kondo-Brown, Kimi. 2015. "Growing up in Hawai'i as Japanese heritage language speakers: Language, culture, and identity." In *Culture and foreign language education: Insights from research and implications for the practice*, ed. Wai Meng Chan, Sunil Kumar Bhatt, Masanori Nagami, and Izumi Walker, pp. 155–177. Boston: De Gruyter.
Kondo, Kimi. 1998. "Social-psychological factors affecting language maintenance: Interviews with Shin Nisei university students." *Linguistics and Education* 9(4): 369–408.
Kondo, Kimi. 1999. "Motivating bilingual and semibilingual university students of Japanese: An analysis of language learning persistence and intensity among students from immigrant backgrounds." *Foreign Language Annals* 32(1): 77–88.
Koole, Tom. 2007. "Review of Ben Rampton (2006) language in late modernity. Interaction in an urban school," *Journal of Pragmatics* 39 (4): 778–780.
Krauss, Michael. 1992. "The world's languages in crisis." *Language* 68: 4–10.
Kress, Gunther, and Robert Hodge. 1979. *Language as ideology*. London: Routledge and Kegan Paul.
Kroskrity, Paul, ed. 2000. *Regimes of language: Ideologies, politics, and identities*. Santa Fe, NM: School of American Research Press.
Kroskrity, Paul. 2009. "Language renewal as sites of language ideological struggle: The need for 'ideological clarification.'" In *Indigenous language revitalization: Encouragement, guidance, and lessons learned*, ed. Jon Reyhner and Louise Lockhart, pp. 71–83. Flagstaff: Northern Arizona University.
Kuykendall, Ralph. 1965. *The Hawaiian Kingdom, 1778–1854: Foundation and transformation*. Honolulu: University of Hawai'i Press.
Labrador, Roderick. 2004. "'We can laugh at ourselves': Hawai'i ethnic humor, local identity and the myth of multiculturalism." *Pragmatics* 14(2/3): 291–316.
Labrador, Roderick. 2015. *Building Filipino Hawai'i*. Urbana: University of Illinois Press.
Laitinen, Denise. 2012. "Political predictions, awards, and networking at annual chamber luncheon." *BigIslandNow.com* (June 29, 2012), Available at http://bigislandnow.com/2012/06/29/political-predictions-awards-and-networking-at-annual-chamber-luncheon/Lakoff, George. 1987. *Women, fire, and dangerous things: What categories reveal about the mind.* Chicago: University of Chicago Press.
Lakoff, George, and Mark Johnson. 1980. *Metaphors we live by*. Chicago: University of Chicago Press.
Lasalle, Melody. 2016. "Caucasian but not white: Race and the Portuguese in Hawaii." *Genealogy Research Journal*. Accessed June 10, 2018, http://www.researchjournal.yourislandroutes.com/2016/07/caucasian-but-not-white-race-and-the-portuguese-in-hawaii/
Latzko, David. 2004. "Tourism and fluctuations in the Hawaiian economy." *Journal of Tourism Studies* 15(2): 67–72.
Ledward, Brandon C. 2007. "On being Hawaiian enough: Contesting American racialization with native hybridity." *Hūlili: Multidisciplinary Research on Hawaiian Well-Being* 4(1): 107–143.

Li Wei. 2008. "Research perspectives on bilingualism and multilingualism." In *The Blackwell guide to research methods in bilingualism and multilingualism*, ed. Li Wei and Melissa Moyer, pp. 3–17. Oxford: Blackwell.

Lind, Andrew. 1980. *Hawaii's people*. Honolulu: University of Hawai'i Press.

Lipe, Kaiwipunikauikawēkiu. 2016. "He 'a'ali'i kū makani mai au: Lessons from struggle and survivance in the Hawaiian language context." In *The journeys of besieged languages*, ed. Delyn Day, Poia Rewi, and Rawinia Higgins, pp. 34–51. Newcastle: Cambridge Scholars Publishing.

Lippi-Green, Rosina. 1994. "Accent, standard language ideology, and discriminatory pretext in the courts." *Language in Society* 23(2): 163–198.

Lockwood, Hannah, and Scott Saft. 2016. "Shifting language ideologies and the perceptions of Hawai'i Creole among educators at the university level in Hawai'i." *Linguistics and Education* 33: 1–13.

Lomawaina, K. Tsiannia, & McCarty, Teresa. 2006. *To remain an Indian: Lessons in democracy from a century of Native American education*. New York and London: Teachers College Columbia University.

Lucas, Paul Nahoa. 2000. "E ola mau kākou i ka 'ōlelo Makuahine: Hawaiian language policy and the courts." *The Hawaiian Journal of History* 34: 1–28.

Lum, Darrell. 1986. "Local literature and lunch." In *The Best of Bamboo Ridge*, ed. Eric Chock and Darrell Lum, pp. 3–5.

Lum, Darrell. 1990. *Pass on, no Pass Back*! Honolulu: Bamboo Ridge.

Mackey, William. 1980. "The ecology of language shift." In *The Ecolinguistics Reader: Language, Ecology, and Environment*, ed. by Alwin Fill and Peter Muhlhausler, pp. 67–74. London: Continuum.

Makihara, Miki. 2004. "Linguistic syncretism and language ideologies: Transforming Sociolinguistic hierarchy on Rapa Nui (Easter Island)." *American Anthropologist* 106(3): 529–40.

Makihara, Miki. 2007. "Linguistic Purism in Rapa Nui political discourse." In *Consequences of contact: Language ideologies and sociocultural transformations in Pacific societies*, ed. Miki Makihara and Bambi Schieffelin, pp. 49–69. New York: Oxford University Press.

Makoni, Sinfree, and Alastair Pennycook. 2005. "Disinventing and (re)constituting languages." *Critical Inquiry in Language Studies: An International Journal* 2(3): 137–156.

Makoni, Sinfree, and Alastair Pennycook, eds. 2006. *Disinventing and reconstituting Languages*. Bristol: Multilingual Matters.

Malo, David. 1987. *Hawaiian antiquities*. Honolulu: Bishop Museum Press.

Mandelbaum, Jenny. 1990/1991. "Beyond mundane reason: Conversation analysis and context." *Research on Language and Social Interaction* 24: 333–350.

Marlow, Mikaela, and Howard Giles. 2008. "Who you tink you, talkin propah? Hawaiian Pidgin demarginalised." *Journal of Multicultural Discourses* 3(1): 53–68.

Marlow, Mikaela, and Howard Giles. 2010. "'We won't get ahead speaking like that!' Expressing and managing language criticism in Hawai'i." *Journal of Multilingual and Multicultural Development*, 31(3): 237–251.

Marshall Carucci, Laurence. 2012. "You'll always be family: Formulating Marshallese identities in Kona, Hawai'i." *Pacific Studies* 35(1/2): 203–231.
Mast, Robert, and Anne Mast. 1996. *Autobiography of protest in Hawai'i*. Honolulu: University of Hawai'i Press.
Matsuda, Mari. 1991. "Voices of America: Accent, anti-discrimination law, and a jurisprudence for the last reconstruction." *Yale Law Journal* 100(5): 1329–1407.
Maynard, Senko. 1999. "On rhetorical ricochet: Expressivity of nominalization and da in Japanese discourse." *Discourse Studies* 1: 57–81.
McCarty, Teresa. 2008. "Schools as strategic tools for indigenous language revitalization: Lessons from native America." In *Can schools save indigenous languages?: Policy and practice on four continents*, ed. Nancy Hornberger, pp. 161–179. London: Palgrave Macmillan.
McDermott, John, and Naleen Naupaka Andrade. 2011. *People and cultures of Hawai'i: The evolution of culture and ethnicity*. Honolulu: University of Hawai'i Press.
McDougall, Brandy Nālani. 2014. "Putting feathers on our words: Kaona as a decolonial aesthetic practice in Hawaiian literature." *Decolonization: Indigeneity, Education and Society* 3(1): 1–22.
McDougall, Brandy Nālani. 2016. *Finding meaning: Kaona and contemporary Hawaiian literature*. Tucson: The University of Arizona Press.
Meissner, Fran, and Steven Vervotec. 2015. "Comparing super-diversity." *Ethnic and Racial Studies* 38(4): 541–555.
Mejer, Jan H. 1987. "Capitalist stages, state formation, and ethnicity in Hawaii." *National Journal of Sociology* 1: 172–207.
Menton, Linda, and Eileen Tamura. 1999. *A history of Hawaii, student book*. Honolulu: Curriculum Research and Development Group, University of Hawai'i.
Merry, Sally Engle. 2000. *Colonizing Hawai'i: The cultural power of law*. Princeton, NJ: Princeton University Press.
Meyerhoff, Miriam, and Nancy Niedzielski. 2003. "The globalization of vernacular variation." *Journal of Sociolinguistics* 7(4): 534–555.
Mishler, Elliot. 1986. *Research interviewing: Context and narrative*. Cambridge, MA: Harvard University Press.
Moerman, Michael. 1988. *Talking culture: Ethnography and conversation analysis*. Philadelphia: University of Pennsylvania Press.
Mohanty, Ajit. 2010. "Languages, inequality and marginalization: Implications of the double divide in Indian multilingualism." *International Journal of the Sociology of Language* 205: 131–154.
Moon, Jade. 2014. "How Hawaiian language almost died." *Midweek*. Accessed June 23, 2018, http://www.midweek.com/hawaiian-language-almost-died/
Muhlhausler, Peter. 1996. *Linguistic ecology: Language change and linguistic imperialism in the Pacific region*. London: Routledge.
Muhlhausler, Peter. 2000. "Language planning and language ecology." *Current Issues in Language Planning* 1(3): 306–367.
Murayama, Milton. 1988. *All I asking for is my body*. Honolulu: University of Hawai'i Press.

Muromoto, Wayne. 1992. "The Shin Issei: The new immigrants from Japan are a mixed lot." *Hawaii Herald* 13(1): A-17.

Mykkanen, Juri. 2003. *Inventing politics: A new political anthropology of the Hawaiian kingdom.* Honolulu: University of Hawai'i Press.

Nagara, Susumu. 1972. *Pidgin English of Japanese in Hawaii.* Honolulu: University of Hawai'i Press.

Ndhlovu, Finex. 2006. "Gramsci, Doke, and the marginalisation of the Ndebele language in Zimbabwe." *Journal of Multilingual and Multicultural Development* 27(4): 305–318.

Ndhlovu, Finex. 2008. "The politics of language and nationality in Zimbabwe: Nation building or empire building." *South African Journal of African Languages* 28(1): 1–10.

Ndhovlu, Finex. 2015. "Ignored lingualism: Another resource for overcoming the monolingual mindset in language education policy." *Australian Journal of Linguistics* 35(4): 398–414.

Nelson, Christian. 1994. "Ethnomethodological positions on the use of ethnographic data in conversation analytic research." *Journal of Contemporary Ethnography* 23(3): 307–329.

NeSmith, Keao. 2005. "Tutu's Hawaiian and the emergence of a neo-Hawaiian language." *'Ōiwi* 3: 68–76.

Nordstrom, Georganne. 2003. "Finding their way to the writing center: Language perceptions of Pidgin speakers and non-native speakers from Asian countries." *The Writing Lab Newsletter* 28(3): 8–11.

Nordstrom, Georganne. 2015. "Pidgin as rhetorical sovereignty: Articulating indigenous and minority rhetorical practices with the language politics of place." *College English* 77(4): 317–337.

Nordyke, Eleanor and Richard K. C. Lee. 1989. "The Chinese in Hawai'i: A historical and demographic perspective." *The Hawaiian Journal of History* 23: 196–216.

Norrick, Neal. 1987. "Functions of repetition in conversation." *Text* 7(3): 245–264.

Ochs, Elinor. 1992. "Indexing gender." In *Rethinking Context: Language as an Interactive Phenomenon*, ed. Alessandro Duranti and Charles Goodwin, pp. 335–358. New York: Cambridge University Press.

Ochs, Elinor. 2012. "Experiencing language." *Anthropological Theory* 12(2): 142–160.

Odo, Carol. 1975. *Phonological processes in the English dialect of Hawaii.* PhD Dissertation, University of Hawai'i at Mānoa.

Odo, Carol. 1977. "Phonological representations in Hawaiian English." *University of Hawaii Working Papers in Linguistics* 9(3): 77–85.

Odo, Franklin. 2008. *Asian American history and culture: No sword to bury: Japanese Americans in Hawai'i.* Temple University Press.

Okamura, Jonathan. 1994. "Why there are no Asian Americans in Hawai'i: The continuing significance of local identity." *Social Process in Hawai'i* 35: 161–178.

Okamura, Jonathan. 2008. *Ethnicity and inequality in Hawai'i.* Philadelphia: Temple University Press.

Okamura, Jonathan. 2014. *From race to ethnicity: Interpreting Japanese American experiences in Hawai'i*. Honolulu: University of Hawai'i Press.
Okamura, Jonathan. 2016. *Imagining the Filipino American Diaspora*. London: Routledge.
Okihiro, Gary. 1991. *Cane fires: The anti-Japanese movement in Hawaii, 1865–1945*. Philadelphia: University of Temple Press.
Oliveira, Katrina-Ann Kapā'anaokalāokeola Nākoa. 2011. "Hō'ike honua: He Mana ko ka 'ōlelo." *Hūlili: Multidisciplinary Research on Hawaiian Well-Being* 7: 51–65.
Oliveira, Katrina-Ann Kapā'anaokalāokeola Nākoa. 2014. *Ancestral places: Understanding Kanaka geographies*. Oregon State University Press.
Olmsted, Francis. 1969. *Incidents of a whaling voyage*. Rutland, VT: Charles Tuttle.
Osorio, Jonathan. 2002. *Dismembering Lahui: A history of the Hawaiian nation to 1887*. Honolulu: University of Hawai'i Press.
Palafox, Neal, Sheldon Riklon, Sekap Esah, Davis Rehuher, William Swain, Kristina Stege, Dale Naholawaa, Allen Hixon, and Kino Ruben. 2011. "The Micronesians." In *People and cultures of Hawai'i: The evolution of culture and ethnicity*, ed. John McDermott, John Andrade, and Naleen Naupaka, pp. 295–315. Honolulu: University of Hawai'i Press.
Pennycook, Alistair. 2010. *Language as a local phenomenon*. London: Routledge.
Pennycook, Alistair. 2011. "The sociolinguistics of globalization (review)." *Language* 87(4): 884–887.
Perez-Milans, Miguel. 2016. "Language and identity in linguistic ethnography." In *The Routledge handbook of language and identity*, ed. Sian Preece, pp. 83–97, London: Routledge.
Perreira, Hiapokeikikāne Kichie. 2013. "He ki'ina ho'okuana'ike mauli ma ke kālailai mo'okalaleo." *Hūlili: Multidisciplinary Research on Hawaiian Well-Being* 9: 53–114.
Poblete, JoAnna. 2014. *Islanders in the empire: Filipino and Puerto Rican laborers in Hawai'i*. Champagne: University of Illinois Press.
Pomerantz, Anita. 1984. "Agreeing and disagreeing with assessments: Some features of preferred/dispreferred turn shapes." In *Structures of social action: Studies in conversation analysis*, ed. John Atkinson and John Heritage, pp. 57–101. Cambridge: Cambridge University Press.
Pons-Ridler, Suzanner, and Neil Ridler. 1989. "The territorial concept of official bilingualism: A cheaper alternative for Canada." *Language Sciences* 11(2): 147–158.
Porteus, S. D., and Marjorie Babcock. 1926. *Temperament and race*. Boston: Gorham Press.
Potter, Jonathan, and Alexandra Hepburn. 2005. "Qualitative interviews in psychology: Problems and possibilities." *Qualitative Research in Psychology* 2(4): 281–307.
Pukui, Mary Kawena, E. W. Haertig, and Catherine Lee. 1972. *Nānā i Ke Kumu. Look to the Source, Volume II*. Honolulu: Hui Hānai.
Pyke, Karen, and Tran Dang. 2003. "'FOB' and 'Whitewashed': Identity and internalized racism among second generation Asian Americans." *Qualitative Sociology* 26(2): 147–172.

Rampton, Ben. 2007. "Neo-Hymesian linguistic ethnography in the UK." *Journal of Sociolinguistics* 11(5): 584–607.

Rampton, Ben. 2015. "Dissecting heteroglossia: Interaction ritual or performance in crossing and stylization." In *Heteroglossia as practice and pedagogy*, ed. Adrian Blackledge and Angela Creese, pp. 275–299. Dordecht, NL: Springer.

Rampton, Ben, Janet Maybin, and Celia Roberts. 2014. "Methodological foundations in linguistic ethnography." *Working Papers in Urban Language and Literacies*.

Rampton, Ben, Karin Tusting, Janet Maybin, Richard Barwell, Angela Creese, and Vally Lytra. 2004. "UK linguistic ethnography: A discussion paper." http://www.lancaster.ac.uk/fss/organisations/lingethn/documents/discussion_paper_jan_05.pdf. Last accessed November 23, 2018.

Reagan, Timothy. 2004. "Objectification, positivism and language studies: A reconsideration." *Critical Inquiry in Language Studies: An International Journal* 1(1), 41–60.

Reichl, Christopher. 2008. "Stories pictures: On the possibility of an incipient level of pictographic writing in pre-contact Hawai'i." *Rapa Nui Journal* 22(2): 117–126.

Reichl, Christopher. 2017. "The Hawaiian petroglyphs: Lesson from incipient levels of pictographic writing." *International Journal of Arts and Humanities* 3(1): 7–16.

Reinecke, John. 1969. *Language and dialect in Hawai'i: A sociolinguistic history to 1935*. Honolulu: University of Hawai'i Press.

Reinecke, John. 1996. *Filipino Piecemeal Sugar Strike of 1924–1925*. Honolulu: University of Hawai'i Press.

Revilla, Linda. 1996. "Filipino Americans: Issues of identity in Hawai'i." In *Pagdiriwang 1996: Legacy and Vision of Hawaii's Filipino Americans*, ed. Jonathan Okamura and Roderick Labrador, pp. 9–12. Honolulu: Student Equity, Excellence and Diversity and Center for Southeast Asian Studies, University of Hawai'i at Mānoa.

Richardson, John. 2007. *Analysing newspapers: An approach from critical discourse analysis*. London: Palgrave Macmillan.

Rickford, John. 1985. "Standard and non-standard language attitudes in a creole continuum." In *Languages of Inequality*, ed. Nessa Wolfson and Joan Manes, pp. 145–159. Berlin: Mouton De Gruyter.

Roberts, Julian. 1995. "Pidgin Hawaiian: A sociohistorical study." *Journal of Pidgin and Creole Languages* 10(1): 1–56.

Roberts, Sarah. 2004. "The role of style and identity in the development of Hawaiian Creole." In *Creoles, contact, and language change: Linguistic and social implications*, ed. Genevieve Escure and Armin Schwegler, pp. 331–350. Amsterdam: Benjamins.

Rohrer, Judy. 2010. *Haoles in Hawai'i*. Honolulu: University of Hawai'i Press.

Romaine, Suzanne. 1994. "Hawai'i Creole English as a literary language." *Language in Society* 23(4): 527–554.

Romaine, Suzanne. 1999. "Changing attitudes to Hawai'i Creole English: Fo' find one good job, you gotta know how fo' talk like one haole." In *Creole genesis, attitudes and discourse*, ed. John Rickford and Suzanne Romaine, pp. 287–301. Amsterdam: Benjamins.

Romaine, Suzanne. 2005. "Orthographic practices in the standardization of pidgins and creoles: Pidgin in Hawai'i as anti-language and anti-standard." *Journal of Pidgin and Creole Languages* 20(1): 101–140.

Romaine, Suzanne. 2013. "The bilingual and multilingual community." In *The handbook of bilingualism and multilingualism*, ed. Tej Bhatia and William Ritchie, pp. 445–465. London: Blackwell.

Rubdy, Rani, and Lubna Alsagoff, eds. 2013. *The global-local interface and hybridity: Exploring language and identity*. Bristol, Buffalo, and Toronto: Multilingual Matters.

Sacks, Harvey. 1992. *Lectures on conversation, Vol. 2*. Gail Jefferson, ed. Blackwell: Oxford.

Sacks, Harvey, and Emanuel A. Schegloff. 1979. "Two preferences in the Organization of reference to persons and their interaction." In *Everyday Language: Studies in Ethnomethodology*, ed. George Psathas, op. 15–21. New York: Irvington Publishers.

Sacks, Harvey, Emanuel A. Schegloff, and Gail Jefferson. 1974. "A simplest systematics for the organization of turn-taking in conversation." *Language* 50 (4): 696–735.

Saft, Scott, Gabriel Tebow, and Ronald Santos. 2018. "Hawai'i Creole in the public Domain: Humor, emphasis, and heteroglossic language practice in university commencement speeches." *Pragmatics* 28(3): 417–438.

Sakoda, Kent, and Jeff Siegel. 2003. *Pidgin grammar: An introduction to the Creole language of Hawai'i*. Honolulu: Bess Press.

San Buenaventura, Steffi. 1995. "Filipino immigration to the United States." In *The Asian American Encyclopedia*, ed. by Franklin Ng, pp. 439–453. New York: Marshall Cavendish.

San Buenaventura, Steffi. 1996. "Hawaii's Filipinos: History and legacy." In *Pagdiriwang 1996: Legacy and vision of Hawaii's Filipino Americans*, ed. Jonathan Okamura and Roderick Labrador, pp. 35–38. Honolulu: Student Equity, Excellence and Diversity and Center for Southeast Asian Studies, University of Hawai'i at Manoa.

Santa Ana, Otto. 2002. *Brown tide rising: Metaphors of Latinos in contemporary American public discourse*. Austin: University of Texas Press.

Sato, Charlene. 1985. "Linguistic inequality in Hawai'i: The post-creole dillema." In *Language of inequality*, ed. Nessa Wolfson and Joan Manes, pp. 255–272. Berlin: Mouton.

Sato, Charlene. 1991. "Sociolinguistic variation and language attitudes in Hawaii." In *English around the world: Sociolinguistic perspectives*, ed. Jenny Cheshire, pp. 647–663. Cambridge: Cambridge University Press.

Sato, Charlene. 1993. "Language change in a creole continuum: Decreolization?" In *Progression and regression in language: Sociocultural, neuropsychological and linguistic perspectives*, ed. Kenneth Hyltenstam and Ake Viberg, pp. 122–143. Cambridge: Cambridge University Press.

Schegloff, Emanuel. 1987. "Recycled turn beginnings: A precise mechanism in conversation's turn-taking organisation." In *Talk and social organisation*, ed. Graham Button and John Lee, pp. 70–100. Clevedon, England: Multilingual Matters.

Schegloff, Emanuel. 1996. "Confirming allusions: Toward an empirical account of action." *American Journal of Sociology* 102(1): 161–216.

Schegloff, Emanuel. 1997. "Practices and actions: Boundary cases of other-initiated repair." *Discourse Processes* 23(3): 499–545.

Schegloff, Emanuel. 1999a. "Naivete vs sophistication or discipline vs self-indulgence: A rejoinder to Billig." *Discourse and Society* 10(4): 577–582.

Schegloff, Emanuel. 1999b. "On dispensability." Paper presented at the 85th Annual Convention of the National Communication Association, Language and Social Interaction Division, Chicago.

Schegloff, Emanuel. 2002. "The surfacing of the suppressed." In *Studies in Language and Social Interaction in Honor of Robert Hopper*, ed. Phillip Glenn, Curtis LeBaron, and Jenny Mandelbaum, pp. 204–223. Mahwah, NJ: Lawrence Erlbaum Associates.

Schegloff, Emanuel. 2007. "A tutorial on membership categorization." *Journal of Pragmatics* 39(3): 462–482.

Schegloff, Emanuel, Gail Jefferson, and Harvey Sacks. 1977. "The preference for self-correction in the organization of repair in conversation." *Language* 53, 361–382.

Schroder, Kim Christian. 2002. "Discourses of fact." In *Handbook of media and communication research*, ed. Klaus Bruhn Jensen, pp. 98–116. London: Routledge.

Schütz, Albert. 1994. *The voices of Eden: A history of Hawaiian language studies*. Honolulu: University of Hawai'i Press.

Scully, Marc. 2010. *Discourses of Authenticity and National Identity Among the Irish Diaspora in England.* PhD dissertation, The Open University.

Shepherd, Susan. 1985. "On the functional development of repetition in Antiguan Creole morphology, syntax, and discourse." In *Historical Semantics/Historical Word-formation*, ed. Jacek Fisiak, pp. 533–545. Berlin: Mouton de Gruyter.

Siegel, Jeff. 1995. "How to get a laugh in Fijian: Code-switching and humor." *Language in Society* 24(1): 95–110.

Siegel, Jeff. 2008. "Pidgin in the classroom." *Educational Perspectives* 41(1–2): 55–65.

Silva, Noenoe. 2004. *Aloha betrayed: Native Hawaiian resistance to American colonialism*. North Carolina: Duke University Press.

Silva, Noenoe. 2017. *The power of the steel-tipped pen: Reconstructing Native Hawaiian intellectual history*. Duke University Press.

Silverstein, Michael. 2003. "Indexical order and the dialectics of sociolinguistic life." *Language and Communication* 23(3–4): 193–229.

Silverstein, Michael. 2010. "Dell Hathaway Hymes." *Language* 86(4): 933–939.

Snyder-Frey, Alicia. 2013. "He kuleana ko kākou: Hawaian-language learners and the construction of (alter)native identities." *Current Issues in Language Planning* 14(2): 231–243.

Speer, Susan. 2002. "'Natural' and 'contrived' data: A sustainable distinction." *Discourse Studies* 4(4): 511–525.

Spradley, James. 1979. *The Ethnographic Interview*. Long Grove, Illinois: Waveland Press.

Stannard, David. 1989. *Before the horror: The Population of Hawaii on the eve of Western contact*. Honolulu: University of Hawai'i Press.

State of Hawaii Department of Transportation. 2014. "Drivers license exams to be offered in multiple languages." http://hidot.hawaii.gov/blog/2014/02/14/drivers-license-exams-offered-in-a-variety-of-languages/.

Stivers, Tanya. 2005. "Modified repeats: One method for asserting primary rights from second position." *Research on Language and Social Interaction* 38(2): 131–158.

Su, Christine. 2011. "The Cambodians." In *People and cultures of Hawai'i: The evolution of culture and ethnicity*, ed. John McDermott, John Andrade, and Naleen Naupaka, pp. 283–294. Honolulu: University of Hawai'i Press.

Su, Christine, and Paul Tran. 2011. "The Vietnamese." In *People and cultures of Hawai'i: The evolution of culture and ethnicity*, ed. John McDermott, John Andrade, and Naleen Naupaka, pp. 270–282. Honolulu: University of Hawai'i Press.

Suchman, Lucy, and Brigitte Jordan. 1990. "Interactional troubles in face-to-face survey Interviews." *Journal of the American Statistical Association* 85(409): 232–241.

Sugita, Megumi. 2000. *Identity and second language learning: Local Japanese learning Japanese in Hawai'i*. Master's Thesis, University of Hawai'i at Mānoa.

Suzuki, Asuka. 2009. "Who is 'Japanese' in Hawai'i: The discursive construction of ethnic identity." In *Beyond yellow English: Toward a linguistic anthropology of Asian Pacific America*, ed. Angela Reyes and Adrienne Lo, pp. 148–166. Oxford: Oxford University Press.

Talmy, Stephen. 2006. "The other Other: Micronesians in a Hawai'i high school." In *Asian and Pacific American education: Learning, socialization, and identity*, ed. Clara Park, Russell Endo, and A. Lin Goodwin, pp. 19–49, Information Age Publishing.

Takabuki, Matsuo. 1998. *An unlikely revolutionary: Matsuo Takabuki and the making of modern Hawai'i*. Honolulu: University of Hawai'i Press.

Takaki, Ronald. 1983. *Pau Hana: Plantation life and labor in Hawai'i, 1835–1920*. Honolulu: University of Hawai'i Press.

Tamura, Eileen. 1993a. "The English-only effort, the anti-Japanese campaign, and language acquisition in the education of Japanese Americans in Hawai'i, 1915–1940." *History of Education Quarterly* 33(1): 37–58.

Tamura, Eileen. 1993b. *Americanization, acculturation, and ethnic identity: The Nisei generation in Hawai'i*. Urbana: University of Illinois Press.

Tamura, Eileen. 1996. "Power, status, and Hawai'i Creole English: An example of linguistic intolerance in American history." *Pacific Historical Review* 65(3), 431–454.

Tamura, Eileen. 2002. "African American Vernacular English and Hawai'i Creole English: A comparison of two school board controversies." *Journal of Negro Education* 71 (1/2): 17–30.

Tannen, Deborah. 1987. "Repetition in conversation: Toward a poetics of talk." *Language* 63(3), 574–605.

Tannen, Deborah. 1989. *Talking voices: Repetition, dialogue, and imagery in conversational discourse*. Cambridge: Cambridge University Press.

Tannen, Deborah. 1995. "Waiting for the mouse: Constructed dialogue in conversation." In *The dialogic emergence of culture*, ed. Dennis Tedlock and Bruce Mannheim, pp. 198–217. Urbana: University of Illinois Press.

Taylor, Jarrod. 2011. "Diversity among Hawaii's children during World War II." *Historia* 100–108. Accessed June 8, 2018, http://www.eiu.edu/historia/2011

Taylor.pdf Tekin, Beyza. 2010. *Representations and Othering in discourse*. Amsterdam: Benjamins.

Teodoro, Luis, ed. 1981. *Out of this struggle: The Filipinos in Hawaii*. Honolulu: University Press of Hawaii.

Tonouchi, Lee. 2001. *Da Word*. Honolulu: Bamboo Ridge Press.

Tonouchi, Lee. 2009. *Living Pidgin: Contemplations on Pidgin culture*. Honolulu: Tinfish Press.

Toolan, Michael. 2003. "An integrational linguistic view of coming into language." In *Ecology of language acquisition*, ed. Jonathan Leather and Jet van Dam, pp. 123–139. Dordrecht, Netherlands: Kluwer Academic Publishers.

Trask, Haunani Kay. 1999. *From a native daughter: Colonialism and sovereignty in Hawai'i*. Latitude 20 Books.

Trudgill, Peter. 1972. "Sex, covert prestige and linguistic change in the urban British English of Norwich." *Language in Society* 1(2): 179–195.

Tsai, Linda. 2001. "Repetition in spoken Chinese: A discourse approach." In *The First Seoul International Conference on discourse and cognitive linguistics: Perspectives for the 21st century*, pp. 781–799.

Tsujimura, Rick. 2016. *Campaign Hawai'i: An inside look at politics in Hawai'i*. Watermark Publishing.

Tsuzaki, Stanley. 1966. "Hawaiian English: Pidgin, creole, or dialect." *Pacific Speech* 1(2): 25–28.

Tsuzaki, Stanley. 1969. "Problems in the study of Hawaiian English." In *Working papers in linguistics*, pp. 117–133. Department of Linguistics, University of Hawai'i.

Tsuzaki, Stanley. 1971. "Coexistent systems in language variation: The case of Hawaiian English." In *Pidginization and Creolization of languages*, ed. Dell Hymes, pp. 327–339. Cambridge: Cambridge University Press.

UNESCO. 2009. "Intergovernmental Committee for the Protection and Promotion of the Diversity of Cultural Expressions." Accessed June 22, 2018, https://en.unesco.org

Van Dijk, Teun. 1993. "Principles of critical discourse analysis." *Discourse and Society* 4(2): 249–283.

Van Dijk, Teun. 1995. "Aims of critical discourse analysis." *Japanese Discourse* 1: 17–27.

Van Dijk, Teun. 2015. "Critical discourse analysis." In *The handbook of discourse analysis*, ed. Deborah Tannen, Heidi Hamilton, and Deborah Schiffrin, eds., pp. 466–485. West Sussex: Wiley.

Van Leeuwen, Theo. 1996. "The representation of social actors." In *Texts and practices: Readings in critical discourse analysis*, ed. Carmen Rosa Caldas-Coulthard and Malcolm Coulthard, pp. 32–70. London: Routledge.

Vellupillai, Viveka. 2003. *Hawai'i Creole English: A typological analysis of the tense-mood-aspect system*. New York: Palgrave MacMillan.

Verschueren, Jef. 2012. *Ideology in language use: Pragmatics guidelines for empirical research*. Cambridge: Cambridge University Press.

Viotti, Vicki. 2003. "Hawai'i's courts dealing with interpreter woes." *Honolulu Advertiser.com*. Accessed July 11, 2017, http://the.honoluluadvertiser.com/article/2003/Jul/21/ln/ln01a.html

Voegelin, Carl, and Florence Voegelin. 1964. "Hawaiian pidgin and mother tongue." *Anthropological Linguistics* 6(7): 20–56.
Voloshinov, Valentin. 1973. *Marxism and the philosophy of language*. Cambridge, MA: Harvard University Press.
Walker, Isaiah Helekunihi. 2011. *Waves of resistance: Surfing and history in twentieth-century Hawaiʻi*. Honolulu: University of Hawaiʻi Press.
Walsh, Michael. 2005. "Will indigenous languages survive." *Annual Review of Anthropology* 34: 293–315.
Watson-Gegeo, Karen. 1994. "Language and education in Hawai'i: Sociopolitical and economic implications of Hawai'i Creole English." In *Language and social construction of identity in Creole situations*, ed. Marcyliena Morgan and Mervyn Alleyne, pp. 101–120. Los Angeles: Center for Afro-American Studies.
Webster, Anthony, and Paul Kroskrity. 2013. "Introducing ethnopoetics: Hymes's legacy." *Journal of Folklore Research* 50(1–3): 1–11.
Weiner, Aaron. 2016. "America's real migrant crisis in the one you've never heard of." *Mother Jones*. Accessed June 25, 2018, https://www.motherjones.com/politics/2016/12/hawaii-micronesia-migration-homeless-climate-change/
Weinstein, Michael, Peter Manicas, and Joseph Leon. 1990. "The Portuguese and Haoles of Hawaii." *American Sociological Review* 55(2): 305–308.
Wetherell, Margaret. 1998. "Positioning and interpretative repertoires: Conversation analysis and post-structuralism in dialogue." *Discourse and Society* 9(3): 387–412.
Wiley, Norbert. 1967. "The Ethnic mobility trap and stratification theory." *Social Problems* 15(2): 147–59.
Wilson, William. 1998a. "The sociopolitical context of establishing Hawaiian-medium education." *Language, Culture, and Curriculum* 11(3): 325–338.
Wilson, William. 1998b. "I ka ʻōlelo Hawaiʻi ke ola, 'Life is found in the Hawaiian language.'" *International Journal of the Sociology of Language* 132: 123–137.
Wilson, William, and Kauanoe Kamanā. 2001. "Mai loko mai o ka 'iʻini: Proceeding from a Dream, the ʻAha Pūnana Leo connection in Hawaiian language revitalization." In *The Greenbook of Language Revitalization in Practice*, ed. Leanne Hinton and Ken Hale, pp. 147–176. San Diego: Academic Press.
Wilson, William, and Kauanoe Kamanā. 2006. "For the interest of the Hawaiians themselves: Reclaiming the benefits of Hawaiian-medium education." *Hūlili: Multidisciplinary Research on Hawaiian Well-Being* 3: 153–182.
Wilson, William, and Keiki Kawaeʻaeʻa. 2007. "I kumu lālā: Let there be sources; let there be branches: Teacher education in the College of Hawaiian Language." *Journal of American Indian Education* 46(3): 37–53.
Wist, Benjamin. 1940. *A century of public education in Hawaiʻi, 1840–1940*. Honolulu: Hawaii Educational Review.
Wong, Alia. 2013. "Fo teach Pidgin o not fo teach Pidgin- Das da question." *Honolulu Civil Beat*. Accessed July 18, 2018, www.civilbeat.com/2013/03/18498-fo-teach-pidgin-o-not-fo-teach-pidgin-das-da-question/
Wong, Jean. 2000. "Repetition in conversation: A look at 'first and second sayings.'" *Research on Language and Social Interaction* 33(4): 407–424.
Wong, Laiana. 1999a. "Authenticity and the revitalization of Hawaiian." *Anthropology and Education Quarterly* 30(1): 94–115.

Wong, Laiana. 1999b. "Language varieties and language policy: The appreciation of Pidgin." In *Sociopolitical perspectives on language Policy and planning in the USA*, ed. Thom Huebner and Kathyrn Davis, pp. 221–237. Amsterdam: Benjamins.

Wong, Laiana. 2006. *Kuhi aku, kuhi mai, kuhi hewa ē: He mau loina kuhikuhi ʻākena no ka ʻōlelo Hawaiʻi.* PhD Dissertation, University of Hawaiʻi at Mānoa.

Wong, Laiana. 2011. "Hawaiian methodologies of indirection." In *Critical qualitative research in second language studies: Agency and advocacy*, ed. Kathryn Davis, pp. 151–170. Charlotte, NC: Information Age Publishing.

Wong, Laiana, and Kekailoa Perry. 2017. "Kū kaʻeo i ke kalaʻihi o Maleka." *Honolulu Star Advertiser*.

Wood, Houston. 1999. *Displacing natives: The rhetorical production of Hawaiʻi.* London: Rowman and Littlefield Publishers.

Woolard, Kathryn. 1987. "Codeswitching and comedy in Catalonia." *IPRA Papers in Pragmatics* 1 (1): 106–122.

Woolard, Kathryn. 1998. "Simultaneity and bivalency as strategies in bilingualism." *Journal of Linguistic Anthropology* 8(1): 3–29.

Woolard, Kathryn. 2004. "Codeswitching." In *A companion to linguistic anthropology*, ed. Alessandra Duranti, Malden, MA: Blackwell.

Woolard, Kathryn A. 2008. "Language and identity choice in Catalonia: The interplay of contrasting ideologies of linguistic authority." In *Lengua, Nación e Identidad. la Regulación del Plurilingüismo en Espana y América Latina*, ed. Kirsten Süselbeck, Ulrike Mühlschlegel, and Peter Masson, pp. 303–323. Madrid; Frankfurt am Main: Iberoamericana: Vervuert.

Yaguchi, Yujin, and Mari Yoshihara. 2004. "Evolutions of 'paradise': Japanese tourist discourse about Hawaiʻi." *American Studies* 45(3): 81–106.

Yamanaka, Lois Ann. 2000. *Heads by Harry.* New York: Harper Perennial.

Yamanaka, Lois Ann. 2006. *Wild meat and the bully burgers: A novel.* UK: Picador.

Yokota, Thomas. 2008. "The 'Hawaiʻi Creole problem': Attitudes about Hawaiʻi Creole." *Educational Perspectives* 41(1–2): 22–29.

Yoshida, Hiromi. 2007. "Language and cultural maintenance of Hawaiʻi-born Nisei." *Educational Perspectives* 40(1–2): 31–35.

Yoshida, Shima. 2014. *Being hafu (Biethnic Japanese) in Japan: Through the eyes of the Japanese media, Japanese University Students, and hafu themselves.* Master's Thesis, University of Utah.

Young, Morris. 2002. "Standard English and student bodies: institutionalizing race and literacy in Hawaiʻi." *College English* 64(4): 405–431.

Young, Nancy. 1972. "Socialization patterns among the Chinese of Hawaii." *Amerasia* 1(4): 31–51.

Young, Vershawn. 2009. "'Nah, we straight': An argument against code switching." *JAC* 29(1/2): 49–76.

Young, Vershawn, Edward Barrett, Y'Shanda Young-Rivera, and Kim Brian Lovejoy. 2013. *Other people's English: Code-meshing, code-switching, and African American literacy.* New York: Teacher's College Press.

Yuuji, Kotaro. 2018. *Ryukyuan language endangerment and revitalization.* Unpublished manuscript, University of Hawaiʻi at Hilo.

Index

Adams, Romanzo, 23
Adelbert von Chamisso, 38
agency (expression of), 17, 76–89, 222
Altheide, David, 199, 210–11
authenticity (of the Hawaiian language), 17, 56, 73–88
Azores, 29

Beaglehole, Ernest, 41
Bingham, Hiram, 39
British Association of Applied Linguistics (BAAL), 11

Cambodian, 6
Cambodian immigrants, 35
Cantonese, 6, 28, 51, 96, 126, 189n2, 204, 224
Captain Cook, 23–24
Captain Philip Spalding, 47
Chinese languages, 2, 4, 6, 33, 36; Chinese language schools, 32
Chinese laborers, 27–28, 37, 42–45
Chock, Eric, 105–6
Chuugokuben (dialect of Japanese), 157–61, 185, 228
Chuukese (as category of people), 199, 200, 216
Chuukese language, 2, 3, 7, 36, 51, 196, 197, 200, 209, 213, 214, 216, 218

Clinton Kanahele, 64, 65
codeswitching, 126, 127, 130, 186, 225
common sense knowledge, 16, 143, 145, 146–49, 226
Compact of Free Association (COFA), 3, 35, 216
conversation analysis, 13, 14, 62–68, 222
court interpreting, 35–36, 196, 206, 213–16, 223–23
court system, 22
covert prestige, 101–3
critical discourse analysis (CDA), 13, 14, 198, 199, 208, 222
crossing, 12
crucial disposition (to revitalize languages), 59

Da Pidgin Coup, 106, 122
Denmark (immigrant plantation workers), 30
diglossia, 8, 9, 15, 56, 102, 221
driver's test, 2, 22, 35–36, 52, 196, 223

education, 4; American system, 7, 36; attitudes toward, 15; changes in Hawai'i, 30–31; Department of, 197, 204, 209; Hawaiian Board of, 102; medium of English, 135, 138, 142,

257

151; medium of Hawaiian, 2, 31, 56–60, 74, 89, 223; multilingualism in, 22; pidgin-free zones, 100; private school, 31
English language, 2, 4, 5, 8, 12, 13, 24, 36; as Indo-European language, 6; as language category, 12, 222; as language of education, 7, 31, 33–34, 165, 228; as language of prestige, 15, 16, 23, 25, 37, 52, 73, 89, 100, 101, 122–23, 223; as official language, 3, 37, 59; as world language, 5; influence on Pidgin, 6, 32, 94–100; language contact, 25, 74; language mixing, 9, 13, 17–18, 76, 110–14, 125–50, 185–86, 224–27; newspapers, 25
English Standard Schools, 33–34, 101
ethnic mobility trap, 48
ethnography of communication, 11
ethnopoetics, 14, 62–63, 222

Filipino, 1, 4, 6; as a person category, 18, 52, 173, 175–76, 191–95, 199–206, 213, 216–19, 231–32; immigrant plantation workers, 35, 37, 49–51, 53, 191–95, 198; languages, 15, 36
Finney, Joseph C., 41
Fishman, Joshua, 60
French language, 36
functional approach (to grammar), 77, 198, 222

generalization (process of), 208–11, 215–16, 222, 231
German language, 6, 36,
German plantation workers, 29–30
Gilbert Islands, 29
Great Mahele, 26
Guam, 3

Haitian Creole, 99
haole, 26, 32–34, 42–44, 46, 48–53, 101, 102, 105, 129, 174, 192–94, 231

Harrison, K. David, 60
Haugen, Einar, 9–11
Hawai'i Creole. *See* Pidgin
Hawai'i English, 94–95, 99, 110
Hawai'i multicultural model, 23, 230
Hawaiian Japanese, 159–60
Hawaiian language, 1, 2–3, 4, 5, 6, 7, 9, 12, 13, 14, 15, 36, 55–91, 204, 223, 224, 228–32; and heteroglossia, 121–34, 135–39, 224–27; as language category, 143–46, 148–52, 222; newspapers, 25, 64, 78, 88
Hawaiian language revitalization, 37, 56, 57–60, 74, 75, 89, 93, 104, 138, 143, 151, 223, 226, 230, 232
Hawai'i Language Roadmap Initiative, 36
Hawai'i Pacific University, 128, 131
Hawaiian place names, 61–62
Hawaiian Renaissance, 17, 36–37, 58–59, 132, 145–46, 230, 232
Hawaiian Sugar Planters' Association (HSPA), 34, 35, 44, 45, 192
heritage languages, 33–34, 164, 189n1
heteroglossia, 12, 13, 17, 18, 125–53, 183, 222, 224–30, 232
Hilo, 1, 9, 19, 56, 107, 115, 121, 125, 144, 161, 165, 167, 168, 221, 226
Honolulu, 26, 28, 46, 160, 163, 197
Honolulu Advertiser, 46, 143
Honolulu Star-Advertiser, 143, 144, 147, 201, 202, 204, 208, 209, 210, 211, 212, 213
Honolulu Star-Bulletin, 44, 46, 143
humor in discourse, 18, 49, 63, 103, 130
humor and Pidgin, 18, 49, 103, 104–6, 109, 114, 132, 133, 134, 147, 150, 151
hybrid forms of language, 18

ideology, 13, 145, 191–219, 222, 230–31, 232; language ideology, 13, 14–16, 22, 59–60, 145. *See also* authenticity

Ilocano, 1, 2, 6, 36, 50, 51, 194, 199, 200, 202–6, 213, 214, 216
immigrant languages, 18, 143, 155, 189n1, 226, 227
indexicality, 17, 127, 139, 222, 229, 230
indigenous knowledge, 5, 60–73, 89
interactional sociolinguistics, 11
interdisciplinary relevance, 13

Japanese Cultural Center, 168–70, 187
Japanese language, 2, 4, 6, 12, 14, 33, 36; schools, 33
Japanese plantation workers, 29, 37, 45–47
Jespersen, Otto, 38

Kamehameha Schools, 18, 31, 82, 85, 128, 135–42, 152, 227
Kanahele collection, 64–66, 90n1
kaona (hidden meanings), 61
Kapena, John, 29
Kauikeaouli, 25
Kenoi, Billy, viii, 9, 13, 17, 93, 94, 99, 105, 107–14, 127, 128–34, 136, 139–43, 150–52, 224, 225, 227, 228, 229, 230
Kimura, Larry, 64, 67, 69, 90n1
King, Martin Luther, Jr., 23
King Kalākaua, 29
King Kamehameha I, 24, 31, 130, 134, 227
King Kamehameha II, 24
King Kamehameha III, 25
Kinubi, 99
Kona, 115, 120, 165, 201, 219f5
Korea, plantation workers, 30, 45
Korean language, 2, 33, 36; schools, 33
Kosraen, 3, 36
Krauss, Michael, 5

Ladd & Company, 26
Lakoff, George, 14, 39
language activism, 13, 104–6, 232
language ecology, 9–11

language families, 6; Austronesian, 6; Indo-European, 6; Micronesian, 6; Polynesian, 6; Sino-Tibetan, 6
language schools, 33
Laotian, 36
linguistic double consciousness, 102, 121
linguistic ethnography, 9, 11–16, 221–22, 232
local (identity), 17, 51, 93–123, 127, 129, 132–33, 139, 150, 174, 187, 193–95, 197, 198, 217, 225, 229, 230, 231
localness. *See* local (identity)
Lum, Darrell, 105–6

Madeira Islands, 29
Malaga Province, 30
Mandarin, 1, 6, 28, 51, 189n2, 204, 224
Marshallese (as a category of people), 207, 215
Marshallese culture, 197
Marshallese language, 1, 2, 3, 6, 36, 51, 196, 199, 200, 206, 213–18, 223
media discourse, 13
melting pot (Hawai'i as), 23
membership category analysis (MCA), 13, 14, 143–45, 156, 169, 198
mercantile houses, 30; Alexander & Baldwin, 30; American Factors, 30; C. Brewer & Company, 30; Castle & Cooke, 30; The Big Five, 30; Theo H. Davies & Company, 30, 44
Merrian report, 47
metaphor theory, 14, 39, 44, 222, 231
Micronesia, 3, 14, 29, 51, 191, 196
Micronesian (as category of people), 35, 189, 191, 192, 195–99, 206–19, 222, 223, 224, 230, 231
Micronesian languages, 6, 7, 15
missionaries, 24–26, 31, 32, 39–41, 57, 74; arrival of, 24, 57, 74, 124; writing Hawaiian, 24–26, 39–41
mock Filipino, 51, 194

monolingualism, 6, 10, 52
multilingualism: definition, 2; enduring quality of, 52; interdisciplinary nature of, 7–8; as social problem, 21–22; multivoiced, 141; recognition of languages, 222–24; situational approach, 150, 151, 227–30; unequal distribution of languages, 55
multivoicedness, 127, 129, 133, 141, 188

narrative analysis, 13
Ni'ihau, 8–9
Norwegian plantation workers, 30

Obama, Barack, 23
Okinawa, 165–67, 173, 179; associations in Hawai'i, 30, 166–67, 180; *Hui Okinawa*, 167, 180–83, 187, 189n8; languages of, 36, 51, 158, 165–67, 180, 181, 182, 183, 187; plantation workers, 30, 165–67
Olmsted, Francis, 42
Orientalism, 22
othering, 18, 22, 44, 51, 201
overt prestige, 101–3

Pacific Commercial Advertiser, 43
Pacific Islanders (as plantation workers), 29
Pidgin, 1, 3, 4, 5, 9, 12, 13, 14, 15, 16, 31–33, 34, 51, 93–123, 143–49, 159–60, 186–88, 194, 223, 224–29; as language category, 143–49, 222; bible, 106; grammar, 95–99; indexical meanings of, 17, 128–35, 139, 150, 222, 229–32; Japanese words, 159–60; lexicon, 94–95; pronunciation, 94–95
Pidgin Guerilla, 148
Pidgin languages, 31–32; macaronic Pidgin, 32, 51
Pohnpeian, 3, 7, 36
Poland planation workers, 30
Porteus and Babcock, 46, 50

Portuguese Cultural Center, 226–27
Portuguese jokes, 103
Portuguese language, 6, 12, 36, 95–96, 126, 185, 226–27
Portuguese immigrants, 29, 37, 45, 46, 47–51, 53, 226–27
post-structuralism, 12
problem frame, 199, 210–13, 217, 231
Puerto Rico: plantation workers, 30, 34, 35; territory of the US, 34
Punahou School, 31

Rapa Nui, 15
reciprocity treaty, 27, 29
repair (in conversation), 63, 64–65, 172
repetition in discourse, 17, 56, 62–73, 76, 89, 93, 222
Reverend Artemus Bishop, 39, 40
Reverend Sereno E. Bishop, 39
Russian, 6, 30, 126, 224
Russian plantation workers, 30
Ryukyuan. *See* Okinawa

sandalwood trade, 26, 27
Sāmoan language, 7, 36, 51, 189, 224; political discourse in, 77
Sāmoan immigrants, 35
self and other, 64
Spanish, 2, 6, 8, 12, 15, 30, 36, 224
Spanish plantation workers, 30
stylizing, 12
sugar plantations, 26–30
sugar planters, 29, 34, 36
superdiversity, 4
Swedish, 6
Sweden plantation workers, 30

Tagalog, 2, 50, 51, 95, 126, 192, 194, 199, 200, 202, 204–6
Tahitian, 7
territorial bilingualism, 8, 9, 221
Thai, 6, 224
Thai immigrants, 35
Tok Pisin, 99

Tongan, 7, 36
Tonouchi, Lee, 105–6, 147–48
tourism, 3–4, 36–37
translanguaging, 12, 126

Uchninanchu, 156, 165–67
UNESCO, 55
University of Hawai'i: at Hilo, 56, 57, 64, 82, 84, 86–87, 104, 128, 133, 143, 168; at Mānoa, 36, 41, 64, 106, 163, 167, 196; Center for Okinawan Studies, 167; system, 3

Vietnamese language, 2, 6, 36, 224
Vietnames immigrants, 35

Waikīkī, 155, 162, 165, 178, 228
Wallace Farrington, 47
whaling, 24, 26, 42
Wong, Laiana, 78, 88, 100, 103, 107
World War II, 34, 47, 159, 160, 167, 192, 195

Yamanaka, Lois Ann, 105–6
Yapese, 3, 7, 36

About the Author

Scott Saft is a professor of linguistics in the Ka Haka 'Ula o Ke'elikōlani College of Hawaiian Language at the University of Hawai'i at Hilo. He received his PhD from the University of Hawai'i at Mānoa in 2000 and after spending time working in Japan, he has been living in Hilo, Hawai'i, since 2004. His research interests include the application of the perspectives of conversation analysis and membership category analysis to Japanese social interaction, and he has most recently been focusing on the situated usage of Hawaiian and Hawai'i Creole (aka Pidgin) and the attitudes toward both languages among people residing in Hawai'i.

www.ingramcontent.com/pod-product-compliance
Lightning Source LLC
Chambersburg PA
CBHW050901300426
44111CB00010B/1328